Stalinism on the Frontier of Empire

This is a fascinating account of frontier Stalinism told through the previously unexplored history of a campaign to attract female settlers to the socialist frontiers of the Soviet Far East in the late 1930s. Elena Shulman reveals the instrumental part these migrants played in the extension of Soviet state power and cultural dominion in the region. Their remarkable stories, recovered from archival letters, party documents, memoirs, press coverage, and films, shed new light on Soviet women's roles in state formation, the role of frontier Stalinism in structuring gender ideals, and the nature of Soviet society and Stalinism in the 1930s. Through these narratives, Elena Shulman offers a nuanced and complex picture of the "subcultures" of Stalinism – generational, regional, and semi-criminal – as well as the complexities of women's lives under Stalin and the limits of Moscow's rule over the periphery and even the Gulag.

ELENA SHULMAN is an independent scholar and has taught at the University of California, Berkeley, and Texas Tech University after receiving her PhD in History from the University of California, Los Angeles, in 2004.

Stalinism on the Frontier of Empire

Women and State Formation in the Soviet Far East

Elena Shulman

CAMBRIDGE
UNIVERSITY PRESS

HQ
1665.15
.Z8
F378
2008

CAMBRIDGE UNIVERSITY PRESS
Cambridge, New York, Melbourne, Madrid, Cape Town, Singapore, São Paulo, Delhi

Cambridge University Press
The Edinburgh Building, Cambridge CB2 8RU, UK

Published in the United States of America by Cambridge University Press, New York

www.cambridge.org
Information on this title: www.cambridge.org/9780521896672

M—

First published 2008

Printed in the United Kingdom at the University Press, Cambridge

A catalogue record for this publication is available from the British Library

Library of Congress Cataloguing in Publication data
Shulman, Elena, 1969–
Stalinism on the frontier of empire : women and state formation in the Soviet Far East /
Elena Shulman.
   p.   cm.
Includes bibliographical references and index.
ISBN 978-0-521-89667-2 (hardback)
1. Women – Russia (Federation) – Russian Far East – History.   2. Migration, Internal –
Soviet Union – History.   3. Women and socialism – Soviet Union – History.   I. Title.
HQ1665.15.Z8F378   2008
305.48′89171057709043 – dc22   2008020509

ISBN 978-0-521-89667-2 hardback

This book is dedicated to the memory of
my grandmother Charna Svider-Shulman and
to my mother Zinaida Khanis-Shulman.

Contents

Illustrations

Illustrators V. Briskin and V. Fomichev, *Komsomol'skaia pravda*,
September 12, 1938.

Acknowledgments

Research for this book was funded by a grant from the International Research & Exchanges Board (IREX) with funds provided by the National Endowment for the Humanities, the United States Department of State, which administers the Title VII Program, and the IREX Scholar Support Fund.

I would like to thank J. Arch Getty, Roshanna Sylvester, and Stephen Frank for discussing this project with me from its inception and reading countless drafts, and for their infinite patience. They are only tangentially responsible for any errors and shortcomings.

I am grateful to Iuri Slezkine, Lynne Viola, Douglas Northrop, Lynn Mally, Robert Edelman, the late Reginald Zelnik, Malgorzata Fidelis, Margaret Kuo, Jeremiah Burke, Nicholas Breyfogle, Wendy Goldman, Gabor Rittersporn, Tim Paynich, and Steven Merritt – participants of the Southern California Consortium for Eurasian, Russian, and Eastern European Studies and the Russian history kruzhok at the University of California, Berkeley – for their insights, help, and advice in the course of my graduate studies and for reading all or parts of this manuscript. Michael Watson at Cambridge University Press has been a joy to work with and is greatly appreciated. I also want to thank the two readers for Cambridge whose suggestions dramatically improved the final product.

I am indebted to the historian Nina I. Dubinina and the staff of the State Archive of the Khabarovsk Region for their assistance during my stay in the Russian Far East and the Kapitsa family for their hospitality and friendship in Moscow. My thanks to the Russian State Archive of Documentary Films and Photographs in Krasnogorsk for permission to reproduce photographs from their collections, and to Allan Gamborg of Gamborg Gallery for permission to use the cover illustration. Routledge Taylor & Francis group has granted permission for publication of an earlier version of chapter 4 from Nicholas Breyfogle, Abby Schrader, and Willard Sunderland (eds.), *Peopling the Russian Periphery:*

Border Colonization in Eurasian History (2007). My thanks also to Eve Levin, editor of the *Russian Review*, where segments from chapters 1 and 2 first appeared as "Soviet Maidens for the Socialist Fortress: The Khetagurovite Campaign to Settle the Soviet Far East, 1937–39," 62:3 (July 2003).

Finally, I want to acknowledge Ruski, the cat, for being born one wintry night in Moscow along with the manuscript.

Glossary of terms

BAMLag	Baikal-Amur road corrective labor camp
Dal'krai	Far Eastern Region
Dal'kraiispolkom	Far Eastern Regional Executive Committee
Dal'kraikom	Far Eastern Regional Committee of the VKP(b)
Dal'Lag	Khabarovsk region corrective labor camp
Dal'stroi	Far Eastern Construction Trust
delo (d.)	file or folder
fond (f.)	collection
GULAG	Chief Administration of Corrective Labor Camps
kolkhoz	collective farm
Komsomol	Soviet Communist Youth League
krai	region
Kraikom	Regional Committee
Kraiispolkom	Regional Executive Committee
kulak	a "strong" or capitalist farmer
list (l.)	folio in archival folder
lespromkhoz	Timber Industry Enterprise
meshchanka	woman with petty-bourgeois views (connoting narrow-minded, chauvinistic or crassly materialistic in the Soviet era)
NEP	New Economic Policy
NKVD	People's Commissariat of Internal Affairs
Obkom	Oblast Committee
oblast	a territorial administrative unit similar to a county
obratnaia (ob.)	verso of numbered folio in archival folder
OKDVA	Special Red Banner Far Eastern Army
opis' (op.)	inventory
Red Army and Fleet Houses	Social and educational clubs directed by Communist party political instructors for officers and their families
RKKA	Worker-Peasant Red Army

RSFSR	Russian Soviet Federated Socialist Republic
sovkhoz	state-owned farm paying wages
taiga	subarctic evergreen coniferous forest
VKP(b)	All-Union Communist party (Bolsheviks)
VLKSM	Soviet Communist Youth League
Zhenotdel	Women's Department of the Communist party

Note on the text

I have adopted a simplified version of the Library of Congress System for transliteration from the Cyrillic alphabet to the Latin alphabet. Terms and names already well known to non-Russian readers have been left in their more familiar spellings.

Idiosyncrasies in translations of primary sources and document titles have been retained to keep the flavour of Soviet bureaucratic jargon in the 1930s and forms of expression typical of this sometimes inadequately educated generation of New Soviet men and women.

Memoirs of Khetagurovites have been dated where the date is known. Undated memoirs were deposited in the Party Archive of the Khabarovsk region between 1974 and 1975.

Introduction

On February 5, 1937 *Komsomol'skaia pravda*, the national newspaper of the Soviet Communist Youth League, published a lengthy article formulated as a letter to the readership. It was ostensibly penned by Valentina Khetagurova, a youth league activist and wife of an army officer living on a far-flung frontier. Her tone sparkled with an odd aura of optimism and lighthearted adventure. It was peculiar. This was, after all, 1937, the nadir of Stalinist terror. The letter had to jostle for attention amid that day's ominous news stories and proclamations decrying the machinations of "enemies of the people" and announcing the arrests of formerly prominent Communist party chiefs and industrial bosses. Nevertheless, diligent readers digesting reports of forthcoming trials and militarist predations in Europe and Asia would also eventually find, at the bottom of page 2, "Join Us in the Far East! Letter of Valentina Khetagurova to the Young Women of the Soviet Union" where Khetagurova beckoned:

> Young women! Sisters-Komsomolki! Far in the east, in the Primor'e and Priamurskaia taiga, we women, together with our husbands and brothers, are reconstructing a marvelous land . . . Millions of brave people struggle there, in the east, with the impenetrable taiga. They are taming the mountains, the forests, and the rivers. But we have few capable hands. Every person, every specialist is on call. And we need many more people to pacify nature, so that all of the region's riches can be exploited for socialism . . . We just need people – brave, decisive, and selfless . . . Wonderful work, wonderful people, and a wonderful future await . . . We are waiting for you, our girlfriends![1]

Several days after this publication, letters from volunteers inundated the newspaper's editorial offices. What began as an engaging article about a young woman's life in the Far East quickly turned into a very real resettlement program. Her invitation effectively tapped into the imaginations of close to 300,000 who wrote in to volunteer over the next several years.

---

[1] Valentina Khetagurova, "Priezzhaite k nam na Dal'nii Vostok!," *Komsomol'skaia pravda*, (*KP* hereafter) February 5, 1937. Valentina Khetagurova (1914–1992).

Its message profoundly changed the life course of approximately 25,000 volunteers who were selected to follow Khetagurova's example. In her honor, those women who went to the Soviet Far East between 1937 and 1939 were officially known as Khetagurovites. Such migrants were instrumental in the extension of Soviet state power across Eurasia.

This book is about the women who yearned to join the ranks of Soviet frontier builders. Their stories, recovered from archival letters, party documents, memoirs, press coverage and films, evocatively illustrate the role of frontier Stalinism in structuring gender ideals and the place of gender in determining the meaning of Stalinism. All these materials exponentially enrich the precious little we currently know about Soviet women's roles in state formation and life on the peripheries, as well as self-perceptions and attitudes among the first female cohort reared wholly under Soviet power.

Tragically, as their stories will make clear, the history of the Khetagurovites is embedded in the history of Stalinist repression. The women wandered into a social landscape rife with hatreds and suspicions born of forced population movements and escalating purges. Everyone struggled to survive the social and environmental by-products of central planning geared almost exclusively toward the development of an industrial-military infrastructure to the detriment of every other need. The resulting absence of basic necessities impacted women in a myriad ways because they were expected to carry on with all household chores and child care even if they worked full-time and took on heavy workloads in public organizations such as the Communist Youth League and Communist party.

In many instances, the stories of the migrants and their ultimate fates in the region are intimately linked with the history of the Chief Administration of Corrective Labor Camps (GULAG), not only because some of the women migrants eventually worked for the repressive organs of the People's Commissariat of Internal Affairs (NKVD), or actually found themselves on the wrong side of the wire in a labor camp, but also because most of the female migrants entered a zone structured by conditions peculiar to this society. As Oleg Khlevniuk has argued, the history of the GULAG is not just the history of totalitarianism or forced labor, it is "the history of . . . creating a distinct social milieu of convicts and their guards and prosecutors. It is the history of a specific camp culture and mentality, which strongly affected the culture, traditions and worldview of Soviet society at large."[2] Thus not only did this periphery reflect larger

---

[2] Oleg Khlevniuk, *The History of the GULAG: From Collectivization to the Great Terror*, trans. Vadim Staklo (New Haven: Yale University Press, 2004), 8.

processes in the rest of Soviet society, but the relationships and practices evolving here reverberated in the rest of the country. Unfortunately for historians, archival sources that can tell us about the social world and the milieu of the region are extremely rare, in part because sources containing such information were systematically destroyed by decree.[3] The materials generated for, by, and about female migrants offer unusual entry points into this frontier of Stalinism.

To think of this region as a "frontier" illuminates its history and Stalinism in surprising ways, even as American historians continue their crusade, more than a century long, to define, debate, denounce, and redefine the term.[4] "Frontier" in this book denotes a sparsely populated region in the grips of acute demographic, social, political, economic, and ecological transformations engendered by its status as a borderland of an expanding

---

[3] *Ibid.*, 3. Studies of special settlements and the GULAG's societies are just beginning to appear. See Lynne Viola, *The Unknown GULAG: The Lost World of Stalin's Special Settlements* (New York: Oxford University Press, 2007); Iu. N. Afanas'ev et al. (eds.), *Istoriia stalinskogo GULAGa: Konets 1920-kh–pervaia polovina 1950-kh godov,* 7 vols. (Moskva: ROSSPEN, 2004–2005); Oksana Klimkova, "GULAG: Ot mifotvorchestva k izucheniiu," *Ab Imperio* 3 (2005), 501–528; Kate Brown, "Out of Solitary Confinement: The History of the GULAG," *Kritika* 8:1 (2007), 67–103; and Stephen A. Barnes, "Researching Daily Life in the GULAG," *Kritika* 1:2 (2000), 377–390.

[4] The literature on the topic of "frontier" in North America is vast, beginning with Frederick Jackson Turner, "The Significance of the Frontier in American History," in *Annual Report of the American Historical Association for the Year 1893* (Washington DC: Government Printing Office, 1894). Subsequent studies include Henry Nash Smith, *Virgin Land: The American West as Symbol and Myth* (Cambridge, MA: Harvard University Press, 1950); William Cronon, George Miles, and Jay Gitlin (eds.), *Under an Open Sky: Rethinking America's Western Past* (New York: W. W. Norton, 1994); Patricia Nelson Limerick, *The Legacy of Conquest* (New York: W. W. Norton, 1988); and Richard Slotkin, *Regeneration Through Violence: The Mythology of the American Frontier, 1600–1860* (New York: Harper Perennial, 1973); Slotkin, *The Fatal Environment: The Myth of the Frontier in the Age of Industrialization, 1800–1890* (New York: Harper Perennial, 1985); Slotkin, *Gunfighter Nation: The Myth of the Frontier in Twentieth-Century America* (New York: Harper Perennial, 1992). For some recent attempts to synthesize, evaluate, or challenge the concept and the myths that surround it, see Gregory H. Nobles, *American Frontiers: Cultural Encounters and Continental Conquest* (New York: Hill and Wang, 1997); Richard W. Etuliiu (ed.), "Myths and the American West," *Journal of the West* 37 (April 1998), 5–107; and Patricia Nelson Limerick, *Something in the Soil: Field-Testing the New Western History* (New York: W. W. Norton, 2000). For other recent works that place women at the center of frontier history and demonstrate the interconnections between gender, class, and race in experiences of the frontier, see Elizabeth Jameson and Susan Armitage (eds.), *Writing the Range: Race, Class, and Culture in the Women's West* (Norman: University of Oklahoma Press, 1997); Richard White, *The Middle Ground: Indians, Empires, and Republics in the Great Lakes Region, 1615–1815* (Cambridge: Cambridge University Press, 1991); and Albert Hurtado, *Intimate Frontiers: Sex, Gender, and Culture in Old California* (Albuquerque: University of New Mexico Press, 1999). Turner's "frontier thesis" has been applied to Russia. See Donald W. Treadgold, "Russian Expansion in the Light of Turner's Study of the American Frontier," *Agricultural History* 26:4 (1952), 147–152, and Mark Bassin, "Turner, Solov'ev, and the 'Frontier Hypothesis': The Nationalist Significance of Open Spaces," *Journal of Modern History* 65:3 (1993), 476–511.

empire. Thus "frontier" by such a definition is an environment and society shaped by violence, forced population movements, and subjugation of outsiders. "Frontiers" as concepts also play a variety of roles in cultures beyond the geographic spaces of borderlands. In political and cultural discourses, including Soviet culture in Stalin's time, "the frontier" proffered fantasies of discovery, progress, reinvention, freedom, and adventure. State-sanctioned histories and cultural representations present its settlement as expansion without imperialism. Despite the odious realities of these zones and the gulf between frontier tales and frontier life, the "frontier" was also a space portending real mobility for migrants and a crucible of complex regional identities. Mythologies surrounding frontier settlement and its heroes often appear in gendered representations of national character.

The female migrants' stories vividly encapsulate patterns of thought, behaviors, beliefs, and life trajectories of women born in the first quarter of the twentieth century. As this cohort reached adulthood, they not only survived a calamitous series of events, they also helped to shape and took part in practices within what we now call Stalinism. "Stalinism" among historians of the Soviet Union, just like "frontier" among historians of North America, is a highly controversial and expansive term that has engendered fiery debates. The term "Stalinism" in this book is indebted to the definition offered by Sheila Fitzpatrick, who employed it "as shorthand for the complex of institutions, structures and rituals" that defined the social, economic, ideological, and political landscape of the Soviet 1930s.[5] "Stalinism on the frontier" connotes an ideological, cultural, political, and economic system emphasizing, at all cost, rapid economic development, extraction of natural resources and militarization of sparsely populated borderlands in response to real and perceived threats on a distant periphery. The use of prison labor and forced population movements in achieving these goals were intrinsic to the workings of the Stalinist system on this frontier because of its difficult climate, insufficient infrastructure, and perennial labor shortages.

Stalinism on the frontier was an exaggerated version of practices and policies associated with Stalinist rule such as terror; untrammeled power of the security police; centrally planned production and distribution;

---

[5] Sheila Fitzpatrick, *Everyday Stalinism: Ordinary Life in Extraordinary Times: Soviet Russia in the 1930s* (New York: Oxford University Press, 1999), 3. In the context of her own work on the history of everyday life in urban Soviet Russia, Fitzpatrick defined Stalinism as "Communist Party rule, Marxist-Leninist ideology, rampant bureaucracy, leader cults, state control over production and distribution, social engineering, affirmative action on behalf of workers, stigmatization of 'class enemies,' police surveillance, terror and the various informal, personalistic arrangements whereby people at every level sought to protect themselves and obtain scarce goods, were all part of the Stalinist habitat" (3–4).

corruption; chronic shortages of goods and housing; absolute monopolization of all public and political life by the Communist party and Stalin's version of Marxism. It was also a world of its own, presenting a poor example of totalitarian control not only because of its distance from Moscow and Stalin's gaze, but also because of its historic role as dumping ground and sometimes refuge for criminals, political prisoners, and nonconformists of all stripes well before the Bolshevik Revolution. It teemed with transients and laborers from all over the Soviet Union, China, and Japan. It was populated by Soviet soldiers, Soviet Koreans, and Soviet indigenous peoples of the North.[6] It held great allure for adventure seekers, gold prospectors, and wilderness enthusiasts. While the worst aspects of Stalinism were magnified here, for thousands in other parts of the Soviet Union, this poorly known and distant region resonated with promises of belonging, heroism, and collective accomplishments.

"Some distant planet"

Seventeen-year-old Ania Alekseeva and her friends in Moscow were diligent readers of the youth paper in the winter of 1937. When they came across Khetagurova's public call to action, they "rushed" to apply. Other young women, such as Communist Youth League activist Efrosina Mishalova working at an orphanage in eastern Ukraine, were also caught up in the excitement of a colorful and purposeful life on the frontier.[7] They imagined the Far East as "some distant planet."[8] The region located along the Pacific Ocean might as well have been another galaxy for teenagers from Moscow or Ukraine. Stretching about 3,000 miles from north to south, the Arctic Ocean is at its northern limits where Alaska rests across the Bering Strait. The Amur and Ussuri rivers demarcate much of the Far East's almost 800-mile border with northern China.

---

[6] Some of the major indigenous groups in the Far East are the Nanai, Udehe, Ul'chi, Nivkhi, Uilta, and Ainu. For more on the subject of indigenous peoples of the Soviet north, see Iuri Slezkine, *Arctic Mirrors: Russia and the Small Peoples of the North* (Ithaca: Cornell University Press, 1994).

[7] When Efrosina Mishalova noticed Khetagurova's letter that February, she read it "ten times and could not sleep till morning. I hurried to find literature about the Far East. I called the district library and asked them to show me everything they had on the Far East: books, newspapers, songs, poems, and plays." Holdings from the former Communist party archive, now under the auspices of the State archive of the Khabarovsk Region, are hereafter denoted as GAKhK P. Memoir of Efrosina Mishalova, "Vospominaia o moei miloi zadornoi trudnoi i schastlivoi komsomol'skoi iunosti [Remembering my dear, fervent, difficult and fortunate Komsomol youth]," February 18, 1976, GAKhK P, f. 442, op. 2, d. 284, ll. 85–85ob.

[8] Memoir of Ania Alekseeva, GAKhK P, f. 442, op. 2, d. 283, l. 14.

Korea and the Sea of Japan border this region on the southeast. Administrative boundaries have undergone frequent reconstitution since the region came under Tsarist control in 1860. By 1906, the Amur, Primor'e, Kamchatka, and Sakhalin oblasts (similar to a county) had come under the Priamur governor-generalship and were collectively known as the "Far East." During the late 1920s and most of the 1930s, the region was called Dal'krai, administered by the Far Eastern Regional Executive Committee (Dal'kraiispolkom). The Dal'krai in the late 1930s included the Amur, Kamchatka, Ussuri, northern Sakhalin, Primorsk, Kolyma, and Jewish Autonomous oblasts. In late 1938 Dal'krai was reorganized into the Primorsk Region and the Khabarovsk Region. Women like Alekseeva and Mishalova for the most part eventually settled in the Far East's southern zones and in or near the towns of Khabarovsk, Vladivostok, Komsomol'sk-na-Amure, and Blagoveshchensk (see figure 1: "Map of the Russian Far East").

Climate and geography conspire to make life in the Far East a challenge. Along its southern periphery in the Vladivostok area, temperatures are considered mild, but as John Stephan, a leading historian of the Far East phrased it, summer humidity "rivals that of Calcutta."[9] In the interior temperatures tend toward the extremes, with global cold records in the north where "steel cracks like glass" and hot summer temperatures in the south "known to carbonize roof shingles."[10] The area is rich in fish, wildlife, minerals, and timber, but it is also gripped by permafrost and riddled with marshlands that necessitate special adaptations to building and provide abundant breeding grounds for all manner of biting insects and hardy mosquitoes (colloquially referred to as "fascists" by longsuffering residents). Difficult climatic conditions and inhospitable soil meant that most Russian and Soviet settlements had the potential to thrive only in the south near the volatile border region. In the Soviet period poor transport links resulted in widespread malnutrition and scurvy during winter on large construction projects for industries such as those in Komsomol'sk-na-Amure. The extreme climate and primitive living conditions were not a secret to the Soviet reading and filmgoing public, having been the backdrop of stories intended to demonstrate the heroism and resolve of Soviet frontier builders.

Alekseeva's father was distraught at her rash decision to volunteer for such a life without his permission, and he warned her that she was heading to a place of "pure suffering."[11] But she was adamant. "We very much

---

[9] John J. Stephan, *The Russian Far East: A History* (Stanford: Stanford University Press, 1994), 9.
[10] *Ibid.*   [11] Alekseeva, 101.

1. Map of the Russian Far East in the twenty-first century.

wanted to try out our own strength; prove that we were not afraid of anything."[12] The allures of its distance and "rumors about all kinds of difficulties: scurvy, harsh climate, a life in tents and lean-tos" captured imaginations.[13] Mishalova was elated when she received an official invitation to fulfill her fantasies of moving to "Kamchatka or Sakhalin . . . where there were mountains, the taiga, and water and where it was difficult to travel from place to place . . . or at least to Komsomol'sk-na-Amure. I dreamed of working where it was very difficult."[14] As a one-time homeless urchin, she recalled, with some sense of irony, that the other teenage

[12] *Ibid.*, 14.   [13] Memoir of Polina Bazarova, GAKhK P, f. 442, op. 2, 283, l. 97.
[14] Mishalova, 86.

girls "were envious that I was an orphan [and] that I could go wherever I wanted, that I did not have to ask anyone for permission or explain myself to anyone."[15] Everything she knew about the region she picked up from movies and books such as *Japan's Secret Agent, The Border Under Lock*, and *The Enemy Will Never Cross the Border*.[16] The prospect of being called up for a higher cause and the opportunity for public displays of self-abnegation in a perilous zone were powerful draws for such urban teenagers. Attempts to dissuade the teenagers from joining up because they were the "weaker" sex were counterproductive. Bazarova and her girlfriends became all the more stubborn when well-meaning relatives exclaimed, "Where are you heading? Lads can't endure it over there!"[17] In fact, they had good reason to worry and probably a much better sense of what lay ahead.

Another of those who read Khetagurova's article was Klava Novikova. Her mother had died giving birth to her in 1921, and in the course of collectivization in the late 1920s her father was executed for being a kulak (a "strong" or well-off peasant) in their village in the Kursk oblast. Novikova was adopted by strangers, completed seven grades at school and went to work in a factory. For years she was ashamed and afraid to tell anyone that she was the daughter of a kulak. In the 1930s it seemed to her that she had to "make amends to our great country" for her family's "indelible guilt," so Khetagurova's invitation to work for the Motherland struck a chord.[18] Aged eighteen, Novikova volunteered to join the builders of Komsomol'sk-na-Amure.

The Komsomol'sk she encountered in 1939 consisted of "barracks, the taiga and dreams."[19] Eventually, she married a "good lad" and had a son, Valerii. Fifteen days after his birth in 1941, his father left for the war front. Alone with an infant, with no relatives to help her, Novikova worked during the day at an exemplary construction site and at night collected undergarments from neighborhood men to launder for a kopek a piece. Because there were too few places for children in the city's crèches, she had to leave her infant alone at home, wrapped tightly and next to a stove to keep from freezing while she worked. Then came what seemed to be a stroke of great luck: she got a job as an accountant at a produce store. But after only a month on the job, she was accused of embezzlement, like many "small fries" who were caught taking home crumbs to feed hungry "tots." She received a sentence of seven and a half years to be served in

---

[15] *Ibid.*, 89.   [16] *Ibid.*   [17] Bazarova, 97.

[18] Ekaterina Sazhneva, "Zhili-byli samurai so starukhoi," *Moskovskii komsomolets*, November 16, 2005, *www.mk.ru/numbers/1912/article64683.htm* (2 of 9).

[19] Aleksandr Iaroshenko, "Klaudia i Iasaburo," *Amurskaia pravda*, March 25, 2004. *www.amurpravda.ru/articles/2004/03/25/4.html?print* (1 of 8).

the labor camps of Magadan, where she "worked as a medical orderly in the sick ward, thank God; it was a good job, not like work felling trees, but in a warm place: my job was to collect samples of phlegm and bodily fluids from prisoners to test for tuberculosis, gonorrhea, and syphilis."[20]

Novikova survived this "hell, and did not crack, I never even said one swear word there."[21] Upon release, she returned to her home in Komsomol'sk to find that her husband, who had returned as a war hero, had married another woman and that her son barely knew her, having been raised by strangers. Others close to her wondered out loud why she bothered coming back. She cried, decided that it was her fault that she had become a stranger to her family, steeled herself to carry on, and went in search of a new life.

Volunteers?

The campaign's success in attracting women like Alekseeva, Mishalova, and Novikova and their attitudes to the world they encountered in the Far East exposes a stratum in Soviet society receptive to official exhortations to build and sacrifice in the name of socialism and patriotic sentiments. A closer look at this stratum, for the most part neglected by scholars, enriches ongoing debates in the Soviet field about women's status under Stalinism. This book also illustrates some of the ways Stalinist society worked, particularly whether and how this regime engendered belief in its mission or whether the totalitarian system relied solely on coercion and passive acquiescence.

Those who subscribe to the idea that all Soviet citizens were oppressed by a terrorist regime see every instance of volunteerism and public expressions of approval as either charades by individuals out to prove their loyalty because of fear or outright falsifications by officials to obscure the truth about wholesale disaffection with the Communists.[22] These scholars contend that the Communist regime was illegitimate and

---

[20] Sazhneva, "Zhili-byli samurai so starukhoi" (3 of 9).

[21] Iaroshenko, "Klaudia i Iasaburo," (2 of 8).

[22] Among those who see all public displays as charades is Jeffrey Brooks in *Thank You, Comrade Stalin!: Soviet Public Culture from Revolution to Cold War* (Princeton: Princeton University Press, 2000). For the school of thought stressing resistance and lack of belief in the system, see Jeffrey Rossmann, "The Teikovo Cotton Workers' Strike of April 1932," *Russian Review* 56:1 (1997), 44–69, and Michael David-Fox, Peter Holquist, and Marshall Poe (eds.), *The Resistance Debate in Russian and Soviet History* (Bloomington: Slavica Publishers, 2003). Stephen Kotkin argues that people wanted to speak the language of the regime and to belong, but this willingness to believe in socialism did not preclude dissatisfaction and resistance to some aspects of the state. see Kotkin, *Magnetic Mountain: Stalinism as a Civilization* (Berkeley: University of California Press, 1995).

unpopular.[23] This fragility in turn generated a reliance on violence and intimidation by ideologues already prone to disregard laws and human rights in pursuit of utopian dreams or boundless power. Others contend that public expressions of support were part of a subterfuge by those who were engaged in impostures or cynical manipulation of slogans, not so much out of fear and certainly not as expressions of real belief in socialism, but in order to secure a slot in an order of estates rather than "a system of social relationships generated by a regime of production."[24] Influential historians, including Fitzpatrick, see the system as a total failure held together by a mixture of inertia, status anxiety, coercion, and rewards for a loyal few.

Fitzpatrick and others, without recourse to debates about the legitimacy of the Bolshevik Revolution or the feasibility of socialist systems in industrial societies, propose that the economic disasters created by Stalin irrevocably warped the dreams espoused by Russian revolutionaries to perfect humanity and forge a new type of social being. What resulted, they argue, was indeed a new person. However, this New Soviet Person was of a different caliber only in that they had incredibly honed "skills" necessary for the "hunting and gathering of scarce goods in an urban environment."[25] Without a doubt, this shoe fits – to a certain extent. However, there is no place in this portrait for those who were not cynical, self-serving, or Communist fanatics. Given such explanations, one is left wondering how a system so utterly reviled by its own citizens survived for another fifty years.

The debate about the nature of Stalinism, voluntarism, and the individual's relationship to the state is far from settled. Lynne Viola's work on the "25,000ers," the factory workers sent to administer newly formed collective farms in the early 1930s, illustrates that among certain groups there was a real commitment to Stalin's policies in the countryside and a willingness to make personal sacrifices for a greater cause.[26] More recently, advocates of the so-called "Soviet subjectivity school" insist that the regime was strong and had a powerful psychological and emotional hold over society.[27] This regime, they argue, was robust not because it

---

[23] See Martin Malia, *The Soviet Tragedy: A History of Socialism in Russia, 1917–1991* (New York: Free Press, 1994), arguing for illegitimacy. On widespread dissent, see Sarah Davies, *Popular Opinion in Stalin's Russia: Terror, Propaganda and Dissent, 1934–41* (Cambridge and New York: Cambridge University Press, 1997).

[24] Sheila Fitzpatrick, *Tear Off the Masks!: Identity and Imposture in Twentieth-Century Russia* (Princeton: Princeton University Press, 2005), 22.

[25] Fitzpatrick, *Everyday Stalinism*, 2.

[26] Lynne Viola, *The Best Sons of the Fatherland: Workers in the Vanguard of Soviet Collectivization* (New York: Oxford University Press, 1987).

[27] Works associated with the "Soviet subjectivity school" include Jochen Hellbeck, *Revolution on My Mind: Writing a Diary under Stalin* (Cambridge, MA: Harvard University

could enforce compliance only through sheer brutal force or only by offering material rewards for blind obedience. The system proved powerful because it was rooted in Communist ideology, which offered sophisticated and diffuse methods of domination through discourse.[28] Their argument is that individuals, otherwise capable of a critical stance, did not wish to live in unresolved tension and resistance to the only world they knew, so they worked on themselves through writing to suppress internal doubts and explain away injustices and shortcomings.

The choices and attitudes of women like Alekseeva and Novikova do not fit neatly into any of these analytical schemas. Whether the women thought that Stalin was an omnipotent leader or that everything was going well in the new socialist state is impossible to say. It appears that a great many believed that enemies were at work to undermine a historic socialist project and were genuinely committed to defending the hard-won accomplishments. Neither Novikova nor Mishalova volunteered in order to improve their material circumstances or to seek an upwardly mobile husband. They did not do it as a form of resistance or to drop out. They were not pressured to volunteer but rather pleaded to be selected.

Despite her tragic childhood, Baba (Granny) Klava, as she was called in her old age, recalled her youth as a happy time. On the wall of the 84-year-old's home hung "like icons" a photograph of Stalin next to one of her second husband, Iasaburo Khachiia. She told a reporter in 2005, with genuine enthusiasm, "We lived joyfully under socialism, even if we were poor, we were all equal – thanks to comrade Stalin!"[29] This was a different sense of self in society, the debates among historians would have it. By focusing attention on the question of how young women came to identify so intensely with this system and volunteer for migration to a "distant planet," we can also get closer to resolving the larger questions of whether this was a weak system, with a despot ruling by force over a cowed population, or whether the regime made great headway in

---

Press, 2006); Igal Halfin, *From Darkness to Light: Class Consciousness and Salvation in Revolutionary Russia* (Pittsburgh: University of Pittsburgh Press, 2000), and Halfin, *Terror in My Soul: Communist Autobiographies on Trial* (Cambridge, MA: Harvard University Press, 2003); and Oleg V. Kharkhordin, *The Collective and the Individual in Russia: A Study of Practices* (Berkeley: University of California Press, 1999).

[28] Because, on the surface, Sheila Fitzpatrick and "young cultural historians of the 'Soviet subjectivity school'" appear to be working on similar questions of identity and "self-fashioning" (though their ultimate conclusions differ), Fitzpatrick has found it necessary to stress dissimilarities between her methodology and those whose "focus is on the self and subjecthood; mine [is] on identity and identification. They are interested in discourse and ideology and have a strong theoretical orientation; I am interested in social practice and the everyday and have a low tolerance for totalizing theory." see Fitzpatrick, *Tear Off the Masks!*, 8.

[29] Sazhneva, "Zhili-byli samurai so starukhoi" (2 of 9).

structuring individual identity and mobilizing thousands to expand state power across Eurasia despite obvious failures and abuses.

For young women, being "Soviet" had different connotations from what it would have meant for men or women of another generation. Clearly, some of the young migrants had cultivated a connection between their sense of self and the Soviet Union's place in history. This identification was rooted in the tremendous leaps in education and perspectives made by women born after the triumph of the Bolsheviks in comparison with the experiences of their mothers. Having been educated under Soviet power, they were the first cohort of working-class women to be literate. Female literacy had never been a priority in the Tsarist educational system, even though great strides were made in spreading literacy among boys and young men. Literate and socially mobile, many young women had a palpable sense of their uniqueness and experienced this as a true personal revolution that catapulted them into a broader world in ways their mothers could never have imagined. Excited by the possibilities of learning through reading and travel, young women were extraordinarily receptive to the frontier fantasies and wilderness adventures coursing through films, music, and literature of the 1930s.[30] This way of seeing women flies in the face of a long-held consensus among historians of Soviet women who argue that women's status underwent a severe degradation in the mid-1930s.[31] Such characterizations of women's status in this period are not entirely convincing. The questions of whether gender roles contracted to a narrow range in the mid-1930s and whether women experienced a drop in status are central to this study.

Debating women's status

Many leading scholars working on Soviet women's history and gender contend that Stalin, with the hearty approval of other men in the Communist party, brazenly betrayed the commitments made by early Bolsheviks when he reinforced gender boundaries by recriminalizing abortion and dismantling programs that previously protected women's

---

[30] Youth culture of the 1920s is the subject of Anne Gorsuch, *Youth in Revolutionary Russia: Enthusiasts, Bohemians, Delinquents* (Bloomington: Indiana University Press, 2000).

[31] For the variety of works taking this position, see Victoria Bonnell, *Iconography of Power: Political Posters under Lenin and Stalin* (Berkeley: University of California Press, 1997); Thomas Schrand, "Soviet 'Civic-Minded Women' in the 1930s: Gender, Class, and Industrialization in a Socialist Society," *Journal of Women's History* 11:3 (1999), 126–150; Lynne Attwood, "Rationality versus Romanticism: Representations of Women in the Stalinist Press," in Linda Edmondson (ed.), *Gender in Russian History and Culture* (New York: Palgrave, 2001), 158–176; and Susan E. Reid, "All Stalin's Women: Gender and Power in Soviet Art of the 1930s," *Slavic Review* 57:1 (Spring 1998), 133–173.

rights. Along the same lines, it has been proposed that the Communist regime in the 1930s actually fostered the evolution of a new and sub-servient middle class by emphasizing consumerism and women's "nat-ural" duties as mothers and housewives. The regime ostensibly wanted women to devote their energies to maintaining sober patriarchal families with throngs of well-groomed and disciplined children. These develop-ments are known in Western historiography as the "Great Retreat."[32]

Historians point to a number of developments they consider to be evi-dence of a retreat. The recriminalization of abortion in 1936 has been seen by historians as a watershed event in the history of Soviet women and as a key feature of Stalinism. However, historians disagree on the impetus for this shift and on whether this was a radical retrenchment and a conservative return to traditional family norms or if this represented a measure wholly congruent with the Bolshevik ideology dating to the early revolutionary period. While Wendy Goldman, a distinguished specialist on Soviet women, sees this as a radical break with the Bolsheviks' early intentions, Richard Stites, another pioneering and influential historian, argued that the family model promoted by the regime in the 1930s was actually compatible with values held by many key Bolsheviks including Lenin and his wife Nadezhda Krupskaia. Others have maintained that the Bolsheviks never intended to liberate women from familial duties. Even before the Revolution, Bolsheviks such as Maxim Gorkii stressed the nur-turing essence of women. Heather DeHaan has pointed out that "[t]he association between the Soviet woman and Soviet motherhood was cer-tainly imbedded in the Bolshevik value system long before the traditional family was 'rehabilitated' in the 1930s."[33] Recently, David Hoffmann has proposed that this emphasis on the family was a reflection of the regime's drive to "manage reproduction" in very similar ways and for the same reasons as other European states in the interwar period, "reflect-ing a new type of population politics practiced in the modern era."[34]

---

[32] The term is associated with Nicholas S. Timasheff, *The Great Retreat: The Growth and Decline of Communism in Russia* (New York: E. P. Dutton, 1946). Timasheff argued that Stalin had abandoned the principles of socialism in exchange for neo-traditional Russian nationalism and patriarchy. Vera Dunham's work is best known for its emphasis on middle-class values and consumerism as defining components of Stalinism; see Vera S. Dunham, *In Stalin's Time: Middle-Class Values in Soviet Fiction* (Cambridge: Cambridge University Press, 1976). For more on the identification of women with consumption in the 1930s, see Sheila Fitzpatrick, "Becoming Cultured: Socialist Realism and the Representation of Privilege and Taste," in her *The Cultural Front: Power and Culture in Revolutionary Russia* (Ithaca: Cornell University Press, 1992), 219–229.

[33] Heather DeHaan, "Engendering a People: Soviet Women and Socialist Rebirth in Rus-sia," *Canadian Slavonic Papers* 41:3–4 (September–December, 1999), 440.

[34] David Hoffmann, "Mothers in the Motherland: Stalinist Pronatalism in Its Pan-European Context," *Journal of Social History* 34:1 (Fall 2000), 36.

Hoffman insists that there was no effort to resurrect "the traditional" family especially since, like other Europeans, the Soviet government, "did not champion the family as a private commitment or as a means to personal fulfillment. Instead it explicitly promoted the maintenance of one's family as an obligation to society and to the state."[35]

Art historian Susan Reid, working on cultural policies and the representation of women, contends that men aggrieved by their inability to limit women's incursions into positions previously associated with masculinity both in the workplace and in the representation of Soviet power were compensated by Stalin in other ways. Thus, according to Reid, while women were shown taking on public roles and positions of authority previously associated with masculine abilities, "[a] variety of narrative and compositional devices reproduced their subjection to patriarchal authority, both specifically as women and as representatives of the 'people.'"[36] Propaganda of this Great Retreat "identified man with culture, woman with nature . . . man with heavy industrial production, and woman with agriculture, food preparation, consumption and reproduction."[37]

Reid and other historians typically see the Movement of Wives (*obshchestvennitsy*) initiated in 1936 as "symptomatic of, and contribut[ing] to, the reaffirmation of gender and class hierarchies."[38] They argue that activist wives were supposed to promote domestic comforts for Soviet professional elite men and elite workers (Stakhanovites).[39] These wives also ostensibly represented the rise of a Soviet middle class, whose values included conspicuous consumption, freedom from the need to work for wives, and a public role for women's "natural" caretaking proclivities. Press and artistic coverage of conferences such as the 1936 All-Union Conference of the Wives of Managers and Engineers of Heavy Industry and the 1936 Conference of the Wives of Red Army Commanders, where

---

[35] *Ibid.*, 45.   [36] Reid, "All Stalin's Women," 148.   [37] *Ibid.*, 147.

[38] *Ibid.*, 154. For other treatments of the wife-activists' movement, see Schrand, "Soviet 'Civic-Minded Women' in the 1930s," 126–150; Robert Maier, "Sovety Zhen as a Surrogate Trade Union: Comments on the History of the Movement of Activist Women in the 1930s," in Kevin McDermott and John Morison (eds.), *Politics and Society Under the Bolsheviks: Selected Papers from the Fifth World Congress of Central and East European Studies 1995* (New York: St. Martin's Press, 1999), 189–198; Fitzpatrick, *The Cultural Front*, 216–237; Rudolf Schlesinger, *The Family in the USSR: Documents and Readings* (London: Routledge, 1949), 235–250; Lewis Siegelbaum, *Stakhanovism and the Politics of Productivity in the USSR, 1935–1941* (New York: Cambridge University Press, 1988), 241; Robert Thurston, "The Soviet Family during the Great Terror, 1935–1941," *Soviet Studies* 43:3 (1991), 557–558. For published excerpts of their conference, see *Vsesoiuznoe soveshchanie zhen khoziaistvennikov i inzhenerno-tekhnicheskikh rabotnikov tiazheloi promyshlennosti – stenograficheskii otchet* (Moscow: Partizdat, 1936).

[39] "Stakhanovites" were workers who had labored at an accelerated rate and were rewarded for their exemplary behavior and record-breaking productivity. For more on this program, see Siegelbaum, *Stakhanovism and the Politics of Productivity*.

Khetagurova gained renown, have been analyzed for their messages about gender and power. Reid has concluded that these public gatherings were orchestrated to "emphasize the emotional bond between the leaders and the people and to arouse fanaticism among those sectors of the population considered most prone to irrational enthusiasm, women and young people."[40] However, by focusing strictly on representations of these public events, historians have paid little attention to women's sense of their role in this spectacle and the paths that brought women like Khetagurova into the national spotlight.

The Movement of Wives was more than a series of large national conferences. Mary Buckley and Rebecca Balmas Neary have demonstrated that the Movement of Wives in Industry, Wives of Red Army Commanders, Wives of Railroad Employees, and wives of rural workers, among others, were more complex than simply venues for middle-class women to boss around inferiors.[41] Women in a variety of industrial sectors organized at their husbands' workplace to improve living conditions for their community as a whole, beginning in 1934. They attempted to use funds allocated to local trade unions to set up nurseries, improve cafeterias, and refurbish workers' dormitories. When necessary, hundreds at a time turned out to help their family members meet production quotas or clear spaces for parks and gardens.[42] The thousands of women who participated were a mixed group. Some had a working-class background and continued to work while participating in the organization. Others had little experience in the workplace and saw an opportunity to gain some experience and renown for charitable activities. Still others were wives

---

[40] Reid, "All Stalin's Women," 154.

[41] Rebecca Balmas Neary, "Mothering Socialist Society: The Wife-Activists' Movement and the Soviet Culture of Daily Life, 1934–41," *Russian Review* 58:3 (July 1999), 396–412 and Mary Buckley, "The Untold Story of *Obshchestvennitsa* in the 1930s," *Europe-Asia Studies* 48:4 (1996), 569–586.

[42] In the Far East the Movement of Wives of Engineers and Technical Personnel and Stakhanovites was active in the fishing industry and among workers in the ports. Activists among Wives of Red Army Commanders in the region tried to ameliorate the shortages of teachers and nurses by recruiting local women into training courses. There were some successes in this venture. One army wife joked in December 1936 that they no longer had to implore young lieutenants on temporary leave from the Far East to marry "a pre-school teacher or a dentist" and bring her back to the frontier. See Liubov' Sud'bina quoted in *Vsesoiuznoe soveshchanie zhen komandnogo i nachal'stvuiushchego sostava RKKA* (Moscow: Gos. Voennoe izdatel'stvo, 1937), 234. Sud'bina's husband was a pilot in the Far Eastern Red Army air squadron. In 1937 there were ninety-five women's councils among the various fish-processing plants, with 4,000 activists. Wives were also well organized on the railroads of the Far East, with a membership roll of about 10,000 women. See El'vira Vasil'chenko, *Sovetskaia gosudarstvennaia politika po preobrazovaniiu sotsial'nogo statusa zhenshchin v usloviiakh Dal'nego Vostoka (1917–1940 gg.)* (Komsomol'sk-na-Amure: Komsomol'sk-na-Amure gos. tekhn. universitet, 2000), 46.

of workers who after joining the organization moved on to develop skills and joined the labor force. The organization that Khetagurova joined after she married Georgii Khetagurov, the Wives of Red Army Commanders, included women from all social ranks and ethnic groups.[43] Many of those who were employees of the Women's Department of the Communist party (Zhenotdel) moved over to work for the Political Administration of the Worker-Peasant Red Army (RKKA) to run their sectors for work among officers' families when the Zhenotdel was disbanded in 1930.[44] As this study will demonstrate, Khetagurova, the daughter of a worker and activist who volunteered for the Far Eastern frontier in 1932, was hardly the epitome of a bored charitable lady.[45]

Anna Krylova concurs with the skepticism expressed by Buckley and Neary about the usefulness of seeing women's lives solely through the prism of the Great Retreat. Krylova argues that the Stalinist 1930s fostered "an unfixed state of gender" when the state "allowed for a construction of non-conventional female dreams, ideals and personalities."[46] She points out that it was, in fact, after the supposed Great Retreat that female pilots attained prominence in the mass media in 1938. The long-distance flight from Moscow to the Far East by Polina Osipenko, Marina Raskova, and Valentina Grizodubova was one of the most intensely covered events in this period.[47] In the course of this coverage and through interviews with journalists, Krylova has found, the female pilots participated in "combining military expertise in war, violence, femininity and redefined motherhood . . . as a new gender constellation at the readers' disposal."[48] Rather than being a period that heralded a return to

[43] For Valentina Khetagurova's speech at the conference and the speeches of other Red Army wives, see *Vsesoiuznoe soveshchanie . . . RKKA* (1937), 172–177. The conference was also extensively featured in *Rabotnitsa* 1 (January 1937). The women who are featured in these texts hailed from many regions, ethnic groups, and social backgrounds.

[44] For an example of this shift in cadres from Zhenotdel to the Army Political administration, see the biographical note on N. F. Iakovleva in *Rabotnitsa* 35 (December 1936), 8.

[45] According to Khetagurova's official autobiography, her father was a factory worker at the Baltiisk Factory in Petrograd when he died in 1918. Her mother was left with four children. Khetagurova's first job was as a draftsman in a machine-building institute. "Personal File: Khetagurova, Valentina Simeonovna for 1938," GAKhK P, f. 35, op. 14, d. 11147, ll. 1–2.

[46] Anna Krylova, "Stalinist Identity from the Viewpoint of Gender: Rearing a Generation of Professionally Violent Women-Fighters in 1930s Stalinist Russia," *Gender & History* 16:3 (November 2004), 640.

[47] In 1937 the percentage of women serving in the armed forces was 0.08 percent (1,142 women). In 1939 their number was slightly lower at 1,038 (0.05 percent) and among that number 51 women were in the naval fleet. In 1937 7,264 women (2.7 percent of the total) were part of the so-called contingent "A," paid employees of the NKVD. See V. B. Zhiromskaia, *Demograficheskaia istoriia Rossii v 1930-e gody: Vzgliad v neizvestnoe* (Moscow: ROSSPEN, 2001), 106–107.

[48] Krylova, "Stalinist Identity," 646.

traditional models of patriarchy, the 1930s "witnessed an attempt to . . . reconcile glaring contradictions between conflicting notions of young womanhood and women's rights."[49] Similarly, Buckley has demonstrated that peasant women continued to be represented as assertive and capable and that many took advantage of opportunities. Despite the discomfort and resistance from men, young peasant women who proved themselves in competitions to raise productivity in agriculture considered themselves to be men's equals.[50]

By implicitly assuming that there was a retreat in women's status, historians risk painting a rosy picture of women's lives and Communist policies before the mid-1930s. It is also essential to remember that just as much as there could never be a singular "male" experience in Soviet history, we cannot talk about women as an undifferentiated category. It is difficult to see how this ostensible new stress on strong patriarchal families worked in everyday life. Seventeen-year-old Alekseeva volunteered for an "independent" life without parental permission and eventually married a man who shared her interests in work and sports. Mishalova dreamed of rugged mountains and was more concerned with spies than motherhood. Novikova's story underscores the degree to which the state disrupted families, rather than strengthened them. All the women limited their fertility by some means despite the withdrawal of contraception from sale and the ban on abortions in the summer of 1936. Although family law was changed in the 1930s, the argument that as a consequence "[w]omen's primary political, social and economic function in society became reduced to producing and rearing children" is not well supported by the historical evidence of the late 1930s.[51]

The impression among scholars that gender boundaries were tightly fixed by the mid-1930s was produced by the questions posed about women in this era. For the most part, historical inquiries have concentrated on how women were represented in a handful of venues; how policymakers tried to control reproduction; and how they exploited women's wage labor. Women, as such, have appeared in scholarship as either victims of the regime or as a backdrop in the theatrics of Stalinism. For many other historians, what women thought and how they related to the state seem peripheral to the seemingly more pressing questions of Communist ideology, totalitarianism, modernization, nationalisms, empire-building, militarism, and so on. Such approaches, of course, presuppose women to be a separate nonpolitical and nonideological

---

[49] *Ibid.*, 641.
[50] Mary Buckley, *Mobilizing Soviet Peasants: Heroines and Heroes of Stalin's Fields* (Lanham, MD: Lexington Books, 2006).
[51] Paula Michaels, "Motherhood, Patriotism, and Ethnicity: Soviet Kazakhstan and the 1936 Abortion Ban," *Feminist Studies* 27:2 (Summer 2001), 327.

category, and gender to be social practice rather than an ideology. As a result, although the published and archival sources of this period brim with such material, most scholars have failed to notice the upsurge of activism and volunteerism among women in the late 1930s in response to the martial culture and their enthusiastic reception of the call to secure Soviet power on a distant frontier.

Women as empire builders

Although women were present at every phase in the history of Russia's eastward expansion, and were targeted for settlement by the Khetagurovite program, their roles and even their very presence are known by few outside the Russian Far East. This exclusion from the narrative of expansion and colonization mirrors the place of women in the narratives of other empire-building projects. According to Anne McClintock, a specialist on the subjects of gender, sexuality, and colonialism, European empire-building projects typically excised women from histories of "direct action as national citizens" while subsuming women "symbolically into the national body politic as its boundary and metaphoric limit."[52] The obfuscation of their roles in empire-building and colonization is ironic because, for young female migrants, it was this geographic mobility and visibility in the expansion Soviet power that offered the greatest potential for realizing their aspirations for respect, autonomy, and incorporation into the narrative of history-making exploits.[53]

The amalgamation of frontier mythologies, the women's perceptions of themselves as grateful products of the Soviet system, and long-entrenched

---

[52] Anne McClintock, "Family Feuds: Gender, Nationalism and the Family," *Feminist Review* 44 (Summer 1993), 62.

[53] Women as migrants and colonizers have not figured as subjects in Western historiography of the Russian or Soviet empires. See Donald W. Treadgold's early and influential treatment of resettlement before 1917, *The Great Siberian Migration: Government and Peasant in Resettlement from Emancipation to the First World War* (Princeton: Princeton University Press, 1957). Indicative of a recent boom in frontier and settlement studies of the pre-Soviet period are Michael Khodarkovsky, *Russia's Steppe Frontier: The Making of a Colonial Empire* (Bloomington: Indiana University Press, 2002); Willard Sunderland, *Taming the Wild Field: Colonization and Empire on the Russian Steppe* (Ithaca: Cornell University Press, 2004); John L. Evans, *Russian Expansion on the Amur, 1848–1860: The Push to the Pacific* (Lewiston, NY: Edwin Mellen Press, 1999); Steven Marks, *Road to Power: The Trans-Siberian Railroad and the Colonization of Asian Russia, 1850–1917* (Ithaca: Cornell University Press, 1991); Alfred J. Rieber and Masha Siefert (eds.), *Extending the Borders of Russian History: Essays in Honor of Alfred J. Rieber* (Budapest: Central European University Press, 2003). The study of the Far East in the national imagination before the Bolshevik Revolution has been pioneered by Mark Bassin, *Imperial Visions: Nationalist Imagination and Geographical Expansion in the Russian Far East, 1840–1865* (Cambridge: Cambridge University Press, 1999).

beliefs that self-abnegation was the ultimate expression of honorable womanhood fueled their desire to take direct action in securing the Soviet system on its most frightening periphery. Self-abnegation in both public and private realms had strong associations with models of womanhood exalted by Russian intellectuals and revolutionaries dating back to the nineteenth century. Exhortations to make sacrifices for collective needs reinforced these ideals among a new generation of women. This widely prized womanly self-abnegation could be expressed in very public ways, such as volunteering for service in the military, which many women like Mishalova considered their duty and within their capacities, or in helping to build new cities in the wilderness.

Women craved postings to a frontier where they could be both real and "symbolic border guards."[54] In their imaginings, their very presence, as representatives of emancipated womanhood and as active agents of the Soviet system, would indelibly mark the borders of the Soviet national collective. They would defend real borderlands from foreign enemies while helping to expose internal ones. Their desire to rehearse fantasies of sacrifice for the sake of Soviet power underscores that there was genuine support for the regime.

This was a symbiotic relationship. The regime needed women's labor on the frontier in many fields and capacities. Far Eastern industries were unable to function without an influx of women with very specific training and professional skills and proven records of activism. Consequently, it was impossible to present a limited vision of women's roles because it would fail to appeal to precisely this kind of activist woman. As an unforeseen benefit, the campaign also became a release valve for pressures created by these restless female activists eager to put into action their revolutionary enthusiasm.

As it turned out, being a symbolic embodiment of Soviet national aspirations carried a heavy price that included intense scrutiny of personal behavior and participation in a system of repression and terror. Many of these would-be empire builders were not prepared to pay that price. Their experiences encapsulate both the positive potential intrinsic to the Soviet regime's programs for female emancipation and the simultaneous dangers and disappointments inherent in conforming to a regime so deformed by paranoia and ruthless exploitation of its own people.

---

[54] Nira Yuval-Davis, *Gender and Nation* (London: Sage, 1997), 23, expanded on the importance of gender in the system of "symbolic border guard" described by John Armstrong, *Nations Before Nationalism* (Chapel Hill: University of North Carolina Press, 1982). Also see the special issue, Lynn Abrams and Karen Hunt (eds.), "Borders and Frontiers in Women's History," *Women's History Review* 9:2 (2000).

Soviet empire-building practices are laid bare in new ways when we look at them from a gendered perspective. When we compare the interplay of race, class, and gender in structuring relationships of dominance and resistance, it is clear that the Soviet Union was a case apart from other imperial systems. The story of women joining empire-building projects by migrating to distant outposts can appear eerily analogous to the histories of women and gender in other empire-building contexts. There are obvious similarities in the way gender ideals infused Soviet motifs of frontier life and Western settlement mythologies.[55] There are also striking similarities in some of the practices and aspirations, described by Elizabeth Harvey, of young German women who set off at almost the same time to define and defend German identity against contamination by Poles and Jews in contested and newly conquered borderlands of Hitler's Reich.[56] However, women's roles on the frontiers of Stalinism differed in profound ways from the roles of women in other empire-building contexts. This divergence was rooted in the ways in which gender and reproduction facilitated Russian and Soviet empire-building agendas.

Nira Yuval-Davis, Anne McClintock, and Elizabeth Harvey, among others working on gender and nationalism, have explored why and how it often fell to German, British, or French women to reproduce nationality on the peripheries by transmitting "ethnic symbols and ways of life to other members of their ethnic group, [and] to serve as signifiers of ethnic/national difference."[57] Soviet women did not engage in similar reproduction of ethnic difference in part because "Soviet" was not a nationality and in part because of women's status in the Communist system. The supposed propensities of women to cling to traditions were not esteemed by Communists but rather reviled. Until the mid-1930s, women's status in the Soviet Union was one of formerly "backward" and oppressed groups that were being emancipated by a socialist

---

[55] For a discussion of the meaning of colonization in the pre-revolutionary context, see Willard Sunderland, "Empire without Imperialism? Ambiguities of Colonization in Tsarist Russia," *Ab Imperio* 2 (2003), 101–114, and James Gibson, "Russian Imperial Expansion in Context and by Contrast," *Journal of Historical Geography* 28:2 (2002), 181–202.

[56] Elizabeth Harvey, *Women and the Nazi East: Agents and Witnesses of Germanization* (New Haven: Yale University Press, 2003).

[57] "Introduction," in Nira Yuval-Davis and Floya Anthias (eds.), *Woman-Nation-State* (New York: Macmillan, 1989), 9–10. On the role of imagining German national difference at "home" and in the colonies through domestic work, see Nancy Reagin, "The Imagined Hausfrau: National Identity, Domesticity, and Colonialism in Imperial Germany," *Journal of Modern History* 73:1 (March 2001), 54–86. On the role of white women as signifiers and enforcers of racial purity, see Susan Kollin, *Nature's State: Imagining Alaska as the Last Frontier* (Chapel Hill: University of North Carolina Press, 2001).

state dedicated to progress and modernity.[58] By the mid-1930s, with the "Woman's Question" purportedly resolved, women came to represent Soviet achievements in Stalinist iconography.[59] This was also the period when women became visible in representations of wilderness adventures and border defense.

In 1937 the rupture between an oppressive and "dark" past was vested in both Communist men and in "New Women" like Khetagurova willing and able to demonstrate patriotism in the context of either labor achievements or securing Soviet power in far-flung regions. While the "New Soviet Woman" did not embody ethnic differences on the frontier, she vividly exemplified a rupture between "backward" women who stayed close to the home or village versus the mobile, modern woman who traversed wide-open spaces and sought out rugged adventures alongside men. The New Soviet Woman, at the center of Galina Shubina's 1938 poster *Oh, My Homeland is a Spacious Country* [*Shiroka strana moia rodnaia*] captures this new placement of women in motion and in the context of "wide" geographic and imaginary spaces.[60] This exaltation of women as travelers and adventure seekers was another instance of divergence between the Soviet case and the representation of female mobility in other colonial and nation-building contexts.

Typically, as Julie Mostov has proposed, "Gender and nation are social constructions which intimately participate in the formation of one another: nations are gendered, and the topography of the nation is mapped in gendered terms (feminized soil, landscapes and boundaries, and masculine movement over these spaces.)"[61] The example of the Khetagurovites turns some of these concepts on their head. The Soviet Far East appeared in popular imaginations and official representations as a thoroughly masculine space. The migrants presented a case of female movement across this space. The mobility of women is a central element

---

[58] The seminal study on the politics of female emancipation in Russia and early Soviet history is Richard Stites, *The Women's Liberation Movement in Russia: Feminism, Nihilism, and Bolshevism 1860–1930* (Princeton: Princeton University Press, 1978).

[59] Women's status as symbols of modernity in the late 1930s is described by Choi Chatterjee, *Celebrating Women: Gender, Festival Culture, and Bolshevik Ideology, 1910–1939* (Pittsburgh: University of Pittsburgh Press, 2002).

[60] Galina Shubina's poster was named for and accompanied by lyrics from V. Lebedev-Kumach and I. Dunaevskii's 1935 "Song of the Motherland," also known by the first line of the tune "Shiroka strana moia rodnaia" written for the 1936 film *Circus* [*Tsirk*]. The song became wildly popular and the melody theme for the broadcast signal of Radio Moscow. For the text of the song and translation, see James von Geldern and Richard Stites (eds.), *Mass Culture in Soviet Russia: Tales, Poems, Songs, Movies, Plays and Folklore, 1917–1953* (Bloomington: Indiana University Press, 1995), 271–272.

[61] Julie Mostov, "Sexing the Nation/Desexing the Body: The Politics of National Identity in the Former Yugoslavia," in Tamar Mayer (ed.), *Gender Ironies of Nationalism: Sexing the Nation* (London: Routledge, 2000), 89.

in the poems and songs dedicated to this campaign (see Appendices 3 to 7). The women's long train journeys across Eurasia played central roles in the publicity surrounding their resettlement and figured prominently as points of wonder and pride in memoirs written years later.

In the case of the Soviet empire, we cannot assume that Russians were the only agents of empire-building. The Soviet women who rushed to the frontiers did not represent Russian ethnic difference and they were not asked to defend or spread Russian neo-traditional culture in the peripheries. In fact, many of those who went were not ethnic Russians. Among volunteers for work on the Far Eastern periphery, a large proportion bore Ukrainian, Jewish, or Belorussian last names or identified themselves as such. (The Far East had been a major destination for Ukrainian peasant settlers since the 1880s). Subsequently, life on a frontier facilitated their attachment to a Soviet identity. The possibility, for some, of being active agents in the narratives of Soviet power trumped the paltry prospects for visibility within the bounds of officially tolerated Ukrainian, Russian, or Belorussian nationalisms in their home regions.

Concerns about race and biological determinism were not preoccupations of Soviet officials as they were for other imperialists in the nineteenth and twentieth centuries because, as Francine Hirsch has argued, "Soviets acted upon the belief that nationalities like classes were socio-historical groups with a shared consciousness and not racial biological groups."[62] This sets the Soviet empire far apart from other modern empires and produced different politics surrounding reproduction. In most imperial contexts, the choice of sexual or marriage partners was of great concern among white settlers and imperial administrators. Often, white women were brought to colonial outposts to keep white men from mixing with native women.[63] In other contexts, white women themselves called for greater participation on their part in imperial ventures to insure the purity of their race or cultural distinctiveness outside the metropole.[64] There is no evidence that Soviet women were enjoined to keep Slavic men from mixing with native women. Soviet women were also not called upon to

---

[62] Francine Hirsch, "Race Without the Practice of Racial Politics," *Slavic Review* 61:1 (Spring 2002), 30.

[63] Many British feminists saw themselves not only as pioneers in the colonies but as heralds of a new imperialism and sought an avenue to greater rights as white settlers in the colonies. See Cecily Devereux, "New Woman, New World: Maternal Feminism and the New Imperialism in the White Settler Colonies," *Women's Studies International Forum* 22:2 (1999), 175–184.

[64] For one example out of many studies finding women wanting to "get involved" in protecting the race, see Adele Perry, "'Fair Ones of a Purer Caste': White Women and Colonialism in Nineteenth-Century British Columbia," *Feminist Studies* 23:3 (1997), 501–524.

civilize or convert natives to a superior creed nor motivated by murderous racial dictates, like young Germans, to sort those unworthy of life from those destined to dominate others.[65] Communist Youth League activists like Mishalova, who was quickly selected to work for the NKVD in the Far East, came to police the social boundaries between those who ostensibly belonged to irreconcilable ideological communities. Many, like Novikova, also went because they considered it their duty to defend a nation they were told was under siege by enemies bent on returning working-class women like themselves to humiliating subservience.

The Khetagurovite campaign and its participants reveal a great deal about the workings of gender in the late 1930s and the mechanisms of Soviet empire-building. These women exemplified and facilitated the rise of a new model of womanhood based on an explicit link to Soviet civilization-building on the peripheries. Such women appeared as active subjects in official culture precisely in the second half of the 1930s. In turn, many women were emboldened to imagine themselves as integral to the Soviet collective in new and broader ways because of the possibilities offered by frontier fantasies. While acknowledging that there were shifts in the status and representation of women in the mid-1930s, this book will nevertheless argue that gender roles continued to be fluid as "the frontier" held out promises of collective and individual fulfillment.

Sources

The source base for a study of Soviet-era migrations and gender dynamics on the Far Eastern periphery is varied and rich. The bulk of documents related to the Khetagurovites are located in Khabarovsk at the State Archive of the Khabarovsk region (GAKhK), which now includes documents from the former Party Archive of the Khabarovsk region (PAKhK).[66] There are also relevant documents in the Russian State Archive of Socio-Political History (RGASPI), the State Archive of the Russian Federation (GA RF), the Russian State Archive of the Economy (RGAE), the Russian State Archive of Literature and Art (RGALI), and archives of Memorial located in Moscow.

---

[65] Women in other empire-building contexts often acted as the "kinder face of the imperial mission." For just one example, see Phyllis M. Martin, "Celebrating the Ordinary: Church, Empire and Gender in the Life of Mère Mari-Michelle Dédié (Senegal, Congo, 1882–1931)," *Gender & History* 16:2 (August 2004), 289–317.

[66] Holdings from the former Communist Youth League archive, now under the auspices of RGASPI, are hereafter denoted as RGASPI M.

The campaign received coverage in central papers like *Komsomol'skaia pravda* and the women's journal *Rabotnitsa* as well as extensive coverage in Far Eastern newspapers such as *Tikhookeanskii komsomolets*, *Tikhookeanskaia zvezda*, and *Krasnoe znamia*. Materials from the former Party Archive of the Khabarovsk region include memoirs of female migrants, correspondence of volunteers with officials, court cases, and official inquiries related to the female migrants, as well as official reports on other events and conditions in the Far East, the progress of resettlement efforts more generally, and the role of the NKVD Corrective Labor Camps in the region.

Memoirs of former participants in the campaign to settle the Far East play an important role in illuminating the experiences and ironies of life for Soviet women in the 1930s. These recollections written forty years after the women arrived in the Far East are critical for understanding the social milieu of those who volunteered for migration. But the memoirs also obfuscate as much as they reveal about lived experiences. Notably absent from their accounts are discussions of anything distasteful about their reception in the region, the ongoing purges and deportations, the labor camp system, and the chaos that reigned in the region. The ability of memoirists to eschew addressing such themes exemplified the practices of self-censorship and selective memories typical of a cohort that found a niche in the Soviet system.

A look ahead

This book is divided into chapters exploring both frontier fantasies and women's real experiences on a frontier of Stalinism. Chapters 1 and 2, "Women and Soviet power" and "Where steel cracks like glass," cover relevant aspects of Soviet history with an emphasis on Soviet women as well as the Far East up to the moment Khetagurova called for young volunteers in 1937. These chapters also illustrate how and why the life courses of women like Novikova, the former labor camp prisoner, and the one-time homeless waif and secret police employee Mishalova were structured by Tsarist colonial and then Soviet empire-building practices.

Chapter 3, "Our famous Valia: The ascent of a Soviet notable," is an exploration of Khetagurova's public persona. Khetagurova was an important public figure and part of a coterie of female notables feted in the pre-World War II period. Khetagurova rose to stardom in part because of her connection to a strategically important frontier and in part because, an ethnic Russian, she was married to a Northern Ossetian Red

Army officer.[67] Her debut as a heroine from a symbolically rich frontier heralded the ascent of a new model of womanhood intrinsically affiliated with the Soviet state as a Eurasian power. This connection distinguished her from other models of womanhood in the Soviet Union and in other European nation-states.

Chapter 4, "'Envy for everything heroic': women volunteering for the frontier," explores the gendered connotations of the Far East as a mythical space in films and press coverage of the late 1930s to understand why Alekseeva, Mishalova, and Novikova were so taken with the possibilities offered by Khetagurova's call-up. This chapter is not simply a discussion of representation. It is also an examination of how such representations shaped the imaginations and aspirations of target audiences by a close reading of letters from volunteers for migration and memoirs of elderly campaign participants.

Chapter 5, "'Bol'shevichki were never ascetics!': female morale and Communist morality," is an exploration of sexuality and marriage as defined by official discourse and as notions and practices of migrants in a region dominated by men and patriarchal relations. Policies such as the ban on abortions in 1936 in the midst of the political and social turmoil engendered by deportations, mass arrests, and purges had a direct bearing on the quality of women's lives. This was also a moment of transition in the symbolic and real status of women in Soviet society. Official investigations, discussions, and letters to authorities in relation to the Khetagurovites provide a unique opportunity for an examination of sexuality and young people's attitudes in this era.

Chapter 6, "Snivelers and patriots," explores the topsy-turvy universe of frontier Stalinism. The reality of life on the frontier crushed more than one eager patriot. Some of their struggles and misfortunes were representative of women's experiences in the patriarchal culture of the Soviet Union and life for most people on its distant and poorly developed frontier. Single women turned out to be vulnerable targets in a social world populated by people who had little use for uppity females or those who already abhorred the Soviet state. The women were doubly exposed in particular if sent to isolated areas where the regime's authority was weak and patriarchal attitudes reigned unimpeded. Other problems were unique to Stalinism on the frontier and women's own expectations. Letters of complaint and debates among activists point to the volatility of

---

[67] Compare this with white women's roles in other colonial contexts. See Ann Laura Stoler, "Making Empire Respectable: The Politics of Race and Sexual Morality in Twentieth-Century Colonial Cultures," in Anne McClintock, Aamir Mufti, and Ella Shohat (eds.), *Dangerous Liaisons: Gender, Nation and Postcolonial Perspectives* (Minneapolis: University of Minnesota Press, 1997), 344–373.

such Stalinist campaigns reliant both on voluntary ardor and on promises of special status.

The Conclusion points to the way these experiences continue to resonate in post-Soviet Russian popular culture and makes a case for the importance of seeing Soviet history through a gendered lens. The Appendix contains poems and lyrics from songs either explicitly dedicated to the Khetagurovite migration or lyrics from songs the women appropriated from Soviet popular culture and considered emblematic of their adventures and aspirations.

1   Women and Soviet power

From its very inception, wracked by World War I and a bloody Civil War, the Soviet Union was an inauspicious stage for forging the communist utopia envisioned by Karl Marx.[1] The improbable triumph of the Bolsheviks amidt the chaos of 1917 left the revolutionaries administering the largest contiguous state in the world armed with powerful Marxist critiques of capitalism but with little guidance on how to build a communist society in the future. Innumerable factors conspired against their success. The Soviet Union was isolated in a sea of capitalist powers antagonized first by the Bolsheviks' decision to take Russia out of World War I and then by their calls to workers of the world to dispense violently with their own capitalist masters. The new society lacked a trained workforce. Its industrial infrastructures and transportation networks were wholly inadequate for effective governance and economic development in the short term. Low literacy, a high proportion of land-starved peasants, and a dizzying array of ethnic groups and national minorities made this a poor laboratory for experiments in socialism.

Every facet of social, political, and economic life in the Russian empire was profoundly transformed by the seemingly ceaseless sequence of war and revolutions even before the Bolsheviks set out to construct a new society.[2] Changes in gender roles and in power dynamics between the sexes followed paths unforeseen by either revolutionaries or defenders of the old order. Mobilizations of men and livestock, mass movements of refugees, the ravages of armies, and occupations in the western borderlands during World War I thrust women into new roles. Millions of women ran households in the countryside on their own, took up jobs in

---

[1] For a recent discussion of this period, see Peter Holquist, *Making War, Forging Revolution: Russia's Continuum of Crisis, 1914–1921* (Cambridge, MA: Harvard University Press, 2002).

[2] For more on the transformations engendered by total war, see Joshua A. Sanborn, *Drafting the Russian Nation: Military Conscription, Total War, and Mass Politics, 1905–1925* (DeKalb: Northern Illinois University Press, 2003), and Peter Gatrell, *A Whole Empire Walking: Refugees in Russia during World War I* (Bloomington: Indiana University Press, 2000).

industries for the first time, and struggled to survive in the cities. Thousands of women took to the streets in protests against war and deteriorating conditions during the February Revolution while others fought on the frontlines against Germany after the Provisional Government accepted female volunteers for all female fighting units.[3] As a result of these experiences, urban and rural women collectively questioned their position in the family and society without support or encouragement from radical revolutionaries.[4] However, there was little likelihood that such profound shifts in gender roles and women's new sense of engagement in questioning the political and social status quo could have garnered the attention of the Bolsheviks. Bolshevik organizers before the revolutionary period did little to appeal directly to working-class women, generally had a difficult time attracting women into their ranks, and attacked efforts by Russian feminists to build coalitions to fight for women's rights.[5] Unable or unwilling to recognize dramatic shifts in attitudes among women, Bolsheviks continued to assume that women were apathetic to revolutionary politics because Tsarist oppression had left them uneducated, conservative, and backward.

Women in the 1920s

Once in power, the Bolsheviks instituted full civil, legal, and electoral equality for women in January 1918. For the most part, the revolutionaries were not preoccupied with launching a wholesale transformation of gender relations because, as Marxists, they believed that the social organization of production shaped values and practices. Thus all inequalities based on sex or ethnicity created by capitalism were supposed to evaporate without prodding once workers came to control the means of

---

[3] Laurie Stoff, "They Fought for Russia: Female Soldiers of the First World War," in Gerard J. DeGroot and Corinna Peniston-Bird (eds.), *A Soldier and a Woman: Sexual Integration in the Military* (New York: Longman, 2000), 66–82, and Melissa K. Stockdale, "'My Death for the Motherland is Happiness': Women, Patriotism, and Soldiering in Russia's Great War, 1914–1917," *American Historical Review* 109:1 (February 2004), 78–116.

[4] Mark Baker, "Rampaging Soldatki, Cowering Police, Bazaar Riots and Moral Economy: The Social Impact of the Great War in Kharkiv Province," *Canadian-American Slavic Studies* 35:2–3 (Summer–Fall 2001), 137–155.

[5] For more on the origins of the Marxists' disdain for feminism, see Marilyn J. Boxer, "Rethinking the Socialist Construction and International Career of the Concept 'Bourgeois Feminism,'" *American Historical Review* 112:1 (February 2007), 131–158. For women in the revolutionary period, see Barbara Evans Clements, *Bolshevik Women* (Cambridge: Cambridge University Press, 1997), and her "Baba and Bolshevik: Russian Women and Revolutionary Change," *Soviet Union* 12:2(1985), 161–184; and Elizabeth Wood, *The Baba and the Comrade: Gender and Politics in Revolutionary Russia* (Bloomington: Indiana University Press, 1997).

production. Meanwhile, the Bolsheviks, having renamed themselves the Communists, were engrossed in fighting the Civil War, reassembling into a union of republics regions that had been part of the Russian empire, and procuring agricultural products from a reluctant peasantry.[6] Experimentations in art and literature and with deliberately nontraditional forms of consensual unions remained the purview of urban intellectuals.

Although there were few prominent female figures in the Communist party, women such as Aleksandra Kollontai, a theorist and activist for women's emancipation, succeeded in convincing Lenin of the need for a special organization for work among women despite the Bolsheviks' dislike for feminism.[7] Nadezhda Krupskaia, Lenin's wife, along with thousands of female Communists, became deeply involved in developing the new Soviet education system and the system of orphanages for children, beginning in the Civil War period and continuing through the 1930s. Other important female figures such as Inessa Armand became the first director of the Zhenotdel formed in 1919. The department crafted special outreach efforts and organized techniques to build support among women for the Bolsheviks and as a way to facilitate women's entry into public life and labor after the Bolshevik victory.[8] The Zhenotdel also coordinated women's involvement in the Civil War when women came to play a significant and novel role. The strain of this conflict was so intense that in 1920 women were conscripted for noncombatant service.

---

[6] For policies toward the peasantry and their reactions to Bolshevik rule, see Orlando Figes, *Peasant Russia, Civil War: The Volga Countryside in Revolution, 1917–21* (Oxford: Clarendon, 1989). For Bolshevik nation-building efforts after the Revolution, see Ronald Suny and Terry Martin (eds.), *Empire and Nation-Making in the Age of Lenin and Stalin* (New York: Oxford University Press, 2001).

[7] Aleksandra Kollontai was the subject of Barbara Evans Clements, *Bolshevik Feminist: The Life of Aleksandra Kollontai* (Bloomington: Indiana University Press, 1979); Beatrice Farnsworth, *Aleksandra Kollontai: Socialism, Feminism, and the Bolshevik Revolution* (Stanford: Stanford University Press, 1980); Eric Naiman, "When a Communist Writes Gothic: Aleksandra Kollontai and the Politics of Disgust," *Signs* 22:1(1996), 1–29; V. I. Uspenskaia (ed.), *Aleksandra Kollontai: Teoriia zhenskoi emansipatsii v kontekste rossiiskoi gendernoi politiki: materialy mezhdunarodnoi nauchnoi konferentsii, Tver'*, March 11, 2002 (Tver': Zolotaia bukva, 2003). Women who were part of the creative intelligentsia in the 1920s and 1930s, such as Nadezhda Mandelstam and Anna Akhmatova, have received generous attention from cultural historians and scholars of Russian literature. This literature is extensive and outside the scope of this study. A good starting point is Beth Holmgren, *Women's Works in Stalin's Time: On Lidiia Chukovskaia and Nadezhda Mandelstam* (Bloomington: Indiana University Press, 1993).

[8] The most authoritative works on Russian feminism and the Communist Party's Women's Department are Richard Stites, *The Women's Liberation Movement*; Carol Eubanks Hayden, "The Zhenotdel and the Bolshevik Party," *Russian History* 3:2 (1976), 150–173; Barbara Evans Clements, "The Utopianism of the Zhenotdel," *Slavic Review* 51:2 (Summer 1992), 485–496; and Wendy Goldman, "Industrial Politics, Peasant Rebellion and the Death of the Proletarian Women's Movement in the USSR," *Slavic Review* 55:1 (Spring 1996), 46–77.

Some women came to hold important positions in the Red Army's political department. Thousands streamed into medical services and combat on every front. They fought using every kind of weapon, including the machine gun.

The New Economic Policy (NEP) instituted by Lenin in 1921, with its free markets, small-scale trade, and some degree of permissiveness in cultural affairs introduced both a period of increasing opportunities for some women and a time of difficult economic circumstances for others. Through the efforts of the Zhenotdel, women in both urban and rural areas learned to read, became more active in the public sphere, and gained experience in local administration. A socialist feminist, Kollontai wanted the new state to radically restructure marriage and divorce, arguing that alimony was "demeaning to women, and that all relations, including casual sexual ties, should receive the same legal consideration."[9] With an eye toward transforming women's lives, Kollontai proposed a general fund to support childrearing and thus liberate women from domestic drudgery and poverty as single mothers. Thousands of women left unhappy marriages when divorce became possible. Single and married women (especially in urban areas of Russia and Ukraine) had more reproductive choices and availed themselves of their right to abortion as a means of birth control.[10]

It is still a matter of debate whether the Bolsheviks ever intended to liberate women in the sense of making them autonomous actors pursuing their personal goals or whether they always meant to free women from the domestic sphere only in order to make their labor available for exploitation by the socialist state.[11] Wendy Goldman has taken the position that although there was a "socialist-libertarian tradition" among Bolsheviks, exemplified by the work of Kollontai, these ideals were "undermined by the material scarcity of the twenties" and finally completely discarded by Stalin in the 1930s, "as the new needs of industrialization became the main arbiter of state policy toward women and the family."[12] Other historians stress that the question is not whether the Communists really

[9] Wendy Goldman, "Freedom and its Consequences: The Debate on the Soviet Family Code of 1926," *Russian History* 11:4 (Winter 1984), 386.

[10] Although unemployed wives of Red Army soldiers and poor laborers could qualify for reduced rates or free service according to the sliding scale at state-run abortion clinics, doctors often denied women abortions if it was their first child or they were beyond their first trimester. The state had provided abortion clinics to keep women from using back-alley methods where they apparently received treatment that threatened their life and their future reproductive capacities.

[11] For more on this, see Thomas Schrand, "The Five-Year Plan for Women's Labour: Constructing Socialism and the 'Double Burden,' 1930–1932," *Europe-Asia Studies* 51:8 (1999), 1455–1478.

[12] Goldman, "Freedom and its Consequences," 388.

intended to liberate women. They argue that the objective was always to transform the domestic sphere and place women's family roles under state control.[13] Zhenotdel activities did target women for liberation from exclusive focus on the domestic sphere by getting them involved in self-improvement, public activities, and wage work to build self-sufficiency and a sense of accomplishment. The Zhenotdel also promised that the state would assist women in their personal evolution and in their ultimate ability to participate in building socialism by establishing easily accessible crèches, communal dining halls, and laundries. For the most part, the Zhenotdel did not seek to restructure the behavior of men in the household. Without a commitment to reconfigure the meaning of masculinity and men's roles in the family, women retained the burdens of caretaking in the home when promised state assistance did not materialize.

Alas, utopian thinking, as Goldman has put it, "came face to face with the material conditions of Soviet social life."[14] Efforts and plans to assist women in developing autonomy, a public role, education, and skills were hampered by the poverty and international isolation of the Soviet Union in the 1920s as well as by the general disinterest of many leading Bolsheviks and rank-and-file party members. This was also a period of high female unemployment, forcing some to abandon their children when easy divorce made it difficult to pursue men for child support. The hoped-for communal dining halls and crèches remained mostly grand promises for the future rather than reality. When asked to comment on family legislation in 1926, it is not surprising that working-class women supported laws to strengthen marriage, discourage promiscuity, and punish male irresponsibility. They in fact demanded, as Goldman explains, "liberation from the social effects of the new sexual freedom."[15]

Few women from among the core of Old Bolsheviks managed to remain important political figures after the early 1920s. Lenin's sisters and his wife were the exceptions because of their relationship to the revolutionary leader. In the public's mind these elderly former underground revolutionaries increasingly appeared as "guardian angel-like figures."[16] On the whole, women were shut out of decision-making circles and remained

---

[13] Michelle Fuqua, *The Politics of the Domestic Sphere: The Zhenotdely, Women's Liberation, and the Search for a Novyi Byt in Early Soviet Russia* (Seattle: Henry M. Jackson School of International Studies, University of Washington, 1996). Soviet-era studies treated the topic of women's history by chronicling the emancipation of women as a task completed by 1937. Soviet authors referred to it as "the resolution of the woman's question." See P. M. Chirkov, *Reshenie zhenskogo voprosa v USSR (1917–1937)* (Moscow: Izdatel'stvo Mysl', 1978).

[14] Goldman, "Freedom and its Consequences," 364.   [15] *Ibid.*, 373.

[16] Katy Turton, "After Lenin: The Role of Anna and Mariia Ul'ianova in Soviet Society and Politics from 1924," *Revolutionary Russia* 15:2 (December 2002), 108.

unwelcome intruders into the symbolic world of proletarian brotherhoods throughout the 1920s.[17]

Future Khetagurovites like Efrosina Mishalova and Klava Novikova were born in the midst of this difficult and tumultuous epoch. The traumas and burdens of this period profoundly affected their life courses. For most of her early life, Efrosina had been on the outermost margin of society and survived a series of calamities by pure chance. Born in 1917, she was never sure whether her mother died when she was ten months or ten weeks old. With her father away fighting in the Civil War, Efrosina was put into an orphanage in Krivoi Rog, Ukraine. Her father never returned and the little girl was taken into the household of a kulak, where for four years, in exchange for food and three rubles per year, she worked as a servant and shepherdess. Bouncing from family to family, she eventually found herself among the ranks of the millions of homeless children roaming in loose bands on the streets. She later recalled that her

[h]omeless gang consisted of seventeen people, six of them girls, two of whom were adults. The older ones "obtained" food, clothing, and money. They took us to the movies and we slept there till autumn. When it became cold we found a basement. We stole clothing to pay for the place. Then one winter night we were all taken away by the "Black Crows."[18]

The militia delivered this crew to an orphanage where Efrosina earned the nickname "Barricade" among the other orphans.

At the same time in the Kremlin, factional struggles among Lenin's followers after his death in 1924 were centered around ways to place the Soviet Union on a quick path to development and eventual self-sufficiency while addressing the restlessness of workers who had grown disenchanted with the NEP.[19] There was a general sense among many workers that the 1917 Revolution's radicalism and promises of a better life had been jettisoned. While factories and institutions, forced to maintain profitability, trimmed their budgets by cutting staff and services, peasants and

---

[17] Eric Naiman working on literature has argued that during the NEP period, anxieties about the course of the Revolution were expressed as anxieties about women and their potential to contaminate men with bourgeois femininity and dissolve revolutionary energy in sexual excess. See Naiman, *Sex in Public: The Incarnation of Early Soviet Ideology* (Princeton: Princeton University Press, 1997).

[18] Memoir of Efrosina Mishalova, "Vospominaia o moei miloi zadornoi trudnoi i schastlivoi komsomol'skoi iunosti [Remembering my dear, fervent, difficult and fortunate Komsomol youth]," February 18, 1976, GAKhK P, f. 442, op. 2, d. 284, l. 82. "Black Crows" were the black cars driven by the Soviet police, at that time called the All-Union State Political Administration (OGPU).

[19] For more on workers' culture and politics during the NEP period, see the collection by L. H. Siegelbaum and R. G. Suny (eds.), *Making Workers Soviet: Power, Class and Identity* (Ithaca: Cornell University Press, 1994).

small-scale merchants (NEPmen) seemed to be thriving. All this appeared all the more insidious to workers observing the begging, prostitution, and thieving of abandoned children like Mishalova's gang on the streets of the first socialist state in history.[20] Workers and new Communist party members demanded a radical turn. Stalin deftly built his constituency out of this impatient mass.

Stalin's revolution

Stalin's subsequent victory over his rivals in the Communist party set in motion a mix of new opportunities, burdens, and calamities for every woman and man in Soviet society. Utopian drives shared by all Communists and Stalin's penchant for violence and paranoia impacted the Soviet population in a variety of ways. Millions suffered while others were caught up in the revolutionary fervor and calls to heroism wrought by major economic, social, and ideological transformations. Men's and women's relationships with the Soviet state in this turbulent period were structured by a multiplicity of factors including generation, ethnicity, social class, and personal inclinations.[21]

In January 1928 Stalin embarked on a course unforeseen by many of those who had helped him outmaneuver his competitors in the Communist party. On a tour of the Urals and Siberia, he expressed dissatisfaction with the power of peasants to withhold grain from the markets in response to low grain prices and lack of manufactured goods. He then ordered the closure of markets that had been a central part of Lenin's New Economic Program and called for the seizure of grain from peasants in a fashion similar to the forced requisition of grain practiced in the period of War Communism, 1919–1921.[22] By the end of 1929, having crushed those who opposed a radical path, the Politburo under his leadership, and large segments of the Communist party impatient with the pace of change,

---

[20] "In 1921 alone, seven million abandoned children [besprizorniki] roamed the towns and countryside." (Goldman, "Freedom and its Consequences," 367). For more on homeless children in the 1920s, see Alan Ball, "The Roots of Besprizornost' in Soviet Russia's First Decade," *Slavic Review* 51:2 (Summer 1992), 247–270.

[21] For the multiplicity of peasant women's experiences and attitudes toward the Soviet regime, see Matt F. Oja, *From Krestianka to Udarnitsa: Rural Women and the Vydvizhenie Campaign, 1933–1941* (Pittsburgh: Center for Russian and East European Studies, University of Pittsburgh, 1996), and Beatrice Farnsworth, "The Rural Batrachka (Hired Agricultural Laborer) and the Soviet Campaign to Unionize Her," *Journal of Women's History* 14:1 (Spring 2002), 64–93. For working-class women, see Anne E. Gorsuch, "'A Woman is Not a Man': The Culture of Gender and Generation in Soviet Russia, 1921–1928," *Slavic Review* 55:3 (Fall 1996), 636–660.

[22] On War Communism and forced requisition, see Lars Lih, *Bread and Authority in Russia, 1914–1921* (Berkeley: University of California Press, 1990).

moved forcefully to implement total collectivization of Soviet agriculture despite ferocious resistance from the peasantry.[23]

Stalin was intent not only on transforming agriculture but also on launching yet another revolution. This revolution, unlike the Revolution of February 1917, was initiated from above.[24] The assault on the peasantry was designed to change the way property, labor, and products were distributed and to revolutionize the structure of rural life by forcing every peasant to join collective farms (kolkhozy). The means of achieving this radical social transformation was an assault on "strong" peasants (kulaks). They were targeted in part because many younger party members – much like Mishalova, who remembered her early years as an exploited laborer for a kulak – had been unhappy with the visibility of well-off peasants in the countryside and their power over other peasants. Others were alarmed by the ability of peasants to withhold or deliver grain to the marketplace according to their personal calculations rather than any interest in socialism. Party leaders assumed that they could undermine opposition in a village to collectivization by crushing the kulaks and letting the poorest among the peasants spearhead collectivization under state direction. Debates about what to do to generate surplus capital and transform Soviet agriculture ended when Stalin ordered the "liquidation of kulaks as a class."

Peasants resisted collectivization by slaughtering their livestock rather than giving it to the collective farms and by taking up arms against the representatives of the regime, including the Red Army, sent to force their acquiescence. In December 1929 and February 1930, the secret police began to deport and execute peasants who resisted the regime in any way, while others were forced to give up all property claims and join the kolkhozy.[25] Thousands of peasant women took active roles in resisting collectivization and the arrests of their priests and men.[26] Forced seizure of grain in Ukraine and the Volga region, in combination with poor weather conditions and the unwillingness of the regime to provide timely aid, led to mass starvation while the rest of the country tightened

---

[23] For more on peasant resistance to collectivization and the regime's repressive measures, see Lynne Viola, *Peasant Rebels under Stalin: Collectivization and the Culture of Peasant Resistance* (New York: Oxford University Press, 1996), and Viola, V. P. Danilov, N. A. Ivnitskii, and Denis Kozlov (eds.), *The Tragedy of the Soviet Countryside: The War Against the Peasantry, 1927–1930* (New Haven: Yale University Press, 2005).

[24] For more on this period, see the collection by Sheila Fitzpatrick (ed.), *Cultural Revolution in Russia, 1928–1931* (Bloomington: Indiana University Press, 1984).

[25] For an account of one such deportation of kulak families, see Lynne Viola, "The Other Archipelago: Kulak Deportations to the North in 1930," *Slavic Review* 60:4 (Winter 2001), 730–755.

[26] For women's role in resistance, see Lynne Viola, "Bab'i Bunty and Peasant Women's Protest during Collectivization," *Russian Review* 45:1 (1986), 23–42.

its belts under a system of rationing. Approximately five million kulaks and their families were deported to places such as Siberia and the Soviet Far East.

The revolution launched by Stalin was an attempt to place the Soviet economy and industrial infrastructure on a par with its capitalist rivals.[27] But collectivization not only did not help the industrialization drive, it hurt it. By 1933, the country had lost 27 percent of its livestock. The most enterprising farmers had been sacrificed without any benefit. Fresh produce and meat disappeared from the shelves of state-run stores for the next fifty years.[28] Hundreds of thousands of families branded as kulaks were taken by force to areas on the Soviet Union's peripheries, where they lived in labor camps and settlements in poorly developed regions without freedom of movement or rights to appeal their deportations. A sullen and uncooperative peasantry fell into patterns of passive resistance and low productivity for the collective farms.

Just as the country descended into chaos and famine, Mishalova's life took on a degree of normalcy. By May 1929, at the age of twelve, she was working in a canteen attached to a coalmine. Access to food in a canteen, in this critical period of the famine in Ukraine, shielded the vulnerable girl from the fate of so many others who succumbed to hunger on the streets and in the countryside. She studied, participated in choirs and drama circles, and finished all seven years at school. Although she witnessed many terrible scenes before becoming an adult, she did not blame the regime that ultimately fed her. In her reckoning, her fellow Ukrainians suffered because "[o]ur country was poor, barefoot, hungry, and bare. There were many internal and external enemies."[29] Another future Khetagurovite, Liubov' Kudriasheva, born in 1915, offered a very similar story on this period in Saratov:

These were our hungry years from 1929 to 1934. In 1932 as a seventeen-year-old girl I went to work on the railroad. They gave me a worker's ration of 800 grams of bread per day. It was hard; people were dying from starvation right on the

---

[27] For recent studies of Stalin, see the edited volume by Sarah Davies and James Harris (eds.), *Stalin: A New History* (New York: Cambridge University Press, 2005).

[28] The topic of collectivization and the resulting famine has generated a great deal of debate among historians. See Mark B. Tauger, *Natural Disaster and Human Actions in the Soviet Famine of 1931–1933* (Pittsburgh: Center for Russian and East European Studies, University Center for International Studies, University of Pittsburgh, 2001).

[29] Mishalova, l. 17ob. She eventually attended courses for school employees and was sent to work as a Senior Pioneer Leader in a large orphanage located in a former nunnery. It was here that she came across the issue of *Komsomol'skaia pravda* with Khetagurova's call-up. The Lenin All-Union Pioneer Organization (1922–1990) was an ideological, sports, and leisure organization for children from ten to fifteen years of age. It was similar to and was supposed to supersede the Boy Scouts.

streets. While they walked around swollen, I was proud of my profession and that I received 800 grams of bread for my labor.[30]

At the crux of the new economic system, which let some starve "right on the streets" and doled out just enough for others in heavy industry, were central planning and controlled goods distribution. Industrial outputs were planned in advance according to targets deemed appropriate rather than popular demand or needs. These targets were laid out in the First Five-Year Plan (1928–1932), intended to increase industrial production by 20 percent, beginning in April 1929.[31] Plans produced by a state agency, Gosplan, with the authority to organize the production of the entire Soviet nation, placed emphasis on capital investment for building industrial capacity in heavy industry and placed light industry on a secondary footing. One of the major elements of these plans was to move the economic geography of the Soviet Union eastward. The shift eastward to take production and populations closer to the sources of raw materials and further from borders with potentially aggressive neighbors initiated a period of giant construction projects such as Magnitostroi in the Urals, Siberia and Soviet Asia.[32] Committees of economists and political bosses also turned their attention to the allocation of labor and to expanding the labor force to meet the needs of rapid industrialization. Despite the disaster in agriculture, First Five-Year Plan targets were reached and even surpassed in some sectors, especially in machine-building industries, the expansion of hydroelectric power, and new railway lines. The plan reduced the Soviet Union's dependence on foreign machinery, though the quality of the output was very low. As soon as the First Five-Year Plan came to a close, the regime announced the Second Five-Year Plan for 1932–1937. The Second Five-Year Plan stressed heavy industry but the pace was moderated to some extent and more emphasis was placed on production of military hardware and railroad construction. As a result, by 1939 Soviet railroads were carrying 91.8 percent more cargo than they had in 1932. A Third Five-Year Plan was disrupted by the Nazi invasion of the Soviet Union in June 1941.

Communists never failed to point out that while the rest of the world slipped into the morass of the Great Depression, men and women in the Soviet Union expected and were able to find work. Workers were

[30] Memoir of Liubov' Kudriasheva, GAKhK P, f. 442, op. 2, d. 284, l. 4.
[31] For more on the politics and social impact of the First Five-Year Plan, see W. G. Rosenberg and L. H. Siegelbaum (eds.), *Social Dimensions of Soviet Industrialization* (Bloomington: Indiana University Press, 1994).
[32] See Kotkin, *Magnetic Mountain*, for an account of the way Stalinism impacted the community that evolved in response to the demands of the industrial and cultural revolution of the 1930s.

guaranteed paid vacations and social benefits such as education, subsidized transportation, and free medical clinics. Some workers and their children experienced the 1930s as a time of upward social mobility through increased educational opportunities and affirmative action programs aimed at promoting workers to positions of authority in the early 1930s.

Forces of push and pull set thirty million peasants on the move to urban areas between 1926 and 1939. The slew of new factories and construction projects needed workers. Technical schools and universities offered crash courses in professions necessary for industry, education, and medicine for young men and women. With the countryside under assault after collectivization young men escaped the deprivations and limitations of life on the kolkhoz by joining the Red Army. Military service led to a Soviet passport and the opportunity to move within the borders of the Soviet Union, rights denied to other kolkhoz members. Determined young peasant women could also find legal escape routes out of kolkhoz life, by enrolling in technical schools and universities. Even the children of kulaks had a right to leave their family's places of forced settlement to attend college or technical schools. Millions of others went to work on a temporary basis in the cities and never returned, even if this was technically illegal.[33] Peasant migrants strained the already limited urban housing stock. Labor in the countryside became overwhelmingly feminized and older, a trend that continued until the collapse of the Soviet Union in the 1990s.

This practically incalculable torrent of migration not only "rusticated" the cities, as Moshe Lewin has argued, but also shaped the political culture of the 1930s and beyond. "Stalinism can only be understood against this background of social flux."[34] Lewin has stressed the central role of these new arrivals in casting a pliant social landscape for Stalinism. "New to their jobs, rank and file and bosses in factories, offices and institutions were socially insecure, frangible, and in most cases still grateful to the system and its leaders for having promoted them. In short, they were followers and clients rather than responsible co-definers of the system's parameters."[35] This explains in part why women like Novikova and Mishalova, along with millions of others, having no experience of any other system, displaced by personal tragedies, and grateful to Stalin,

---

[33] For a full treatment of peasant life in the 1930s, see Sheila Fitzpatrick, *Stalin's Peasants: Resistance and Survival in the Russian Village After Collectivization* (New York: Oxford University Press, 1994).

[34] Moshe Lewin, "Russia/USSR in Historical Motion: An Essay in Interpretation," *Russian Review* 50:3 (1991), 259–260.

[35] *Ibid.*, 260.

believed that this system was truly equal because hardships were shared for a higher cause and that it operated ultimately in their best interests.

However, this equality was in fact a mirage in the centralized system. Soviet workers who thought that their time had come actually suffered a decline in their standard of living because of the manmade famine raging in the country in the early 1930s, the institution of rationing, and the reinvestment of surplus capital from their labor into ever grander industrial projects rather than into improving working and living conditions for the workers of a socialist state. Worse still, access to goods depended on your status in a variety of hierarchies, and on corruption. Elena Osokina and Sheila Fitzpatrick have deftly traced the origins and rules of these systems and the creation of new "social hierarchies based not on production but consumption."[36] Initially, one's access was dependent on social rank, profession, and place of residence in a period of shortages. Even when rationing formally ended in 1934, the hierarchical system persisted and expanded. Throughout the 1930s, a system of "closed distribution" was in force. Every city and town had its own special stores and cafeterias where only certain groups of customers could shop and eat. As Alena Lebedeva has demonstrated, this centralized system operated in tandem with the practice of "blat," the use of personal connections to outwit the centralized system and obtain better rations or privileges.[37] Although all forms of trade outside of the state apparatus were made illegal in the early 1930s, a "black market" quickly developed in which hard-to-find goods and food could be acquired at a price and at some risk of arrest.

Gender politics in the 1930s

Stalin's crash industrialization program transformed women's lives in innumerable ways. They were targeted as a source of labor for a wide variety of sectors during the First Five-Year Plan. According to Goldman, as a result of this conscious effort to either force or entice women into the labor force, "Between 1929 and 1935, almost four million women began to work for wages, 1.7 million of them in industry . . . By 1935, forty two percent of all industrial workers would be women."[38] This

[36] Fitzpatrick, *Everyday Stalinism*, 13. The workings of this hierarchical system and corruption within it are thoroughly covered by Elena Osokina, *Our Daily Bread: Socialist Distribution and the Art of Survival in Stalin's Russia, 1927–1941* (The New Russian History, ed. Kate Transchel), trans. Transchel and Greta Bucher (Armonk, NY: M. E. Sharpe, 2001).

[37] Alena Lebedeva, *Russia's Economy of Favors: Blat, Networking and Informal Exchange* (Cambridge: Cambridge University Press, 1998).

[38] Wendy Goldman, *Women at the Gates: Gender and Industry in Stalin's Russia* (Cambridge: Cambridge University Press, 2002), 1.

large-scale entrance of women into the labor force "undercut the strict hierarchies of skill and gender within the factories," forcing men "to reexamine their ideas about skill, 'masculine' and 'feminine' work, and the role of women in the workplace."[39] Tensions between men and women escalated. Even before Stalin's revolution, women's entry into the industrial workforce and public life was fraught with contradictions and met with outright hostility from men. Diane Koenker has summed up these dynamics as: "Garden-variety [common] misogyny, ubiquitous in prerevolutionary workplaces, carried over into the socialist period, despite official policies."[40] Even though there were no attempts to change men's roles in the household, attempts were made to change attitudes toward women in the workplace. These attempts, according to Koenker, mostly failed and "divisions between men and women in Soviet work places became more distinct, not less, by the eve of the First Five-Year Plan."[41] When the Zhenotdel was disbanded in 1930, women were set adrift without an organization dedicated to their interests and left surrounded by men disgruntled by their intrusion into formerly men-only spaces and professions. Also, with the end of Zhenotdel, as Goldman has underscored, women lost their only forum for articulating grievances and had no way to influence policies just when Soviet planners were working to "regender" the labor force. Consequently, "Although they did enter traditionally male industries in record-breaking numbers, Soviet industry retained both vertical and horizontal patterns of sex segregation."[42]

In the mid-1930s women continued to work in the labor force, trained in a variety of sectors, and became prominent symbols of Soviet achievements in educating and "liberating" previously oppressed groups. Conflicting messages about women's autonomy and abilities versus their duties and special roles as mothers were difficult to reconcile in reality. As more women and children arrived in the cities, the authorities failed to maintain a coherent program to provide childcare and other services. Women continued to carry all responsibilities for household chores and childcare while rubbing shoulders with irritated and irritating neighbors. Millions shared kitchens and bathrooms in the forced intimacy of communal apartments without labor-saving devices and without indoor plumbing. At work, a glass ceiling kept even the most

---

[39] *Ibid.*
[40] Diane P. Koenker, "Men Against Women on the Shop Floor in Early Soviet Russia: Gender and Class in the Socialist Workplace," *American Historical Review* 100:5 (December 1995), 1439.
[41] *Ibid.*   [42] Goldman, *Women at the Gates*, 68.

ambitious women out of top ranks of industry and party before and after 1936.[43]

The state had exacerbated women's burdens by creating skewed systems of distribution and shortages for those who did not have the right status or connections. Subsequently, another kind of "New Woman" developed in the Soviet Union, but it was not the woman envisioned by Kollontai. This New Soviet Woman could easily become a huntress for a husband who possessed the right connections or social status. If she was unlucky enough to have a child and a low social status, she could just as easily transform into a tired, overworked, and apathetic beast of burden, concerned mostly about making home life more comfortable and obtaining scarce food and clothing for her children on the black market. None of these developments meshed very well with either dreams of women's liberation or utopian intentions to eviscerate the domestic sphere. These developments also predated the so-called Great Retreat in 1936 that ostensibly ushered in a new emphasis on strong families, demographic growth, and domesticity as women's natural calling.

As women entered the urban labor force, divorce rates stayed high, birth rates dropped, and abortions outnumbered live births. Urban women in the European regions of the Soviet Union had come to rely a great deal on abortion as a method of family planning. Authorities also noted a spike in juvenile crime and disorder in schools, which they attributed to poor parental supervision.[44] Officials chose to address such problems with harsher punishments for underage offenders and by strengthening the family as a legal unit, beginning in 1934. A publicity campaign explicitly rejected the concept of free love and linked it to a bourgeois morality foreign to a socialist state. Subsequent changes in family law in 1936 not only made abortion illegal but granted awards to mothers of large families and made divorce more expensive. Although there were increasing shifts toward an emphasis on women's domestic duties and the criminalization of abortion impacted many women in profound ways, it remains unclear how women perceived these shifts.[45] Throughout the 1920s and 1930s,

---

[43] There were 600 women factory directors in the country in 1939; only 156 women among agricultural administrators, and 22,000 female apparatchiks. Among administrators of cultural-educational institutions, 31 percent were women; only 91 women were in charge of institutes of higher learning in 1939 in the whole of the Soviet Union. See Zhiromskaia, *Demograficheskaia istoriia*, 105–106.

[44] There were 57,000 births and 154,584 abortions in Moscow in 1934 (*Izvestiia*, July 12, 1936). See Hoffmann, "Mothers in the Motherland," 51n.39.

[45] Most scholarship so far has explored representations of women rather than reception among women. For studies of representation, see Elizabeth Wood, "The Trial of the New Woman: Citizens-in-Training in the New Soviet Republic," *Gender & History* 13:3 (November 2001), 524–545; Attwood, "Rationality versus Romanticism,"

many women actually supported laws to strengthen families and make wayward fathers more responsible for their offspring.[46]

Yet young women like Ania Alekseeva could nevertheless choose to work in any number of professions and fantasize about their future exploits. Many people imbibed ideas about revolution, heroism, and adventures through literature, film, and music produced under the rubric of Socialist Realism. Young women read about the achievements of women their age in industry, agriculture, and aviation. Books and films were filled with stories of female heroines unmasking spies and helping to achieve production records. All art and literature in the 1930s was supposed to portray life not as it was but in revolutionary development, or "Life as it was becoming." In general, all art was meant to promote the masses' ideological reeducation. Such efforts found a fertile soil. More than one of the memoirists mentioned the role of literature and fictional heroes as inspiration for their decision to leave. Mariia Koliasnikova, living in a small town and working at a factory, wanted to join "something grandiose, demanding from you all of your strength and knowledge. Demanding nothing in return, we wanted to be just a bit like our heroes from Ostrovskii's *How the Steel was Tempered* and Makar Nagul'nov and Semeon Davidov from Mikhail Sholokhov's *Virgin Soil Upturned*."[47]

Anna Krylova, in her work on this cohort, found a similar pattern and showed how literature and films representing fictional women heroes and

158–176; Frances L. Bernstein, "Envisioning Health in Revolutionary Russia: The Politics of Gender and Sexual-Enlightenment Posters of the 1920s," *Russian Review* 57:2 (April 1998), 191–217; Tricia Starks, "A Fertile Mother Russia: Pronatalist Propaganda in Revolutionary Russia," *Journal of Family History* 28:3 (July 2003), 411–442; Elizabeth Waters, "The Modernization of Russian Motherhood, 1917–1937," *Soviet Studies* 44:1 (1992), 123–135; and Chris Burton, "Minzdrav, Soviet Doctors, and Policing of Reproduction in the Late Stalinist Years," *Russian History* 27:2 (Summer 2000), 197–221.

46 One of the ways historians have tried to understand other women's reactions to shifts in policies has been to collect oral history interviews and diaries from those who lived through this period. These sources more than anything illustrate the diversity of experiences and responses to Stalinism rather than a clear shared sense of betrayal or support for the regime. See Barbara Alpern Engel and Anastasia Posadskaya-Vanderbeck (eds.), *A Revolution of their Own: Voices of Women in Soviet History*, trans. Sona Hoisington, (Boulder, CO: Westview Press, 1998), and Sheila Fitzpatrick and Iuri Slezkine (eds.), *In the Shadow of Revolution: Life Stories of Russian Women from 1917 to the Second World War*, trans. Iuri Slezkine (Princeton: Princeton University Press, 2000).

47 Memoir of M. N. Koliasnikova (Koturanova), GAKhK P, f. 442, op. 2, d. 283, l. 85. Sholokhov's 1932 novel is about the arrival of an urban worker to administer collectivization, while Ostrovskii's wildly popular 1933 novel depicted a Civil War hero, Pavel Korchagin. For an analysis of this latter novel and an explanation of its popularity among the Soviet reading public, see Katerina Clark, *The Soviet Novel: History as Ritual* (Bloomington: Indiana University Press, 1981), 131–133, and Evgeny Dobrenko, *The Making of the State Reader: Social and Aesthetic Contexts of the Reception of Soviet Literature* (Stanford: Stanford University Press, 1997).

fighters encouraged real young women to "construct and fashion themselves as fighters in war and life."[48]

It is clear from the Khetagurovite story that many women continued to have confidence in their abilities and, as Mary Buckley has demonstrated, demanded better treatment despite strong resistance from a variety of men and institutions.[49] A new generation of women searched for role models that could reconcile their desires for autonomy, recognition, and the duties associated with Soviet womanhood. Women like Alekseeva and Mishalova thought they had choices, that motherhood was not an overriding preoccupation, and that they could prove themselves to be equal to men on the frontier and in national defense.

To overcome all obstacles, the regime stressed willpower and discipline at the core of the New Soviet Person. Propagating such values and disciplining young adults between the ages of fourteen and twenty-eight had been the task of the Communist Youth League (Komsomol) since its founding in 1918. It was a network of town, regional, republic, and all union-level committees working in conjunction with and mirroring the organizational structure of the Communist party. The Komsomol had cells in all workplaces and educational institutions. Once in the League, members were expected to attend meetings, complete assignments of the organization, participate in defense training, and prepare to join the Communist party.

Of course, many young people felt especially torn between their families' histories and the allure of taking part in the grand historical drama of building socialism. Those who wanted to accelerate their own metamorphosis into new men and women (like Novikova and the diarists analyzed by Jochen Hellbeck) distanced themselves from their pasts by "refashioning" their internal and external selves.[50] Persistent in their attempts to atone for past sins, such individuals hid their personal histories, learned to "speak Bolshevik," and began to think of themselves not as victims but as the linchpins of a new "civilization."[51] Those who were eager to fit into the grand narrative of socialism, like Valentina Khetagurova and Mishalova, engrossed themselves in the Komsomol.

Recent studies of Soviet youth and the Communist Youth League have stressed youthful nonconformism or careerism and concluded that the Communists failed to create a coherent Soviet youth culture. However,

---

[48] Krylova, "Stalinist Identity from the Viewpoint of Gender," 638.

[49] Buckley, *Mobilizing Soviet Peasants*.

[50] The concept of refashioning comes from Jochen Hellbeck, "Fashioning the Stalinist Soul: The Diary of Stepan Podliubnyi, 1931–1939," *Jahrbücher für Geschichte Osteuropas* 44:3 (1996), 344–373.

[51] The process by which some began to "speak Bolshevik" and the concept of Stalinism as a civilization are the subjects of Kotkin, *Magnetic Mountain*.

the role of films, newspapers, and literature in firing their imaginations and the willingness of thousands to sacrifice themselves on the frontier suggest that Communist ideals reached their target audiences to a significant degree.[52] Having missed both the revolutionary days of Lenin and the heady days of the First Five-Year Plan, some young people craved their own opportunities to display heroism and commitment to socialism. These sentiments were especially strong among female activists in the Communist Youth League.

It was the Komsomol that was in charge of programs to resettle young women in the Soviet Far East. Although membership of the Komsomol was not a prerequisite for migration, about half the women who became Khetagurovites were active members of the organization.[53] This was at the same time that the Komsomol struggled to retain female members, who, according to Anne Gorsuch, found themselves alienated "by the masculinized culture" of the organization and overall lack of interest in women's issues among fellow members.[54] Those who went as Khetagurovites would have gone with some degree of exposure to such discrimination, if not in the workplace, then within the Komsomol. This group was not the sort to be discouraged by "[g]arden-variety misogyny."

In this social cauldron, gender and generation determined how the messages of Communist ideologues and Soviet popular culture were received. According to Krylova, such messages were crafted by officials and journalists with the intent of providing "different models and combinations of Soviet femininity intended for different generational audiences."[55] This remaking of the possibilities for Soviet womanhood was fused with the push to develop an aura of "romance" awaiting those who rushed to the peripheries to build a new civilization. The building of new cities in the forests in fact produced genuine enthusiasm among young people. This is one of the more tragic paradoxes of this period. On the one hand, there was genuine enthusiasm among young people of both sexes for exploits on the peripheries and a willingness to work very hard to build and defend a new civilization. On the other hand, the use of forced laborers on these very same projects, and the brutality, injustice, and low productivity

---

[52] For these arguments, see Corinna Kuhr-Korolev, *Gezähmte Helden: Die Formierung der Sowjetjugend* (Essen: Klartext, 2005), and Kuhr-Korolev (ed.), *Sowjetjugend 1917–1941: Generation zwischen Revolution und Resignation* (Essen: Klartext, 2001).

[53] Out of the 11,000 who arrived in 1937, 214 were members of the Communist party and 4,756 were members of the Komsomol. Khetagurovites expanded the ranks of the regional Komsomol organization, adding 9,000 new members by 1938 to an organization that numbered 55,500 in January 1937. See Nina Dubinina, *Dal'nevostochnitsy v bor'be i trude: Istoricheskii ocherk, 1917–1941* (Khabarovsk: Khabarovskoe knizhnoe izdatel'stvo, 1982), 111. Dubinina refers to GAKhK P, f. 618, op. 1, d. 304, l. 47.

[54] Gorsuch, "A Woman is Not a Man," 637.   [55] Krylova, "Stalinist Identity," 648.

that accompanied them, corrupted dreams and eclipsed the genuine voluntary sacrifices of young people.

The Great Terror

The political system that developed under Stalin in the 1930s was a product of systematic terror and force. The state was run by Stalin, a small circle of Communist party leaders, and the secret police under the cover of a democratically phrased constitution. With the personality cult in full swing, no criticism of the "Great Leader" could be voiced. Visible deprivations, plan failures, epidemics, shortages, and every manner of manmade calamity were explained away as consequences of enemy predations and plots. Good citizens were supposed to maintain a cheerful disposition and patience while making sacrifices for the greater cause of building the first socialist society in history. Faced with a myriad problems in their quest to fulfill unrealistic plan targets, factory administrators and political leaders berated subordinates and set ever higher quotas. They also fabricated charges of sabotage against convenient targets such as managers trained during the prerevolutionary period and former oppositionists.

By the 1930s, there were few members of the party who knew much about alternative strategies of development or had ever experienced the open debates within the party that had been allowed under Lenin. Young workers like Mishalova had no trouble believing that all ills were the work of enemies. Other workers, more cynical about ideological exhortations or perhaps uninterested in abstract explanations, responded to the intensification of production and poor working and living conditions by avoiding personal responsibility and innovation. All this bore little resemblance to the promised "joyful" life under socialism. The system, rife with tensions, corruption, and denunciatory practices in the context of Stalin's unlimited power, exploded into a senseless bloodbath known as the "Great Terror."[56]

The period commonly referred to as the "Great Terror" began in July–August 1937, subsiding in November 1938 when Stalin ordered a halt to mass repression. With the approval of the Politburo, Stalin initiated

---

[56] There is a long-running and far-ranging debate about the impetus behind and the scale of the Great Terror. See J. Arch Getty, *The Origins of the Great Purges: The Soviet Communist Party Reconsidered, 1933–1938* (Cambridge: Cambridge University Press, 1985); Getty and R. T. Manning (eds.), *Stalinist Terror: New Perspectives* (Cambridge: Cambridge University Press, 1993); Getty and Oleg V. Naumov, *The Road to Terror: Stalin and the Self-Destruction of the Bolsheviks, 1932–1939* (New Haven: Yale University Press, 1999); Robert W. Thurston, *Life and Terror in Stalin's Russia, 1934–1941* (New Haven: Yale University Press, 1996); and Robert Conquest, *The Great Terror: A Reassessment* (New York: Macmillan, 1990).

these punitive actions as a strike against what he perceived to be a "fifth column." Although historians continue to debate his intentions in orchestrating events in this period, recent archival revelations have led to some consensus. According to Oleg Khlevniuk, the Great Terror, while not inevitable and "seemingly chaotic," should be understood as "a series of centrally directed punitive actions against various groups that the Soviet leaders perceived as real or potential enemies."[57] In the Far East the Terror had a particular significance because it severely impacted prisoners already in the labor camps and national minority groups such as the Soviet Koreans. The rapid influx of prisoners into the labor camp system as a result of mass arrests also aggrandized the power of the NKVD. The Great Terror then dramatically increased mortality among prisoners in the Far East because the camps were unable to accommodate the hundreds of thousands of new arrivals between 1937 and 1938. Many others already in labor camps and prisons were summarily executed before the new waves of convicts arrived.[58]

As the terror unfolded, Stalin first targeted Old Bolsheviks by falsifying charges of treason and murder against them. Thus the first set of victims publicly tried and executed were Lenin's colleagues and those who had competed with Stalin for leadership in the 1920s. In order to carry out his attack on real and potential opposition, Stalin promoted individuals loyal to him to influential positions and relied on them to discredit and repress men such as Grigorii Zinoviev, Lev Kamenev, and those associated with the exiled Leon Trotsky. One such figure, Nikolai I. Yezhov, came to orchestrate and symbolize mass repressions. Yezhov's organization of the first show trial in August 1936 was a significant turning point. According to Khlevniuk, the course of this trial signified the impending "intensification of repression against everybody who had supported, directly or indirectly, any political opposition."[59] Yezhov's success in handling this trial was noted and earned him a new post. He was appointed People's Commissar of Internal Affairs to replace the former chief, Genrikh Yagoda, in September 1936.

Yezhov continued to develop cases against other prominent targets and another show trial took place in January 1937. In the dock were prominent Bolsheviks who had been Stalin's colleagues but in his mind had the potential to marshall forces against him. The defendants were

---

[57] Khlevniuk, *The History of the GULAG*, 140.

[58] In 1938 a special commission sentenced 5,866 prisoners to death and another 12,566 to extended sentences (*ibid.*, 171).

[59] *Ibid.*, 141. For Yezhov's career, see J. Arch Getty and Oleg V. Naumov, *Stalin's "Iron Fist": The Times and Life of N. I. Yezhov* (New Haven: Yale University Press, 2008).

convicted of organizing a "parallel anti-Soviet Trotskyist center" and were sentenced to be shot. The scale of the Terror quickly expanded after the second trial. A plenum of the Communist Party Central Committee meeting in late February–early March 1937 expanded the list of enemies by calling for the arrest of former figures of the "right deviation" N. I. Bukharin and A. I. Rykov. The final show trial was staged a year later in March 1938, when Bukharin and others were convicted of plotting to destroy the Soviet Union and kill Stalin, on the evidence of forced confessions and falsified documents.

However, top Bolsheviks were not the only targets for expulsion, arrest and execution. In May 1937 the Politburo resolved to exile from Moscow and other important Soviet cities all former oppositionists and Communists expelled from the party. Family members of former oppositionists were also ordered exiled from important urban centers and expelled from the Communist party. By 1937, repression and arrests were well under way among the military and members of the Communist party apparatus at all levels and in all regions, as well as defense industry employees. Key Soviet military leaders such as the Deputy People's Commissar of Defense M. N. Tukhachevskii and high-ranking generals were arrested in 1936 and ordered to be executed at a June 1937 trial of the "anti-Soviet Trotskyist military organization." The purge and Terror spread to every level of the party and state apparatus. Regional party secretaries fell in rapid succession, accused of lack of vigilance or of being co-conspirators in anti-Soviet conspiracies. The NKVD was simultaneously the instrument for implementing the Terror and its personnel potential targets in the search for enemies. Such pressure on the secret police further fueled the hunger among investigators to uncover ever larger plots lest they be accused of lacking vigilance or worse. Other sectors of the population swiftly began to feel the blows from the repressive measures.

It is unclear why the purge spread to encompass groups outside of the party, military, or government apparatuses but by July 1937 the government moved to mass repression. At the end of July 1937, the Politburo endorsed an operational order from the NKVD. The infamous Order No. 00447 outlined the mechanisms and scope for mass operations against "former kulaks, criminals and other anti-Soviet elements." Targets of this order included former kulaks, both those who had escaped from exile and those who had completed their sentences, former oppositionists, political prisoners already in labor camps, Tsarist officers and non-Bolshevik party members from the pre-revolutionary period, along with criminals. There were separate fates for these groups. Some were to be arrested and immediately shot. Others were to be arrested and incarcerated in camps or prisons for eight to ten years. Khlevniuk has described the process and the results: "Each province, territory and republic was assigned quotas for both categories. In total, the order commanded the arrest of 268,950 people, of which 72,950 (including 10,000 camp prisoners) were to be shot."[60] Shortly after the beginning of this operation, the regime turned its attention to arrests and executions of national minority groups, especially those living in territories along the Soviet borders such as Poles, Finns, and German nationals. In September and October 1937, another large operation against populations in the borderlands targeted the Korean population of 170,000 in the Far East for deportation to Kazakhstan and Uzbekistan, ostensibly to "stop the penetration of Japanese spies."[61]

Mass repression also engulfed relatives of the arrested. Order no. 00486 in August 1937 called for the arrest of wives of men accused of treason. The women were sent to labor camps for long sentences. Thus, although few women were in top leadership posts, they could be arrested even if they had never held an important post, for guilt by association as wives or close relatives of the accused. Their children over the age of fifteen were driven into special orphanages or corrective labor colonies. Women with their own pedigree as Communists were stunned not only by the arrests of their husbands but by their own arrest, not for any crimes they had committed but simply for being "wives." Mariia Gol'dberg, arrested in January 1938 and sent to KarLag in Kazakhstan along with other wives of enemies of the people, was initially "shocked by the senselessness, the inanity of exactly this issue. We, Soviet women, who had our own place in the building of our country, having our own public persona, were turned into a thing, an appendage."[62] In some cases, young women who worked closely with recently "unmasked" enemies were accused of illicit sexual relations with the enemy. In Khabarovsk K. Gracheva was working for the regional Komsomol Committee when a series of leaders were expelled and arrested. Gracheva in turn was expelled from the organization and lost her job when she was accused of sexual relations with these recently exposed "enemies" and general "depravity." Unable to prove her innocence in any other way, the frantic Gracheva obtained a doctor's note testifying to her virginity. Her case eventually reached the Komsomol Central Committee. Her sad story, sans the virginity test, appeared in

---

[60] Khlevniuk, *The History of the GULAG*, 146.

[61] *Ibid.*, 147. The Korean order is reprinted on 148.

[62] Memoir of Mariia M. Gol'dberg, "Story about what will never be repeated, 1962–63," Memorial, f. 2, op. 1, d. 47, l. 5. There are a number of published works on women prisoners of the camps; for one example, see Meinhard Stark, *Frauen im GULAG: Alltag und Überleben, 1936–1956* (Munich: DTV, 2003). Women were 23.4 percent of the prisoner population in 1937; in 1939 their proportion fell slightly to 22.8 percent. See Zhiromskaia, *Demograficheskaia istoriia*, 107.

Komsomol'skaia pravda.[63] A few days after the article, the Khabarovsk regional Komsomol removed accusations against her for "ties with enemies." However, she was reprimanded by squeamish Komsomol members for pleading her case via "the vulgar course" of obtaining a doctor's note to disprove previous sexual relations.[64] Gracheva was willing to do whatever it took to clear her name because the stakes were high.

Having turned a blind eye to overzealous NKVD organs and allowed locals to ask for additional target numbers, Stalin let the repression reach astronomical proportions. The final numbers of those arrested and executed were much higher than the initial quotas because local NKVD operatives began to compete to "unmask" traitors. They first turned to arresting those who had prior convictions. When this proved inadequate, they tortured and used other scare tactics to force unfortunates, sometimes people picked at random on the streets, to sign confessions of crimes against the Soviet state qualifying them for the death penalty. Confessions obtained by torture or by those wishing to settle personal scores produced lists of new people slated for arrest, imprisonment, and execution. Without any real evidence of criminal or anti-Soviet activities, "more than 500,000 people were convicted under Order no. 00447 in 1938."[65] Secret memorandums from the archives reveal that in the period of the Great Terror about 1.5 million people were sentenced to various prison terms and about 680,000 people were shot.[66] The Soviet secret police did not employ any means of "mass extermination" such as gas chambers, which means that on average, "1,500 executions conducted each day were individual."[67] Hundreds of thousands of others lived under threat of arrest as outcasts, losing jobs, access to education, and homes on account of having "connections with enemies of the people," relatives living abroad, or an "alien" social background.[68]

The "Great Terror" ended when on November 17, 1938, the Politburo adopted a resolution "On arrests, procuratorial supervision, and investigative procedure," blaming the NKVD for "excesses" and forbidding further operations and deportations.[69] Yezhov was replaced by Lavrentii Beria on November 25, 1938. Yezhov and other NKVD employees were then arrested in a new purge of the Commissariat. Every employee of the NKVD could theoretically have been accused of breaching "socialist legality." But there was no second wave of wholesale repression against state security workers, and according to Khlevniuk, only "7,372 officers

---

[63] T. Karel'shtein, "Vrazheskaia kleveta," *KP*, January 22, 1938.
[64] "Protocol of the meeting of the Far Eastern Regional VLKSM bureau," January 26, 1938, GAKhK P, f. 618, op. 1, d. 322, ll. 18–22.
[65] Khlevniuk, *The History of the GULAG*, 161.   [66] *Ibid.*, 168.   [67] *Ibid.*, 166.
[68] *Ibid.*, 169.   [69] *Ibid.*, 186.

of state security were fired that year (twenty-three percent of the total), and 937 of those were arrested," under the slogans of "Restoring socialist legality" and "Liquidation of wreckers."[70] For the next several years, a small number of cases of those sentenced to death and to the camps were reviewed. For the most part, those already in the camps had less chance of having their cases reviewed than the lucky souls whose cases were still under investigation at the moment mass operation came to an end at the close of 1938.[71] As the mass operations wound down, the camps in the Far East still teemed with hungry, ill, and bewildered victims of the Terror with no way to clear their names. Their presence and their forced contribution to the building of the region became the unspoken but decisive undercurrents on the frontiers of Stalinism.

While the Khetagurovite campaign was initiated before the crest of the Great Terror packed labor camps with doomed convicts, the fate of the female migrants was irrevocably marked by these events. Far Eastern industries, already short of labor and endemically mismanaged and corrupt, became even more desperate for qualified, untainted, responsible and disciplined people to restore some semblance of order as the Terror and mass deportations swept away waves of trained cadres and denizens. The need for female labor in particular became all the more acute because Soviet Koreans and Chinese migrant laborers were deported leaving vacant positions reserved by state decree for female labor. The NKVD's expanding empire of camps demanded their own armies of accountants, nurses, and typists. Women and qualities identified with female labor finally appeared as obligatory keystones in Stalinist state building and national security on the frontier.

[70] *Ibid.*, 187.   [71] *Ibid.*, 195.

2   "Where steel cracks like glass"

Women were scarce in the frontier societies of the Far East. The region's sex ratio – seventy-three women for every hundred men in 1937 – was a major improvement on the state of affairs in previous decades, but, such an imbalance still generated dilemmas unknown in other rural areas of the Soviet Union.[1] The shortage was touted by journalists as a veritable Achilles' heel of a critical border zone. A deficit of women affected family and community formations, and it proved detrimental to the functioning of industries and regional institutions where quotas for female labor went unfilled. Moreover, the visible absence of women tended to add an air of impermanence and ambiguity to the Soviet claims on the Far East because women's presence as wives and mothers often serves to "mark" the boundaries of the nation in patriotic discourses.[2] The dictates of full-scale industrialization in the 1930s and international tensions made the dearth of women on this frontier a matter requiring attention at the highest levels of the Stalinist regime.[3]

The imbalance between the sexes and its economic and social ramifications were, to a large extent, fallouts of state policies. Now Soviet bureaucrats, spurred by plan targets for rapid Far Eastern development, tried to engineer an immediate solution by appealing to young female activists. There was nothing remarkable about this intervention into settlement dynamics – hundreds of years before the Bolshevik Revolution,

[1] Figures from Nina I. Dubinina, *Dal'nevostochnitsy v bor'be i trude. Istoricheskii ocherk, 1917–1941* (Khabarovsk: Khabarovskoe knizhnoe izdatel'stvo, 1982), 102. This ratio was similar to the urban ratios of Soviet Russia in 1923.

[2] For a discussion of women's bodies in struggles over national identity and territory, see Mostov, "Sexing the Nation/Desexing the Body."

[3] For more on the gendered division of labor and women in the Soviet labor force, see the pioneering and influential work of Wendy Goldman, *Women, the State, and Revolution: Soviet Family Policy and Social Life, 1917–1936* (Cambridge: Cambridge University Press, 1993). Other works on this subject include Melanie Ilic, *Women Workers in the Soviet Interwar Economy: From "Protection" to "Equality"* (New York: St. Martin's Press, 1999), and Schrand, "The Five-Year Plan for Women's Labour," 1455–1478.

the Russian state sought to control, channel and exploit planned and anarchic population movements on the peripheries[4] – except for the special appeal to women.

Tsarist officials in the nineteenth century were concerned with border security and the possibilities of using such spaces to allay population pressures in central Russia. Government officials, along with Russian and foreign entrepreneurs, also hoped to exploit the region's rich resource base.[5] The first Russians to occupy the Far East permanently were soldiers stationed along its borders with China in the 1850s and 1860s. Once the region was open for voluntary settlement in the 1860s, the authorities concentrated on attracting settlers for agriculture and left the needs of other economic sectors to develop with temporary migrant labor. State servitors in the Far East were willing to make significant concessions to attract certain categories of settlers. One of the groups officially welcomed were Old Believers. These religious dissenters had long forsaken the official Orthodox Church and rejected governmental authority. Often the state punished them with forced exile and the first contingent of Old Believers arrived in the Far East by force in 1859. However, in 1863 Governor General of Eastern Siberia, M. S. Korsakov, began encouraging the voluntary resettlement of Old Believers. The invitation to resettle was embraced by such non-conformists because they could find refuge in the isolated region from the state and shield their children from the corrupting influences of modern life. The subsequent disinterest of regional officials in persecuting these and other non-Orthodox Christians, despite loud protestations from the Orthodox Church, shaped a space that in practice tolerated religious diversity decades before religious tolerance became law in the Russian Empire.[6]

Although the Far East was not open for settlement until after the emancipation of the serfs in the 1860s, it shared many of the same settlement patterns experienced in the history of Siberian settlement dating back

---

[4] See the collection of essays in Nicholas Breyfogle, Abbey Schrader, and Willard Sunderland (eds.), *Peopling the Russian Periphery: Borderland Colonization in Eurasian History* (London: Routledge, 2007).

[5] For further reading on settlement and contemporary debates surrounding it, see A. A. Kaufman, *Pereselenie i kolonizatsiia* (Sankt.-Peterburg, 1905).

[6] M. B. Serduk, "Religioznye pereseleniia na iuge Dal'nego Vostoka Rossii," in A. I. Krushanov and V. L. Larin (eds.), *Dal'nii Vostok Rossii v kontekste mirovoi istorii,* (Vladivostok: DVO RAN, 1997), 241–244. For further reading on the subject of Old Believers in the Far East, see the recent work of Iuliia V. Argudiaeva, *Staroobriadtsy na Dal'nem Vostoke Rossii* (Moscow: Institut etnologii i antropologii RAN, 2000) and her: "Khoziaistvennaia adaptatsiia staroobriadtsev v Primor'e," in A. S. Vashichuk (ed.), *Adaptatsiia etnicheskikh migrantov v Primor'e v XX v.* (Vladivostok: DVO RAN, 2000), 8–26.

to the seventeenth century.[7] It was also associated with Siberia in the Russian and later Soviet imaginations. Travelers and Russian intellectuals have long insisted that Siberians were of a different character from ordinary Russians. Alexander Herzen wrote that "Familiarity with danger and the habit of prompt action have made the Siberian peasant more soldierly, more resourceful and more ready to resist, than his Great Russian brother."[8] These observations became recurrent tropes in Soviet literature about Siberia and the Far East by implication. The idea that Siberians were a special group who carved out "free" spaces pervaded the writings of village prose authors such as Valentin Rasputin in the mid-twentieth century.

For peasants, Siberia as a geographic space offered less exploitation and potentially fewer intrusions into their lives. In the eighteenth and nineteenth centuries, just as serfdom and natural calamities made life ever more difficult for peasants in European Russia, Siberia was becoming more accessible. Serfs who managed to cross the Urals to escape from their landlords settled in Siberia to become state peasants. As such they paid only a quitrent (a preset payment often in kind instead of the more fluid and onerous labor obligations that peasants resented) and were supervised by a state bailiff rather than a master. Social status was relatively less important and private property more secure in these wide-open spaces where landed nobility never gained control of land and labor and where government officials were few and far between.

However, while Siberia held out the possibility of "freedom" from the repressive state and landlords, it was a place of punishment and exile and had a well-deserved reputation for fostering abuses by government officials. Intellectuals sent into exile to Siberia, such as Fyodor Dostoevsky,

---

[7] On Siberian settlement, see Steven G. Marks, "Conquering the Great East: Kulomzin, Peasant Resettlement and the Creation of Modern Siberia," in Stephen Kotkin and David Wolff (eds.), *Rediscovering Russia in Asia. Siberia and the Russian Far East* (Armonk, NY: M. E. Sharpe, 1995), 23–39; Treadgold, *The Great Siberian Migration*; Alan Wood, "Sex and Violence in Siberia: Aspects of the Tsarist Exile System," in John Massey Stewart and Alan Wood (eds.), *Siberia: Two Historical Perspectives* (London: GB-USSR Association and School of Slavonic and East European Studies, 1984), 35–61; Wood, "Russia's 'Wild East': Exile, Vagrancy and Crime in Nineteenth-Century Siberia," in Wood (ed.), *The History of Siberia: From Russian Conquest to Revolution* (London: Routledge, 1991), 117–139; and Leonid M. Goryushkin, "Migration, Settlement and the Rural Economy of Siberia, 1861–1914," in *ibid.*, 140–157.

[8] Quoted in James R. Gibson, "Paradoxical Perceptions of Siberia: Patrician and Plebeian Images Up to the Mid-1800s," in Galya Diment and Iuri Slezkine (eds.), *Between Heaven and Hell: The Myth of Siberia in Russian Culture* (New York: St. Martin's Press, 1993), 89; Iuliia V. Argudiaeva (ed.), *Sem'ia i semeinyi byt v vostochnykh regionakh Rossii* (Vladivostok: Dal'nauka, 1997).

provided "the consummate image of Siberia as hell."[9] Because of the difficulty in governing Siberia from Moscow, regional governors had broader powers than their counterparts in European Russia. Governors such as Ivan Pestel (Governor General of Western Siberia from 1806 to 1819) was the most notorious among them for cruelty, abuse of power and avarice. According to Harriet Murav, who analyzed the myths about Siberia among Russian intellectuals in the nineteenth century, Anton Chekhov did not try to resolve the contradiction inherent in his observations of Siberia. For him, it was a place of exile, desolation, and punishment and, at the same time "the site of greatest freedom."[10] All the contradictory, frightening, yet nevertheless alluring ideas about Siberia as a space and Siberians as a special type shaped by the natural environment and distance from the state were inherited and in some ways exaggerated when they were transposed onto the Russian and then Soviet Far East.

Pre-revolutionary images and practices of using Siberia and the Far East as destinations for convict labor and punishment outlived the Romanov dynasty. Other practices of empire in Eurasia also crossed the revolutionary divide. Far Eastern industrial and party bosses ran their enterprises as fiefdoms much like their Tsarist predecessors, either because their distance from the center dictated such tactics or because they took advantage of the leeway they found. Most of all they focused attention on fulfilling plan targets to secure their status in the Soviet system. They also showed little interest in providing the services necessary to improve conditions for laborers and their families. The decision-making power and lack of interest among local bosses in living up to the promises of socialism contributed a great deal to the poor performance of the region in turning migrants into residents.

Throughout the history of its settlement, two interrelated problems worked to undermine sustained regional growth. First, although settlers and migrants came to the region, few stayed to become permanent residents. Second, the low percentage of women among the settlers and seasonal migrants itself fueled the high settler turnover rate, setting up a vicious circle in which the shortage of women and the restlessness of the population were blamed for the low quality of life in general and the tendencies of settlers to abandon their plans to stay and create a stable community life. Such demographic patterns also had a direct impact on the status of women who put down roots in the region.

In the pre-revolutionary period a steady flow of temporary male migrants, together with the number of troops stationed in the region,

---

[9] Harriet Murav, "'Vo Glubine Sibirskikh Rud': Siberia and the Myth of Exile," in Diment and Slezkine (eds.), *Between Heaven and Hell*, 103.

[10] *Ibid.*, 108.

made the Far East an overwhelmingly male zone. Critical components of Tsarist settlement policies and the strategies of voluntary migrant families were at the root of an imbalance between the sexes.[11] Statistics demonstrate that officials selecting peasant migrant households for resettlement preferred subsidizing families with a preponderance of male laborers. Compounding this preference were peasants' own strategies. Peasant families tended to choose migration if they had a disproportionate number of adult men in the family.[12] Both officials and peasants shared the assumption that the arduous physical work necessary to transform the taiga into arable lands made ample male labor power essential. Sons rather than daughters were more likely to stay within the household after marriage and could be expected to support the extended family in the first difficult years. Families with a higher number of men were further favored by a 1901 shift in resettlement policy. Henceforth settlers received land based on the number of males in their household, as opposed to a previous standard of 100 desiatiny (one desiatina equals roughly 2.7 acres) per family allotment.

Despite a system of material incentives to promote settlement initiated in the 1860s, the population of the Far East grew slowly, reaching approximately 140,000 by 1880.[13] The pace picked up in the 1880s and 1890s but was sluggish in comparison with the rate at which settlers were moving to Siberia in the same period. Of the 1,400,000 settlers who registered at resettlement points on their way eastward, only 63,000 were heading for the Far East between 1890 and 1899.[14] Throughout this period, regional agriculture, severely limited by natural conditions and a small population base, could not guarantee a local source of food at the best of

---

[11] The 1897 Russian Imperial Census showed that even in comparatively well-populated areas of the Far East, like the Iuzhno-Ussuriisk okrug, women accounted for only 34.5 percent out of a population of 55,875 peasants and 44.2 precent among the Cossack soslovie's (service estate) total of 11,763. The situation did not improve among peasants in subsequent decades. In 1910–1912 in so called "old-settler" agricultural communities (those who came before 1901) there were 93.3 women for every 100 men; in settlements made up of new migrants, there were 87 women for every 100 men. Figures from Iulia V. Argudiaeva, "Demograficheskaia situatsiia i demograficheskoe povedenie krest'ian u vostochnykh slavian Dal'nego Vostoka Rossii (60-e gody XIX–nachalo XX v.)," in Elena Chernolutskaia (ed.), *Voprosy sotsial'no-demograficheskoi istorii Dal'nego Vostoka v XX veke* (Vladivostok: DVO RAN, 1999), 6–7.

[12] "Among those settlers who came at the expense of the government between 1883 and 1892 for every 100 men there were 93.88 women. Among peasants who came without government assistance there were 88.57 women for 100 men" (Argudiaeva, "Demograficheskaia situatsiia," 6).

[13] Leonid L. Rybakovskii, *Naselenie Dal'nego Vostoka za 150 let* (Moscow: Nauka, 1990), 52.

[14] *Ibid.*, 53.

times.[15] Grain was regularly imported from potential international rivals. The inability of locals to support garrisoned frontier troops was one of the main impetuses for the construction of the Trans-Siberian Railroad.[16] By 1900, the population of the Far East stood at an unimpressive 430,000. A quarter of this figure was non-Slavic: migrants from Asian countries and 55,000 indigenous Tungus and Nivkhi.[17] With the availability of the Trans-Siberian Railroad, the population grew by another 440,000 in the period between 1900 and 1910. By the time the Revolution of 1917 swept away the Romanov dynasty, the Far East was home to just about one million officially registered denizens.[18]

Social stability and demographic growth in the region were not simply undermined by an anemic agricultural base. Many of those who came to the region did not live long enough to escape the difficulties they found. Natural increases were unlikely to become a major factor in expansion of the population base when in 1900 child mortality among the agrarian population of the Amur oblast was an abysmal "740 for every 1000 born."[19] The Primor'e region was especially vulnerable to epidemic diseases because of merchant and settler traffic as well as population movements from Asia. By 1908, 612 commercial ships were coming into the port of Vladivostok, increasing the frequency of plague. Despite efforts to inspect incoming ships by a newly formed sanitary service, plague hit the city in 1910 and again in 1921.[20] Squalid living conditions and a lack of elementary sanitation in cities like Vladivostok with a population of 90,000 quickly generated mass outbreaks. Cholera struck the city in 1895, 1902, 1909, and 1910. A catastrophic shortage of doctors in the cities and the absence of medical care in the countryside meant that the region faced outbreaks of smallpox every six to seven years, even though vaccinations were available. Typhus was common and epidemics lasted for years. The largest typhoid epidemics were in 1889, 1890, 1904, and 1907–1908. Diphtheria raged in 1886, 1889, 1907, and 1912–1914. Illness among children was widespread and whooping cough was especially bad in 1911, and 1916. Scarlet fever broke out in 1911, lasting until 1912. The last typhoid epidemic began in 1918 and lasted four years.

---

[15] V. M. Kabuzan calculated a total of 488,700 peasant settlers between 1850 and 1916 and 499,205 for all other kinds of settlers such as demobilized soldiers and nonagricultural settlers. See Kabuzan, *Dal'nevostochnyi krai v XVII–nachale XX vv. (1640–1917): Istoriko-demograficheskii ocherk* (Moscow: Nauka, 1985), 157.

[16] For more on this, see Marks, *Road to Power.*

[17] Rybakovskii, *Naselenie Dal'nego Vostoka*, 57.   [18] *Ibid.*, 67.

[19] *Ibid.*, 38. Rybakovskii cites from *Obzor zemledel'cheskoi kolonizatsii Amurskoi oblasti* (Blagoveshchensk, 1913), 260.

[20] E. B. Krivelevich et. al. (eds.), *Ot shamanskogo bubna do lucha lazera (Ocherki po istorii meditsiny Primor'ia)*, Chast' 1 (Vladivostok: Vladivostokskii gosudarstvennyi meditsinskii universitet, 1997), 136–137.

In the early twentieth century, the migration of laborers heading for work in industries and mining grew more intensively than that of agricultural settlers. When the number of workers arriving in the region began to catch up with the number of peasants, sex ratios were skewed even further.[21] A survey in 1913 found that male migrants tended to be married men, but only 1 percent brought their families.[22] Women were actually barred in contracts from accompanying men to work in Far Eastern gold fields. Consequently, the percentage of women was especially low in urban areas and among those engaged in nonagricultural occupations.[23] The shortage of women in the labor force was so acute that female convicts released from Sakhalin Island were sent to work in Far Eastern hospitals and as servants in private homes.[24] With wives and children left behind in other areas, men were unlikely to invest energy and resources in permanent housing, form social networks, or treat this experience as anything other than a temporary stage.

Unlike Europeans in other colonial contexts, Russian and Soviet officials were not concerned about interracial unions or miscegenation on the frontier.[25] Intermarriage with populations on the peripheries had been

[21] For instance, women constituted 34.5 percent of the population in the Primor'e oblast in 1896. By 1913, the proportion of women in the Primor'e oblast had actually fallen – that year they constituted only 25.6 percent of the population. See L. I. Galliamova, *Dal'nevostochnye rabochie Rossii vo vtoroi polovine XIX – nachale XX vv.* (Vladivostok: Dal'nauka, 2000), 22. Galliamova agrees with the figures of Soviet-era historian B. V. Tikhonov in *Pereseleniia v Rossii vo vtoroi polovine XIX v. (Po materialam perepisi 1897 g. i passportnoi statistiki* (Moscow: Nauka, 1978), 103, 164. Women made up 42.6 percent of the population in the Amur oblast as a whole.

[22] Galliamova, *Dal'nevostochnye rabochie*, 136.

[23] In the city of Khabarovsk, Slavic women were only 17.2 percent of the population and an even more striking 15.4 percent in Vladivostok in 1896. Meanwhile, gender ratios in European Russia in the 1890s stood at 100 men to 103 women. Even Siberia, a region known for a longstanding shortage of women, had 95 women for every 100 in this period. Figures from Goryushkin, "Migration, Settlement and the Rural Economy," 143.

[24] By 1897, women constituted 7.2 percent of the Far Eastern workforce and just 2.2 percent of the workforce if servants were not included. This is at a time when women's share in industrial labor in the European parts of Russia was 27 percent. See Galliamova, *Dal'nevostochnye rabochie*, 120.

[25] Although gender as a category of analysis or women as migrants and colonizers, for that matter, have not figured prominently as subjects in studies of Russian or Soviet history, scholars in a variety of other fields have scrutinized the workings of gender, class, and race in the practices and structures of empires. The secondary literature on gender and empire is vast and continues to expand. See Philippa Levine (ed.), *Gender and Empire* (Oxford: Oxford University Press, 2004); Catherine Hall, *Civilizing Subjects: Metropole and Colony in the English Imagination, 1830–1867* (Chicago: University of Chicago Press, 2000); Ann Laura Stoler, *Carnal Knowledge and Imperial Power: Race and the Intimate in Colonial Rule* (Berkeley: University of California Press, 2002); Julia A. Clancy-Smith and Frances Gouda (eds.), *Domesticating the Empire: Race, Gender and Family Life in French and Dutch Colonialism* (Charlottesville: University Press of Virginia, 1998); Katie Pickles, *Female Imperialism and National Identity: Imperial Order Daughters of the Empire*

integral to Russian empire-building since at least the seventeenth century. Authorities and observers actually applauded a tendency among Far Easterners to intermarry across ethnic and confessional divides. Soviet historians continued this tendency and argued that the regions' reputation for a more tolerant and less hierarchical society was in part a result of the bride shortage and high intermarriage rates leading to the "dilution of *soslovie* [social estates] and ethnic boundaries."[26] These government-sanctioned practices of integration through intermarriage survived the 1917 rupture and were further boosted in the Soviet period.[27]

There were no official or entrepreneurial efforts to encourage non-agricultural female laborers to go to the Far East before the 1930s.[28] Tsarist officials, entrepreneurs and later Soviet managers were not anxious about the absence of female laborers for industry. They reasoned that a low level of mechanization in the Far East dictated an almost exclusive reliance on male labor, obviating the need for women in wage labor beyond the service sectors.[29] There was also little training and few jobs

---

(Manchester: University of Manchester Press, 2002); Louis Montrose, "The Work of Gender in the Discourse of Discovery," *Representations* 33 (Winter 1991), 1–41; Lora Wildenthal, *German Women for Empire, 1884–1945* (Durham: Duke University Press, 2001); Elizabeth Vibert, "Real Men Hunt Buffalo: Masculinity, Race and Class in British Fur Traders' Narratives," *Gender & History* 8 (1996), 4–21; Margaret Strobel, *European Women and the Second British Empire* (Bloomington: Indiana University Press, 1991); Angela Woollacott, *Gender and Empire* (New York: Palgrave, 2006); Richard Phillips, *Sex, Politics and Empire: A Postcolonial Geography* (New York: Palgrave, 2006); Clare Midgley (ed.), *Gender and Imperialism* (Manchester: Manchester University Press, 1998).

26 El'vira Vasil'chenko, "Gosudarstvennaia politika po formirovaniiu, razvit'iu i organiza-tsiiu deiatel'nosti zhenskogo sotsiuma na DV (1860–1940)," unpublished PhD dissertation, Ivanovskii gos. universitet (2000), 25. The process of ethnic dilution among Eastern Slavs in the Far East is at the crux of Argudiaeva's argument. Iu. Argudiaeva, *Krest'ianskaia sem'ia u vostochnykh slavian na iuge Dal'nego Vostoka Rossii (50e-gody XIX v. – nachalo XX v.)* (Vladivostok: DVO RAN, 1997).

27 This study will be one of the first efforts to explore gender dynamics of Soviet empire-building while addressing questions about women's agency in the Stalinist system of the late 1930s. Douglas Northrop addresses gender and empire in his *Veiled Empire: Gender and Power in Stalinist Central Asia* (Ithaca: Cornell University Press, 2004).

28 Russian imperial authorities in the nineteenth century considered ways to encourage banished men to marry so that wives and families would "lend a more orderly cast to Siberia's settlement." See Abby M. Schrader, "Unruly Felons and Civilizing Wives: Cultivating Marriage in the Siberian Exile System, 1822–1860," *Slavic Review* 66:2 (Summer 2007), 230–256.

29 Historians in the Russian Federation have given some attention to women's roles in the settlement history of the Far East in highly empirical works delving into the structure of the migrant peasant families before 1917 and patterns in the participation of women in the labor force throughout the twentieth century. Other Russian scholars have examined the status of women on Sakhalin Island in the nineteenth century because it was so well known for its shortage of women and the reputed moral dissolution of its residents. See Argudiaeva, "Demograficheskaia situatsiia,"; El'vira A. Vasil'chenko, "Semeino-brachnye otnosheniia dal'nevostochnogo krest'ianstva v

for women outside of agriculture and domestic service, at a time when in central Russia women were working in textile manufacturing.

In the 1930s the Communist party, the Red Army, and the NKVD directed all aspects of development and resettlement in a sparsely populated region in the shadow of a looming confrontation with the Japanese empire.[30] The region garnered relatively little attention and resources from the Soviet regime until the end of the First Five-Year Plan in the early 1930s. Funds appeared as the Politburo grew increasingly alarmed by Japanese activity in Manchuria. Japan's determination to fortify and settle the area just south of the Soviet border was all the more alarming considering the variety of problems on the Soviet side, not the least of which was low population density.[31] Just like settlers and soldiers in the prerevolutionary period, the residents of the Soviet Far East continued to

seredine XIX-nachale XX veka," in Vasil'chenko (ed.), *Nauchno-metodicheskie problemy gumanitarnykh nauk*, ch. 1 (Komsomol'sk-na-Amure: Komsomol'sk-na-Amure gos. tekhn. universitet, 1999), 24–28; Vasil'chenko, 'Zhenshchiny-katorzhanki i spetsposelenki na Dal'nem Vostoke', in *ibid.*, 43–47; Vasil'chenko, *Sovetskaia gosudarstvennaia politika*; and M. I. Ishchenko, "Spetsifika brachnykh otnoshenii na Sakhaline (konets XIX–nachalo XXv.)," in Argudiaeva (ed.), *Sem'ia i semeinyi byt*, 35–45. Nina I. Dubinina, a Khabarovsk-based historian, was the first to publish a study of the Khetagurovite migration using archival sources. Dubinina's scholarship, published in the 1980s, though based on archival research, was limited in the questions asked because of Soviet-era censorship and self-censorship. Constraints of censorship dictated a highly descriptive production with a laudatory tone for the accomplishments of female participants and the organization that ran the campaign. See Dubinina, *Dal'nevostochnitsy v bor'be i trude*, and for her study of the Khetagurovite campaign, see her, *Ty pozovi, Dal'nii Vostok!* (Khabarovsk: Khabarovskoe knizhnoe izdatel'stvo, 1987).

30 For more on the Soviet Far East's political history, strategic significance, and use as a zone for the exploitation of convict labor, see Stephen Kotkin and David Wolff (eds.), *Rediscovering Russia in Asia: Siberia and the Russian Far East* (Armonk, NY: M. E. Sharpe, 1995); Steven E. Merritt, "The Great Purges in the Soviet Far East, 1937–1938," unpublished PhD dissertation, University of California, Riverside (2000); I. D. Batsaev and A. G. Kozlov, *Dal'stroi i Sevvostlag OGPU-NKVD SSSR v tsifrakh i dokumentakh* (Magadan: SVKNII DVO RAN, 2002); Aleksandr Suturin, *Delo kraevogo masshtaba: O zhertvakh stalinskogo bezzakoniia na Dal'nem Vostoke* (Khabarovsk: Khabarovskoe knizhnoe izdatel'stvo, 1991); O. P. Elantseva, *Obrechennaia doroga, BAM (1932–1941)* (Vladivostok: Dal'nevostochnyi gos. universitet, 1994); and Elantseva, *Stroitel'stvo No. 500 NKVD SSSR: Zheleznaia doroga Komsomol'sk–Sovetskaia Gavan' (1930–1940 gg.)* (Vladivostok: Dal'nevostochnyi gos. universitet, 1995).

31 The Far East had a density of 0.7 individuals per square kilometer in 1932, while Japan had 154 individuals per square kilometer and China 48 individuals per square kilometer. Japan was indisputably winning the race to foster permanent settlements in disputed regions. In the 1920s in the northern half of Sakhalin Island, divided at the 50th parallel between the Soviet Union and Japan, there were only 10,630 Soviet citizens residing in an area of 40,986 kilometers. At the same time, the Japanese population below the 50th parallel, thanks to "effective" colonization efforts, stood at 293,000. See M. S. Vysokov, "Sovetskaia kolonizatsiia Sakhalina na rubezhe 20–30 kh godov: Vybor puti," in Vysokov, *Slaviane na Dal'nem Vostoke: Problemy istorii i kul'tury. Doklady i soobshcheniia nauchnoi konferentsii* (Iuzhno-Sakhalinsk: Sakhalinskii tsentr dokumentatsii noveishei istorii, 1994), 101.

depend on grain shipments from Manchuria because of poor transport links and low agricultural productivity. With the advance of the Japanese military into Manchuria in the 1930s, such dependency could not continue.

Worse still for the Soviet government, planned migration to the region had ceased entirely with the start of World War I.[32] Repression sapped labor and resources. The population declined by 200,000 between 1913 and 1926 when large groups of former White Army officers, former gentry, and members of the clergy were stripped of their citizenship and deported to China.[33] Cossacks and an unknown number of peasants crossed into China throughout the 1920s and 1930s to flee the Soviets. Finally, thousands were deported from the region during the dekulakization campaign in the early 1930s or forced off their productive farms and into special regime camps. Henceforth these "special settlers" lived in horrendous conditions and worked under duress clearing roads and felling trees.[34] By the late 1920s, the population had grown by 500,000 despite the ebbs and flows of refugees, foreign occupation, diseases, migrants, and forced relocations, bringing the total to just above one and a half million in 1930.[35]

After the early 1930s, the pace of state investment rocketed. Investment in the Far Eastern economy was eight times higher in the Second Five-Year Plan than in the period between 1928 and 1932. By 1934, Far Eastern development was receiving almost half of all capital investment in the USSR. While thousands were brought to the region by force as a result of Stalin's attack on kulaks and their families, attention also turned to voluntary resettlement programs. As an indication of the national security interests inherent in this undertaking, a resettlement administration in existence under the Council of People's Commissars USSR was liquidated and its functions appropriated by the NKVD, forming the

---

[32] Paradoxically, because of the instability caused by the Civil War and refugee populations, as of 1923 Russian women outnumbered Russian men 100:90 (742,052,000 women and 481,691,00 Russian men) in the Far East. The presence of numerous other nationality groups such as Ukrainians and Belorussians pushed the final tally to reflect a shortage of women. See Vasil'chenko, *Sovetskaia gosudarstvennaia politika*, 21.

[33] Figures from Stephan, *The Russian Far East*, 163. Rybakovskii offers different figures (originating from V. G. Udovenko, *Dal'nii Vostok* (Moscow, Gos. izd-vo geogr. lit-ry, 1957), 71. Rybakovskii found a population increase from 875,000 in 1910 to 1,281,700 in 1926. See Rybakovskii, *Naselenie Dal'nego Vostoka*, 99–100. For a recent survey of settlement patterns and policies in the Soviet period, see Iurii V. Pikalov, *Pereselencheskaia politika i izmenenie sotsial'no-klassovogo sostava naseleniia Dal'nego Vostoka RSFSR (noiabr' 1922–iiun' 1941 gg.)* (Khabarovsk: KhGPU, 2004).

[34] See Elena Chernolutskaia, "Protivorechivost' migratsionnoi politiki na Dal'nem Vostoke SSSR v 20–30-e gody (na primere Primor'e)," in *Istoricheskii opyt osvoeniia vostochnykh raionov Rossii.* Kniga II (Vladivostok: DVO RAN, 1993), 90.

[35] Rybakovskii, *Naselenie Dal'nego Vostoka*, 110.

Resettlement Department of the NKVD.[36] Despite this turmoil, the population finally showed some substantial increases, coming close to three million in 1940, a number that included the 300,000 labor camp inmates in the area.[37]

Plans for an infusion of new permanent settlers in the 1930s went hand in hand with tactics to stop the influx of so-called undesirable labor. Laborers from Asia had long been prominent in a number of Far Eastern industries such as fishing and timber, and in the education sector. There were different kinds of Asian migrants working in the region. Many Koreans in the Far East were immigrants who were in the region as permanent residents and possessed Soviet citizenship.[38] Chinese and Japanese laborers were less likely to possess Soviet citizenship or to seek it out, coming to the region to work for a short period. Estimates of Chinese seasonal laborers in the 1920s are based on poor data but they numbered somewhere between 50,000 and 70,000.[39] With the beginning of the First Five-Year Plan, the Soviet government sought to cap the numbers of Chinese migrants entering and the total leveled off at about 47,800 by the early 1930s.[40] The first to be targeted for outright expulsion were

[36] The Resettlement Department of the NKVD administered, in conjunction with the Communist party, both forced and voluntary resettlement programs between 1936 and 1939. The People's Commissariat of Agriculture USSR worked along parallel lines with the NKVD to coordinate voluntary agricultural resettlements. However, the transfer of responsibility for voluntary resettlement into the hands of the NKVD between 1936 and 1939 actually led to stagnation in the pace of agricultural settlement. Three years later, on May 27, 1939, the NKVD Resettlement Department and the resettlement sector of the People's Commissariat of Agriculture USSR were liquidated and their functions combined into a Resettlement Administration under the Council of People's Commissars USSR. As soon as responsibility for resettlement was transferred back to the auspices of the Council of People's Commissars USSR in May 1939, the number of free settlers rocketed, even though plans and results continued to be at odds. See "Introduction to archival inventory [Predislovie k opisi]," Russian State Archive of the Economy (RGAE), f. 5675, op. 1.

[37] Rybakovskii, *Naselenie Dal'nego Vostoka*, 110. Rybakovskii cites 2,739,000. Natural increase accounts for one-third of this number, the rest were migrants and convict laborers.

[38] For more on the Koreans in this area, see Hyun Ok Park, "Korean Manchuria: The Racial Politics of Territorial Osmosis," *South Atlantic Quarterly* 99:1 (2000), 193–215, and I. O. Sagitova, "Etnokul'turnaia i sotsial'no-ekonomicheskaia adaptatsiia koreiskoi diaspory na territorii Primorskogo kraia v dorevoliutsionnyi period," in Vashchuk (ed.), *Adaptatsiia etnicheskikh migrantov*, 55–68. Korean immigration to the Soviet Union was initially welcomed and had increased "significantly during the 1920s with close to 150,000 arriving during the decade," then leveled off to about 10 percent of total new arrivals in the region. See Rybakovskii, *Naselenie Dal'nego Vostoka*, 78.

[39] *Ibid.* For more on the Chinese in the region, see G. N. Romanova, "Ekonomicheskaia deiatel'nost' kitaitsev na rossiiskom Dal'nem Vostoke: Torgovlia, predprinimatel'stvo, zaniatost' (konets XIX-nachalo XX v.)," in Vashchuk (ed.), *Adaptatsiia etnicheskikh migrantov*, 83–101.

[40] This number is for the whole of the Far Eastern region. See Rybakovskii, *Naselenie Dal'nego Vostoka*, 80.

Japanese seasonal laborers in the fishing and timber industries. In 1933 they were no longer allowed to work in Kamchatka. Subsequently, Slavic women filled the resulting void.[41]

During the Great Terror, the secret police deported, arrested, or expelled East Asian legal and illegal migrants as well as others branded politically untrustworthy. Japanese, Chinese, and Korean laborers, many of whom had Soviet citizenship, became victims of this ethnic cleansing. Chinese and Japanese laborers were arrested or deported to their home regions, while Koreans with Soviet citizenship faced forced relocation to Central Asia. Consequently, the Primor'e region lost 200,000 residents, or a fifth of its population, in the course of 1937–1939.[42] These policies not only devastated the lives of hundreds of thousands but also undermined key social and economic sectors long reliant on Asian laborers. Thousands of positions were left vacant, especially in food preparation, education, and fish processing. These were also occupations officially classified as female and reserved for women by Soviet planners.

Rural areas had a different set of gender dynamics because of policies that took forced settlers to the region. The region was home to thousands of fatherless families taken there by force as part of the dekulakization campaign.[43] In 1938 there were 24,266 special settlers in the Khabarovsk region living within forty to a hundred kilometers of the Soviet border with Manchuria. One kolkhoz in the Jewish Autonomous Zone was 95 percent female. Officials grumbled that under such circumstances, "All the work is done by women."[44] In another kolkhoz twenty-four out of thirty adults were family members of repressed kulaks. Because the heads of these households were either shot or imprisoned in the early 1930s, there were only eight adult men on this farm. Six were new members who

---

41 The number of women as seasonal workers in the fishing industry, formerly dominated by Japanese labor, grew from 12,000 in 1929 to 29,000 in 1932. The number of Slavic women laborers also increased in the timber industry from almost none to 12,000 in 1932. See Vasil'chenko, *Sovetskaia gosudarstvennaia politika*, 37.

42 On the deportation of other "suspect" groups, see Elena N. Chernolutskaia, "'Ochistka' Primor'ia ot 'Neblagonadezhnogo' naseleniia v 1939 g. kak element stalinskoi repressivnoi politiki," in Chernolutskaia (ed.), *Voprosy sotsial'no-demograficheskoi istorii*, 95–112. On ethnic cleansing as a policy on the Far Eastern borderlands, see Terry Martin, "The Origins of Soviet Ethnic Cleansing," *Journal of Modern History* 70:4 (December 1998), 840–842, 851.

43 For a recent study of special settlers throughout the Soviet Union, see V. N. Zemskov, *Spetsposelentsy v SSSR, 1930–1960* (Moscow: Nauka, 2003). By 1932–1933, the Primor'e had 40,500 such special settlers. See Chernolutskaia, "Protivorechivost'," 90.

44 "Memorandum notes and short reports on questions of completing the April 19, 1938 resolution of the Central Committee VKP and SNK," GAKhK P, f. 2, op. 8, d. 192, l. 32.

had recently joined the kolkhoz under the auspices of a program to settle army veterans in frontier zones.[45]

Throughout the 1930s, a program to settle demobilized men actually contributed to skewed sex ratios. The program was initiated with the idea that trained and disciplined veterans would be available at a moment's notice for defense against Japanese incursions. Between 1937 and 1939 agricultural settlement in the Primor'e region was mostly based on this program.[46] Demobilized soldiers were offered 2,000 rubles and housing to stay in the region.[47] This poorly studied program has been mischaracterized as involuntary by Pavel Polian, one of the few scholars to examine the subject thus far. Some soldiers may have felt pressured by their commanding officers to sign up for settlement when superiors looked to fulfill plan targets.[48] However, secret reports to Far Eastern Communist party leaders reveal that even if officers pressured subordinates, the men who did not want to stay had plenty of opportunity to slip away or never appear at their designated place of residence. Of the 1,000 men who agreed to settle in 1936, authorities could locate only 500 a year later.[49] Their quick departures were considered unfortunate by top Communist party officials and sorry reflections of broken promises on the part of local administrators to provide good housing, but not crimes requiring further punitive attention.

---

[45] Their proximity to the border slated them for further suffering in 1938 when they were forcibly removed by the NKVD and relocated further north to prevent them from potentially collaborating with invaders. See "Memorandum notes, reports on the work of NKVD organs," January 11, 1939, GAKhK P, f. 35, op. 1, d. 313, ll. 262–263. In 1938 the NKVD conveniently "uncovered" an "ROVS underground" among special settlers in these Lespromkhozy supposedly formed in 1936. The "Rossiiskii obshche-voennyi soiuz" (Russian military union) was an organization of former Tsarist army officers formed in 1924 and initially headed by General Wrangel. The organization was an umbrella structure for a variety of émigré military formations and groups located in China, France, Turkey, etc.

[46] "On plans for resettlement of demobilized Red Army men and their families and young people of the Khetagurovite call-up in 1938 into kolkhozy, industries, enterprises and institutions of the region. Protocols of the meeting of the Far Eastern Regional Bureau of the Communist Party," April 25, 1938, RGASPI, f. 17, op. 21, d. 5446, l. 58.

[47] "Resolution 2045–446s – On release of funds for setting up households of demobilizing commanders of the RKKA in the Far East. Sovnarkom resolution signed by Molotov," November 17, 1937, GAKhKP, f. 553, op. 3, d. 4, l. 180.

[48] P. Polian, Ne po svoei vole: istoriia i geografiia prinuditel'nykh migratsii v SSSR (Moscow: OGI-Memorial, 2001).

[49] In 1937, 13,000 demobilizing soldiers settled in the region. Three thousand went to work in kolkhozy, another 3,000 were hired by the railroad, more than 3,000 were slated for administrative work at a variety of levels, and 5,000 were employed by other industries in the region. The veteran soldiers assigned to agriculture often did not tarry in their new homes. Before the end of the year, 300 of the 3,000 had already fled to parts unknown. See "Stenographic text of the Far Eastern Regional Communist Party Conference," May 29 to 31, 1937, RGASPI, f. 17, op. 21, 5385, l. 162.

Despite setbacks, military and civilian authorities were determined to rely on the veterans for agricultural settlers. The plan for 1938 projected the settlement of 30,830 demobilized soldiers in regional kolkhozy.[50] The need was particularly dire because hundreds of productive farms lay abandoned after the forced deportation of Soviet Koreans at the close of 1937.[51] Although some of the demobilized soldiers were sent to low-status jobs in the countryside, many were picked for quick upward mobility. Efrosina Mishalova's future husband was one of these demobilized soldiers who volunteered to stay in the region and was eventually selected to work in the NKVD. The regional procurator's office, chronically short of employees, especially during and after the purges, also sought out these men for jobs as investigators and regional procurators.[52]

"We are not building . . . a male monastery"

Settling demobilized men along the border was one thing. Having them stay required at least a promise of viable communities in isolated villages and construction zones. Army officers who were approached to stay in the region after demobilization were sometimes unwilling to make that commitment because of the fierce competition among them for available women.[53] Komsomol organizers worried that even enthusiastic and patriotic young workers tended to dissipate quickly in all-male company, turning to gambling, drinking, and desertion.[54] More than one commentator hypothesized that a significant increase in the number of women would transform the atmosphere, make men at least think twice about their poor hygiene, and inspire others to imagine themselves as long-term residents.

[50] "On plans for resettlement of demobilized Red Army men and their families and young people of the Khetagurovite call-up . . ." April 25, 1938, RGASPI f. 17, op. 21, d. 5446, l. 58.

[51] For example, to facilitate the replacement of Korean farmers by demobilized soldiers, the Regional Party Committee presented a request to the Communist Party Central Committee and the Council of People's Commissars USSR to order the Dal'Lag GULAG NKVD to prepare enough wood for 400 new homes (*ibid.*, 61).

[52] 'Report: On the condition of work and tasks of the organs of the procurator in accordance with the decisions of the February plenum of the Central Committee and the Stalin Constitution," December 28, 1937, GA RF, f. 8131, op. 14, d. 4, l. 10.

[53] The military's presence had increased in the region between 1932 and 1936 from six to fourteen divisions, about "300,000 men or 15 percent of the Red Army." See Stephan, *The Russian Far East*, 183.

[54] In 1939 the population of the Far East had the highest percentages of people between the ages of 20 and 29, making up 28.7 percent of the population in the Khabarovsk region and 29.7 percent in the Primor'e region. At the same time, the percentage of people in this age group in the Russian Republic of the Soviet Union was 17.7 percent. See Zhiromskaia, *Demograficheskaia istoriia*, 104.

Workers in Komsomol'sk, where women were initially barred by factory bosses from joining the first contingent of builders, shared the sentiments of army officers. At a meeting in 1935 between workers and newspaper editors, "one young builder" sent a note to the conference presidium with a question: "Will young women be coming this year?" The city's newspaper, *Udarnik Komsomol'ska* published the note and the answer: "Of course the work site will gain more young women in tandem with the kind of professions needed on site. Besides all this, we need to remember that we are not building in Komsomol'sk a male monastery, but a socialist city, where life must be in full swing."[55] Army commanders and party bosses were under some pressure to assuage such concerns and retain valuable personnel.

There were other reasons to focus on promoting female migration. Because this frontier of Stalinism, bordering Japanese-occupied Manchuria, was destined to be a frontline in case of war, regional military and party leaders worried that they needed more women along the border where they could step into jobs left vacant in the case of full-scale mobilization of men.[56] The Far Eastern regional party Committee reminded lower-level organizations that they had to both facilitate the resettlement of demobilized soldiers in frontier areas and place more emphasis on recruiting and retaining female participants of the Khetagurovite campaign: "In case of a mobilization many enterprises and institutions will be left without employees and a labor force and you are obligated . . . to develop a plan to take Khetagurovites and organize for them the necessary courses to prepare them to be drivers, tractor and combine mechanics etc."[57] An immediate arrival of single women, unhindered by husbands and children in their choice of postings, was an expeditious way to address cadre shortages in such circumstances.

A chronic deficit of cadres plagued every organization but certain sectors were particularly reliant on trained female labor. Industries and the NKVD needed experienced accountants. Towns needed librarians, teachers, and nurses. Neighborhoods and factories needed staff for their cafeterias, stores, laundries, and public baths. All these needs went unmet because the women who were already in the region had few opportunities to gain professional training. Technical schools and universities were

---

[55] "Survey of the Press," *Tikhookeanskaia zvezda*, March 9, 1935.

[56] Japanese women were also encouraged to identify at this time as frontier heroines and "active agents of Japan's colonial mission" in Manchuria. See Louise Young, *Japan's Total Empire: Manchuria and the Culture of Wartime Imperialism* (Berkeley: University of California Press, 1998), 368–369.

[57] "Protocol of the meeting of the Far Eastern Communist Party Committee Bureau," March 10, 1938, RGASPI, f. 17, op. 21, d. 5445, l. 53.

practically nonexistent.[58] To make matters worse, across the country men were no longer trained in sectors such as retail, kindergarten education, accounting, food services, communications, and a whole host of other "lower service personnel" positions deemed exclusively female.[59] This state-authorized gendered division of labor became an unforeseen impediment to Far Eastern development. An influx of more trained women would quickly address the shortages produced by this regendering of the Soviet labor pool.[60]

The rest of the country had long relied on the work of female Communist party members in education, medicine, and second-tier positions in local and regional administrations. Yet, in the Far East there were only five thousand female Communists out of the forty-five thousand registered Communist party members in 1933.[61] Authorities in Moscow were well aware of this cadre crisis and that it undermined settler retention efforts. In 1934 the All-Union Resettlement Committee under the Council of People's Commissars USSR concluded that in the Far East

There are not enough workers for the party-Komsomol and the administrative-industrial sectors at the regional and local level. If this issue of providing cadres for the region's social and consumer services is not decreed a special problem, along with the settlement of an agricultural and industrial labor force, . . . all of those who settle will be candidates for returnees.[62]

Of course, after 1937 some viewed the women as a reserve of activists to replenish the ranks of organizations recently devastated by the purges.

Even in the Stalinist system, there were competing and sometimes contradictory interests for every facet of decision-making and implementation. The Khetagurovite campaign was not an exception. When the government resolutely turned its attention to resolving the difficulties that made the region such a poor performer at retaining arrivals, ameliorating skewed gender ratios appeared feasible and essential. It was 1937 that became the first year since 1934 to have any significant numbers of new planned voluntary arrivals for permanent settlement and the

[58] As a result, during the First Five-Year Plan, although the number of women in the workforce grew by eight times, from 25,000 to 200,500, they were concentrated in low-skilled jobs in heavy industry. See Dubinina, *Dal'nevostochnitsy v bor'be i trude*, 58.

[59] Wendy Goldman charts the emergence of this gender-based division of labor and argues that it was "planned from above, by the state . . . re-gendering the economy beginning in 1930." For a list of professions reserved for women, see Goldman, *Women at the Gates*, 171, 283.

[60] This regendering of the Soviet labor force by governmental fiat is the topic of Goldman, in *ibid.*

[61] Dubinina, *Dal'nevostochnitsy v bor'be i trude*, 43.

[62] "Memorandum notes on the review of Far East settlement," RGAE, F. 5676, op. 1, d. 138, l. 7ob.

first time that Soviet state planners attempted to ameliorate the sex ratio imbalance.

Communist party and Komsomol authorities had a more heterogeneous vision for women in the region than the young workers in Komsomol'sk or the veterans considering permanent settlement. Because it was the party and the Komsomol that structured the Khetagurovite campaign, they made the program one that focused on selecting qualified professionals and exemplary activists rather than pliable young brides to cheer up lonely border guards. Authorities were compelled to consider how to attract female migrants, as well as to ascertain and acknowledge women's roles on the frontier. Of course, the need to define and articulate the role of women on the frontier did not translate directly into a uniformly shared vision of their role.

"We are waiting for you!": the Khetagurovite campaign

All these agenda coalesced to produce Valentina Khetagurova's appeal in *Komsomol'skaia pravda* on February 5, 1937.[63] Six weeks after its publication, the authorities established a Khetagurovite Committee for the Resettlement of Young People in the Far East in Khabarovsk under the auspices of the Far Eastern Regional Executive Party Committee and the Far Eastern Regional Komsomol.[64] The Khetagurovite Committee was nominally composed of important regional functionaries who were expected to take part in processing applications, determining regional labor needs, and supervising the progress of new arrivals.[65]

---

[63] Valentina Khetagurova-Zarubina, "Priezzhaite k nam na Dal'nii Vostok!," *KP*, February 5, 1937. This was not her first public appearance, as she graced the front cover of *Rabotnitsa*'s 1937 January issue devoted to the Conference of Red Army Wives. Anna Krylova has also identified 1937 as a pivotal moment in the evolution of gender roles when *Komsomol'skaia pravda* published letters from young women articulating their right to participate in combat and also containing "a disavowal of motherhood as an essential need and duty." See Krylova, "Stalinist Identity," 640.

[64] The bureau of the Far Eastern Regional Communist Party Committee first addressed the needs of the voluntary migration on March 17, 1937. It was resolved to form a temporary committee to organize the reception of the migrants. See "Protocol 333/20–352/39 of the meeting of the Far Eastern Regional Communist Party Committee Bureau, March 2, 1937–April 11, 1937: Decision by poll – 18. On rules for receiving young women in the Far East," GAKhK P, f. 2, op. 1, d. 1055, l. 133. The temporary committee consisted of Gregory Krutov (head of the Regional Executive Committee) as chairman, Il'ia Slinkin (First Secretary of the Khabarovsk oblast Communist Party Committee), Cherniavskii from the Far Eastern Komsomol, head of the regional soviet of trade unions Andrionov, and a representative of the People's Commissariat of Heavy Industry, Ivanov. Directors and administrators of regional soviet and economic enterprises were ordered "to immediately and personally report to the Committee how many and what kind of workers were needed and where the arriving women were to be sent." Krutov and Slinkin were arrested shortly thereafter during the purges (Slinkin on March 26, 1937).

[65] By October 1937, with 10,000 women already in the region, this migratory pipeline was finally compelling enough to warrant a lengthy discussion and resolution at a Far

The Khetagurovite Committee orchestrated a publicity campaign through newspapers and Komsomol organizations in large industrial centers of the country, as well as in institutes and universities in Moscow, Leningrad, Kiev, and other cities. The objective was not simply to find young women, but to specifically recruit "teachers, agronomists, livestock experts, doctors and others that are in short supply in the region."[66] No doubt there were underlying assumptions that these nurses and teachers would also "naturally" provide all sorts of other unpaid productive and reproductive labor.[67]

Data that exists on numbers of applications, arrivals, and their final destinations offers sufficient information to reconstruct the campaign's scope and trajectory. Sources disagree on the number of application letters sent between 1937 and 1939. Final tallies for letter totals ranged from 121,473 to 160,000. And because many letters contained more than one submission to migrate, the number of applicants was higher than the number of letters. For instance, in a span of eight months in 1937, there were 42,000 letters from 67,000 individuals.[68] This is why official estimates of actual applicants rather than letters ranged from 250,000 to 300,000.[69]

Arrivals began in April 1937. From then until the end of the year, more than 11,000 young women arrived as Khetagurovites, both alone and in groups of co-workers from all parts of the Soviet Union ranging from Moscow, Leningrad, and Khar'kiv to small towns in Ukraine and

Eastern Regional Communist Party Committee Bureau meeting of October 10–14, 1937. Internal documents suggest that officials considered the campaign an expression of genuine enthusiasm rather than a mobilization engineered by their own hands. This is clear in the formulation of their resolution: "The call of Komsomolka Khetagurova initiated in the whole country a movement of tens of thousands of young women who love their Motherland. Komsomolki and youth [are] expressing intense desire to work in the Far East, in the sphere of developing and mastering the grand natural riches of the region, as well as in the sphere of strengthening its defenses as the socialist country's fortress in the East." See "Protocols 48–56 of the Far Eastern Regional Communist Party Committee, January 4, 1938 to February 25, 1938: Appendix to Protocol no. 41, October 14, 1937," RGASPI, f. 17, op. 21, d. 5444, l. 48.

[66] Ibid., 49.

[67] For a discussion of women's reproductive and productive labors in other frontier societies, see Hurtado, *Intimate Frontiers*.

[68] "Far Eastern Regional Communist Party Committee ORPO: Memorandum notes, short reports, information sent to the Regional Communist Party Committee: On the status of the movement of youth of the Khetagurovite call-up to the Far East, March 20, 1938: Summary for eight months of 1937," GAKhK P, f. 2, op. 6, d. 358, l. 4. For further details of migrants' destinations and occupations in the regions, see Appendix 1.

[69] "Memorandum notes, short reports and other documents of the Komsomol Central Committee's commission and other organizations on the status and potentials of the Khetagurovite commission's activities and on the mobilization of young people for the construction of the Far East," April 29, 1939, RGASPI M, f. 1, op. 23, d. 1351, l. 12.

Belorussia (see Appendix 2). Large contingents came from Ukraine and major industrial cities in Russia, while smaller groups came from regions such as Azerbaijan, Georgia, and Kazakhstan.[70] Eventually, more than 25,000 women and 5,000 men had migrated as Khetagurovites by the time the campaign ended at the close of 1939.[71] This influx contributed significantly to the number of young women in the region.[72] In the first year of the campaign, 27 percent of the newcomers were younger than twenty and 66 percent were between the ages of twenty and thirty.[73]

Most of those who eventually left for the Far East were not lonely spinsters, economic migrants, or consciously seeking to sit out political storms in the isolation of the peripheries. There is no clear pattern to explain the push to migrate. Women came from many different regions, large cities, and small towns; some were orphans like Klava Novikova while others came from intact urban families like Ania Alekseeva. Many were already employed as teachers and nurses while others were just finishing school.

Some contemporaries and scholars who have discussed the Khetagurovites have assumed that they embarked for a region known for its overabundance of men because of a shortage of eligible men in their home regions. A series of violent periods – World War I, the Revolution, Civil War, and collectivization – had indeed dramatically skewed male: female ratios in all parts of the Soviet Union. Consequently, the overall percentage of women in the Soviet Union was disproportionately large in 1937, standing at 52.7 percent. However, this was due to the imbalance

---

[70] Seven nursing students came from the city of Dzhambul, Kazakhstan. They applied to become Khetagurovites as a group and in March 1938 moved to Khabarovsk, where they stayed together. The Khetagurovite Committee assigned them to the railroad administration's hospital in Khabarovsk. See the complaint from Nadezhda Kravchenko, February 14, 1939, GAKhK P, f. 78, op. 1, d. 895, l. 144. Another group of eight women came together from Kazan upon graduation from a teachers' college. Some were directed to work in the city of Komsomol'sk-na-Amure. See "Letters and requests of laborers received by the Regional Communist Party Committee from the Central Party Committee, 1939," Complaint from Shura Baranova, October 9, 1938, GAKhK P, f. 2, op. 6, d. 341, l. 11.

[71] The final tally is from "Resolution of the Komsomol Central Committee 'On the work of the Khetagurovite Commission," October 13, 1939, RGASPI M, f. 1, op. 23, d. 1351, l. 69. About 10,000–12,000 arrived in the Far East using invitations and funds of the Khetagurovite Committee but bypassed the Committee in Khabarovsk and found work elsewhere in the region. See "On the situation with letters at the Khetagurovite Committee," April 1940, RGASPI M, f. 1, op. 4, d. 288, l. 43.

[72] "Far Eastern Regional Communist Party Committee March 20, 1938: Summary for eight months of 1937," GAKhK P, f. 2, op 6, d. 358, l. 3. Khetagurovites were widely distributed in the region. Definitive numbers for final destinations were not located, though data for industries/institutions exist for 1937. See Table 1 in Appendix 1 for their destination in 1937.

[73] *Ibid.*

among older age groups.[74] Moreover, most of the Khetagurovite cohort, ages 15–19 and 20–24, born during the Revolution and the Civil War, were only 8.21 percent and 9.02 percent respectively of the total Soviet population in 1937. It was an inordinately small group reflecting the low birth rate and high infant mortality during the war years.[75] Besides, in 1939 men in the age group they were most likely to marry (25–34) made up more than 50 percent of the urban population.[76] Later studies of marriage patterns for this cohort confirm this, "showing only minor effects of . . . excess male mortality on the propensity of women to marry and on their mean age at marriage."[77] A typical Khetagurovite, between eighteen and twenty-two, would have had no sense that she had diminished marriage prospects and thus needed to seek out grooms in some distant and inhospitable land.

Employed factory workers and members of professional groups such as teachers, secretaries, and nurses in high demand everywhere were typical Khetagurovites. There were also many women with experience in heavy industry and mining. Iulia Druzhevich, a teacher, became a locomotive driver in the Far East. Mariia Komarova was a compressor operator in a coalmine. Valentina Parimova was a factory worker but was delegated to run a kolkhoz affiliated with her factory. Eventually, she also chaired the village soviet for five years. Tamara Zabelina had been a tractor driver, then a welder, and in the Far East she became a political instructor in a technical school for sailors and a political instructor on riverboats.

Increasingly, the Khetagurovite Committee had to fight with enterprises at the point of departure for certain professionals. Teachers were especially hard to bring out, not because they did not apply but because their home organizations refused to release them from their contracts even under penalty of sanctions from party organizations.[78] Khetagurovites were not enticed with bonuses and special pay scales like other types of

---

[74] The gender imbalance in Soviet cities, with 52.2 percent women in 1937, does not reflect the balance between genders in urban areas for those between the ages of 15 and 29. For that age group, the balance was almost even with 49.2 percent men and 50.8 percent women. Women were 59 percent of those between the ages of 50 and 59. See Zhiromskaia, *Demograficheskaia istoriia*, 92, 95.

[75] *Ibid.*, 96.   [76] *Ibid.*, 103.

[77] Sergei Scherbov and Harrie van Vianen, "Marital and Fertility Careers of Russian Women Born Between 1910 and 1934," *Population and Development Review* 25:1 (March 1999), 131–132, 134.

[78] There were numerous "requests to take action against such organizations" (there were forty letters from teachers in 1938 bemoaning their inability to leave for the Far East). Teachers were invited to come with families because they could be offered apartments if they taught in village schools and because they were so badly needed. See Valentina Khetagurova, "Organizovat' dvizhenie molodykh patriotov," *KP*, January 26, 1938.

skilled laborers recruited for work in far-flung regions. In fact, they often suffered a loss of rank at their new job and had to make do with lower salaries.[79]

Individuals who might have thought that the campaign offered an escape route from the reverberations of the Great Terror actually exposed themselves to background checks and interactions with the NKVD. Hava Volovich from Mena in Ukraine had long romanticized the prospect of "felling trees in the snowy taiga [or] expeditions to the Arctic."[80] After reading Khetagurova's letter, "I decided I would go. I was tired of merely reading about great construction projects: I wanted to go along and build something myself."[81] Her mother pleaded with her not to expose herself to official scrutiny because she had connections with recently arrested co-workers. Just as her mother feared, Hava never returned from one of her visits to the NKVD to obtain travel documents. She subsequently spent numerous harrowing years in labor camps, where she had more than her fill "of woodcutting in the taiga [and] Arctic cold."[82]

Frontier Stalinism

The Khetagurovite campaign unfolded simultaneously with an unprecedented escalation of state repression in 1937–1938. The Far East was hit hard by party purges, arrests, mass terror and deportations. Just as the Khetagurovites began to arrive, every institution in the Far East was ravaged by waves of arrests and flushed with paranoia. The Komsomol, charged with facilitating their resettlement, was in the grip of a purge affecting every rung of its structure.[83] The women's chances of making an easy transition were severely curtailed by such circumstances. Young factory workers excited by the prospect of dedicating themselves to strengthening a distant border land because they were "sure that Soviet power was

---

[79] The Komsomol Central Committee's Sector for Work among Women asked the All-Union Central Council of Trade Unions to resolve the problem related to the loss of seniority for Khetagurovites and the lack of consistency in their pay. The problem persisted without resolution while the Khetagurova campaign was in existence. See "Memorandum notes, short reports and other documents of the Komsomol Central Committee's commission and other organization on the status and potentials of the Khetagurovite commission's activities and on the mobilization of young people for the construction of the Far East," July 5, 1939, RGASPI M, f. 1, op. 23, d. 1351, l. 49.

[80] Hava Volovich, "My Past," in Simeon Vilensky (ed.), *Till My Tale is Told*, trans. John Crowfoot (Bloomington: Indiana University Press, 1999), 241.

[81] *Ibid.*, 246.   [82] *Ibid.*, 241.

[83] The expulsion of Komsomol leaders in the region and calls to pursue other "enemies" left in the organization were announced in "Decree of the V Plenum of the Far Eastern Regional VLKSM," August 27–29, 1937, GAKhK P, f. 618, op. 1, d. 310, ll. 216–218.

the most righteous, the most just, most necessary for people and ready to sacrifice ourselves to make it so" embarked on a collision course with an alternate reality.[84]

The migrants also arrived at a moment of transition and expansion in the population and administration of the labor camps. The size of camp populations and life within the camps in the Far East changed drastically during the period of the Great Terror. At the height of the Great Terror between 1937 and 1938, there were five autonomously administered corrective labor camps in the Khabarovsk region: Dal'Lag, Raichikhlag, Ushosstroi, Novo-Tambovsk Corrective Labor Camp, and Administration of Camps for Railroad Construction (ZhDSU) NKVD for the Far East. In 1938 the five camps together held 201,926 prisoners and 15,597 free employees.[85] Even with significant capital investment, the camps became impossible to administer and the workforce incapable of work because of illness and malnutrition.[86] Torrents of new arrivals during the Terror transformed labor camps into "extermination centers" rather than labor camps.[87]

The Far Eastern Construction Trust (Dal'stroi) formed in 1931 but liquidated in 1953 was one of the biggest and most important of the five labor camp systems.[88] The administration of its Dal'Lag camps was located in Khabarovsk, with nine departments engaged in a variety of building projects. One section ran state collective farms with prison labor, others such as the Birokan and Birsk were assigned to lumber production. Convicts working under the auspices of Dal'stroi cleared forests, drained swamps, built roads and railroads, worked in the goldfields of Kolyma, and built the city of Magadan, among many other tasks.[89] Other departments under Dal'Lag had prisoners working on construction projects in

---

[84] Memoir of M. N. Koliasnikova, GAKhK P, f. 442, op. 2, d. 283, l. 85a.

[85] Other subcamps in the railroad system were located in places such as Ulan-Ude and in the Primorsk region. See "Memorandum notes, reports on the work of NKVD organs," February 3–11, 1939, GAKhK P, f. 35, op. 1, d. 313, ll. 1–4.

[86] With 800,000 new prisoners arriving in the camps across the Soviet Union in 1938, death rates exceeded anything "in previous years (except during the 1933 famine). According to the NKVD, 25,376 people died in the camps in 1937 and 8,123 died in prisons and colonies. In 1938, these numbers were 90,546 and 36,039, respectively." These numbers were incomplete because of falsifications and because those who died in transit in between camps were not counted. See Khlevniuk, *The History of the GULAG*, 179.

[87] *Ibid.*, 185.

[88] For the widespread use of convict labor to build railroads, see O. P. Elantseva, "Stroitel'stvo zheleznykh dorog na vostoke Rossii v 1930-e gody," *Rev. Etud. Slaves* 71:1 (1999), 93–112.

[89] For more on this topic, see Paul R. Gregory and Valery Lazarev (eds.), *The Economics of Forced Labor: The Soviet GULAG* (Stanford: Hoover Institution Press, 2003), and Galina M. Ivanova, *Istoriia GULAGa, 1918–1958: Sotsial'no-ekonomicheskii i politiko-pravovoi aspekty* (Moscow: Nauka, 2006). For detailed histories of Dal'stroi and the building of Magadan, see V. G. Zeliak, *Piat' metallov Dal'stroia* (Magadan: Kordis, 2004); David J.

the cities of Khabarovsk, Komsomol'sk, Nikolaevsk-na-Amure, on Sakhalin and Kamchatka. Many of the new prisoners were assigned to work in the timber industry because it was relatively easy to set up, required minimal investment, and supplied much-needed timber. These camps in the forests were also some of the most difficult to survive in, becoming, as Oleg Khlevniuk described them, "provisional death camps."[90]

By 1939, Dal'stroi employed 6,841 free laborers in both the Khabarovsk and Primorsk regions.[91] Of the 589 women who worked as free employees for Dal'Lag in the Khabarovsk region, 312 had come to the region as Khetagurovites.[92] Efrosina Mishalova and others like her would learn only after arrival that they would have to work for the NKVD, ruling over thousands of starving prisoners. Even when the women did not work directly for the camps, they often found themselves working in organizations that used current and former prisoners, some in positions of authority and wielding power over the migrant women. Those who were slated to work in the GULAG NKVD plunged into a murky social and political world manipulated by a motley group of misfits, scoundrels, and brutes clothed in the authority of NKVD uniforms.

Their co-workers in the secret police hardly inspired a great deal of confidence. NKVD employees were at the bottom of the Soviet achievement ladder. In the Far East many were functionally illiterate. In this period no more than 35 percent of NKVD personnel had finished high school and only 5 percent had earned a degree above high school level. These numbers were far below the national average. For example, on average in the Soviet Union about 30 percent of Red Army recruits had some education beyond primary school, this was true for only 10 percent of NKVD troops in 1939.[93]

Nordlander, "Capital of the GULAG: Magadan in the early Stalin Era, 1929–1941," unpublished PhD dissertation, University of North Carolina (1997); and Batsaev and Kozlov, *Dal'stroi i Sevvostlag.*

[90] Khlevniuk, *The History of the GULAG*, 178.

[91] Because the Far East was divided into two administrative units, reports meant for the Khabarovsk Regional Communist Party First Secretary included a breakdown on the numbers of those within the Khabarovsk region and the Far East as a whole. Thus as of January 1, 1939, Dal'Lag had 34,723 prisoners and 1,732 free employees in the camps located in the Khabarovsk administrative region. Petrov, Chief of the Political Department Dal'Lag NKVD, reported on the number of free employees for Dal'Lag NKVD in the Khabarovsk region on January 1, 1939. See "Memorandum notes, reports on the work of NKVD organs," GAKhK P, f. 35, op. 1, d. 313, l. 63.

[92] Another massive system, the Administration of Camps for Railroad Construction, with seven subsections, had 135,872 prisoners, in the territory of the Khabarovsk region. These railroad camps had 11,165 free employees, 7,857 of them prison guards in 1939. *Ibid.*, 1–4.

[93] Zhiromskaia, *Demograficheskaia istoriia*, 124–125. Lack of education and professional qualifications were also a problem in the regional procuracy. The regional procurator's

Working for the NKVD in the Far East pushed many men to desperate acts or stirred the worst instincts. The guards assigned to the railroad construction camps gained attention in 1939 as a particularly troubled group. Regardless of explicit prohibitions by the chief of the NKVD against using female prisoners as household servants, an inspection of conditions concluded that at least five thousand women were used as servants in the homes of camp employees of every rank in this camps system.[94] Men with guns or with favors to dole out were also not averse to forcing female prisoners into sexual relationships. When one such guard, Gribchenko, received a severe reprimand from the Komsomol for sexual relations with a prisoner, he slashed her throat in the woods in retaliation.[95] Violence was ubiquitous. Among these guards, in the period between January 1, 1939 and July 1, 1939 there were thirteen suicides, seven attempted suicides, two incidents of guards murdering their wives, and two incidents of bodily injury during incidents of domestic abuse. Four guards deserted and twelve died from accidental causes. In one incident a guard murdered another and another died "by accident" at the hands of a fellow guard.[96]

Those who were unfortunate enough to be assigned as a guard lived in deplorable conditions not much better than those they guarded. In 1939 guards of BurLag and their families suffered from scurvy because they could not get milk, vegetables, or protein.[97] On the Kamchatka peninsula, the most requested posting of young volunteers from Moscow, there were fifteen suicides and several attempted suicides among employees of the NKVD and border guards between 1935 and 1937. Commanders of the border patrol spent their time drinking and forcing women from the

office had a shortfall of about 150 assistant procurators, investigators, and other "technical" employees such as secretaries and bookkeepers in 1937, partly because of the purges and partly because there was always a shortage of qualified people in the region. Of the 112 procurators, 50 percent had worked there for less than three years, while 63 of the 112 had only an elementary education and only 20 percent had legal training. Among the investigators, 68 of 111 had no more than an elementary education and only 9 percent had any legal training. See "Report: On the condition of work and tasks of the organs of the procurator in accordance with the decisions of the February Plenum of the Central Committee and the Stalin Constitution," December 28, 1937, GA RF, f. 8131, op. 14, d. 4, l. 8.

[94] "Report: Results of inspection of conditions of construction of the UZhDS GULAG NKVD in the Far East in relation to completing the resolution of the Regional Party Committee of June 1, 1939. Totals of free employees for UZhDS in the Khabarovsk region, as of December 1939," GAKhK P, f. 35, op. 1, d. 315, l. 35.

[95] "Report on the conditions in the military guard of the UZhDS GULAG NKVD in the Far East," August 25, 1939, GAKhK P, f. 35, op. 1, d. 314, l. 156.

[96] One guard was murdered by a civilian, while guards murdered four civilians and injured two others. Guards were punished for inappropriately killing three prisoners and wounding fifteen others. *Ibid.*, 11.147–148.

[97] *Ibid.*, 172.

native Chukchi population to drink, then imposing "collective cohabitation and humiliation."[98]

Despite resolutions from the Communist party and the Administration of the NKVD, the severe shortage of qualified people meant that camps in the Far East employed those who were either current or former prisoners convicted for "counterrevolutionary" crimes, the most serious offense in the system. In the context of the Great Terror, such employment practices, previously allowed by Moscow, produced a rush to root out those who made their way into responsible positions.[99] Subsequently, in 1938 the NKVD's apparatus in the Far East was almost completely renewed with the arrest or removal of former prisoners in positions of authority. They were replaced by "Communists, Komsomol members and those who came on the Khetagurovite call-up."[100] Yet former and current prisoners continued to assist in the administration of NKVD camps throughout the Great Terror and beyond. For instance, despite the recent purge, in 1939 AmurLag had 2,503 employees, of whom a massive 1,113 were former prisoners and 105 had convictions for "counterrevolutionary" activities under Paragraph 58 of the Soviet Criminal Code. Other camps had similar proportions of former prisoners among their current employees working as specialists.[101]

Prisoners and former prisoners provided all kinds of services in milieus far from the eyes of officious ideologues in Moscow. Former kulaks escaping special settlements or peasants unwilling to stay on their collective farms sometimes made a living as "tavern keepers" deep in the taiga,

---

[98] "Reports, notes addressed to the first secretary of the Far Eastern Regional Party Committee VLKSM. Extracts from protocol no. 36 meeting of the Kamchatka oblast Communist party Committee – 2. Information on the political-moral condition of the border patrol and regional administration of the NKVD," October 4, 1937, GAKhK P, f. 2, op. 1, d. 1295, l. 202. Chukchi are one of the largest native circumpolar groups in the northern territories of this region. On circumpolar people in the Soviet Union, see Slezkine, *Arctic Mirrors*.

[99] Prisoners in NKVD camps could sometimes earn early release for days worked if they were not convicted of political crimes. Prisoners could also be released if they were not considered "politically dangerous"; if they volunteered to stay in the territories and work to develop "virgin lands" in colonies of former prisoners; and if their families were willing to join them. See Khlevniuk, *The History of the GULAG*, 110.

[100] "On economic activity of Dal'Lag NKVD for 1938 and plans for 1939," GAKhK P, f. 35, op. 1, d. 313, l. 54.

[101] Of the 1,326 personnel in the administration of the railroad construction system, 414 were former prisoners and 119 were serving under Paragraph 58. See "Report: Results of inspection of conditions of construction of the UZhDS GULAG NKVD in the Far East in relation to completing the resolution of the Regional Party Committee from June 1, 1939: Number of free employees in the system UZhDS in the Khabarovsk region, December 1939," GAKhK P, f. 35, op. 1, d. 315, l. 26.

specializing in supplying liquor to labor camp inmates and their guards.[102] Some convicts offering shady services were protected by camp administrators. For instance, one prisoner, Kovrigin, by profession an engineer but serving a sentence in BAMLag for counterrevolutionary activities, was a favorite of some Communist party members in the camps' administration. His services included "complicated surgeries, treating the seriously ill and performing abortions." Eventually, he was blamed for the deaths of several patients. "Others have been maimed and made into invalids." Amateur surgery was not his only hobby: Kovrigin also served as a "priest, blessing, casting spells and kissing the ill." When his home was searched, police found "a chasuble, religious books and etc." Despite the protestations of some NKVD employees, there were Communists who "expressed their gratitude to him."[103]

Life in the Far East heralded a new type of family structure for Soviet women. Young women who became mothers had a very hard time staying in the workforce because of a severe shortage of daycare facilities. They had become the first generation to navigate wage work, chores, and childrearing in a strictly nuclear family setting cut off from extended kin and grandparents. Newly formed families with working and activist mothers, like Novikova and Alekseeva, were forced to leave their children alone or take them with them. There was little alternative in the labor-starved region where "[t]hose who can even afford it cannot find a nanny because there are no people."[104] Women were also suffering from a new law allowing bosses to fire workers for missed days. Any lucky enough to find childcare were often forced to stay at home when the daycare facilities closed under quarantines. As a result, women were particularly vulnerable to termination of their employment and black marks on their record because wives, rather than husbands, tended to children at home in those circumstances.[105]

---

[102] For a short period in 1934, exiled kulaks and members of their families were permitted to apply for a restoration of their civil rights and for the right to leave exile (before serving out five years) if they had proven themselves to be "most distinguished" workers. This "liberalism" did not last long when NKVD authorities noted a large outflow of families from their labor settlements. The regime moved to stop this outflow by disconnecting the restitution of civil rights from the right to leave exile. From February 1936, labor settlers were bound to exile indefinitely even if they had full civil rights. See "Report to the Secretary of the Khabarovsk Communist Party Committee Donskoi from the Chief of the Nizhnii-Amur camp NKVD, Uspenski, 1939," GAKhK P, f. 35, op. 1, d. 314, l. 94.

[103] "Materials of the court and procurator of the Far East region," May 13, 1937, GAKhK P, f. 2, op. 1, d. 1329, l. 69.

[104] "Protocol of the I Khabarovsk regional conference of the VLKSM," February 11–15, 1939, Artiushina, GAKhK P, f. 617, op. 1, d. 3, l. 144.

[105] *Ibid.*, l. 145.

Miserly investment in urban infrastructure and services could impact women in more direct ways than men. Those who came to the region with children or started families in the Far East contended with malnutrition and lack of services available in other parts of the country. Conditions for women with children actually deteriorated in the mid-1930s. The number of outpatient clinics in the Khabarovsk oblast decreased in 1937 from thirty-eight to thirty-five.[106] The number of daycare centers also fell, from thirty-six to twenty-nine in 1937.[107] Getting around was a challenge in itself, especially while pregnant or with small children. Vladivostok lacked sidewalks on all or part of its major streets in 1937. City bridges regularly collapsed under the weight of automobiles. Only central streets were cleaned and the few existing roads were impassible because of potholes and cracks. Streets that had been officially renamed still bore their old names, leading to endless confusion.[108] Even in the Soviet period, Vladivostok never fully expurgated its reputation for the exotic and dangerous. Occasionally, the local newspaper included brief mentions of police activity aimed at disbanding "pritony" (dens) of thieves and morphine addicts.[109]

In the Far East, right under the noses of the ostensibly fearsome and omniscient NKVD, a criminal underworld not only persisted but blossomed. At a school attached to a mine in the town of Artem, a group of students "regularly beat up . . . girls and pioneers, ripping off their ties, cutting up twelve coats, breaking the display glass at the store and stealing wine and snacks."[110] In Khabarovsk boys at a school of NKVD employees beat up and stabbed the "best and most civic-minded" student at the school. School children in the town of Iman whiled away their time with "declassed" prisoners of BAMLag who supplied some of the female students with alcohol. In the city of Komsomol'sk, fourth graders at an elementary school "run by a former prisoner of BAMLag . . . , stole money from their parents, worked as pickpockets, and took money out of the till in the store to buy sweets and wine."[111] Another group of students, after expulsion from their school in a suburb of Khabarovsk, organized parties in the basement of a mill where intoxicated girls were sometimes raped. A slew of schools reported swastikas on their walls,

---

[106] "Protocol III Khabarovsk oblast Communist party conference," June 4–9, 1938, RGASPI, f. 17, op. 21, d. 5463, l. 77.
[107] The number of children in the daycare network consequently decreased by 25 percent from 1,095 to 829. *Ibid.*
[108] "Privesti v poriadok ulitsy," *Krasnoe znamia,* October 10, 1937.
[109] "Proisshestviia," *Krasnoe znamia,* March 9, 1936.
[110] "Memorandum," April 8, 1937, GAKhK P, f. 2, op. 1, d. 1107, l. 8.
[111] *Ibid.,* l. 9.

obscenities scrolled across portraits of Marx, and damage to portraits of Molotov and other leaders.

The cities also teemed with displaced relatives of the recently arrested and those under suspicion. Residents were subject to forced relocation at any given moment. The living conditions were chaotic even in relatively well-established cities like Vladivostok and Khabarovsk and competition for housing in the region was ruthless. With the expansion of the military forces stationed in the Far East and the command personnel in the city of Khabarovsk, the housing situation became particularly tense. NKVD chief Yezhov had to issue a special order to force Far Eastern Regional Party Committee members to assist the command and political staff of the military in obtaining housing. Locals were ordered to prepare housing previously occupied by now-arrested military personnel for newly arrived officers, instead of hoarding it for themselves. They were also supposed to present "at least seventy percent" of the apartments made vacant by arrests of civilians and deported Chinese. The plan was to force out forty-three families of arrested men to make room for newly arrived officers.[112]

Initially, Komsomol'sk-na-Amure was supposed to be built and settled by volunteers from the Komsomol. However, recruiting and retaining a free labor force became nearly impossible in the difficult conditions presented by a city planned and developed strictly according to defensive priorities, as Jon Bone put it, "without any thought for labor or logistical matters."[113] Convict labor compelled to stay on site was selected as the only option for authorities disillusioned with free labor.[114] As Bone has shown, one year after the project got under way, for every one Komsomol volunteer there were eleven prisoners building the city of youth.[115]

Komsomol'sk-na-Amure from its inception and through the 1930s had no general urban development plan. One of the first factories built provided housing for its workers by encouraging self-built lean-tos as a temporary measure in the city's first year (1932–1933). These were still in use when the Khetagurovites arrived in 1937–1938. The first construction chief, Kattel', who masterminded the use of lean-tos in 1932, also ordered the removal of all trees in the territory of Dal'promstroi (Far Eastern Industrial Construction Trust). Komsomol activists complained that construction chiefs "considered themselves fully empowered owners

---

[112] "On measures to provide apartments to the command and political staff and soldiers of the OKDVA. Resolution of the Far Eastern Bureau VKP(b)," June 3, 1938, RGASPI, f. 17, op. 21, d. 5446, l. 315.
[113] Jonathan A. Bone has traced the origins of Komsomol'sk-na-Amure. See Bone, "Who Really Built Komsomol'sk-na-Amure, and Why," *Rev. Etud. Slaves* 71:1 (1999), 59–92.
[114] *Ibid.*, 92.   [115] *Ibid.*, 90.

and built whatever they saw fit. . . . This anarchy and lack of a building plan for the city has led to the fact that the city in the taiga does not have a single tree except for the settlement near Factory No. 126 and now it must be made green again."[116] Storehouses for fuel and fish-processing plants were placed upriver from the city, with predictable consequences for the waters along the city's shores. Each industrial complex had plans to build its own parks and small hospitals instead of consolidating resources.[117] Construction chiefs could not agree on which organization should build a bridge across a minor Amur tributary, the Silenka, separating the settlements surrounding two construction projects. For years, residents were unable to travel overland between the two settlements except in the winter when ice covered the stream. At all other times of the year, the fifteen thousand residents of the settlement around Aviation Factory No. 126 (a hydroplane factory also known as Aviastroi) needing to access any city institution in the territory of Dal'promstroi had to travel seven kilometers by land and eleven kilometers down river.

An investigation of conditions for children in Komsomol'sk-na-Amure in 1936 revealed "an extremely alarming situation."[118] Workers and their children lived in barracks with several families sharing one room, sleeping together on bunks. In a city of approximately 50,000 in 1936, there were only two pediatricians, no dentists or eye specialists, no milk stores, and five kindergartens that could accommodate 215 children but not able to serve any fruits or vegetables throughout that year. There was no way to prevent the spread of diseases in these circumstances. Many children died in 1936 from scarlet fever and measles. Although birth rates were high, with 125–160 babies born per month, death rates among children under twelve months were also astronomical. Of the 2,257 children born in 1936, 1,110 – almost half – died; 624 of these were under the age of one.[119] In January 1937 alone, there were 202 births and eighty-six deaths, forty-four of them infants under one.

Most houses in Komsomol'sk did not have "elementary" services such as a sewer system and electricity throughout the 1930s.[120] It was difficult to buy seafood in the city even though plants on the Amur had a surfeit of fish. Milk products, potatoes, onions, and cabbage continued to be

[116] "Memorandum," May 26, 1937, A. Kosarev, RGASPI M, f. 1, op. 23, d. 1254, l. 37.
[117] Report on conditions in Komsomol'sk for A. Andreev, "Resolution of the Komsomol Central Committee, January–December 1936," RGASPI M, f. 1, op. 23, d. 1182, l. 19.
[118] "Memorandum," May 26, 1937, RGASPI M. f. 1, op. 23, d. 1254, l. 38.
[119] Ibid.
[120] "Requests received by the Regional Communist Party Committee," March 4, 1939–October 26, 1939, GAKhK P, f. 35, op. 1, d. 351, l. 117.

shipped all the way from Ukraine or Novosibirsk.[121] A liter of milk cost six to ten rubles at a time when some of the migrant women earned two hundred rubles per month. The large factories in the city had their own state farms but their produce was reserved for the administrative staff and not their workers. The food crisis in the city was so dire that the secretary of the Far Eastern Komsomol proposed that 300–400 cows be brought into the city from disbanding state farms so that they could be sold to individual workers in Komsomol'sk.[122]

There was a large outflow of young people from the city because it did not have a technical college or a university. In 1939, when labor discipline laws had severely limited worker mobility across the Soviet Union, nothing could keep people there. While Komsomol'sk's Aviation Factory No. 126 hired 5,048 workers in 1939, it also "lost" 2,670 in the same period, 369 of them badly needed engineers. In the first two months of 1940, another 476 workers left the factory, mostly because of unsatisfactory housing.[123]

There were few venues for after-work activities that did not involve drinking. Komsomol organizers in the city carried on a thankless struggle with alcoholism and in particular the residents' propensity to brew their own moonshine. Most of the time the organizers turned a blind eye to these practices among their own members, even when the Komsomol Central Committee passed a special resolution at its IV plenum pointing to the consumption of alcohol as the primary cause of "moral dissolution" within the organization. An investigation of several neighborhoods in Komsomol'sk revealed that workers were not only brewing beer (braga) for personal consumption, but also selling their concoctions at "illegal" prices. Every neighborhood had moonshine available. The homebrew, made more potent with the addition of low-grade tobacco (makhorka) regularly "poisoned" the denizens of the city of youth.[124]

Women like Mariia Koliasnikova who came to the region as a Khetagurovite, like many of the memoirists, painted a portrait of tight-knit communities and collaborative neighbors. However, she was one of the few to admit that a significant number of young people in Komsomol'sk did not live up to the ideal of patriotic Soviet builders and that prisoners worked alongside voluntary laborers. The unenlightened and unpatriotic mostly

---

[121] Letter from M. P. Savenko to *KP*. "Requests received by the Regional Communist Party Committee," March 4, 1939, GAKhK P, f. 35, op. 1, d. 351, ll. 117–118.

[122] "Materials of the Far Eastern regional Komsomol," April 17, 1937, GAKhK P, f. 2, op. 1, d. 1300, l. 18.

[123] Lobanov, head of the Soviet cadre department of the Regional Party Committee. "Memorandum notes, 1939," GAKhK P, f. 35, op. 1, d. 172, l. 87.

[124] Comments by Fedorov from Komsomol'sk at a meeting of the regional Komsomol organization," January 3, 1938, GAKhK P, f. 618, op. 1, d. 321, l. 176.

[l]aughed at us, drank, fought, etc. But we just took no notice of them. In general, most of the young people on the construction site were good. There was insignificant hooliganism despite the fact that prisoners from Dal'Lag worked on the site. The gals never feared walking late at night on the streets. No one ever offended them.[125]

Nevertheless, the presence of prisoners, and the paranoia and tragedies of mass repressions, added to the deprivations of life on the frontier of Stalinism, proving too much for many who did not find supportive networks. Their stories and the implications of their travails are the subjects of subsequent chapters.

"Everything had been made with love"

Alekseeva and her friends, blissfully uninformed about life in the Far East, were amazed that young women such as themselves were genuinely wanted to "fasten cadres" and "to populate the cities with permanent residents."[126] As they signed up, organizers explained that they had to be prepared for "an independent life." A departure date of April 28, 1937 was set with a special train reserved for a contingent of four hundred female volunteers headed for Komsomol'sk-na-Amure. That sunny day, "all of Moscow had come out to see us off. The platform was packed with people singing, playing music, talking and many hands were filled with the first flowers of the year, mimosas. There were touching moments, with young men crying."[127] At some stations along the Trans-Siberian Railroad, the well-publicized train was met with more fanfare and in some spots where clusters of bachelor Red Army men predominated, the locomotive driver had to fend off entreaties "to leave behind at least one wagon."[128] Press coverage was lavish. Images from this first large wave of

---

[125] Memoir of M. N. Koliasnikova, GAKhK P, f. 442, op. 2, d. 283, l. 89a. Convicts played a central role in the timber industry across Russia. See Judith Pallot, "Forced Labor for Forestry: The Twentieth-Century History of Colonization and Settlement in the North Perm Oblast," *Europe-Asia Studies* 54:7 (2002), 1055–1083. There were large populations of prisoners working in and around Komsomol'sk-na-Amure. One autonomous camp, the Novo-Tambovsk camp, was located in Komsomol'sk. Most of its prisoners worked in the timber industry and lived in forest camps. The Novo-Tambovsk camp itself was divided into ten separate camps in the forests and surrounding the city. There were about 11,000 prisoners in these camps in 1938, with another 4,000 expected to arrive in 1939. The camps also employed 700 free laborers. See "Memorandum notes, reports on the work of corrective-labor camps NKVD USSR in the Far East: On the number of camps located in the Komsomol'sk district and their assignments, May 28–October 3, 1939," GAKhK P, f. 35, op. 1, d. 317, l. 35.
[126] Memoir of Ania Alekseeva, GAKhK P, f. 442, op. 2, d. 283, l. 14.
[127] *Ibid.*, 15.   [128] *Ibid.*, 16.

2. "Just off the train from Moscow to Khabarovsk," April 1937.
Left to right: Z. M. Makarova, metro builder; A. D. Afonina, metro
builder; M. M. Nastas'kina, employee of the Communist party Central
Committee; N. F. Ishchenko, employee of the Institute of Nutrition;
T. I. Mekhal'chenko, metro builder.

arrivals, such as figure 2, "Just off the train from Moscow to Khabarovsk"
and figure 3, "Goodbye," found their way to newspapers across the Soviet
Union.[129]

After arriving in Khabarovsk, the group boarded the riverboats *Kosarev*
and *Chicherin* to sail to their final destination on the Amur River. En route
to Komsomol'sk, the women took in the scenery along the riverbanks and
sang tunes from polar exploration films that seemed apropos.[130] Rallies
held on the boat whipped up the women's enthusiasm and unexpectedly
produced an impression among some that they had volunteered for the

[129] "On the *Chicherin*," along with "Song of Young Women – Far Easterners" dedicated
to the Khetagurovites, appeared in *Rabotnitsa* 17 (June 1937), 18. All photographs of
the Khetagurovites and Valentina Khetagurova are from the Russian State Archive of
Film-Photographic Documents (RGAKFD) in Krasnogorsk, Russia. See Appendix 6
for the text of the song.

[130] A popular song among the women was from the 1936 film about polar explorers, *Semero
smelykh* (*The Brave Seven*): "Leisia pesnia, na prostore" (Song – Go Flutter Through
the Air). See Appendix 8 for the lyrics.

3. "Goodbye"
Large group of women aboard the *Chicherin* for the trip to Komsomol'sk-na-Amure from Khabarovsk on the Amur River in April 1937. This is the boat trip that brought the first large group of 400 women to Komsomol'sk, including Ania Alekseeva.

ultimate sacrifice. One young woman pledged, "Although we are going to a sure death, I will not retreat!"[131]

As their boats neared the shore of Komsomol'sk-na-Amure, the passengers heard an orchestra and saw a large crowd of young men rushing along the river to greet them. The men had decked themselves out in their "best outfits and shaved (which they did rarely)." The impatient

[131] Memoir of Polina Bazarova, GAKhK P, f. 442, op. 2, d. 283, l. 98.

and fidgety throngs of men quickly filled the shores of the Amur where the riverboats would moor. Alekseeva recalled how, "When the boats arrived, a diverse group of gals streamed onto the shore. There were blondes and brunettes (future brides and wives). The lads immediately livened up, became happier and completely involuntarily fixed the flaps on their shirts and tightened their silk belts and timidly offered their services in helping to unload belongings."[132]

With expectations nourished by rumors and adventure stories, the new arrivals prepared to live in tents. None of them expected their assignment to a three-story apartment building supposedly constructed in anticipation of their arrival by young factory workers during their free time. In a rush to finish on time, the workers had to leave some things unfinished and improvised in other details. For instance, there were no locks on doors and windows. Workers used whatever was to hand on their shopfloor to furnish the new accommodation. As a result, everything was made of steel. "It was all very pretty but heavy to lift. You couldn't move a chair from its place!"[133] The women were touched by all the attention. "Everything had been made with love."[134]

Seventeen-year-old Anna Plaskina, who arrived on the same boat with Alekseeva, was assigned to the first floor. On their first night in the city, unable to lock out visitors, she and her new roommates were besieged until one in the morning by "groups of five to six lads" posing as representatives of different organizations. These "representatives" covertly slipped notes to the women in which they opined "mostly about love at first sight and named a time and place for a rendezvous." Their otherwise impressive effort was not fully convincing. None of the notes included the name of the enchantress who ostensibly inspired such adulation, having been composed several days before the women's boats moored in Komsomol'sk.[135] When the lads finally left, "the gals started joking that they may get kidnapped and taken into the taiga, never to see each other again. Only one thing comforted us: there were many knights, but no horses, just one camel circling the building, but they wouldn't get very far on him and whisk away their intended."[136] Eventually, the authorities were forced to put a guard by their rooms to keep men from trying to sneak in and some of the young women from sneaking out.

The next day, the women were taken to their new jobs. "There was no time to be bored."[137] Not everything went smoothly. Some among the Muscovites had "never seen a factory and had no idea about machines.

---

[132] Alekseeva, 19.   [133] *Ibid.*   [134] *Ibid.*, 103.
[135] Memoir of Anna I. Plaskina, GAKhK P, f. 442, op. 2, d. 283, l. 52.
[136] *Ibid.*, 53.   [137] *Ibid.*

They came to work wearing their fancy dresses. The old workers watched them in shock. Of course, their surprise was understandable, considering that some of the women mistook machine oil for cows' milk."[138]

Alekseeva dived into a myriad activities besides working at the factory. She was active in the Komsomol, was in charge of organizing young women, edited her factory's wall newspaper, took part in antireligion campaigns and trained to use a gun. "Back then we felt that we were really needed people and never turned down any assignment and we were proud" of managing such a heavy load.[139] She was also the captain of her shopfloor soccer team. Sports were at the center of her life. She eventually married a ski and soccer enthusiast in 1939, the same year she became a candidate member of the Communist party at the tender age of nineteen.

Mishalova, like Alekseeva, traveled to the Far East on a train reserved for Khetagurovites. En route there were a series of official "chats" about "morality." The young women were told that they had to be especially vigilant on the border and that "over there at every step one could meet people alien to our Soviet reality. We needed to recognize in such a person the stranger and not provide cause to drag us into their enemy nets."[140] Because she had experience of working with orphans, she accepted an assignment to work in orphanage No. 1 in the regional center of Khabarovsk, though this foreclosed the possibilities of mountains in Kamchatka. Eventually, she and other Komsomol members were selected to work for the Khabarovsk Regional Administration of the People's Commissariat of Internal Affairs (UNKVD), where she stayed until 1941. She met her future husband, Dimitrii, a teacher and four years her senior, at the orphanage in Khabarovsk.

Despite the cheerful memories of former Khetagurovites, after almost three years the Khetagurovite campaign was declared a failure because it was deemed a cumbersome way to resettle young people. Some of the young migrants, like Alekseeva, made the Far East their permanent home and were recognized as pioneers and "first-builders." Others, like Mishalova, left the Far East to follow their husbands, to join the army in the fight against the Nazis, or for other personal reasons. There were some who found their new surroundings so unbearable that they left at the first opportunity or took even more drastic steps. And of course, some, like Novikova by the luck of the draw, stayed in the region as prisoners. Such sinister possibilities were worlds away from the magical landscapes depicted in publicity promoting migration to the frontier of Stalinism.

[138] *Ibid.*   [139] Alekseeva, 103.
[140] Memoir of Efrosina Mishalova, February 18, 1976, GAKhK P, f. 442, op. 2, d. 284, l. 93a.

3 "Our famous Valia": the rise of a Soviet notable

Magical landscapes needed pioneering men and women like Valentina Khetagurova. Evgenii Petrov (the famous writer and journalist of the Ilf and Petrov fame)[1] assisted in the manufacture of Khetagurova as a representative of frontier heroism and a Soviet celebrity, having met her while on tour in the Far East in 1937. His article extolling her virtues simultaneously applauded her abilities to resist becoming "dizzy" from the "huge and deafening fame" and reinforced her notoriety by comparing her to famous Western movie stars. According to Petrov, Khetagurova's capacity to handle fame exemplified a general ability of "our" young people not to let "popularity ruin them." This resilience was "understandable" in a generation that had grown up for twenty years under Soviet power to become "spiritually pure and unspoiled."[2] In other countries, Petrov opined, "Any kind of movie star celebrity would immediately mean furs, diamonds, personal yachts and villas – the noses of those women instinctively turn up to the sky, the eyes squint, as though the famous one has become nearsighted, her walk loosens."[3] Khetagurova, by contrast, seemed to carry her fame with the "dignity of a philosopher. This is not an act. There's not the slightest hint of posing."[4] Although on the inside, Petrov assumed, she enjoyed her popularity, "You would not notice this on the outside. It is difficult to retain mental equilibrium, when a person experiences fame. It is even harder not to display real or imagined superiority. This is evidence of great tact."[5] Petrov's ode to Khetagurova's poise as a representative of a new Soviet personality was not unusual.

Khetagurova represented an emerging generation of women who had grown up entirely under Soviet power. Contemporaries and later commentators recognized that she was a person "with whom a whole epoch

---

[1] Ilia Ilf and Evgenii Petrov were famous journalists and satirists in the 1920s and 1930s. They published *Twelve Chairs* (1928), which became a canonical satire of Soviet society and a sequel in 1931, *The Golden Calf*. They also drove across the USA in the winter of 1934–1935, chronicling their impressions of the "capitalists" for their Soviet audience.

[2] Evgenii Petrov, "Khetagurovki," in G. Akopian (ed.), *Zhenshchiny strany sotsializma*, (Moscow: OGIZ, 1939), 46.

[3] *Ibid.*   [4] *Ibid.*, 47.   [5] *Ibid.*

85

in our country is forever tied."[6] Her personality was at the forefront of her image and conveyed not only by recounting her achievements, but by displays of her temperament, tastes, and humor. According to Tatiana Fedorova, another prominent figure from the 1930s who subsequently developed a friendship with Khetagurova when they were both Supreme Soviet Deputies, "There is much to be said about her, our famous Valia, because this would be the story of young women of that now distant time, about their dreams, their ambitions, about the makings of a Soviet woman's personality."[7]

The success of the publicity campaign that ensued after the publication of Khetagurova's call-up in February 1937 and her subsequent fame should be understood as the result of several factors. First, the text itself evocatively tapped into widespread attitudes and myths about the Far East. Second, the letter was a personal appeal from a figure who not only touted the importance of the Far East for national defense but whose life story embodied a newly emerging model of womanhood. This model was intrinsically linked to the Soviet Union's status as a Eurasian power. The women who answered Khetagurova's call proved eager to fit the new mold because it offered a sense of potency and of belonging to a grand narrative of Soviet state-building. Finally, the other important ingredient was Khetagurova herself. She was not simply a marionette in someone else's theatrics but rather an active participant in crafting her career and image. Her activities and reception after capturing the national spotlight provide instructive glimpses into the gender politics of Soviet stardom.

Khetagurova rose to prominence when women's symbolic roles were shifting as public culture changed from an emphasis on socialist revolution to the defense and development of Soviet power across Eurasia. This shift did not bring about a reinforcement of gender boundaries but rather some unexpected expansion of possibilities for women. These shifts also produced waves of disaffection on the part of men when young women assumed they had been invited to participate as heroic equals in national defense.

Khetagurova's Soviet "personality," confident in enunciating women's special contributions and in its portent of geographic and social mobility, provided an alternative to several established models of womanhood. Her new personality supplanted and subsumed the officially sanctioned and valorized models of female revolutionaries. The female revolutionary model had been one of self-abnegation for Marxist and international revolutionary causes, with an almost total lack of interest in the accoutrements

---

[6] Aleksandr Kochukov, "Uroki Khetagurova," *Krasnaia zvezda*, May 8, 2003.
[7] T. V. Fedorova, *Naverkhu Moskva* (Moscow: Sov. Rossiia, 1975), 6.

associated with femininity or domestic comforts. The embodiments of this model were particularly prominent in the Zhenotdel. However, by the mid-1930s their star was fading. These figures were leaving the public stage because of their advancing age and because their generation became suspect during the purges that began at this time.

Two other archetypes with negative connotations informed official policy and dominated cultural representations of women. One was that of the backward and oppressed woman, usually associated with the peasantry or non-Slavic peoples of the empire. Presumably, more conscious comrades toiled to enlighten and liberate these benighted and ignorant women and draw them into the collective project of building socialism. In the 1930s these figures were still potent symbols illustrating the progress made by the victory of communism in liberating those most oppressed by Tsarism and capitalism.[8]

The second and more problematic figure was that of the meshchanka. Solidly associated with the relics of pre-revolutionary society, she had no interest in socialism and was potentially harmful to society as a whole through her pernicious influence on husband and children. The meshchanka became an elastic label assigned to women who through apathy or antipathy or by virtue of difficult economic circumstances failed to engage in public life. None of these figures offered compelling role models for a generation of women anxious to fit in as they reached adulthood at the end of the 1930s.

Urban, educated, and celebrated women like Khetagurova, an indisputable product of the Soviet system, increasingly eclipsed older archetypes. The new archetype of Soviet womanhood, like Khetagurova, worked outside of the domestic sphere yet simultaneously drew gratification from family life. She enjoyed public acclaim, though she was not supposed to seek it out at the expense of male egos. This new heroine was geographically mobile and literally appeared in a different environment. Her story played out against a backdrop of wide-open spaces and dramatic natural settings where she operated as a multidimensional professional, activist, and personable friend. These theaters for dramatizing facets of Soviet womanhood differed considerably from the symbolic and real confines of factory shopfloors, podiums, and kitchens figuratively populated by older, static, and humorless archetypes of Soviet laboring women.

Khetagurova as a wife and an activist embodied other markers of the officially lauded modern woman-citizen. Her stardom was directly related to her work on the frontier of Stalinism. Her marriage, as a Russian

---

[8] This is an argument most fully elaborated by Choi Chatterjee in *Celebrating Women*.

woman, to an Ossetian officer represented an officially welcome dilution of ethnic boundaries through intermarriage.[9] Subsequently, the couple also exemplified a model of marriage as partnership in the service of the Soviet state.

Khetagurova did not disappear from the national stage after the publication of her appeal. Rather, she became a prominent female figurehead, a well-respected member of the Far Eastern Komsomol and military circles, and a patron of thousands of young women. Her career as a public figure demonstrates that at least this female superstar was not simply an inert pawn manipulated by the propaganda machine. She took an active part in building her own credentials as an activist long before authorities in Moscow placed her at the center of the campaign to attract young women to the Far East.

Her life story is not an easy one to reconstruct: unlike her husband, she never published a lengthy memoir. While Khetagurova was the more prominent member of her family before World War II, her star and visibility was almost fully eclipsed afterwards when her husband's military career and wartime service seized the spotlight. Nevertheless, she did turn up on numerous occasions in the press after 1945 and left behind some reflections on her life, especially on the occasion of the fiftieth anniversary of the Khetagurovite campaign.[10]

In the late 1930s Khetagurova was a highly visible media figure, appearing as a subject in articles and photographs and as a columnist in Far Eastern and national newspapers. She was also a member of the Far East's Komsomol Regional Committee and took an active part in the management and popularization of the Khetagurovite campaign. The resulting archival trail permits some insights behind the façade of published sources. We also learn something about her road to stardom from her husband's memoirs and from her friend Fedorova's memoir.

Khetagurova's public appeal for migrants and subsequent publications were peppered with autobiographical vignettes from the life of an independent young woman. The autobiographical format allowed plenty of room to delineate the tropes of a fully "Soviet" cohort including an emphasis on a working-class background and an impoverished childhood without a father. Of course, at times, such sources present insurmountable challenges. They reveal few details that could suggest a critical stance

---

[9] For the implications of this on the structure of families in the late twentieth century, see Nikolai Botev, "The Ethnic Composition of Families in Russia in 1989: Insights into the Soviet 'Nationalities Policies,'" *Population and Development Review* 28:4 (December 2002), 681–706.

[10] Valentina Khetagurova, "K 50-letiiu khetagurovskogo dvizheniia – Veriu v derzost' molodykh," *Dal'nii Vostok* 2 (1987), 127–133.

on events or personages of the period. Khetagurova's recollections, as well as those of her husband and friend, were also written many years later and reflected their present-day concerns and agreed-upon stories within a close-knit circle. However, even within the narrative conventions of Soviet autobiographies there are clues to the meaning of activism and authority for ambitious women like Khetagurova.

A Soviet woman

Khetagurova was born in 1914 into the Zarubin family in St. Petersburg. Four years later, her father, a Putilov factory worker, died, leaving a widow and four children just as the Civil War began to grind down vulnerable families. As a teenager, Valentina Zarubina thrived on multitasking. She studied at night and worked during the day, played sports, and participated in several organizations. She studied drafting in the evening at a technical school in 1931–1932 while working in a machine-building plant during the day.[11] Although she claimed to have been happy in Leningrad, real gratification eluded the young Komsomol member. "Magnitka, Dneprogas, uninhabited spaces beyond the Urals beckoned to us. We were sure that our hands were needed in precisely those places."[12] Unlike women from another generation, she was not the subject of successful efforts to enlighten or to train. Rather, she took her place in socialist construction without prodding.

When her Komsomol cell was ordered to drum up three volunteers for Far Eastern work, the young Valentina jumped at the chance. Her decision was an act of insensitive disobedience. Her older sister had died during a study-related trip to a construction project and the tragedy weighed heavily on the family. Outsiders tried to dissuade her, reminding her of the inevitable heartache that her departure would inflict on her mother and trying to deflate her frontier fantasies with stories about dreary isolation and the dangers of life in the wilds. The seventeen-year-old only grew more thrilled at the prospect. Aware of the potential blow to her mother, Valentina nevertheless volunteered for the Far East without her consent.

The need for volunteers took precedence over parental authority. The district Komsomol leaders, clearly thinking of their quotas, did not ask for parental permission. Fearing that her mother would be crushed if she thought her daughter was voluntarily abandoning the family, Valentina

---

[11] Valentina delayed further study after completing school because "she had to help her mother. She went to work as a draftsman in an institute." She omitted this explanation from her story. See Fedorova, *Naverkhu Moskva*, 6.
[12] Khetagurova, "K 50-letiiu," 127.

claimed that she had been compulsorily "mobilized." The ruse was discovered. Although shamefaced, Valentina persisted. To soften the blow, she pledged to make their separation a brief one. This was a promise she was able to keep, for later, as a married woman, she brought her mother to live with her in the Far East. Such devotion and the wish to live together were not just expressions of affection and family bonds. Valentina acknowledged that many of her later achievements were made possible only by the presence of her mother, who took care of her small children and ran the household while her famous daughter traveled extensively and worked.

After settling these irksome family issues, young Valentina, with a group of thirteen others, boarded a train bound for the Far East. The train journey and her adventures en route to her new home play a prominent role in her recollections. She remembered her "modest" send-off in the spring of 1932. She also felt it necessary to point out that there was no greeting party for her group in Khabarovsk. "We believed that great deeds in honor of the Motherland awaited us. This faith did not proclaim itself with loud declarations but dwelled in our hearts. Patriotism, as wisely noted by L. N. Tolstoy, is a chaste emotion."[13] The fact that Khetagurova later helped to organize festive greeting parties for "young patriots" did not interfere with her desire to stress the purity of her own aspirations. The homage to patriotism and the lack of fanfare surrounding her departure and arrival underscored that migration to the Far East was an exemplary act of sacrifice for the cause of national defense.

Her new employer was the engineering section of the Special Red Banner Army of the Far East (OKDVA). In its administrative offices she and the two other young women in her group were offered jobs in the city offices while the men were assigned to remote destinations. The women protested that they had "not come all this way to sit in an office." Valentina felt compelled, in her later years, to justify this militant reaction to such distinctions in assignments between men and women. She explained to the potentially bewildered readers of the 1980s that "[i]n those days we fiercely reacted to the smallest manifestation of unequal rights with men."[14]

In the dormitory where her group stayed, the young women heard stories of pristine wilderness and the great potential of a hitherto obscure but strategically vital settlement called De-Kastri where "important things are being initiated." The women were determined to see the place for themselves; the commanders were sure that the young women would make a quick getaway once they encountered "a real bear's

---

[13] *Ibid.*   [14] *Ibid.*, 128.

corner" (an isolated area). There was a brief standoff and a gleeful triumph. Khetagurova also remembered the men's cagey smirks as they relented in the face of the young hotheads' zeal. To underscore the point that women were just as capable as men and perhaps even more committed to their mission, Valentina told of a distasteful incident when she passed a group of men abandoning a project in the wilderness. They shouted to the women to turn round and go home, otherwise they would "perish for nothing."[15] Disturbed by the cowardice of the weak-willed men, she carried on. After a grueling journey in a variety of river crafts and on horseback, she fell asleep in her new home in De-Kastri, a dugout lit by a contraption fueled by castor oil and potato skins. When she made her appeal as a Far Easterner five years later, she told her readers that of course as a seventeen-year-old girl embarking for the frontier she had "dreamed about romantic adventures, knew that there, far away from my Motherland, in the taiga, an interesting and captivating life awaited me. But life turned out to be not only more difficult than I had imagined, but much more marvelous than the dream."[16]

Shortly after arrival, Khetagurova made herself indispensable to the tiny settlement, her high energy and enthusiasm establishing her at the center of community life. Although she was a newcomer, membership of the Komsomol and status as a volunteer empowered her to plunge into every aspect of public life, since "We Komsomol members 'got into' everything." In her recollections as well as in her speeches and articles in the 1930s, she dwelled on the difficult conditions of life and work as well as her amazement at the "highest moral qualities of people of my generation." In her understanding of Komsomol culture "no one was indifferent" and all her activities exemplified the Komsomol's ethos of activism. Besides working as a draftsman, she took on so many other projects that "it was impossible to list them all." Some of her activism took the form of commonsense suggestions. "Instead of continuing to live in barracks overrun by cockroaches, she suggested moving to tents while the barracks were disinfected," according to Fedorova.[17] Other initiatives reflected how well Khetagurova had internalized the Communist zeal for organizing and formalizing leisure and perhaps monitoring venues for expression. "Instead of just singing songs, Valia insisted that locals organize a drama circle."[18] Her propensity to volunteer and high degree of involvement were recognized and further bolstered. Only just having turned eighteen, she became a deputy in the settlement's soviet.

[15] *Ibid.*, 129.
[16] Valentina Khetagurova, "Priezzhaite k nam na Dal'nii Vostok!," *KP*, February 5, 1937.
[17] Fedorova, *Naverkhu Moskva*, 6.   [18] *Ibid.*

Energetic, selfless, and "into everything," she epitomized the Komsomol heroine of the early 1930s as the women joined the ranks of shock (exemplary) workers and trained to use a submachine gun.

Khetagurova's choice of marriage partner also made her stand out from others and may have contributed to her eventual selection as a representative of modern Soviet womanhood. After all, the intermarriage of different ethnic groups brilliantly embodied the family of nations tropes at the center of Soviet national identity. Her future husband, Georgii Khetagurov, had his own revolutionary story to tell. Born in 1903, Georgii was the son of a Northern Ossetian railroad mechanic on the Georgian Military Highway. True or not, he claimed that his father was involved in the Caucasian revolutionary underground. To underscore his impoverished but radical pedigree, Georgii recalled that "Our homely dwelling, made up of rocks, was a conspiratorial meeting place for many years. When I was very little we were sometimes visited by our distant relative Kosta Khetagurov – the famous Ossetian poet." After completing church school, he worked in a zinc-mining concession owned by a French company and did a variety of odd jobs in Vladikavkaz. Under the tutelage of an uncle, he joined a Red partisan unit fighting against White Cossacks in the Kassar Valley, then formally enlisted in the Red Army's Second Caucasian infantry regiment in 1920. He joined the Communist party in 1921 while taking Red Army commander courses in Piatigorsk. By the time he met Valentina, Georgii had accumulated a reputation and awards for exemplary service during conflict with Chinese troops over the Chinese Far Eastern Railroad in 1929, receiving the Order of the Red Banner.

Georgii's status as an exotic "other" among his fellow officers provided plenty of material for friendly ribbing. Many of his friends in the officer corps called him Khatabich because "he looked and walked like the fairy tale hero."[19] "Khatabich" was the old "Oriental" magician in the fairytale movie *Starik Khatabich*. The nickname hardly signified a valiant military hero – he was rather a kindly genie who flew on rugs and granted wishes. "Khatabich" most of all implied a quixotic character, and it suggests that Georgii came across as a person who had been taken from a "traditional" context and functioned as best he could in the supposedly "modern" world of Slavs and Communists.

Khetagurova was prone to stress his "otherness" by remarking on his special skills on horseback and agility with swords and dances associated with mountain tribes in Southern Russia and Georgia. When asked to describe her first impression of her husband, she told a reporter that she remembered seeing not only a "good-looking Dzhigit – but one that

---

[19] Kochukov, "Uroki Khetagurova."

danced the *lezginka* like a master."[20] Fedorova, the family friend, did not forgo mention of his "sparkling dark Caucasian eyes."[21]

Even the story of their romance as told by Georgii contains the contrast between his own "traditional" proclivities and Valentina's emancipated disposition. Georgii explains that soon after he was posted to De-Kastri, a group of engineers arrived from Leningrad. "Among them was a vivacious young woman, Valia Zarubina, the daughter of a Putilov factory worker." Soon after meeting, their friendship turned to love. "I offered Valia, as they used to say in the past, my hand and heart. She started laughing, and then said seriously, 'I did not come here for this.'" Georgii later recalled that his wife belonged to "[t]hat renowned generation of Soviet youth who built Magnitka and Dneprogas, Komsomol'sk-na-Amure, our first tractor and shipbuilding plants. These youths and young women considered all personal concerns secondary because they were so taken with enthusiasm for labor."[22] Valentina finally relented and married Georgii in 1933. The marriage presents one of the many ironies in her life story.[23] The fact that she invited young women in part to encourage men to stay and form families contrasted sharply with her own reaction to a marriage proposal. This may explain why she skipped over the incident in her own recollections.

"On her own initiative?"

Unlike most famous female notables of the 1930s, Khetagurova did not represent the evolution of a backward or oppressed woman into the light of Soviet liberated womanhood. She was also different from the many military wives who had to adjust to their husbands' postings in some distant periphery. She had volunteered to live in a remote outpost as a single woman and only later married an officer. She did not disengage from activism but metamorphosed from the persona of an ardent young Komsomol activist to that of an organizer among the wives of officers in her husband's military district. She also continued to work as a secretary in the voentorg (military goods distribution system) after marriage. It was this activism that eventually took her to the Kremlin.

---

[20] A "Dzhigit" is a horseman. The "lezginka" is the traditional folk dance of the Lezgin, one of the ethnic groups of present-day Dagestan. It is both a couples' dance and a male solo dance, often performed with a sword.

[21] Fedorova, *Naverkhu Moskva*, 6.

[22] Georgii Khetagurov, *Ispolnenie dolga* (Moscow: Voenizdat, 1977), 35.

[23] While both her husband and friend Fedorova included the story of her initial refusal of the marriage proposal, Valentina never mentioned this vignette. Fedorova writes that Georgii "fancied the smart and serious Valia. When he tried to court her she angrily told him that 'We did not come here for this.'" See Fedorova, *Naverkhu Moskva*, 6.

The rise of a female heroine out of the experiences of Far Eastern life was not an expression of a wholly new emphasis on the uses of women's labors to supplement the personnel of military outposts in sparsely populated areas – the wives of Red Army officers had been the subjects of organizational efforts that began in 1929. This work among wives was an initiative of the political departments in the Red Army who sought to politicize and organize them into a cohesive and readily mobilized social group.[24]

How and why Khetagurova came to the attention of the authorities and became the figurehead of the migration campaign are difficult questions to answer because most sources erroneously stress that women's activism in public works was the result of individual initiative. The notion that the wives movement in her settlement was started at the initiative of the eighteen-year-old newly married Khetagurova was well entrenched by 1937. In articles surrounding her candidacy for appointment to the Supreme Soviet, readers were informed that "Based on the initiative of Valia in the division of major Khetagurov, the wonderful movement of commander's wives began, accomplishing truly great deeds in Red Army dormitories, cafeterias, and clubs."[25] However, these accomplishments, presented as the result of her personal initiatives, were in fact part of a much broader organizational effort to keep women like Khetagurova engaged in public life and to make use of their labor after marriage.

The scheme for organizing the wives of officers was delineated at a meeting of the All-Army Conference of Political Workers in February 1929. Among a series of resolutions on the work of the Red Army and Fleet Houses (Clubs) were general guidelines for work among families. Officers' wives were invited to participate in activities sponsored by the Red Army Houses where they could organize a variety of social and educational circles and listen to lectures on topics ranging from politics and literature to hygiene. Wives were supposed to become familiar with the goals and activities of the Soviet government and the party and to offer assistance in organizing public canteens and laundries. All of this work was to be

[s]tructured around spontaneity and the initiative of the women themselves, taking into account their interests and requests, for which it is necessary to pick out a female activist group that could be called together periodically to discuss their work. Commissions on Work among Women and Children are to be created

---

[24] "Rezoliutsii i soveshchaniia po rabote domov Krasnoi Armii i Flota, February 4–7, 1929: Resolution 121 – Rabota s sem'iami: Rabota sredi zhen," in *Vsearmeiskie soveshchaniia politrabotnikov, 1918–1940 (rezoliutsii)* (Moscow: Izdatel'stvo Nauka, 1984), 275–276.
[25] M. Severnaia, "Kandidat Komsomol'skogo okruga," *Tikhookeanskii komsomolets,* October 30, 1937 (hereafter *TK*).

within Red Army Houses. These commissions should include both men and women. Directors of Red Army Houses will chair such commissions.[26]

The resolution on Work among Officers' Wives noted that previous attempts to organize wives had been unsatisfactory. There were "objective" factors such as the women's responsibilities for children and household duties. As a result, Red Army House directors were supposed to set up laundries and canteens to relieve some of the burdens on wives so that they could participate in public activities. Other obstacles were deemed to be of a "subjective character." Clearly, this sort of work was a low priority for officers. They not only ignored orders to organize among women, but there had been instances of "outright opposition to this work." Evidently the worst of all "subjective" impediments, and so pervasive that it merited repeating, was "the backwardness of women, [and] the existence of a whole series of meshchanskii [petty-bourgeois] prejudices and moods, including withdrawal into circles of equal rank."[27] The Red Army and Fleet Houses were expected to prosecute "the struggle against backwardness, meshchanstvo, prejudice and gossip."[28] A subsequent resolution produced by the First Conference of Officers' Wives on March 9, 1930 explained that the movement of wives' "fundamental goals were . . . to struggle with the remnants of meshchanstvo, active participation of wives in defense circles . . . , and to attract members of officers' families from national groups into public work."[29]

Red Army House libraries were instructed to include books on women's movements and to order women's periodicals. Furthermore, work among wives included training courses in nursing, communication, and sharp shooting. Newspapers produced by the Houses were also supposed to include women's "columns" where they could publish articles on issues of relevance to families. Red Army wives groups were initially seen as a complementary formation in the work of the Zhenotdel. All their work was to be conducted "in a tight connection with the zhenotdely of party committees."[30] In general, it was expected that zhenotdel meetings would include groups of Red Army wives. After the Zhenotdel was disbanded, wives groups continued to function in army units, convening at regional and national levels throughout the 1930s.[31] Organizers among Red Army

---

[26] "Rezoliutsii i soveshchaniia . . . , February 4–7, 1929," 275–276.   [27] *Ibid.*, 276.

[28] *Ibid.*, 277.   [29] *Vsesoiuznoe soveshchanie . . . RKKA*(1937), 315.

[30] A Zhenotdel representative was expected to be part of the commissions for work among families. The Red Army Houses were to encourage women to join in the activities of the Zhenotdel through delegate meetings and as interns (*praktikantki*) in sectors of the city soviets. See "Rezoliutsii i soveshchaniia . . . , February 4–7, 1929," 276.

[31] For instance, see "Soveshchanie zhen nachal'stvuiushchego sostava RKKA, March 8, 1930," in *Vsearmeiskie soveshchaniia politrabotnikov 1918–1940*, 315. Officers' wives

wives trumpeted a direct connection between the activities of wives in the 1930s and the record of women's support and work alongside husbands during the Civil War as auxiliary personnel. They were also justified in considering themselves the forerunners of the movement of wives that was associated with the patronage of the Ministry of Heavy Industry.[32]

By the mid-1930s, worries about meshchanstvo among wives receded, but they were replaced with an emphasis on the uses of women's labor on the peripheries. By 1936, the activities of wives in the Far East garnered special attention because they were so badly needed. During a meeting with a commission charged with organizing the national conference of army wives in 1936, it was significant that a representative from the Far Eastern Army was the first to make a report to the People's Commissar for Defense, Kliment Voroshilov. "You know that in the Far East every person is valued like gold," Osnovina explained. "That is why so many wives of commanders and political workers work not only in divisions and headquarters but also in various posts in the Party and in soviet and economic organizations of the region. Not a few wives work in the divisions as teachers."[33]

Voroshilov, the obvious "patron" of the officers' wives, provided official reinforcement of the prevailing emphasis on women's labor. It was simply indispensable, "especially in distant garrisons where we must achieve the maximum involvement of women and family members of serving men for permanent work in divisions in cultural, educational, and service organization (clubs, schools, crèches); administrative and economic organizations and military supply systems [*voentorg*] (headquarters, stores, warehouses, cafeteria, etc.)."[34]

During the Fourth All-Union Conference of Red Army Officers and Command Staff Wives in December 1936, where Khetagurova was elected to the conference's presidium, press coverage of the conference summarized these objectives. "The wives of commanders have provided a huge army of cultural-political workers for the army units, a significant number of whom are far from the center, in garrisons located in border

---

groups reappeared for similar reasons in the 1960s through to the 1980s in isolated garrisons. See El'vira B. Ershova, "Garnizonnye zhensovety v Sovetskoi Armii v 60-e–80-e gody," in *O nas i nashem dele* 3–4 (September 1999), web-based journal, *www.womnet.ru/aboutus/3-4/index.htm.*

[32] For more on the Wives Movement in Industry, see Balmas Neary, "Mothering Socialist Society: The Wife-Activists' Movement and the Soviet Culture of Daily Life, 1934–41," *Russian Review* 58 (July 1999), 396–412; Mary Buckley, "The Untold Story of *Obshchestvennitsa* in the 1930s," 569–86; and Schrand, "Soviet 'Civic-Minded Women' in the 1930s," 126–150.

[33] "Priem t. K. E. Voroshilovym zhen komandirov i nachsostava RKKA," *Krasnoe znamia*, August 16, 1936.

[34] *Ibid.*

zones."[35] This stress on wives in the peripheries explains to some degree why Khetagurova was selected to the presidium and placed on the cover of *Rabotnitsa*, and why her remarks were given so much weight.

Although there were variations in the several narratives surrounding the impetus and role of Khetagurova in the wives' movement of her garrison, all the activities described neatly embodied the orders outlined in 1929 for work in Red Army Houses. Like the authors of the resolutions on army wives, she sensed that the experience of an officer's wife in isolated circumstances could nurture the worst qualities associated with the presumably backward proclivities of women. When she moved from De-Kastri to the military garrison, she encountered "the well-known lot of army wives. Their husbands are engrossed in their duties, and the wives are left to wait for them on their porches. The prospect of such a life, it goes without saying, did not suit me and the other wives shared my attitude."[36] The wives, just as had been hoped, helped by filling in breaches in services for military personnel.

At some point, fed up with delays in establishing a public laundry in the garrison, a group of commanders' wives washed, repaired, and ironed thousands of pairs of linens.[37] Georgii and Fedorova thought that such selfless labor reflected the spontaneous initiatives of enthusiasts like Khetagurova. "Instead of withdrawing from public life, Khetagurova gathered the other officers' wives and organized a collective laundry when the laundress fell ill."[38] In the spring they organized *subbotniks* (semivoluntary work on Saturdays), "forcing" everyone to clean up the settlement. The women also tackled "the scourge of the North": scurvy. Soldiers and officers "at our insistence" consumed a broth made from tree bark and ate the wild onions and cranberries the women obtained in the taiga. "And in the end the dangerous disease retreated."[39] The soldiers' gratitude was the reward for the women's backbreaking toil.[40]

---

[35] "Vsearmeiskoe soveshchanie zhen komandirov Krasnoi Armii," *Rabotnitsa* 35 (December 1936), 7.

[36] Khetagurova, "K 50-letiiu," 131.

[37] Various reasons are given for the need of officers' wives to do laundry. One version offered by Fedorova was that the laundress fell ill. Khetagurova explained that the ship that ferried dirty laundry for the soldiers had become disabled. While Georgii claimed that his wife and others washed 12,000 pairs of underwear, Khetagurova recalled a more believable number of several thousand pairs.

[38] Fedorova, *Naverkhu Moskva*, 6.   [39] Khetagurova, "K 50-letiiu," 131.

[40] Later, Khetagurova explained that the women "gained courage and started their own farms." In a year the women's labor produced more than "thirty tons of pork, forty thousand eggs and fully supplied milk for our children and those who were ill. Other divisions copied our example." Fifty years after these events, Khetagurova failed to mention that the wives of De-Kastri actually began individual gardens in response to a directive of K. Voroshilov and Ian Gamarnik. Army units were ordered to establish their own sources

The wives also organized a drama club, while at the army club they arranged Voroshilov sharpshooter circles along with other defense training. They trained to be radio and telegraph operators and learned to ride horses under Georgii's tutelage. He proudly boasted forty years later, "It is still delightful to recall that the best rider turned out to be my Valentina. More than once she came out the winner in equestrian sports against the men."[41]

Despite some confusion surrounding the initiatives that eventually brought her into the national spotlight, there are clues in Khetagurova's story toward a better understanding of how such careers were constructed. Simeon V. Rudnev appears as a key figure in Khetagurova's retelling of her activism and rise to prominence. In 1932 Rudnev was the Commissar and Chief of the Political Department of the De-Kastri military district. Khetagurova "was proud all of my life that he gave me my recommendation to join the party."[42] Rudnev's role in promoting Khetagurova can be read on one level as a trope of Socialist Realism and Soviet propaganda. In a conventional plot of this genre, an older and wiser Communist serves as a guiding hand in the formation of young workers and heroes. But it would be a mistake to assume that this nod to Rudnev was an undeserved artifice of Communist etiquette. Conversely, it would also be a mistake to assume that Rudnev was acting on his own initiative to promote the work of army wives. Khetagurova's zeal for activism would have fizzled out without the active encouragement and patronage of a well-connected Commissar. Rudnev, for his part, did not ignore his duty as a Political Commissar to foster an organization of army wives.[43]

---

of agricultural supplies in response to the miserable state of the food distribution system in the years following collectivization and the general problems of nutrition in northern climates. After they put their own gardens in order, the women helped out on the farm of the division. Khetagurova explained these orders in Khetagurova, "Taiga otstupila," *Rabotnitsa* 1 (January 1937), 11.

[41] G. Khetagurov, *Ispolnenie dolga*, 38.

[42] Besides being a seemingly capable and resourceful manager of people, Rudnev had impeccable revolutionary credentials – he had taken part in the storming of the Winter Palace in 1917. He and Georgii Khetagurov also successfully avoided the devastating purge of Far Eastern military officers. Rudnev went on to head a famous partisan unit in Ukraine and died in a battle with anti-Soviet Ukrainian units in 1944, for which he was posthumously awarded the title of Hero of the Soviet Union. See Khetagurova, "K 50-letiiu," 129.

[43] Similarly, Pasha Angelina was supported by a local political department (Politotdel) chief not simply because he was sympathetic to the idea of female tractor drivers but because he was "pursuing the party's policy." See Praskovya Angelina, *My Answer to an American Questionnaire* (Moscow 1951), 24, quoted in Oja, *From Krestianka to Udarnitsa* 35. Credit for initiative in famous campaigns depended on who was the subject of the biography. The origin of the wives movement among Red Army officers' wives was also presented as the work of one individual in the biography of Simeon Rudnev. But in this

Khetagurova eventually became a figurehead for the campaign because she had taken up opportunities presented by the active promotion and support of Political Commissar Rudnev. He followed and facilitated the work of wives and also "indefatigably popularized our experience and even motivated us to publish in the army's press." He also introduced her to visiting dignitaries. Khetagurova recalled that "Ian Gamarnik, the head of the Political Administration of the RKKA, visited our garrison twice, praised us and also expressed the opinion that it would be difficult to develop and reliably defend the Far East without drawing in young women."[44] Gamarnik was known for his ability to "spot talent."[45] Eventually, V. K. Bliukher and the head of the Political Administration of the OKDVA, N. E. Donenko, were made aware of the wives' efforts. After becoming acquainted with men like these, Khetagurova offered suggestions for improving conditions in the Far East. She had good timing. She joined a dialogue already initiated by military planners like Bliukher and Gamarnik who were endowed with sweeping powers to engineer not only the defensive but also the social and economic capacities of the region in this period. Gamarnik had been working on plans to promote settlement since 1926 and developed a plan to bring 400,000 peasants from Ukraine.[46]

"From the shores of the Pacific"

No resolution or directive outlining a plan for a campaign to attract female migrants to the Far East has been located. It is probable that none existed. Subsequent accounts reveal the haphazard way this campaign began and hence the opportunities for an articulate woman with an active patron to

version it was Rudnev who was credited with the idea as a spontaneous response to the adverse conditions of the region. A participant in the partisan unit under the command of Rudnev during World War II, Peter Vershigora jumbled the Khetagurovite movement and the movement of wives in a biographical sketch composed to hail the fallen hero. "Who remembers the Khetagurovite movement of wives of the command staff in the Far East? It was born and grew in the De-Kastri district where Rudnev was the Commissar." Vershigora explained that the settlement suffered from scurvy and lack of activities to satisfy cultural needs. "And Rudnev finds a reserve – the caring hands of women. This is how the movement of commanders' wives was born." See Vershigora, *Liudi s chistoi sovest'iu* (Moscow: Moskovskii rabochii, 1946), 45.

[44] Khetagurova, "K 50-letiiu," 131. Ian Gamarnik was also Deputy Defense Commissar and chairman of the Special Commission for Far Eastern Development and Defense beginning in 1931, traveling "frequently to the region as the plenipotentiary of the Politburo" (Stephan, *The Russian Far East*, 179). Khetagurov also remembered Gamarnik's remarks that "the care of women's hands is especially necessary here, in this sparsely settled region, where the riches of the Far East cannot be conquered without the participation of women" (G. Khetagurov, *Ispolnenie dolga*, 38).

[45] Stephan, *The Russian Far East*, 176.   [46] *Ibid.*, 177.

grab the spotlight in the Soviet system. Khetagurova claimed that the idea to attract more women was sparked when "We saw the usefulness of our work, and we felt the necessity of our presence here in this distant garrison. We noticed that just our being here improved the mood of soldiers."[47] According to Fedorova, the call-up was purely Khetagurova's idea and stemmed from a concern with family formation as well as the need for cadres in female-dominated professions. In this version, Valentina,

[t]ogether with her husband and friends, often thought about the seriousness of the Far East to national defense. Many soldiers and officers having served their time would stay here in this marvelous region forever but one has to start a family – that's life. Besides this, how many female laboring hands are needed for the Far East! There are advertisements in schools, clubs and construction projects: we need teachers, librarians, cooks, hairdressers . . . That is when Valia had an idea to call young women to come to the Far East – the Komsomol and party organizations heartily supported her.[48]

These ideas found a receptive audience and helped Khetagurova attain a prominent place at the Fourth All-Union Conference of Red Army Officers' and Command Staff Wives in December 1936.[49] There she was awarded the Red Banner Order of Labor and bestowed with a gold watch by the Commissar of Defense, Voroshilov. Her authority was further boosted when she appeared in a photograph next to Stalin on the front page of *Pravda* (see figure 4, "*Rabotnitsa* cover," figure 5, "Next to Stalin," and figure 6, "On the podium with Voroshilov").[50]

Khetagurova not only appeared seated next to Stalin, which was no doubt staged at the behest of the authorities, but at the critical moment

---

[47] Khetagurova, "K 50-letiiu," 131. Rudnev had a hand in preparing Khetagurova to make a speech that would set her apart from the rest. According to Georgii, it was Rudnev who asked her "to be sure to make a speech at the conference and explain how women are helping to make the taiga habitable . . . and how many more female hands are needed for the Far East!" G. Khetagurov, *Ispolnenie dolga*, 39.

[48] Fedorova, *Naverkhu Moskva*, 6.

[49] Her name was first on the list of awardees among the wives who received the Red Banner Order of Labor. See "O nagrazhdenii ordenami . . . ," *Pravda*, December 26, 1936; and G. Khetagurov, *Ispolnenie dolga*, 39. Although Khetagurova claimed later that parts of her speech at the Red Army Wives Conference touched upon the issue of the need to stimulate the migration of women to the Far East, the published transcript of her speech at the conference made no mention of this issue. See Khetagurova quoted in *Vsesoiuznoe soveshchanie zhen komandnogo i nachal'stvuiushchego sostava RKKA*.

[50] *Pravda*, December 24, 1936. She had already appeared next to Voroshilov on the cover of *Pravda*, December 21, 1936. The photograph shown here was printed in the *Rabotnitsa* issue dedicated to the conference. She was the main focus of a major article on the Wives' Conference by N. Iakovleva and B. Fonareva, "Patriotki sovetskoi strany," *Pravda*, December 20, 1936. For more on the practice and significance of depicting women activists in proximity to Stalin in visual propaganda, see Reid, "All Stalin's Women," 133–173.

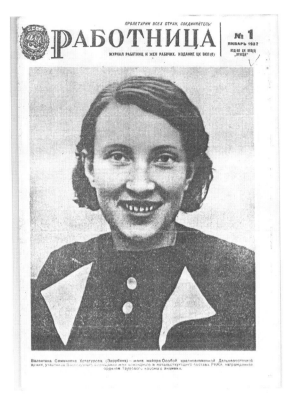

4. "*Rabotnitsa* cover"
Rabotnitsa 1 (January 1937). Issue dedicated to the Conference of Red
Army Command Staff's Wives in Moscow, December 1936.

when all the other women turned to the camera, she is shown turned
to Stalin, suggesting a moment of friendly banter and a special status.
After the conference, she was appointed as an instructor in the Army's
political department for work among families of the command staff.[51] In
publications written in the 1930s, Khetagurova stressed her proximity to
Stalin and Voroshilov, and she did not fail to note the gold watch from
Voroshilov in her Communist party autobiography.

Her memories of those days at the conference were still vivid forty years
later. The contrast between life in the Far Eastern forests and the spotlight
on a tribune next to Stalin produced anxiety and elation. Khetagurova
explained that she and the other activists spent a lot of time thinking

[51] "Personal file – Khetagurova, Valentina Simeonovna for 1938," GAKhK P, f. 35, op.
14, d. 11147, ll. 1–2.

Товарищи Сталин И. В., Молотов В. М., Ворошилов К. Е., Гамарник Я. Б., Буденный С. М. и Егоров А. И. среди членов президиума Всесоюзного совещания жен командного и начальствующего состава Рабоче-крестьянской Красной армии.

Фото Н. Кулешова

5. "Next to Stalin"
Conference of Red Army Command Staff's Wives in December 1936.
The photograph appeared on the front page of *Pravda* and in *Rabotnitsa*.

6. "On the podium with Voroshilov"
Conference of Red Army Command Staff's Wives, December 1936.
Valentina Khetagurova is on the right next to People's Commissar for
Defense Kliment Voroshilov.

about what to say at the conference about the need for women. However,
"When I came up to the tribune, just like Alexandra Sokolova in the film
Chlen pravitel'stva [*Member of the Government*, 1939], I immediately forgot
everything on earth."[52]

---

[52] Khetagurova, "K 50-letiiu," 132. In the film a poor, uneducated woman joins a collective
farm, overcomes social ridicule and an abusive husband, and is eventually elected a

Just think, from the deep taiga – straight into the Kremlin! . . . Then they call my name! As though in a dream I go up into the presidium and take a place next to the leading Soviet marshals and distinguished party members and statesmen. I understood that this honor was bestowed on me only because I came from the most distant garrison – from the shores of the Pacific Ocean.[53]

Only the sight of a giant map of the Far East brought her out of her trance and she "simply said that without young women the Far East could never be developed . . . They must help the men make it habitable." Other Far Eastern delegates supported her point. The idea to turn to all Soviet young women with a call-up in *Komsomol'skaia pravda* was "born" later. Shortly, her face appeared on the front cover of *Rabotnitsa*'s issue dedicated to the conference.[54] A month later, her call-up for female participation in the settlement of the Far East was published in *Komsomol'skaia pravda*.[55]

Officials never elaborated on how Khetagurova was selected to become a figure to promote Far Eastern migration. The best clue to her selection appears in a description of her meeting with Voroshilov and Stalin at the Red Army Wives conference. A member of the Komsomol's Central Committee's (TsK) sector for Work among Young Women and a journalist for *Komsomol'skaia pravda*, Elena Kononenko, explained that members of the Komsomol TsK knew about Khetagurova before she arrived in Moscow. After she was selected for the conference presidium, "It happened that she sat next to comrade Voroshilov." When Voroshilov found out that she was from the Far East, he knowingly inquired, "Are you the Komsomolka who went there in 1932?" He then introduced her to Stalin, who "firmly shook her hand."[56] Rudnev's efforts to publicize the work of Far Eastern wives and to fashion a female heroine out of Khetagurova had paid off.

Official party directives followed rather than preceded the massive display of enthusiasm for her invitation:

Most, me included, did not anticipate that events after the publication of my appeal would take on such a scale [*razmakh*]. Those gals went to the Far East

---

deputy to the Supreme Soviet. Khetagurova alludes to the film because it is another instance of a woman rising from obscurity to be the center of attention and adulation among Soviet leaders.

[53] *Ibid.*, 131.

[54] See *Rabotnitsa* 1 (January 1937), front cover and p. 3. Khetagurova's photograph appeared in *Rabotnitsa* several times: *Rabotnitsa* 28 (October 1938), 9; *Rabotnitsa* 4 (February 1938), 7; and (behind Stalin), *Rabotnitsa* 5 (February 1937), 5.

[55] Khetagurova managed the production of her own image in photographs. Although memoirists remember her as a plump woman, her photographs never reveal this. She is either shown in a head shot or standing at a slight angle to downplay her width.

[56] Elena Kononenko, "Plamennaia patriotka," *TK*, December 6, 1937.

despite fear and the risk, alone and in whole trainloads, at their own expense and at the expense of the state. After this first surge there was a special governmental decision on all measures of support for the patriotic initiative.[57]

Deafening fame

As the campaign evolved, Khetagurova took an active role in the affairs of the organization created to facilitate the migration. She also retained her position as a political instructor and organizer of wives in the headquarters of the Far Eastern Army. By the end of 1937, Khetagurova was not only on the committee for the Khetagurovite movement of youth to the Far East but also a deputy in the Supreme Soviet USSR.[58] Throughout this period, her articles appeared in national and regional newspapers on topics related to the migration of young people and patriotic pieces.[59]

Once the Khetagurovite campaign took on a life of its own, Khetagurova was positioned within the ranks of other well-known female stars of Soviet production and achievement. In the opening address to a regional Khetagurovite conference, the speaker asserted, "This country, comrades, is proud of patriots like Maria Demchenko, like Valentina Khetagurova, Pasha Angelina, Polina Osipenko, Dusia Vinogradova, Tat'iana Fedorova and hundreds of others like them."[60] Publicity about the activities of famous Soviet heroines created the impression that all the famous women made up an intimate community.[61] The representation of Khetagurova along with other female notables was a common

---

[57] Khetagurova, "K 50-letiiu," 132.

[58] Her election and duties as a deputy also generated a series of articles and photographs in the press throughout 1938: photograph and article by Valentina Khetagurova, "Privet podrugam!," *Tikhookeanskaia zvezda*, May 5, 1938 (hereafter *TZ*); "O registratsii kandidata v deputaty soviet soiuza Valentiny Simeonovny Khetagurovoi," *TK*, November 29, 1937; photograph with another famous woman Stakhanovite, T. V. Fedorova, in their roles as deputies, *TZ*, June 8, 1939; "Kandidat Komsomol'skogo okruga," *TK*, October 30, 1937; full page dedicated to Khetagurova, with photograph and biographies, *TK*, December 6, 1937; another page dedicated to Khetagurova was "Deputat – sluga naroda," *TK*, December 12, 1938.

[59] She appeared in a publication dedicated to important Soviet women, E. Petrov, "Khetagurovki," in *Zhenshchiny strany sotsializma* (Moscow: Gos. izd. polit. lit., 1939), 46–51, and in the book dedicated to the Conference of the Wives of Red Army Commanders in 1936, *Vsesoiuznoe soveshchanie . . . RKKA* (1937) 172–177. Her articles in the press include Valentina Khetagurova, "Zavoevannoe nikomu ne otdadim!," *TZ*, August 1, 1938; "Nashi besstrashnye sestry," *KP*, November 11, 1938; "Organizovat' dvizhenie molodykh patriotov," *KP*, January 26, 1938; and "Po-stalinski vospityvat' molodezh'," *TZ*, February 15, 1939.

[60] "Stenographic text of the regional Khetagurovite conference," September 15, 1938, Ovchinnikov, GAKhK P, f. 618, op. 1, d. 325, l. 9ob.

[61] Vinogradova made much of her friendships with Demchenko and Angelina. See E. Vinogradova, "Moi podrugi," *KP*, March 8, 1938. The notables sent public letters to

practice in public culture in which prominent female heroes were presented in relationship to one another. These virtual communities evoked the image of a female sphere to which ordinary women could turn for support and understanding. A photograph depicting three female notables "on vacation" in a speedboat illustrated these themes with the three notables appearing in a new backdrop of open spaces, relaxed camaraderie, and mobility associated with Khetagurova as a frontier heroine.[62]

In some instances, famous female heroines developed genuine long-lasting friendships. The friendship between Fedorova and Khetagurova was well known. The emphasis on a woman's sphere and women's networks is strong in Fedorova's story about her first encounter with Khetagurova. They were introduced by an even greater elder female figure, Nadezhda Krupskaia, in the Kremlin during the first session of the Supreme Soviet.[63]

Meanwhile, the hundreds of letters addressed to Khetagurova and the laudatory articles in national newspapers that followed the publication of her call-up engendered unease at home. She herself was apprehensive. "All of these unknown-to-me young men and women were calling themselves Khetagurovites and Khetagurovki. I remember that initially this kind of an unexpected popularity of his name disturbed Georgii Ivanovich, but later he became accustomed to it."[64] There were several reasons for his discomfort. It was a perilous moment for all army officers as the Great Terror was devastating their ranks. This kind of notoriety could go either way in the senseless course of the Stalinist terror: it could protect the famous family or induce unwelcome scrutiny.[65] There is no way to know if Georgii survived because of his famous wife. Perhaps officer Khetagurov was more concerned that the "unexpected popularity of his name" was not in recognition of his own feats, but those of his young wife. It could not have been easy for Georgii, known to his friends as a man out of sync with the present day, to watch his 23-year-old wife ascend to stardom under his family name. In the end, whatever he may have thought, he did not stand in her way.

---

each other. For an example, see "Perepiska deputatov. Pis'mo Pashi Angelinoi Valentine Khetagurovoi," *TZ*, April 22, 1938.

[62] The photograph, entitled "On Vacation," shows Angelina, Khetagurova, and Fedorova on a speedboat in 1939. See Fedorova, *Naverkhu Moskva*, 31.

[63] This meeting subsequently led to a lifelong relationship built on a rapport of sharing both "joy and grief." In 1973 Khetagurova and Fedorova accepted an invitation from the Kamchatka Komsomol for sightseeing and festivities as "Komsomol veterans" to celebrate its fiftieth anniversary. See, *ibid.*, 6.

[64] Khetagurova, "K 50-letiiu," 132.

[65] For more on the military purges, see V. S. Mil'bakh, "Repression in the Red Army in the Far East, 1936–1939," *Journal of Slavic Military Studies* 16:4 (2003), 58–130.

On another occasion, Khetagurova claimed that she was uncomfortable with the use of her married name as a moniker for a campaign. "From the very beginning I did not like this convention, dreamed up by one of the journalists. This was not the point of it all. It was the spirit and enthusiasm of young gals, who really believed in their ideals, knew how to work, as they say to the seventh sweat, who dreamed about bright futures."[66] Indeed, this discomfort was apparent in the late 1930s. Khetagurova avoided using the term "Khetagurovite" in most of her public appearances. In articles she referred to Khetagurovites as "young patriots, who came here voluntarily."[67] Others noticed this tendency. One memoirist was struck by the fact that during a meeting at which Khetagurova delivered a report on the movement, she "did not call it Khetagurovite."[68]

As a local celebrity in the 1930s, Khetagurova was marshaled to play prominent roles in well-publicized Far Eastern events, especially those related to issues of defense and female achievement.[69] During the conflict at Lake Khasan in August 1938, she headed a delegation of young women Khetagurovites to visit wounded soldiers and was "the first one to offer her blood."[70] This trip, orchestrated by the regional Komsomol Committee, was hailed as a deed "worthy of the highest order of commendation."

Once in the Far East as a Supreme Soviet deputy and regional Komsomol secretary, Khetagurova was promoted as a figure of some stature. On the first anniversary of the Khetagurovites' arrival in Komsomol'sk-na-Amure, *Tikhookeanskaia zvezda* dedicated several articles to praising their achievements and showcased Khetagurova. The caption to the photograph proclaims her new titles: "Deputy of the Supreme Soviet USSR, initiator of the patriotic movement of Youth to the Far East."[71] As a Supreme Soviet deputy Khetagurova was a voice of authority on a wide range of matters and governmental affairs including issues of resettlement. In one piece she announced that it was "[t]ime to seriously sum up the first experience with the resettlement of young

---

[66] Aleksander Kochukov, "Uroki Khetagurova," *Krasnaia zvezda*, May 8, 2003.

[67] Valentina Khetagurova, "Volnuiushchie vstrechi. V gostiakh u boitsov," *KP*, September 11, 1938. For other examples of this, see Khetagurova, "Organizovat' dvizhenie molodykh patriotov," *KP*, January 26, 1938, and, "Po-stalinski vospityvat' molodezh'," *TZ*, February 15, 1939.

[68] Memoir of Efrosina Mishalova, February 18, 1976, GAKhK P, f. 442, op. 2, d. 284, l. 113ob.

[69] She was present to greet the all-female crew of the airplane *Rodina* (Polina Osipenko, Marina Raskova, and Valentina Grizodubova) when they were rescued in the Far Eastern taiga at the end of their record-breaking flight in 1938. See "Protocol of the I Khabarovsk regional Komsomol conference," February 11–15, 1939, GAKhK P, f. 617, op. 1, d. 3, l. 158.

[70] "Stenographic text of the regional Khetagurovite conference," September 17, 1938, Sobolev, GAKhK P, f. 618, op. 1, d. 325, l. 392.

[71] "Valentina Khetagurova," *TZ*, May 5, 1938.

7. "Portrait of a deputy"
Valentina Khetagurova, 1938.

patriots in the Far East and take away the bureaucratic barriers that interfere with the movement and to resolve certain, in my opinion, governmental issues connected to this movement."[72] Khetagurova was presented to
the country as both a Supreme Soviet Deputy carrying out her duties to
the "people" and as a partner in a marriage of equal patriots, as in figure
7, "Portrait of a deputy," 1938, and figure 8, "The Khetagurov couple at
home in Khabarovsk," 1938.[73]

Khetagurova's role as a "leader" meant concern for the smooth running of the campaign and the discipline of those who carried the title
Khetagurovite. Morale and morality within the Komsomol was one of
the most common themes in her public statements. In general, she placed

[72] Valentina Khetagurova, "Organizovat' dvizhenie molodykh patriotov," *KP*, January 26,
1938.
[73] The photograph of Khetagurova reading was published in *Rabotnitsa* 28 (October 1938),
9.

8. "The Khetagurov couple at home in Khabarovsk, 1938"

young women's issues at the center of her speeches and articles. At the
conference of Khetagurovites in September 1938, she focused a great
deal of criticism on Komsomol organizations for their failure to attend
to Khetagurovites and provide proper guidance and activities for young
women more generally. "Among young women Khetagurovites in their
work there are special conditions. Many are already mothers. But some
of them are having children for the first time and simply do not know
how to handle them. They do not know how to combine the duties of
motherhood and public activism."[74] Of course, she herself was able to
"combine" these duties only because her mother had come to live with
her in the Far East.

Her employment in the political administration of the Far Eastern
Army also gave her an unusual standing among Komsomol activists
who were under orders to highlight their collaboration with the military. This was evident during the discussion surrounding the selection of
Khetagurova as a member of the Far Eastern Regional Komsomol Bureau
in the summer of 1938. The transcript of the plenum reveals that she did
not want the position. She tried to persuade those present that there
had to be "many other comrades who can be brought into the regional

[74] "Stenographic text of the regional Khetagurovite conference," September 18, 1938,
Khetagurova, GAKhK P, f. 618, op. 1, d. 325, l. 339.

Komsomol Committee."[75] She pleaded that she was inordinately busy as a Supreme Soviet Deputy and "moreover the basis of my work in the political administration of the military requires a great deal of travel."[76] But the plenum chairman did not allow her to decline the nomination, because "[w]e need tighter connections with army organizations . . . Comrade Khetagurova works directly in the political administration [of the army] and thus has a close familiarity with the interests of the army . . . The fact that she has a heavy work load is not a sufficient justification."[77]

Khetagurova functioned as an information conduit explaining party directives to young women. This was especially true of explaining thorny policies on women in the military. Although there were many more professions and activities open to women, the demarcations between men's and women's duties to the nation remained controversial. Women's insistence that they were the equal of men in every field including the military produced a backlash at the very top of the Communist party at the close of the 1930s. After the publication of the 1939 "Law of General Military Duty," Khetagurova appeared as the author of an *Izvestiia* column on November 22, 1939. In "Woman and the Country's Defense," she tried to make clear how the new law applied to women who had been barraging military authorities with requests to enlist in the military. Her message was couched in the form of a vignette from a conversation with Voroshilov. She had come to report on the accomplishments of women in military sharpshooting and equestrian sports, but instead of praising the women, Voroshilov remarked that this was "[w]rong. We have plenty of men for such things."[78] Women preparing for war were supposed to dedicate their attention to feminine professions such as nursing and communications. Voroshilov even claimed that Khetagurovites had performed badly during the fighting at Lake Khasan. This was a radical turn. Just one year earlier, the women had been praised for their work! According to Voroshilov's new version of events, young women had wasted their time cultivating military skills, instead of medical training. As a result, they could list all the parts of the submachine gun and all types of bombs, "but could not help the doctor during blood transfusions." Khetagurova tried to sustain some balance in the way she summed up this awkward about-face on the issue of women and combat readiness:

I do not want to say that women should not study the machine gun, that they should not know how to shoot. All of this is necessary. But we must not forget that

---

[75] "Stenographic text of the III Plenum of the Far Eastern Regional Komsomol Committee," July 19–22, 1938, GAKhK P, f. 618, op. 1, d. 320, l. 10.
[76] *Ibid.*   [77] *Ibid.*, 11.
[78] Valentina Khetagurova, "Zhenshchina i oborona strany," *Izvestiia*, November 22, 1939. Quoted in Dubinina, *Ty pozovi, Dal'nii Vostok!*, 106.

the main places of women in war are in the hospitals, infirmaries, repair shops, in communication units. And we must prepare for this.[79]

Ironically, Khetagurova felt the sting of such attitudes when she volunteered for active duty after the German invasion in 1941. She applied to enter the army as a commissar of an all-female communications regiment, a duty well within the range of appropriate female roles outlined in her own public statements. However, she was "summoned by the party Central Committee and told 'There is no need for you at the front. Your husband is fighting there, and doing it well. We are offering you a very responsible position in the organization for families of service men.'"[80]

Khetagurova's work as a local and national notable is illustrative of the benefits and pitfalls for ambitious women in the late 1930s. Internal documents from the regional Komsomol organization reveal that she clashed with male Komsomol leaders. At the same time, she developed supporters within the organization and avoided the often tragic fates of her male rivals in this period when relations were anything but amicable within the leadership.

Despite her misgivings, Khetagurova was appointed as a Third Secretary of the Far Eastern Komsomol Regional Committee on August 13, 1938. However, she served for just over a month.[81] Her brief stint and sudden departure generated a heated debate among activists about her treatment in a series of finger-pointing sessions.[82] The consensus among activists was that the First Secretary, Ovchinnikov, "hated her."[83] It was understood that he "feared that she would eclipse his authority."[84] The First Secretary was himself a new arrival from Moscow. He struggled to make his mark and clumsily grabbed an opportunity for a well-publicized appearance as the opening speaker at the regional conference of Khetagurovites. It backfired. The participants were indignant that their Valia stood in the background. "After all, Khetagurova is the initiator of this movement, but he was not even embarrassed and told Khetagurova to write the speech for him, and then even with a written speech he could

---

[79] *Ibid.*   [80] Khetagurova, "K 50-letiiu," 133.

[81] "Meeting of the Far Eastern Regional Komsomol Committee Bureau: Protocol 59," September 26, 1938, GAKhK P, f. 618, op. 1, d. 323, l. 195. The Third Secretary is usually responsible for the propaganda work of the committee.

[82] "Stenographic text of regional Komsomol activists in Khabarovsk," January 4, 1939, GAKhK P, f. 618, op. 1, d. 321, l. 123.

[83] "Meeting of the Organization Bureau of the Far Eastern Regional Central Committee, December 9, 1938: On the question of practices in the work of the Organizational Bureau," GAKhK P, f. 618, op. 1, 324, l. 195.

[84] "Protocol of the I Khabarovsk regional conference of the Komsomol," February 11–15, 1939, GAKhK P, f. 617, op. 1, d. 3, l. 157.

not say it properly. You could ask the gals from the conference. He spoke for thirty minutes and screwed up the whole speech."[85]

Ovchinnikov was not the only man in the Komsomol's leadership unwilling to stand in the shadow of a female superstar. "On the part of certain other employees there were also abnormal attitudes toward Khetagurova. For instance, Kozlov told her that she was abusing her status as a medal winner." The men could not resist treating her as a child. Ovchinnikov "used to say to her, 'You know, you act like a girl.'"[86] The reaction of potential male competitors seems to have been generated in part by Khetagurova's air of experience and competence. There is some indication that she expected to be treated with greater deference than she received. Her supporters thought she wanted to leave because "[e]veryone addressed her in the informal 'you,' absolutely not taking into account that comrade Khetagurova is a person-patriot, a medal recipient; a Deputy of the Supreme Soviet USSR . . . Khetagurova told me that she would have stayed if her treatment had not been so boorish."[87] Perhaps, after more than a year of celebrity, Khetagurova had cultivated some degree of aloofness that did not serve her well among men.

Those who worked with Khetagurova generally held her in high esteem and bemoaned her departure, because she had been "[a] person with a soul, she was loved, people came to her, people asked her for advice."[88] Moreover, a celebrity like Khetagurova had great value for the Far Eastern Komsomol. One activist observed that the Komsomol Central Committee in Moscow usually ignored his requests, until "Khetagurova wrote to comrade Molotov with a series of inquiries regarding the creation of pioneer and sports clubs, the construction of a dormitory, and about student stipends. An answer arrived immediately from the Central Committee of the Communist party."[89] An air of deference was also part of the

---

[85] "Stenographic text of the meeting of regional Komsomol activists in Khabarovsk," January 4, 1939, GAKhK P, f. 618, op. 1, d. 321, ll. 90–91.

[86] Ibid., 45.

[87] Remarks of Monakhov, employee of the Organizational Bureau of the Khabarovsk region's Komsomol Central Committee. See "Meeting of the Organization Bureau of the Far Eastern Regional Central Committee, December 9, 1938: On the question of practices in the work of the Organizational Bureau," GAKhK P, f. 618, op. 1, 324, l. 176.

[88] "Stenographic text of the regional Komsomol activist meeting in Khabarovsk," January 4, 1939, GAKhK P, f. 618, op. 1, d. 321, l. 90.

[89] "Protocol of the I Khabarovsk regional conference of the Komsomol," February 11–15, 1939, GAKhK P, f. 617, op. 1, d. 3, l. 158. Similar sentiments are clear in the comments of another female employee of the Komsomol Kraikom: "The whole Komsomol organization wondered why Khetagurova was let go from work in the kraikom and sent to Army Headquarters to strengthen the work of the Headquarters. This is not right, Army Headquarters is strong enough, but Valentina Khetagurova is necessary for the Komsomol kraikom. She has shown herself to be a tactful employee." (Ibid., 201.)

9. "Valentina Khetagurova chatting with new arrivals, Khabarovsk, 1937"

mystique that Khetagurova cultivated among a more receptive audience of female activists in the region. It appears that an aura of belonging to a pantheon of female notables carried its own set of benefits and pressures that Khetagurova proved capable of handling.

"We were sent by you"

One of the most obvious messages embedded in the presentation of Khetagurova was that of a patroness of women in need.[90] Typical of this representation was a series of columns in a Far Eastern newspaper highlighting her care and attention to the needs of women and photographs such as figure 9, "Valentina Khetagurova chatting with new arrivals, Khabarovsk, 1937." Other female notables were also promoted as patrons of young women. As deputies to the Supreme Soviet, women such as Vinogradova and Fedorova received a large number of letters from

---

[90] When life proved unbearable in the Far East, some Khetagurovites apparently persevered because Khetagurova had told them what to expect and had suffered the same deprivations. For an example of this, see "Stenographic text of the Regional Khetagurovite Conference," September 17, 1938, Opryshko, GAKhK P, f. 618, op. 1, d. 325, l. 295.

10. "Valentina Khetagurova reading letters from constituents, 1938"

women.[91] Archives support the impression that in Khetagurova's case at least, they took to heart their role as interlopers on behalf of women.

Cultivating such a mystique had its price. Excessive stress on Khetagurova as a female leader brought with it pressure from Komsomol activists and Khetagurovites. Consumers of public culture did not see in her just a figurehead or simply a model for proper behavior. They expected her to take an active role in the undertaking that bore her name and to have a special understanding of young women's needs in the conditions of the Far East. Their letters illustrate strategies of supplication and the workings of patronage networks in the Soviet system. The photograph of her in figure 10, "Valentina Khetagurova reading letters from constituents," appeared not just in Far Eastern newspapers but in the national journal, *Rabotnitsa*.[92]

Migrants who wrote to Khetagurova to complain about their living and working conditions were prepared to remind her that, "[h]aving read your autobiography, we gave ourselves a firm word to follow in your footsteps to give all of our knowledge and work experience toward the improvement of life for Far Eastern laborers."[93] Many explicitly

[91] For an example of this, see Vinogradova, "Moi podrugi."
[92] *Rabotnitsa* 28 (October 1938), 9.
[93] Collective letter of complaint from the Krasnoiarsk rice sovkhoz, GAKhK P, f. 2, op. 1, d. 399, l. 114.

demanded that Khetagurova be more than a figurehead for the campaign they had joined. Khetagurovite Molchanova, dissatisfied with the treatment of Khetagurovites, took aim at Khetagurova herself. "What must be done? Here young women have noted that we have been called for this great deed and that Valia Khetagurova put out this call-up. But now we do not feel leadership, real leadership on the part of comrade Khetagurova."[94] Similar grumbling about Khetagurova's commitment to the Khetagurovites continued to surface in other venues.[95]

One group of young women underscored that Khetagurova was partially responsible for their present miserable circumstances. "We were sent by you to Zernozhivtrest who sent us to the Krasnoiarsk rice sovkhoz." Although there was a hint of recrimination and disappointment with their placement, the letter was couched in amicable terms. The women wrote to her "personally for advice and aid, as a dear friend." They pleaded, "Teach us how to be. We have reached complete despair, our only hope is with you and we are very sure that we will receive an answer and we will not be tossed onto the vagaries of fate and we will be helped to live and work."[96] There were supplicants who applied another kind of pressure by threatening suicide. "Valentina Simeonovna, we ask for some advice, what should we do? [If something does not change] there is no reason to continue living. We ask that you not refuse us a written reply, we turn to you like our own sister."[97] Khetagurova subsequently arranged better conditions. This was not a singular instance of her ability to act on behalf of Khetagurovites.[98] Photographs like figure 10 of Khetagurova reading letters from her admirers and constituents encouraged others to seek her intervention.

Some wrote baleful letters to their "Most Dearest and Kind" with full name and patronymic.[99] Others addressed her in the familiar "you," using "Valia" throughout the letter to underscore their closeness to her

---

[94] "Stenographic text of the regional Khetagurovite conference," September 17, 1938, Molchanova, GAKhK P, f. 618, op. 1, d. 325, l. 266.

[95] "Stenographic text of the meeting of regional Komsomol activists in Khabarovsk," January 4, 1939, GAKhK P, f. 618, op. 1, d. 321, l. 165.

[96] Collective letter of complaint from the Krasnoiarsk rice sovkhoz, GAKhK P, f. 2, op. 1, d. 399, l. 114.

[97] Letter of complaint from Mariia Panasenko, GAKhK P, f. 2, op. 6, d. 341, l. 128.

[98] Khetagurova's intervention is evident in the investigation and resolution of numerous cases. For instance, see the letter of complaint by Volodin and correspondence of officials in GAKhK P, f. 35, op. 1, d. 339, ll. 8–11.

[99] Collective letter of complaint from the Krasnoiarsk rice sovkhoz, GAKhK P, f. 2, op. 1, d. 399, l. 114. For another example of a letter to Khetagurova as a patron, see "Memorandums, letters addressed to the secretary of the Far Eastern Regional Komsomol on the question of work of Komsomol organizations: Collective letter of complaint from the Vostochny grain sovkhoz," September 19, 1938, GAKhK P, f. 618, op. 1, d. 326, l. 85.

and therefore their expectations that she would take an interest in their fates:

Valia! Do not be surprised that there has not been correspondence between us before, we have corresponded with other organizations. But now we have not received any answers and concrete directions or aid in response to our reports about outrageous goings-on and abnormalities. And now we have decided as a last hope to write to you. Valia, even though we did not want to worry you with our requests since as a deputy of the Supreme Soviet you have not a few cares and concerns, . . . we thought that you are still interested in your Khetagurovites and will not leave our letter without attention and you won't consider it laborious to answer . . . We are waiting, really waiting.[100]

Khetagurova reacted promptly. Shortly, an inspector traveled to the problem state farm (*sovkhoz*), confirmed the dire state of affairs, and forced administrators to address the women's concerns, providing proper clothing, shoes, and better living conditions.[101]

Emblematic of Khetagurova's response to such letters was a note she composed for a regional-level Komsomol sector to accompany another complaint about abhorrent conditions endured by Khetagurovites in a state grain farm (*zernosovkhoz*). "I am forwarding you a copy of a letter for investigation so that you can take immediate necessary measures. I ask to be informed of the measures you have taken. Deputy of the Supreme Soviet, V. Khetagurova."[102]

Other women wrote to ask for help in receiving alimony payments from wayward fathers. Belova, who came to the Far East as a Khetagurovite, explained that she had met and married another Komsomol member on one of her assignments. However, as soon as he found out she was pregnant, he accused her of "promiscuity to find a reason to deny paternity."[103] Now alone with a newborn, Belova was "helpless and unemployed." Khetagurova responded by helping her to find a "good" job in the Dal'Lag system, where she was given an apartment and her child placed in daycare. In other cases, Khetagurova helped women to obtain medical treatment they could not otherwise get.[104]

---

[100] *Ibid.*

[101] "Memorandums, letters addressed to the secretary of the Far Eastern Regional Komsomol on the question of work of Komsomol organizations: Report: On the investigation of letters from Khetagurovite combine drivers from the Vostochny grain sovkhoz," GAKhK P, f. 618, op. 1, d. 326, ll. 87–88.

[102] Note sent to the Peasant Sector of the Regional Komsomol Committee," October 7, 1938, GAKhK P, f. 618, op. 1, d. 326, l. 84.

[103] Letter written to Khetagurova in her capacity as a Deputy of the Supreme Soviet, GAKhK P, f. 618, op. 1, d. 326, l. 178.

[104] Letter of complaint written to Stalin from N. F. Savotina, GAKhK P, f. 35, op. 1, d. 357, l. 80.

On one occasion Khetagurova was able to affect the availability of merchandise on a significant scale. When she visited Komsomol'sk-na-Amure in 1937 and 1938, she performed the role of patron to young mothers.[105] Young families were desperate, as Komsomol'sk was utterly bereft of crèches, cribs, and children's clothing. The situation, well known in the Far East and long the subject of letters to Moscow officials, was temporarily ameliorated when "Khetagurova came to visit us" with a case of the much-needed merchandise. "And that was all that was done."[106]

Khetagurova's interest in women's issues and ability to act on behalf of women did not survive into the war years and post-war period. Sometime in 1940, Khetagurova's Far Eastern story came to an end, when her husband was reassigned to Moscow. Her departure from the Far East, after becoming so well known for inviting others to make it their permanent home, was clearly a source of some embarrassment. There is a note of guilt in her self-justifications. "Georgii Ivanovich . . . was a military man and he received orders from Moscow. I was, of course, his helpmate in struggle [*boevaia podruga*] and moreover the time had come for me to study. I entered the Promacademy."[107] Her status as a wife of an army officer had finally trumped her status as a Far Eastern celebrity.

When the German invasion began in June 1941, the Khetagurov family was separated.[108] The husband and wife saw little of each other for the next five years. Khetagurova continued to play a prominent role in the political departments of the military and in the apparatus of the Sovnarkom RSFSR, working as a member of a governmental administrative department coordinating assistance for families of service personnel. She also ran the Youth Fund for Orphans, distributing donations from young workers to subsidize thirty-three orphanages and ten clinics. Her articles appeared in the military's newspaper *Krasnaia zvezda*. In the last years of the war, she worked under Aleksei Kosygin, chairman of the Sovnarkom RSFSR. After the War, her celebrity status was eclipsed by the military exploits of her husband. Nevertheless, when groups of young people were dispatched with great fanfare to distant construction

---

[105] Before being nominated to become a deputy to the Supreme Soviet, Khetagurova had no connections to Komsomol'sk-na-Amure. Her appeal, though, drew a large contingent of young women to Komsomol'sk and then her duties as a Deputy meant that her name was closely connected with that city. For her appearances in Komsomol'sk, see the publicity surrounding the Supreme Soviet elections, "Vstrecha rabochikh zavoda No. 126 s tov. Khetagurovoi," *TK*, December 6, 1937.

[106] "Stenographic text of the Regional Khetagurovite Conference," September 15, 1938, Vochkova, GAKhK P, f. 618, op. 1, d. 325, l. 57.

[107] Khetagurova, "K 50-letiiu," 133. The examples of Lenin's wife, Nadezhda Krupskaia, and Voroshilov's wife, who worked as an auxiliary to the army during the Civil War, established the honorific appellation "helpmate in struggle" (*boevaia podruga*).

[108] G. Khetagurov, *Ispolnenie dolga*, 38.

projects in the 1970s and 1980s, Khetagurova appeared alongside other dignitaries to see them off.

In a conventional nod to humility, Khetagurova stressed in her later years that she was not exceptional: "I have lived a life indistinguishable from the life of the Soviet people."[109] But clearly she *was* different and she relished her unusual past. She obviously missed the days when she was a public figure and bemoaned that there was "[n]o way to return to the golden pre-war 1930s."[110] She still received correspondence from young people. Schoolchildren sent letters from De-Kastri with requests to help them write about their town. These faint echoes of her celebrity offered some comfort to the widow (Georgii had died in 1975 at the age of seventy-two). "Now that Georgii Ivanovich is not among us, I am not lonely. Letters . . . letters . . . letters . . . They say so much, warming the soul with the sense of eternal regeneration."[111]

The occasion of her death prompted a short column in the Far Eastern *Tikhookeanskaia zvezda*. A chairman of the regional soviet of Veterans of War and Labor, A. Kengurov, recalled his last meeting with Khetagurova in Moscow at the end of November 1991, while he was attending the All-Russian Conference of Veterans. Friends of hers in Komsomol'sk-na-Amure asked him to convey a few gifts. After "traditional hospitality, tea and bliny" Khetagurova asked about the city. She wanted to know how the elderly "first-builders" of Komsomol'sk were treated and wondered if its sixtieth anniversary would be celebrated. She complained about the lot of the elderly in Moscow and lamented that her party card was now a meaningless relic. Then she asked him to pass on her greetings to everyone who knew and remembered her at this "most difficult and anxious time."[112] Although she dreamed about visiting the Far East just once more, she never had the chance, passing away in January 1992.

Conclusion

It is easy to forget that Valentina Khetagurova was only twenty-three years old when she became a national celebrity. Although young, she was able to make an impression on those who mattered and was genuinely popular among Komsomol activists. She used to her advantage all the attributes

---

[109] Khetagurova, "K 50-letiiu," 133. Matt F. Oja discusses this trope in the memoir of Pasha Angelina in *From Krestianka to Udarnitsa*, 18.

[110] Valentina Khetagurova quoted in Aleksandr Kochukov, "Uroki Khetagurova," *Krasnaia zvezda*, May 8, 2003. Kochukov, a military journalist for *Krasnaia zvezda* in 2003, met Georgii and Valentina Khetagurova in 1975 when Georgii, apparently seriously ill, was working on his memoirs in a hospital.

[111] Khetagurova, "K 50-letiiu," 133.

[112] A. Kpengurov, "K pamiati Valentiny Khetagurovoi," *TZ*, January 24, 1992.

entitling her to full membership of the Soviet collective: a working-class and Komsomol pedigree, an exotic married name, and a record illustrative of an eagerness to sacrifice herself in the name of the Motherland.

While campaigns to mobilize workers and heroic exploits were common, none of the well-known campaigns carried the name of a woman before or after Khetagurova arrived from the taiga. She had become a modern Soviet heroine for young women who sought adventures and recognition for their labors and activism. Those who migrated operated under the conviction that a prominent person like Khetagurova was more than just a spokesperson. Rather, they saw in her a female patron who understood their needs. Khetagurova responded to this pressure by getting involved when she could. She was not an inert archetype publicized by the propaganda establishment for its own ends. She took advantage of the opportunities available and inserted her own "personality" into the making of a Soviet heroine.

In addition, Khetagurova presented a model of a successful marriage. She was not a dependent or submissive appendage. Rather, driven by her own ideals, she appeared as the partner of Georgii Khetagurov, an exemplary "helpmate in struggle." Whether those who followed her call-up could reproduce such relationships became a topic of great concern. We will never know what she thought about the horrendous realities of life on the frontier for hundreds of thousands working on all those "grand projects." Nor is it clear how close her husband and their family came to being one of those prisoners, like so many Red Army officers in that era. It might have been a matter of luck.

The image of a woman who could do everything but asked for little in return was dramatically reinforced by events in the 1940s. During World War II, women of her generation volunteered for active duty, fought in partisan units, carried the tremendous burdens of the home front, and cared for the wounded men who returned from battle. Afterwards, they helped to rebuild the ravaged country. Khetagurova also belonged to a generation that, having survived the "golden" 1930s and the war, lived to see a lifetime's work destroyed and long-held ideals debased. She died in the early 1990s along with the Soviet empire she had played a notable role in building.

4   "Envy for everything heroic": women volunteering for the frontier[1]

The Far Eastern landscape – pristine, primordial, and on a permanent war footing – functioned as a congenial backdrop for patriotic fantasies. Events and conditions along the borders of the Soviet Union attained increasingly greater prominence as topics in speeches, articles, and editorials in newspapers and as subjects of film, literature, and song in the late 1930s.[2] Soviet citizens arrived with notions of the region that they had picked up from official propaganda and from popular beliefs about Siberia and its natural world.[3] It was in this period between 1936 and 1939 that the Soviet Far East came to play a dominant role as a stage for dramatizing threats to national integrity and as a seedbed for a crop of heralded patriots who struggled against a chaotic natural world while participating directly in securing Soviet territorial claims. Such heroes either contributed to border defenses or fortified the nation's might by their very presence in a forbidding environment where they endowed former culturally and ideologically marginal spaces with elements of the Soviet civilization-building project.[4]

Hundreds of thousands volunteered for migration in response to such publicity. Why? What were the cultural and emotive dynamics motivating Soviet voluntary migrants, and young women in particular, to embark for a precarious life thousands of miles from home? How did prospects of frontier life structure women's self-image and expectations?

Documents produced for and by those who participated in this migration process – including official publicity materials, letters, and memoirs

---

[1] A version of this chapter appears as "'Those Who Hurry to the Far East': Readers, Dreamers and Volunteers," in Breyfogle, Schrader, and Sunderland (eds.), *Peopling the Russian Periphery*, 213–237.

[2] For more on this, see Emma Widdis, *Visions of a New Land: Soviet Film from the Revolution to the Second World War* (New Haven: Yale University Press, 2003).

[3] For images of Siberia in the pre-revolutionary period, see James R. Gibson, "Paradoxical Perceptions of Siberia: Patrician and Plebeian Images up to the Mid-1800s," in Diment and Slezkine (eds.), *Between Heaven and Hell*, 67–93.

[4] Although forced labor was widely exploited in the area, the laborers were not expected to be the first line of defense in case of war or to serve as the backbone of long-term demographic growth.

of settlers – reveal gendered aspects of Stalinism on the frontiers of empire. In addition, letters written in response to mobilization campaigns lend themselves to an examination of reader reception and a better understanding of how men and women digested official messages and deployed them in their displays of patriotism.

Despite or perhaps because of the Far East's aura of danger and challenge, young women were determined to play a role in the construction of a new Motherland and the defense of the nation. The prospect of impending war with the Japanese, especially on a distant frontier known for its shortage of women, drew attention to women's roles in the event of full-scale mobilization. Women's labor in the workforce and the military appeared indispensable for a nation at war. Even if women were not called to the front, they could imagine themselves as a ready reserve trained and available to replace men there if needed. After all, Valentina Khetagurova held out the prospect of "honorable" service for women. In her appeal she asked her readers whether they wanted to "be among the first to defend our great Motherland, the way it was defended by the Far Eastern Bolsheviks and partisans in the memorable 1920s?" Those who answered yes would join in the "We" who were going to "permanently knock out our enemies' cravings for our Soviet Socialist Far East."[5]

Women's possible contribution in the event of total war became an arsenal in the women's demands for entry into previously all-male spheres. The dream of frontier exploits also effectively struck a chord among young women because it was one of the few spaces where womanly virtues seemed to be a decisive force in history and in revolutionary struggles against nature and enemies. Yet many of those who went had wildly distorted expectations and the reality they found was a disappointment: once the migrants arrived, they quickly discovered that the Far East would indeed test their resolve, but not in the way they had imagined.

When the *Columbus* came to Komsomol'sk

All public appeals for resettlement emphasized that migrants should come out of a sense of patriotic duty in order to assist in the exploitation of natural resources for the good of the nation. Although the state maintained and periodically adjusted material incentives (*l'goty*) to facilitate permanent settlement, migrants who came only in search of better pay were potentially less desirable and possibly politically suspect. Promotional literature avoided discussions of monetary gain in part because they were reminiscent of pre-revolutionary resettlement campaigns that were

---

[5] Valentina Khetagurova, "Priezzhaite k nam na Dal'nii Vostok!," *KP*, February 5, 1937.

squarely based on promises of self-enrichment for enterprising peasants and merchants. On a more practical level, in the 1930s financial inducements did not adequately compensate migrants for the abysmal living conditions they found on the frontier. The lack of goods, a catastrophic housing shortage, and the high cost of living in the Far East offset most gains in salaries and benefits. Moreover, material rewards for resettlement were offered to only a limited number of highly skilled workers and professionals and few headed to the extreme northern regions of the Far East where special incentives were in effect in any case. Those who went to the region strictly in search of better pay quickly discovered the inadequacy of such incentives and often left at the first opportunity.

A predetermined scheme for explaining the need for resettlement and for writing about the Far East was always at work in promotional literature. When necessary, the concepts informing it were reshuffled to fit the relevant audience, but they did not alter significantly between 1936 and 1939. *Pravda*'s November 11, 1936 issue dedicated to the Far East presented these tropes most fully. Its articles are telling illustrations of the mix between patriotic culture and frontier mythologies commonly encountered by Soviet readers.

The leading editorial piece took great pains to differentiate the Bolsheviks' rights of possession and exploitation from the claims of Asian neighbors and capitalist predecessors. The Far East was presented as an empty land where nature beckoned for a ruler. Although themes of civilizing missions existed in occasional articles about the relatively small number of native people living in the area, literature promoting resettlement generally glossed over their existence. The empty land served as the dramatic canvas where Bolsheviks triumphed in a clash of civilizations. "Before the Bolshevik Revolution, capitalists – both native and foreign – were only hunters here. They took only what was strewn around."[6] According to this logic, capitalists and all others represented a lower level of human evolution and as hunters and gatherers they forfeited their right of possession by their lack of industriousness. Moreover, "[c]apitalists lacked the will and technology" to exploit natural resources. The Bolsheviks, on the other hand, had "a deeper feeling for the region" and dispelled its undeserved reputation as a "place of death" perpetuated by their possibly effete and certainly fainthearted predecessors. *Pravda*'s editors concluded that "[t]he Bolsheviks, armed with technology and culture, were the first real discoverers of the Far East and thus its rightful masters [*khoziaeva*]."[7]

The Japanese, their activities in Manchuria, and their predatory nature were recurrent themes in publicity soliciting migration to the Soviet–Manchurian border. Far Eastern commanders reported to *Pravda*'s

---

[6] "Forpost sotsializma na Vostoke," *Pravda*, November 11, 1936.   [7] *Ibid.*

readers that the Japanese were well on their way to establishing a Manchurian infrastructure with the intention of using it as "a platform for war against the Soviet Union."[8] Indeed, part of the appeal of the Far East was that it was a geographic space that fostered a direct and visceral sense of competition with Japanese rivals. Those who stood on the banks of the Amur River, in the city of Blagoveshchensk, could observe Japanese troops and fortifications across the water with the naked eye. Thus an ordinary person could measure up "the power in development and culture of the capitalist world with the socialist world, and to be one of the builders in the Far East is to be a leading soldier of a new society on one of the most important sectors of the front."[9]

Soviet citizens were summoned to observe the predatory essence of Japanese militarism and the natural world on the "other" side. National boundaries supposedly coincided with stark differences in fauna and flora. Yellow tinged the enemy landscape. "The Manchurian side has thick low bushes, egg-yellow flowers cover its steep cliffs; tiny fields reach to the river bank. Here is the settlement of Japanese reservists – dusty, cheerless, with gray metal roofs."[10] Readers could have easily picked up repeated references to "yellow" as a subtle echo of "Yellow Peril" anxieties so common in pre-revolutionary discourses in reference to the region's Asian neighbors, but no longer fit to print in their most brazen form in Soviet-era publications.

Journalists employed metaphors from Russian folk tales in appeals for resettlement and in descriptions of the frontier. Magic keys, enchanted taigas, fantastic natural treasure troves, and mighty *bogatyri* (mythical Russian warrior-knights) populated the gallery of mottoes about the Far East under Bolshevik rule. Although late to join the Soviet Union because of the prolonged Civil War and Japanese occupation of the region, the Far East "would make up for this tardiness with *bogatyr'*-like growth." Bolsheviks were the true masters of the area because they brought with them "socialism, the enchanted key to the region's treasures." Having brought this magic key to the wilderness, the new masters were the first to really unlock its "innumerable riches." Once "the spell of backwardness" was dispersed by its Bolshevik *khoziaeva*, "the taiga receded . . . Just like in a fairy tale, roads and railroads now run across bottomless marshes and places where no human had ever set foot."[11]

[8] L. Aronshtam, "Osobaia Krasnoznamennaia," *Pravda*, November 11, 1936.
[9] D. Zaslavskii, "Na Tikhom okeane," *Pravda*, November 11, 1936.
[10] B. Lapin and Z. Khatsrevin, "Vverkh po Amuru. Putevye zametki," *Pravda*, June 25, 1939.
[11] "Forpost sotsializma na Vostoke."

Throughout this period, films set in the Far East reiterated the themes outlined in newspaper coverage. The Arctic and the Far East served as "key heroic spaces" in the increasingly common adventure-frontier films of the Stalin era.[12] Intrepid male partisans and keen-eyed border guards joined forces with burly working men to tame the wilderness on the silver screen. These images of powerful *bogatyri*, whether in the guise of border guards or of unflinching Arctic explorers, were representations of the Far East that left no room for archetypes of female heroism. If one took the *bogatyr'* theme to its logical conclusion, women could have no place in magical spaces because in Russian fairy tales they never accompanied men on their quests. Rather, the maiden sat wistfully in a tower awaiting liberation by her knight. However, by the late 1930s the practical necessity of populating the region dictated the promotion of Khetagurova to carve out at least a niche for women in frontier myths and to capture women's imagination. The frontier of Stalinism, the likely frontline of a global conflict, needed female "[s]teel workers and welders, teachers and draftswomen, typists and accountants, clerks and performers, everything in the right proportion."[13]

The immediacy of the threat from the Japanese created an arena in the Far East where women could defend the Motherland.[14] The very first contingent of young women to go to the Far East consisted of several dozen young women slated for work for the Far Eastern procurator's office in Khabarovsk. As they prepared to depart from Moscow, they met privately with the Chief Procurator of the USSR, Andrei Vyshinskii, who told them that as they were going to the Far East they had to be extra careful, because in this region "[c]onditions are especially difficult, where, more so than any other place, we have dealings with an enemy that is especially practiced in the art of deceit and in harming Soviet power." They should also expect a particularly large number of "spies, diversionists, [and] White Army officers" who "jumped" across Soviet borders.[15]

---

[12] Emma Widdis, "Borders: The Aesthetic of Conquest in Soviet Cinema of the 1930s," *Journal of European Studies* 30:4 (December, 2000), 405.

[13] *Ibid.*

[14] It is worth noting that Karen Petrone found that confrontations with the Japanese in the Far East offered both Tsarist and Soviet-era publicists platforms for elaborating upon "military-heroic masculinity." See Petrone, "Masculinity and Heroism in Imperial and Soviet Military-Patriotic Cultures," in Barbara Evans Clements, Rebecca Friedman, and Dan Healey (eds.), *Russian Masculinities in History and Culture* (New York: Palgrave, 2002), 172–193.

[15] "Speech of Procurator of the USSR A. Ia. Vyshinskii at the meeting with young women assigned to investigative work in the Far East," April 17, 1937, GA RF, f. 8131, op. 14, d. 5, l. 2.

Women and frontier landscapes

In publicity aimed at young men and women, the frontiers were billed as extraordinary spaces for personal growth and character formation, where "conditions [were] especially conducive to the education of strong, hard characters, and to fortifying the will."[16] The natural bounty of the region demanded special reverence and required special dedication from people who eschewed avarice and the "long ruble." Only those truly loyal to their Motherland and their professions were capable of understanding the region and becoming its masters. Personal growth was paired with conquests of a natural world that was at once fascinating and threatening. "Those who come here are the sort interested in the struggle for socialism in new, unique conditions, those who want to open up their own personal horizons and those who are bewitched by ocean storms."[17]

Khetagurova certainly evoked images of men versus nature to underscore the sense of drama and excitement for those willing to test their resolve and prove their fealty:

By the will of our Motherland and our party, cities and settlements are now being created. Roads are being laid. Indestructible concrete strongholds – fortresses of socialism – are rising on the Pacific coast in the darkest woods, where until recently roamed only Manchurian deer, bears, and tigers. Here we are building, creating in the name of socialism, a new life in the region that odious killers and spies from the anti-Soviet Trotskyite gang tried to sell to the Japanese militarists, in this land, against which our Far Eastern enemies have a grudge. It is difficult to write about all of this grand, exciting work. One has to be a poet or artist for this.[18]

Khetagurova's letter carefully detailed the role of a womanly touch in transforming rugged woods into resplendent outposts of Soviet civilization. She explained that women's arrival made possible the formation of families and introduced familiar comforts such as clean sheets and curtains into the disarray of settlement life. Women's labor literally and symbolically "filled in" the cracks and produced homes and home life. "At first many among us – workers and specialists – lived in lean-tos and unfinished houses. There was not enough labor power and so we women collected moss to fill in the cracks and poured ash on the roofs, and finished constructing the houses."[19]

Khetagurova stressed that because this region was untouched, those who wished to see the immediate fruits of their labors could be readily satisfied. "It is gladdening to think and know that this recently wild

---

[16] Zaslavskii, "Na Tikhom okeane."   [17] *Ibid.*
[18] Khetagurova, "Priezzhaite k nam!"   [19] *Ibid.*

and barren frontier is being transformed into one of the marvelous corners of our wonderful country by the strength of our own hands."[20] She described how a collection of unfinished structures became quintessential models of Soviet urban *kulturnost'* (cultured behavior). Electric lights – the unmistakable mark of Soviet progress – twinkled along the coastline now that both sexes worked in unison to claim the taiga. She also enumerated the amenities created through the settlers' efforts: schools, water mains and sports arenas. Here symbolic connections between womanhood and socially stabilizing elements emerge in frontier mythology as the ultimate linchpins of successful settlement and frontier defense.

The women in her settlement were always busy with activities of direct relevance to national priorities, and everyone would "be of use in case of war. If necessary we can find nurses, communications workers, radio operators and machine gunners among them. Many of our young women have become avid hunters." Participation in the defense of Soviet civilization was not the only reward of frontier life. Breathtaking landscapes were the backdrop for embryonic frontier societies where relationships were warmer and collective life was richer. Khetagurova reassured her readers that

[h]ere in the struggle with nature, we discover our best qualities. Here we know how to really help a comrade, to be a friend in happy and troubled times. Difficulties bring us together . . . I am not calling on you to renounce life . . . Young women bring into this severe and often coarse life things that ennoble and lift up people, inspiring them to new heroic deeds. But remember, we are only calling brave, decisive people who are not afraid of difficulties . . . Everything that is difficult, but needed for our Motherland, is honorable.[21]

The appeal to women made in promotional literature such as Khetagurova's letter held out the possibility of entry into heroic realms but in gendered terms. Khetagurova claimed that her work in the taiga was more difficult and perhaps more meaningful than the work of women in other regions.[22] Women's labor on the frontier beyond the realms of production appeared as anything but the irrelevant daily drudgery of housekeeping. Their activities, whether at home or as voluntary workers in communal institutions, were lauded as the most visible expression of women as "a second army" standing in the path of invaders. Khetagurova reasoned that "[l]ads of course can cut down trees, build roads. But only women's hands can make the region really lived in. Life runs somehow superficially, in a suitcase mood, if caring hands, the cheerful laughter of

---

[20] *Ibid.*   [21] *Ibid.*
[22] This sentiment was later repeated by those who came as Khe-tagurovites. See Khetagurova quoted in *Vsesoiuznoe soveshchanie* . . . *RKKA*, 174.

young women, and the eyes of a caretaker are missing."[23] A chance to publicly display commitment to belonging and good citizenship by self-lessly employing their "women's hands" proved to be an effective draw for female volunteers.

Many of the cinematic and press representations of frontier life also tried to mirror frontiersmen from other historical contexts. Soviet exploration myths were often consciously patterned on interpretations of American experiences. The "discovery" of America and Western adventure stories à la Jack London were familiar to and extremely popular with Russian readers and resurfaced in narratives about Soviet settlement life.[24] Europeans and Americans had come to imagine the exploration of the far north as a particularly masculine undertaking because of "the physical duress involved in the conquest of the Arctic and because exploring was regarded as the conquest of virgin territory."[25] And in a similar vein, just as the themes of masculine endurance versus the ravages of a hostile natural world dominated Western tropes about the Arctic, so it was among ordinary Soviets, who idolized Soviet Arctic male daredevils and aviators.[26]

The urge to recreate motifs of discovery in the Far East was obvious to the first contingent of young people who came to build what would become Komsomol'sk-na-Amure in 1932. They sailed to their destination on the riverboat *Columbus*, a detail that was not forgotten by the makers of the popular 1938 film *Komsomol'sk*.[27] The film's main female protagonist, Natasha, pens a letter to the young women of the Soviet Union inviting them to join her in building the city of youth in the taiga, in a conscious reference to the Khetagurovite campaign.[28] After years of "imagining" Siberia and the Far East as rugged masculine adventure zones, newspaper coverage of the Khetagurovites, films like *Komsomol'sk*

---

[23] Valentina Khetagurova, "Zdravstvui, iunost' 30-kh!," *Rabotnitsa* 8 (1967). Quoted in Dubinina, *Ty pozovi, Dal'nii Vostok!*, 73.

[24] For more on reading habits and the popularity of Jack London, see Dobrenko, *The Making of the State Reader.*

[25] Linda Bergmann, "Women Against a Background of White: The Representation of Self and Nature in Women's Arctic Narratives," *American Studies* 34:2 (Fall, 1993), 53.

[26] See John McCannon, "Positive Heroes at the Pole: Celebrity Status, Socialist-Realist Ideals and the Soviet Myth of the Arctic, 1932–1939," *Russian Review* 56:3 (July 1997), 346–365.

[27] A. V. Kiparenko, "Na stroitel'stve goroda iunosti," in A. V. Artiukhina et al. (eds.), *Uchastnitsy velikogo zasedaniia* (Moscow: Gos. Politizdat, 1962), 145–156.

[28] The film director Sergei Gerasimov explained the connection in "Fil'm *Komsomol'sk* gotov," *TZ*, April 4, 1938. The role of women in the plot received attention in other publications, see N. Likhobabin, "Kino *Komsomol'sk*," *TZ*, June 15, 1938. For a discussion of gender and frontier films in other historical contexts, see Wendy Webster, "Domesticating the Frontier: Gender, Empire and Adventure Landscapes in British Cinema, 1945–1959," *Gender & History* 15:1 (2003), 85–107.

and *Gal with a Personality* (*Devushka s kharakterom*) (1939) were foregrounding female characters. Nevertheless, women's representations in such films and the publicity surrounding Khetagurova did not alter the terms used to describe the mission of Soviet power in the Far East or the gender of its possessors. Although women and their valuable contribution were central elements in the plot of *Komsomol'sk*, its theme song, "March of the Komsomol," turned to the Far East's natural elements and decreed that it was time to "Submit! Your master [*khoziaen*] has come!" The reiteration of the word *khoziain* gave a particularly masculine flavor to the imagery of frontier settlement, since it meant not only master of the house, or boss, but also husband and man.[29]

Despite some of the obvious similarities with Western tropes, there were important differences shaping the collective imagination about Soviet frontier life. Siberia and Far Eastern regions had reputations as simultaneously zones of freedom from the intrusion of the state and dangerous zones teeming with criminals and penal colonies. The darker themes competed with the motifs that promised autonomy and renewal until the 1930s. Paradoxically, all public discussion of the region as a place of punishment disappeared at the same time as the NKVD exponentially expanded its empire of camps. By the mid-1930s, the harsh natural worlds of Siberia and the Far East were presented unambiguously as testing grounds in which to prove one's stamina born out of revolutionary commitment rather than as places of suffering or untrammeled freedom from the state.

The content of gender ideology in Soviet exploration and settlement narratives also departs from important components of Western experiences. First, the role of women differed because the accumulation of wealth and property, and other inducements for mass participation in expansion and settlement in other territories, were not supposed to be central elements in this Soviet patriotic migratory process. In literature such as Vera Ketlinskaia's 1938 novel *Courage* (*Muzhestvo*) (depicting the first builders of Komsomol'sk), Soviet women embarked for distant lands to demonstrate their resolve, strength, and commitment to the nation rather than as companions of pioneering men or to improve their material circumstances. Second, Russian and Soviet ideals of womanhood exalted women's self-abnegation for the collective good. Highly dramatic acts of self-denial were especially respected. Khetagurova garnered the national spotlight after she volunteered to abandon cosmopolitan Leningrad to

---

[29] A striking shortage of women in Komsomol'sk-na-Amure received attention in the coverage of the city's five-year anniversary in January 1937. See V. Malev, Iu. Zhukov, L. Los' et al., "Komsomol'sk segodnia. O iunom gorode, psevdoromantike i nasushchnykh potrebnostiakh 'Taezhnoi stolitsy,'" *KP*, January 14, 1937.

live in a remote forest where she faced scurvy and predatory wildlife. Her public appeal to encourage young women's migration was replete with stories of her subsequent life on the frontier where she labored self-lessly in a struggle against low morale and an unforgiving natural world to provide sustenance for garrisoned troops. These ingredients of Soviet gender ideology, unlike motives that might have pulled women in other national contexts to the peripheries, propelled young women's enthusi-asm for this venture and shaped their sense of accomplishment and social worth.

Khetagurova's life story, which made up the bulk of her famous letter, was not one commonly found in official narratives about women's lives. She was not a woman who had been oppressed or illiterate. Although the piece was probably substantially produced by the editorial staff of *Komsomol'skaia pravda*, Khetagurova's letter told the story of adaptation from the perspective of a woman who acted on her own to take advantage of a chance to travel to an exotic land. Her adventure story also alluded to the peripheral status of women in revolutionary and frontier mytholo-gies by positioning them as envious observers. Khetagurova remarked that "Soviet young women are ruled by a great envy, envy for every-thing heroic."[30] When she first volunteered to go, unsympathetic men in authority tried to keep her from going because it was "no place" for a young woman. Almost unable to fulfill her fantasy of living in the taiga because she was a woman, Khetagurova now pronounced that women were finally welcome in the geographic space of the Far East and by extension into the grandiose epic of Soviet history.

Women like Khetagurova ultimately found that there was a price to pay for claiming recognition in nation-building projects based on a spe-cific feminine contribution. Soviet women were not the first to confront this dilemma. A wide body of literature on women's participation in expansionist projects in other historical contexts illustrates how gendered ideology punctuated and structured these undertakings.[31] For instance, according to historian Catherine Cavanaugh, suffragists construed Cana-dian women's participation in settlement as a potential avenue toward political equality. They "saw women's settlement work as the basis of their claim to a voice in the future of the West."[32] However, women's bid for public authority based on their role in a "pioneering partner-ship" also "had the effect of reinforcing dominant gender conventions,"

---

[30] Khetagurova, "Priezzhaite k nam!"
[31] For examples, see Montrose, "The Work of Gender in the Discourse of Discovery," 1–41.
[32] Catherine Cavanaugh, "'No Place for a Woman': Engendering Western Canadian Set-tlement," *Western Historical Quarterly* 28 (Winter 1997), 509.

because they stressed the specificity of their feminine contributions in a masculine project.[33]

Similarly, women's claims to their rightful place alongside men in Soviet civilization-building projects emphasized the uniqueness of women's contributions and thus could likewise potentially reinforce gender boundaries. However, Soviet women like the Khetagurovites pushed those boundaries by appropriating the omnipresent Stalinist emphasis on the inevitability of a total global conflagration. Unaware of any likely reversal of policy should war break out, they continued to expect and sometimes demand equality and visibility because of women's indispensability as trained workers, professionals, and potential fighters in times of war.

Although thousands of migrants traveled to the Far East in this period, the sight of single young women embarking for the frontier received the most coverage and appeared most curious. Once volunteers surfaced in response to Khetagurova's appeal, Soviet journalists did not hesitate to publicize their example as yet another sign of socialist triumph. A column on the front page of *Komsomol'skaia pravda* in April 1937 aimed at publicizing the success of the Khetagurovite call-up also attempted to distinguish this migratory process from those in capitalist countries. The author underscored the special significance of spatial movement for young women. While migration in capitalist countries was a product of "unemployment, hunger and cold, boundless sacred love for their mighty socialist Motherland" propelled Soviet migrants to the Far East.[34] Examples of whole families, who had good jobs in good conditions but were moving to the Far East, "where difficulties and deprivations awaited them," served as proof that only the most "noble" motivations explained such decisions.

Women's resolve to "move to the borderland with Manchuria" was placed in explicit contrast with the fate of Japanese women. This theme was encouraged to take on sensational overtones by the use of a letter from a Japanese farmer supposedly published by a Japanese news service and cited by *Komsomol'skaia pravda*. In the excerpt presented to Soviet readers, the Japanese farmer Kisaragi was offering to sell his sixteen-year-old daughter Khanae. As he explained, "Life is so difficult that it is impossible to continue in this way . . . She cried a great deal but has now agreed. She does not need luxuries. If necessary, send her to Formosa or to Manchuria. Save our home!"[35]

The fate of the Japanese farmer's daughter, forced by hunger "into a public house in Manchuria," afforded the polar opposite of the voluntarism of Soviet young women streaming to the other side of the

---

[33] *Ibid.*, 506.   [34] "Molodye patriotki svoei rodiny," *KP*, April 11, 1937.   [35] *Ibid.*

border. Just in case the lesson was not clear enough, the column ended with yet another exemplary letter from young women wishing to go to the Far East and an invocation to readers:

Contrast this with the wholly limitless grief and profound drama in the letter of the Japanese farmer we introduced to you. It is hard to find a more striking contrast for a graphic illustration of the state of affairs in the two worlds. The fate of a sixteen-year-old Japanese girl – this is the fate of all children of laborers in the capitalist world. The noble urge of young women patriots traveling to the Far East on the call-up of Khetagurova – these are the dreams and thoughts of the glorious and fortunate daughters of the socialist Motherland.[36]

The voluntary spatial mobility of Khetagurovites appeared in favorable contrast with the lives of contemporary women in Japan and in a temporal contrast with the supposed immobility of Russian women in the pre-revolutionary period. In a column several weeks later, a correspondent quoted from a young woman thrilled to be traveling where she was "needed. Me, a small, inconspicuous person, I am going to do a great deed. They wait for me! Just think of how great that is!"[37] Rejecting her family's long urban history, the young woman repudiated the notion that the world revolved around Moscow:

I want to see other cities, rivers, forests and mountains. I want to look into all the corners of my Motherland. My mother lived all of her life in Moscow; my granny was born and died in a house within the gates of Moscow, not having seen more than one city. Life, after all, is just too short to sit for years on end in one spot on a huge geographic map.[38]

Photographs of new migrants in dramatic natural settings, in warm collectives of like-minded young people, or in jobs previously associated with rugged frontiers worked to attract new waves of volunteers throughout 1937 and 1938. For examples, see figure 11, "Fishing", figure 12, "Departing for Komsomol'sk", 1937, and figure 13, "Finally on Sakhalin Island," 1937.

"I just read the newspaper"

Hundreds of thousands of people willing to move across the Eurasian continent stood behind the propaganda campaign on the pages of *Komsomol'skaia pravda*. They labored to write enthusiastic letters, sometimes more than once, volunteering to become Far Easterners. Thousands

---

[36] *Ibid.*   [37] *Ibid.*   [38] *Ibid.*

11. "Fishing"
Khetagurovite Kupeshkina at the Fish Trust of Vladivostok, 1937.

boarded eastbound trains to prove their loyalty and to explore heroic possibilities on the frontier. According to *Tikhookeanskaia zvezda*, in March
and April 1937 more than 4,000 young female Muscovites responded to
Khetagurova's call-up and mobbed the offices of the selection committee. The claim that the offices were mobbed was not an invention of the
propaganda establishment: those who later wrote memoirs about their
experiences as Khetagurovites also recalled the exceedingly large number of young women crowding the Moscow offices of the Far Eastern
representatives that spring.

Although the campaign was initially aimed at women, men disregarded
this and applied to become Khetagurovites as well. Some were eventually
accepted into the program. Subsequently, a male participant was called a

12. "Departing for Komsomol'sk, 1937"
Four women leaving Khabarovsk and heading to Komsomol'sk-na-
Amure on the riverboat *Chicherin*, 1937.

Khetagurovets and a female a Khetagurovka. The men's failure to notice
that the program was meant for women provides an opportunity to compare responses from men and women to a distinct promotional campaign
with overt gender connotations.

Letters from volunteers and memoirs reveal some of the ways in which
volunteers digested the themes described above. What they selected to
note or remember about their decision to migrate offers a glimpse into the
public's imagination about the Far East and the role women expected to
play in Soviet frontier life. Of course, these sources do not offer unmedi-
ated access to the migrants' motivations and experiences; even so, they are
still valuable indicators of the durability of formative perceptions. Certain
themes that appeared in the 1930s reappeared almost unaltered in the
women's memoirs forty years later. These memoirs also indicate something about the personalities most likely to find life in the Far East attractive. They reveal commonly held aspirations among this female cohort to
position themselves in the most public forums where they could display
their standing as pivotal agents in securing Soviet power.

Letters from resettlement applicants in the 1930s contained information on age, education, work history, and sometimes statements of preference for future work and duties on the frontier. Single women, women

13. "Finally on Sakhalin Island"
Group of new arrivals in Okha, Sakhalin Island, 1937. The woman in a polka-dot dress with white collar is a pioneer leader, Evdokia Proletarskaia.

with children, single men, and men writing on behalf of their families sent inquiries. A large proportion of correspondents came from towns (of all sizes) in Ukraine, Belorussia, and central Russia. Statistics on those who eventually arrived as Khetagurovites in 1937 and 1938 support the impression that although most applicants were under the age of forty, there was no rigid uniformity among them in terms of region of origin, profession, and party or Komsomol membership.[39] Nevertheless, significant patterns emerged. About one-third of both men and women were currently or had once been propagandists and organizers, either in their workplace or in their military regiments. Some of the women, in their thirties, had experience in Communist party zhenotdely and Soviet sectors for work among women. Many of the older women had worked as orphanage administrators. A significant proportion of male respondents had a background in journalism or had been factory newspaper correspondents (*rabkory*) or village correspondents (*sel'kory*). There is no indication in the archival record of whether these letter writers were eventually selected for migration, or their subsequent fate.

[39] "Report: On the status of youth of the Khetagurovite call-up," March 20, 1938, GAKhK, P, f. 2, op 6, d. 358, l. 1.

Letter writers did not apply on a soon-forgotten whim. There are many instances in which applicants indicated that they had applied before but were rejected or never received a reply. Yet they continued to inquire and reapply by post and telegram at considerable personal expense. Typical of this persistence were three female employees of the Southern Ural Railroad. Because they "burned with desire to work in the Far East stirred by the appeal of Valentina Khetagurova," they refused to accept numerous rejections from the Khetagurovite Committee.[40] The Khabarovsk archive retained their telegram, which reiterated their suitability and right to participate. A married couple were so eager to be accepted that they enclosed an extra sheet of blank paper and a stamped envelope in their correspondence with the Khabarovsk regional Communist Party Committee to expedite their invitation.[41]

Readers of promotional materials about the Far East understood such texts as categorical invitations to participate in revolutionary acts. Keenness to perform heroic deeds and exaggerated emotions were typical sentiments in letters. After reading *Muzhestvo*, with its story of the building of Komsomol'sk-na-Amure by resilient male and female Komsomol members, Ketlinskaia's readers, like Vera Nikitkina, wrote asking for advice on how to become a Khetagurovite.[42] The tone and urgency of Nikitkina's letter underscores the emotional allure of migrating to a place where she could feel useful:

I have wanted to go to the Far East for a long time in response to the call of Valentina Khetagurova . . . I thought that I would not be useful there, but now after reading this book [*Muzhestvo*] I think that even I could be of use . . . I ask you to write to me and tell me if I can go there and how to get there and please do not deny this to me. I want to get to Komsomol'sk so much.[43]

On the whole, though, women tended to be laconic in their letters of application, often offering only vague reasons for their enthusiasm. Typically, women like Tatiana Sharaia, from the Chernigov oblast of Ukraine, explained merely that she "already had a long-term desire to resettle for permanent residence and work in the Far East."[44] Igalkina, a 22-year-old

[40] They addressed their letter to the First Secretary "personally." Letter from Fedorova, Gladkova, and Ryzhnikova, April 7, 1939, GAKhK, P, f. 35, op. 1, d. 185, l. 160.

[41] Letter from Dodoka and Svistula, March 1939, GAKhK P, f. 35, op. 1, d. 185, l. 296.

[42] Letters to Ketlinskaia are in Rossiiskii gosudarstvennyi arkhiv literatury i iskusstva, RGALI, f. 2816, op. 1, d. 362–364. For a discussion of women writers, the portrayal of women, and V. Ketlinskaia in the 1930s, see Rosalind Marsh, "Women Writers of the 1930s: Conformity or Subversion?," in Melanie Ilic (ed.), *Women in the Stalin Era* (New York: Palgrave, 2001), 173–191.

[43] Letter from Vera Nikitkina, Vol'nogorsk village collective farm (sel'kolkhoz), RGALI, f. 2816, op. 1, d. 363, ll. 73–73ob.

[44] Letter from T. Sharaia, May 1939, GAKhK P, f. 35, op. 1, d. 339, l. 272.

from the Smolensk oblast, volunteered because "all the time I notice in newspapers interesting things about our beloved Motherland. Especially interesting to me is life in the Far East."[45]

Women were also more candid than men about mundane personal reasons to relocate. Selezneva, thirty-seven, volunteered for "work of any kind" in the Far East. She explained that "[h]ere I have nothing to hold me. I have no family." Press accounts compelled her to "give over all of [my] strength and energy for the Far East."[46] Khatukhina sent two different letters to the Khetagurovite Committee. In one letter she stressed that she wanted to move to the Far East to extricate herself from some unspecified family circumstance and to follow her acquaintances who had recently moved to Komsomol'sk-na-Amure.[47] Molchanova wished to live in Komsomol'sk and "this desire was especially strong" because she had a "good comrade serving in Komsomol'sk in the Red Army." She listed her attributes as a member of her Komsomol cell, an assistant to the First Secretary, and an avid sportswoman.[48] "I have a great desire to enter nursing courses, over there I can probably do so," wrote Valentina Glevskaia.[49] Four young women in the Komsomol in Smolensk were impatient to be officially invited. This group of friends "wanted to live in the Far East and to receive a specialization." One of them expressed a desire to study for a professional degree and to "strengthen the power of the Soviet Union."[50] It is not clear why the women thought that they had a better chance of studying on the periphery than in Smolensk. They were wholly misinformed. A severe shortage of institutions of higher learning was one of the major factors pushing young people to abandon the region.

Women were most adept at visualizing themselves as defenders of the Soviet border. Glevskaia from Nikolaevsk, Ukraine, wrote a typically enthusiastic and jingoistic letter to the Khetagurovite Committee in September 1939:

[45] Letter from Igalkina, GAKhK P, f. 35, op. 1, d. 174, ll. 159, 159ob, 160, 160ob.

[46] "Applications and short reports from Communist party members wishing to work in the Far East and correspondence." Letter from Selezneva, March 1937, GAKhK P, f. 2, op. 2, d. 146, l. 126.

[47] Letter from Khatukhina, May 17, 1939, GAKhK P, f. 35, op. 1, d. 250, l. 38. In another letter written just one month earlier, she claimed that although she had personal reasons for migrating, these were superseded by her desire "to work in a new construction site." See also letter from Khatukhina, April 2, 1939, GAKhK P, f. 35, op. 1, d. 185, l. 68–68ob.

[48] Letter from Molchanova, GAKhK P, f. 35, op. 1, d. 185, l. 299. Molchanova applied first in November 1938, then sent this letter in March 1939.

[49] Letter from Glevskaia, March 1939, GAKhK P, f. 35, op. 1, d. 339, l. 270.

[50] Pegov personally forwarded their letter to the Khetagurovite Committee chairman: "Comrade Lapshin, I ask you to answer the young women with haste and help them move here to work," May 3, 1939. Letter from Ivantseva, Ivanova, Egorenkova, and Lukovnikova, GAKhK P, f. 35, op. 1, d. 359, ll. 95–97.

I just read the newspaper about the Far Eastern region and I've read it now so many times, I have a desire and such a grand desire, that was born a long time ago, to go to the Far Eastern region . . . I am twenty-four years old, but now I only want to go to the Far East, all my desires and aspirations [*sic*]. I have a five-year-old son, I say to him, "Son, let's go to the Far East," and he replies, "Yes, to butcher the fascists!"[51]

Glevskaia pledged "to work in the Far East honestly and bravely and to defend my Motherland, beloved country."[52] This was the one theme that regularly appeared in women's otherwise brief explanations of their desire to resettle. T. Zhurikhina from Ivanov addressed her letter's recipients in a chatty tone. "Dear comrades, border-guards of the Far East. I come to you with a true desire." She explained that she wanted to work with them "in unison, in the defense of the Motherland from an enemy attack."[53] Lotikova, thirty-one, "burned with desire to put my own share of work into the task of strengthening our Far Eastern borders."[54] Mariia Glupikhina, eighteen, called herself "a loyal *patriotka*" who wanted to be included in the ranks of those who longed to work in the Far East.[55] Chashchina from Cheliabinsk wrote to the Khabarovsk Communist Party Committee because she "wanted to work in the Far East. To join you, if it is at all possible."[56] Schoolteachers were the most proficient at applying eloquently, as demonstrated in a collective letter from four teachers from Smolensk. Their letter stressed their eagerness to educate youth on a distant periphery as part of the Far Eastern patriotic family. They wanted to "contribute our selfless labor together with the best people to strengthen the power of our Motherland, strengthen our borders against our enemies."[57]

What such women sought were conditions where they could immediately impact the quality of life. The frontier needed them to model Soviet habits and practices. Only such selfless patriots could be counted upon to persuade others to withstand deprivations and remain committed to national goals. Poligonova explained, "We were called here by Valia Khetagurova not just to work in industry or help in public works. Valia

---

[51] Letter from Glevskaia, GAKhK P, f. 35, op. 1, d. 339, l. 270.   [52] *Ibid.*
[53] Letter from Zhurikhina, March 8, 1939, GAKhK P, f. 35, op. 1, d. 185, l. 192.
[54] Letter from Lotikova, GAKhK P, f. 2, op. 8, d. 146, l. 116.
[55] Letter from Glupikhina, September 28, 1938, GAKhK P, f. 2, op. 6, d. 341, l. 139. Glupikhina was rejected for resettlement by the Khetagurovite Committee Secretary because she did not have a professional background; selection criteria had become more narrowly focused on skilled workers after initially accepting any politically vetted applicant.
[56] Letter from Chashchina, August 29, 1939, GAKhK P, f. 35, op. 1, d. 336, l. 43.
[57] Letter from schoolteachers Nikol'skaia, Gavrilova, Fedorova, and Novikova, November 24, 1939, GAKhK P, f. 35, op. 1, d. 358, l. 87.

Khetagurova called us to strengthen, to instill culture in the Far East, so that our people will not run from the Far East, so that they stay here as permanent residents."[58]

Khetagurovites were sure that they were needed and their presence was a requirement for permanent conquest of a disputed territory. They were not unique in the 1930s in their expectation of participating alongside men in combat. Women across the country were training to use weapons, fly airplanes, and sky-dive.[59] Women's sense of themselves as linchpins of defense was so powerful that it pervaded their statements in this period, and figured prominently in memoirs written forty years later. Efrosina Mishalova in her memoir recalled the adulation with which the audience of new arrivals listened to the speech of V. K. Bliukher, the Far Eastern commander. The speech was apparently exhilarating for women like Mishalova, who remembered the atmosphere in the hall when the famous war hero called on "dear young women" to never forget that

Although at this time you are wearing civilian dress, you are actually soldiers in the Red Army, defenders of the Far Eastern borders. Remember this always and everywhere . . . You are now residents of the Far East and we are all now on the border with Japan. Japan is a very sneaky and insidious enemy . . . Always be prepared to join the ranks of the defenders of our sacred Far Eastern borders.[60]

The audience broke into tumultuous applause. "Everyone was in such a mood that one wanted to grab a rifle at that moment and go to fight the samurai. If a samurai was to have fallen into our hands at that moment he would not have escaped alive."[61] This was precisely the kind of rhetoric that many of the women found most exhilarating and easily integrated into their visions of their future in the Far East.

Women's peripheral status in the prevalent mythologies of revolutionary bravado explains the appearance of "envy" as a motivating force among them. They may have picked up on this theme when Khetagurova mentioned it, and since they discarded so much else, like the rhetoric of mighty warrior knights and enchanted forests, it clearly spoke to their own attitudes. Igalkina was "pleased and envious that other young women

---

[58] "Stenographic text of the regional Khetagurovite conference," September 17, 1938, Poligonova, GAKhK P, f. 618, op. 1, d. 325, l. 316. Similar understanding of the need for women appeared in the memoirs. For an example, see Memoir of M. N. Koliasnikova, GAKhK P, f. 442, op. 2, d. 283, l. 86.

[59] Women's emphasis on taking up arms and readiness to participate in violence is a common theme in this period. See Krylova, "Stalinist Identity from the Viewpoint of Gender," 626–653.

[60] Memoir of Efrosina Mishalova, February 18, 1976, GAKhK P, f. 442, op. 2, d. 284, ll. 114ob–115.

[61] *Ibid.*, 114ob.

were going to the region."[62] She initially thought it was not possible for her to join them because she was in the retail industry, which seemed to lack relevance to historic missions. Claiming to be writing on behalf of other young women in her workplace, she promised that they would respond with great happiness if invited and pledge to become Far Eastern Stakhanovites. She also "promised not only to work but if necessary to go along with our fathers and brothers to the border and defeat the enemy on their territory."[63] E. Iuzhina, thirty-one, also wrote out of a sense of "envy for the younger women who I see leaving for the Far East" in response to Khetagurova. She explained, "I am not an engineer, nor a doctor, I am a party worker and I have an immense desire to work in the Far East."[64]

In other scholarly studies of letters from this period, Soviet women figure prominently as victimized supplicants who emphasize their weakness, ill-health, poverty, or motherhood to implore action on the part of the powerful.[65] None of these letter-writing strategies was evident in letters from female volunteers. On the contrary, women presented themselves as adaptable and energetic, and specifically defined themselves as patriotic. Motherhood in fact appeared to applicants as a possible disadvantage, with the potential of sabotaging their dreams of moving to the Far East. Thus a divorced single mother, living with her own mother worried that her family circumstances could undermine her application, so she felt it necessary to reassure party authorities that "[m]y family does not interfere with my work."[66] Such volunteers made explicit offers to put patriotic undertakings above familial duties. These were not victims appealing for aid. Rather, these women assumed that they were needed to defend the frontier and to "bring everything to life that will win patriotism."[67] The presence of such strategies belies the notion that a Great Retreat pushed women into the confines of the domestic hearth. These sentiments also indicate a fervent current of support for the Soviet regime.

---

[62] Letter from Igalkina, GAKhK P, f. 35, op. 1, d. 174, ll. 159, 159ob, 160, 160ob.

[63] *Ibid.*

[64] Cadre Department Correspondence. Letter from Iuzhina, December 25, 1938, GAKhK P, f. 35, op. 1, d. 185, ll. 87, 88.

[65] For more on such strategies, see Golfo Alexopoulos, *Stalin's Outcasts: Aliens, Citizens and the Soviet State, 1926–1936* (Ithaca: Cornell University Press, 2003).

[66] Cadre Department Correspondence. Letter from Iuzhina from Orel, where she was the Third Secretary of a Communist Party District Committee, GAKhK P, f. 35, op. 1, d. 185, ll. 87, 88.

[67] "Stenographic text of the regional Khetagurovite conference," September 16, 1938, Shukhman, GAKhK P, f. 618, op. 1 d. 325, l. 100. Similar pride in restructuring the behavior of men in rough settlements is prominent in the Memoir of Anna Plaskina, GAKhK P, f. 442, op. 2, d. 283, l. 52.

This ideological system was effective in forging strong emotional bonds. Among women, the prospect of being explicitly called to defend the system had a particular pull. Calls for acts of self-abnegation on the frontier for the cause of collective defense or the march of humanity toward a better world were emotionally rewarding and simultaneously worked to cement women's identification with the Soviet state.

In hindsight, elderly memoirists offered a wide range of explanations for their eastward trek to the shores of the Pacific. Some were attracted by prospects of autonomy from parental control and exotic landscapes. Others considered resettlement a test of their personal resolve precisely because few acquaintances and relatives believed that women could abide the difficult conditions of the frontier. All these sentiments were mixed with a determination to participate in important national projects. Nina Asikritova and her friends were drawn to the frontier of Stalinism because of young people's "natural" propensity to "dream about great feats and about extraordinary voyages."[68] According to Iuliia Druzhevich, the primary driving force was not "a search for intense personal sensations"; rather, it was a test and exploration of "one's moral strength" and a chance to "live a life of purposefulness with passion in the name of the Motherland."[69]

"Doesn't the Far East need us?": male volunteers

The emphasis on women in the early call-up period was greeted with some confusion. Unperturbed by Khetagurova's appeal to women, men turned to this migratory pipeline to fulfill their own patriotic aspirations and wanted to enlist as heroic Khetagurovites.[70] Correspondents remarked that

It is characteristic that in response to the appeal of Khetagurova, women were not the only ones to answer. Every day the Far Eastern Plenipotentiary Minaichenkov has to listen to dozens of complaints from male Komsomol'tsy. "Why is it only women? Doesn't the Far East need us?" . . . The "aggrieved" were directed to the People's Commissariats and organizations that were recruiting labor.[71]

---

[68] Memoir of Nina A. Asikritova, "Sorok odin god na Dal'nem Vostoke [Forty-one years in the Far East]," October 1978, GAKhK P, f. 442, op. 2, d. 298, l. 2.

[69] Memoir of Iuliia Druzhevich, March 8, 1975, GAKhK P, f. 442, op. 2, d. 284, ll. 31–50. Quoted in Dubinina, *Ty pozovi, Dal'nii Vostok*!, 159.

[70] "Correspondence with the Communist Party Central Committee: On the status of work on the Khetagurovite movement of youth to the Far East," April 11, 1939, GAKhK P, f. 35, op. 1, d. 344, l. 78.

[71] N. Rodin, "Na Dal'nii Vostok! Vydany pervye putevki devushkam stolitsy," *KP*, March 26, 1937. "Far Eastern Regional Communist Party Committee: ORPO: Memorandum notes, short reports, information sent to the Regional Communist Party Committee:

Men, just like female migrants, presented themselves as potential equals in a common struggle to defend the borders. Three male workers from a railroad factory in the city of Magnitogorsk wrote asking to resettle because they wanted to work on a new construction site, "where they need labor." They told the First Secretary that his speech at the Eighteenth Party Congress "moved their hearts." Now they impatiently sought to

work in the Far East, together with you and with all the working class and peasantry of the Far Eastern Region, to strengthen its might. [We desire] with you struggling to build new constructions, to struggle for the full dawn of our flowering, unbeatable Motherland. And if the Japanese fascists try to stick their beastly paws into our loved unbeatable Motherland, then we are always ready at the first call of our government, at any minute, at any second to come to the defense of our border.[72]

There are numerous examples of this loquacious style in the letters from men. Karpov-Karaev was the most extreme, if not the most adept, of those who enthusiastically consumed and then reworded texts to display his own standing as a conscious citizen. He claimed to have participated in the revolutionary struggle and the Civil War, and in 1937 wrote that the call of the Communist party, government, and Khetagurova

forced every honest citizen of the Soviet Union to think about being battle-ready everyday and in any sector of work . . . The Far Eastern taiga is now being remade into a marvelous region by the will of our wonderful Fatherland [*otechestvo*], by our valiant Party of Bolsheviks in the thickest of forests where until recently roamed ferocious beasts, bears and tigers, [and] at this moment grows the construction of cities, villages, the building of railroads and roads, the building of fortresses of socialism near to the Pacific Ocean.[73]

K. Dodoko, thirty-two, explained that when he and his wife read about the region in the newspapers, "we decided to go and live in your region and work for the good of our Motherland. If we are needed then we will come at any minute to the defense of our Motherland and the Far Eastern

On the status of the movement of youth of the Khetagurovite call-up to the Far East, March 20, 1938: Summary for eight months of 1937," GAKhK P, f. 2, op. 6, d. 358, l. 1. Of those who arrived by the end of 1937, there were 868 men (203 demobilized from the army), in part because the Khetagurovite Committee coordinated its operation with efforts to settle demobilized members of the Far Eastern Army in the region. Not all the men came from units stationed in the Far East; while 75 came from the OKDVA, 58 came from military districts in the Ukraine, 18 from the Moscow or Leningrad districts, 25 from Belorussia, 13 from the Caucasus, etc.

[72] Letter from Zemnukhov, Semenychev, and Chushkin, March 25, 1939, GAKhK P, f. 35, op. 1, d. 185, l. 366.

[73] Letter from Karpov and family, June 14, 1937, GAKhK P, f. 2, op. 2, d. 146, l. 142.

border."[74] Dodoko was in charge of a department in a sovkhoz and his wife was a village teacher in the Vannov district of Krasnodar region. His use of a collective "we" is noteworthy because it was unusual for men to write in the plural on behalf of themselves and their families when volunteering the whole family for relocation.

Female and male teachers were the most engaged in elaborating their interests and seemed to be the most enthusiastic consumers of Soviet-frontier mythologies. Teacher Pavel Martynov from the Gor'kovskaia oblast was keen to teach in a Far Eastern school but had little luck getting hired by writing to the regional education department. After reading several articles in newspapers about the Far East, he wrote to the region's First Secretary. Thirty-three, with a wife and two children, Martynov taught geography and natural history to fifth, sixth, and seventh graders. His wife was a preschool teacher who also ostensibly wanted to work in the Far East. Martynov stressed that he was "committed with my whole soul to my grand obligation – the education of children. I want to give my still young strengths to the education of children of the Far East, the future defenders of our mighty fatherland, the future builders of social-ism." This geography teacher was also the only one to demonstrate a cognizance that the region was not an empty wilderness or filled with wild savages, but was populated by a variety of indigenous people who sent their children to school. Martynov indicated an interest in teaching in a national minority school and although he had no special knowledge of these cultures, he was ready to learn any language necessary for the job.[75]

Bookkeeper Nicholai Emel'ianov, thirty-three, was the only man among the letter writers to mention mundane motivations for resettle-ment. He wanted to leave the only area he had ever known because "I have only one reason for leaving the Donbass, and this is to change cli-matic conditions and at least slightly fulfill my duty to help our country in the matters of development of the Khabarovsk region."[76] His search for a better climate in the Far East was profoundly misguided because the Khabarovsk region is better known for its climatic extremes. His mis-perception of what was in store highlights the extent to which the region figured as a veritable Garden of Eden in the imagination of the nation's most dutiful sons.

---

[74] Letter from Dodoka and Svistula, March 1939, GAKhK P, f. 35, op. 1, d. 185, l. 296.
[75] Letter from Martynov, March 25, 1939, GAKhK P, f. 35, op. 1, d. 185, l. 351.
[76] Letter from Emel'ianov, March 28, 1939, GAKhK P, f. 35, op. 1, d. 185, ll. 125–126.

"The whole country knew!"

If a superstar such as Khetagurova emerged out of the periphery, there was also apparently the potential for young women to gain their own acclaim. One of the inescapable benefits of becoming a Khetagurovite was the publicity lavished on participants. Becoming a Khetagurovite meant repeated appearances in photographs and articles in hometown newspapers as well as in their new place of residence. Khetagurovites starred in a documentary film, *Khetagurovki* (1938), and were eulogized in Matvei Blanter's 1939 operetta *On the Banks of the Amur* (*Na Beregu Amura*). Some of the real-life migrants then watched the operetta performed in Khabarovsk.[77] There were other productions based on the Khetagurovites. There was the 1939 musical comedy *Gal with a Personality* with a plot revolving around an officer's wife and a Far Eastern heroine inviting the women of Moscow to join them on the frontier. There were obvious references to Khetagurova in the 1938 film *Komsomol'sk*.[78] A theatrical work, the 1938 play *Tania* by Aleksandr Arbuzov, told the story of a woman's personal growth through selfless labor and migration to the Far East as a Khetagurovite. Arbuzov and his collaborator continued to focus on frontier builders with the collectively written *City at Dawn* of 1940–1941 about Komsomol'sk. There were also poems and songs (see Appendices 3–7). All these works undoubtedly afforded extraordinary outlets for public affirmation. Journalists boosted the migrants' sense of self-importance with suggestions that letters from volunteers should be carefully archived and preserved for posterity. "Years will pass – and these tomes will be read by historians and writers and they will write books about these young women."[79] Photographs such as figure 14, "Getting to know the Far East," 1937, and figure 15, "Meeting new arrivals," 1937, depicting the supposedly smooth welcome in Khabarovsk reinforced fantasies of adventure, geographic mobility, and limitless possibilities.

Those who migrated had often already garnered a certain degree of limelight at their place of origin as either exemplary workers in production or as prominent activists. Many Khetagurovites genuinely enjoyed public speaking and displays of their own authority. For instance, one

[77] Matvei Blanter was also famous for the song "Katiusha." Efrosina Mishalova recalled how much she loved seeing the operetta in Khabarovsk in the late 1930s (Mishalova, 119ob). *Komsomol'sk* was filmed on location by Sergei Gerasimov.

[78] The main heroine in *Gal with a Personality*, played by the rising star Valentina Serova, also helps border guards to catch a spy who crossed the border to undermine Soviet power, while in the film *Komsomol'sk* Natasha, played by Tamara Makarova, helps to expose internal enemies plotting to derail the construction of the new city.

[79] T. Karel'shtein, "Sotni devushek edut na Dal'nii Vostok," *KP*, July 11, 1937.

14. "Getting to know the Far East"
Looking at a map of the Far East. New arrivals learning about the region
at the Khabarovsk office of the Khetagurovite Committee, 1937.

woman loved being an "agitator." She enjoyed visits to workers' homes
for talks and relished the times when "[w]hole families listened to
me."[80] The opportunities for such prominence were thoroughly welded
to public rituals affirming national loyalties. Most of all, she delighted
in appearing on a tribune: "I was so small but so proud that I was
giving orders to such a large mass of people to raise the flag."[81] In
Khabarovsk she became the Secretary of her Komsomol factory organization, something she "had dreamed about" from her earliest days in the
Komsomol.

Part of this longing for the limelight is obvious in the pleasure the memoirists experienced during the fanfare surrounding their departures and
their arrivals in the region. Memoirists dedicated inordinate amounts of
space in their recollections to descriptions of their first journey to the
frontier. Mariia Koliasnikova not only felt elated at the public festivities when she left her hometown, but was also taken by surprise and at
the same time pleased by her reception in Khabarovsk where "we were

---

15. "Meeting new arrivals"
Group of migrants at the office of the Khetagurovite Committee with posters describing the industries of the Far East in the background, Khabarovsk 1937.

greeted with great warmth. An orchestra played once more, there were fine speeches. We were very uncomfortable because we had not done anything yet and we were being greeted as heroes."[82] Polina Bazarova was also proud of the exciting sendoff and reception. "The whole country knew! We were even presented with a song 'Goodbye, young women.'" (see Appendix 3.)[83] Before Kapitalina Kostina left her Gor'kii factory for the Far East, she was given a grandiose sendoff by her factory and drama circle comrades. In Khabarovsk her group was "greeted even better than they were sent off. The orchestra played, there were masses of people there and we smiled and cried from joy."[84] All the greetings and special festivities along the way made women like Levina feel that they were "traveling as people who are needed in the Far East."[85]

Popular stereotypes and official representations of the Far East laid great stress on the primitive living conditions awaiting hardy frontier

[82] Koliasnikova, 87.
[83] "Goodbye, Young Women!," 1938. Music by Isaak Dunaevskii, words by L. Levin. See Appendix 3. Memoir of Polina Bazarova, GAKhK P, f. 442, op. 2, d. 283, l. 98. A similar focus on the fanfare of their sendoff is found in the Memoir of Ania Alekseeva, GAKhK P, f. 442, op. 2, d. 283, l. 15.
[84] Kostina, l. 6.   [85] Memoir of Levina, GAKhK P, f. 442, op. 2, d. 283, l. 44.

pioneers.[86] Of course, before journeying to the Far East young women knew only what they had read in novels such as P. Pavlenko's 1936 *In the East* and similar stories and films.[87] Friends and acquaintances inadvertently added to the mystique and the drama. When Asikritova decided to volunteer, she was told by acquaintances, "You'll perish there at the edge of the world. And there are savages living there who walk around naked, and there are shamans beating on their tambourines, and beasts. And misfortune awaits young women at every step [where they are] surrounded by nothing but convicts."[88] Twenty-year-old Bazarova explained that she and her friends used to read everything they could about Komsomol'sk-na-Amure but only knew that "[t]here somewhere at the edge of the world a new city has been born made by the hands of the Komsomol."[89]

Subsequently, the allure of heroic acts in this exotic space contributed to a widespread experience of dashed hopes after the women reached their destinations. Iliukhina and her friends were "expecting to see in Komsomol'sk not only the wild taiga with beasts, but also half-savage people, with whom we would be forced to struggle."[90] Bazarova remarked that the women who traveled to Komsomol'sk "were bothered by pangs of conscience since it was like we had come to something already made. We were greeted with a five-year-old city and not a remote taiga."[91] Anna Plaskina, who left for Komsomol'sk at the age of seventeen, remembered that when she and her group arrived, "[w]e saw finished houses and we became very disillusioned because we did not see the tents the way we had fantasized. We imagined tents and the taiga and impassible paths. Later we understood that we would get our share of good and bad."[92] Valianskaia from Kiev "used to dream about the Far East. The taiga, the hills and the beauty of it all appeared in front of us."[93] She and her friends "especially wanted to end up in the taiga, in the real taiga. When we arrived we became disillusioned. Instead of the taiga, we saw three or

---

[86] This was a prominent theme in the recollections of participants as well as in comments made in the 1930s. See Memoir of P. Egorova, GAKhK P, f. 442, op. 2, d. 283, l. 9, 2 April 1974.

[87] "Stenographic text of the regional Khetagurovite conference," September 16, 1938, Beliakova, GAKhK P, f. 618, op. 1, d. 325, l. 88. The novel is set in the Far East and concerns a young heroine, Olga, who confronts a variety of impediments including the natural world to aid border guards and security officials in tracking down spies.

[88] Asikritova, 3.

[89] Memoir of Polina Bazarova, GAKhK P, f. 442, op. 2, d. 283, l. 97.

[90] "Stenographic text of the regional Khetagurovite conference," September 15, 1938, Iliukhina, GAKhK P, f. 618, op. 1, d. 325, l. 17. Khetagurovite Iliukhina was working in Komsomol'sk's Factory No. 126.

[91] Bazarova, 95.   [92] Plaskina, 53–54.

[93] "Stenographic text of the regional Khetagurovite conference," September 15, 1938, Valianskaia, GAKhK P, f. 618, op. 1, d. 325, l. 62.

four trees. But we had dreamed of seeing a real taiga, where snakes and animals are roaming."[94]

Khetagurovites hoped to find a sparsely developed land that would function as a conspicuous platform on which to display the indispensability of women's work inside and outside of the domestic sphere. The common experience of disappointment also suggests that women sought public feats, encounters with savages, and primitive conditions in which they could demonstrate their citizenship and sacrifice. The more savage the locals or the more uncouth the workers, the more visible their own status as patriots and the more secure they felt themselves to be as agents of the nation.

Activists in the 1930s blamed behavioral problems among some Khetagurovites, poor work performance, and unreasonable demands on the fact that they "did not meet savages but ordinary people and a city under construction."[95] Instead, they saw the tens of thousands of prisoners and their guards who were doing most of the building around them. The presence of prisoners must have contributed to the feelings of disappointment, but it was not possible for the women – neither at the time nor in later memoirs – to mention such realities as a source of their disillusionment.

The women were, however, able to discuss another source of their eventual disappointment: skeptical reactions among their new neighbors and co-workers. The female-headed campaign and the image of young women embarking for a land known for its overabundance of men complicated the meaning of migration and put many women on the defensive. Having stressed the specificity of their feminine contributions, the Khetagurovite campaign reinforced a sense that women's essential differences might also render them ill-equipped to act out of purely patriotic sentiments. If there were doubts about their motivations, there were doubts about the ultimate worth of their apparent sacrifices.

The Far East continued to retain a strong association with rugged masculinity, notwithstanding efforts to interject women into the mythical landscapes in official culture. The women who volunteered to invade such masculine spaces exposed themselves to ridicule. Female participants could never overcome their anomalous place in frontier mythologies. Their intentions remained suspect and observers assumed that women could be motivated only by the search for husbands or wealth, rather than patriotism. When Opryshko prepared to leave for the Far East with two

---

[94] *Ibid.*, 64.
[95] "Stenographic text of the regional Khetagurovite conference," September 15, 1938, Iliukhina, GAKhK P, f. 618, op. 1, d. 325, l. 18.

of her factory co-workers, "[p]eople laughed at us because [they said] we were going only to get married because there are many lads there. Or for a long ruble. But those who sympathized with us, and knew what awaited us along the way, told us that we would meet with great difficulties. We would have to be hungry and go without" the basics.[96] Druzhevich felt it necessary to reject the notion that young women came in search of husbands or personal gain. "We answered precisely because it was more difficult there. We were not offered any material incentives. There was a one-off travel subsidy. All of us were workers, after all. At the time, of course, marriage was not an end in itself for us."[97]

Having succeeded as a locomotive driver, an occupation traditionally dominated by men, Druzhevich remained cognizant of the treatment women received when they trespassed into male spheres. In this context, she acknowledged that "[c]ertain narrow minded people often with malicious smiles and crafty airs judged and measured us only as women who came to the Far East to get married."[98] Forty years later, she continued to encounter people who demeaned "the most pure, exalted and beautiful." The sting of such mockery was so tangible that it elicited a lengthy rejoinder:

I will say it briefly: in our youth, and today, there was never and is not now a shortage of young men. However, to find a friend, to build with him a beautiful life like singing a song, is not always possible. If you are going to look for this specifically, then you won't find this in the Far East, and you can't write away for it "across the border." There are probably people today who crave to "earn" and to return home in their own *Volga* [a car] . . . These are apparently the types who yearn to "get married" and "advantageously" no less. These sorts were always around with or without the call-up.[99]

Only partially able to realize their hopes of sustained and genuine acclaim for their sacrifices, Khetagurovites continued to draw prestige by stressing how tightly their life paths intertwined with the evolution of Soviet society. Despite the contentious meaning of their sacrifice, those who settled in the region garnered real satisfaction from the development of their new hometowns. Egorova, who settled in Komsomol'sk-na-Amure, continued to identify herself and her group of friends as former Khetagurovites who were respected members of their community and authentic pioneers. Several dozen former Khetagurovites were still prominent public figures in the 1980s. They had formed not only life-long friendships but also a strong civic pride in the urban landscape they

[96] "Stenographic text of the regional Khetagurovite conference," September 17, 1938, Opryshko, GAKhK P, f. 618, op. 1, d. 325, l. 295.
[97] Druzhevich, quoted in Dubinina, *Ty pozovi, Dal'nii Vostok!*, 159.
[98] *Ibid.*, 158.   [99] *Ibid.*, 158–159.

inhabited. As Egorova explained, "The 'gals' meet often and now we call ourselves pioneer pensioners but we participate in the public life of our city and do not get sad. Our city has become unrecognizable, flowering, and we all love it because our share has been put into its construction."[100] Mariia Komarova, who originally hailed from Ukraine, concluded her memoir with this reflection on her decision to migrate. "I am very pleased that I ended up in the Far East. This is my second Motherland. I might even say that I love Russia more than Ukraine."[101] A visceral sense of having participated in turning a wilderness into a city made it possible for women like Komarova to identify her interests with a grander nation-building project transcending her former allegiances.

Khetagurova's invitation to create a new society on a blank slate of wilderness was a genuinely popular sentiment that served the interests of the Communist party in the immediate prewar years and had the potential to further reconfigure gender boundaries. The search for recognition and a space where they felt needed suggests a profound sense of social isolation experienced by some young women in a society that promised equality but often denigrated traits and jobs associated with femininity. The invitation to join frontier builders appeared as a welcome opportunity for women to interject themselves totally and publicly into a project of great national import. Such demonstrable sacrifices for the national good promised to bestow upon them the kind of social worth they craved. It also integrated women more fully in a wider Soviet collective by offering participation in the expansion of Soviet power in Eurasia.

[100] Egorova, 91.
[101] Memoir of Mariia Komarova, GAKhK P, f. 442, op. 2, d. 282, l. 145ob.

5   "Bol'shevichki were never ascetics!": female morale and Communist morality

In *Adres podviga – Dal'nii Vostok: Muzhestvo Komsomol'ska*, a 1974 book lionizing the heroic builders of Komsomol'sk-na-Amure, a vignette about three inseparable girlfriends who went to the region as patriotic volunteers captures something of the unease about sex and marriage that seems to have existed and echoes experiences revealed in archival documents. A young woman rushes to her dormitory to tell her friends about a marriage proposal. The subsequent fictional dispute between the girls encapsulates, to a surprisingly accurate extent, the qualms about and contentious nature of sexual behavior and marriage forty years earlier. One of the friends welcomed the news, but the other, Taisa, did not hide her displeasure and exhorted, "What did we come here for? To work, build a city, study, to defend the border. What will happen if we all jump into marriage? Have you thought of that?" Her friends rejected this position as ridiculous. Taisa persisted, "I'm speaking like a revolutionary, like a Bol'shevichka . . ." Her friends fired back, "Bol'shevichki were never ascetics!" Taisa was undaunted. "Marriage is a sign of weakness!" The woman who planned to marry cut off the debate: "'It is love, girls . . .' she said firmly but quietly. 'The time will come and you will fall in love.'" Eventually, all the friends married and moved out of the dormitory. The authors interjected, "And such is life. Its laws are eternal."[1]

In fact, love, sex, and marriage were anything but uncomplicated symbols of the "eternal" for female migrants who had participated in the Khetagurovite Campaign for Resettlement of Young People in the Far East. Because the campaign was initially aimed specifically at women and because the region suffered from an overabundance of men, contemporaries and modern scholars have assumed that female Khetagurovites departed for the Far East in search of husbands.[2] With a female figurehead in the person of Valentina Khetagurova and the prominence it gave

---

[1] Gennadii Khlebnikov and Efim V. Dorodnov, *Adres podviga – Dal'nii Vostok: Muzhestvo Komsomol'ska* (Khabarovsk: Khabarovsk. knizh. izd.-vo. 1974), 146.
[2] Stephan, *The Russian Far East*, 197–198.

to seemingly autonomous single women, the Khetagurovite campaign made its participants vulnerable to insinuations of sexual iniquity. Accusations of sexual voraciousness comprised a large part of the repertoire of those who sought to diminish women's authority upon their arrival in previously all-male spheres.[3] The choices of women in their private lives and marriage partners once in the region came under intense scrutiny.

The task for Communist educators and officials was formidable. Before the Bolshevik Revolution, marriage had remained a matter regulated by religious authorities, communities, and family elders.[4] Because church authorities were in full control, the state and its officials never established practices, discourses, or authority in this domain.[5] The regime that came to power in 1917 discarded religious dictums on personal morality and disparaged the insularity of petty-bourgeois unions until well into the 1930s. How could educators and organizers in the 1930s guide young people on the subjects of marriage, sex, and morality in a society that had officially rejected religion and all its signposts for the conduct of personal life? What were the rules for personal behavior and sexuality in a society with diluted communal institutions and kin groups splintered by migration and urbanization?[6]

Young adults, who predominated numerically in newly built industrial settlements like those in the Far East, stumbled into nebulous social zones where they made up their own rules and developed a variety of attitudes concerning sexual unions and the institution of marriage.[7] This anonymity gave young people greater control over their sexual lives and choices in the selection of marriage partners. However, for women, new autonomy in other spheres did not translate into an equal degree of choice

---

[3] For a discussion of anxiety about female sexuality arising out of women's "colonization" of new spaces, see Phil Goodman, "'Patriotic Femininity': Women's Morals and Men's Morale during the Second World War," *Gender & History* 10:2 (August 1998), 278–293.

[4] The church established and enforced guidelines not only on personal behavior but limited choices of marriage partners based on confessional affiliations. For instance, Orthodox and Roman Catholics were forbidden from marrying non-Christians. For the rules, see the Articles of vol. 10, Part 1 of *Svod Zakonov Rossiiskoi Imperii*, reproduced in Ia. A. Kantorovich, *Zakony o vere i veroterpimosti* (Sankt-Peterburg, 1899).

[5] Laura Engelstein has described the abortive efforts of Russian liberals to secularize and professionalize the regulation of sexuality through legal reforms. See Engelstein, *The Keys to Happiness: Sex and the Search for Modernity in Fin-de-Siècle Russia* (Ithaca: Cornell University Press, 1992).

[6] This discussion is indebted to the notion of the "quicksand society" explored by Moshe Lewin in *The Making of the Soviet System: Essays in the Social History of Interwar Russia* (New York: New Press, 1994).

[7] Sheila Fitzpatrick has discussed the changes in behavior among university students in the late 1920s. See Fitzpatrick, "Sex and Revolution: An Examination of Literary and Statistical Data on the Mores of Soviet Students in the 1920s," *Journal of Modern History* 50:2 (1978), 252–278.

16. "The Khetagurovite dormitory"
Dorms for Khetagurovites in Komsomol'sk-na-Amure, 1937. In reality, few women were lucky enough to have a room like this in Komsomol'sk. Left to right: Ania Klimova, Tania Artamonova, and Zoia Shuvalova.

or control over sexual relationships. The contours of these dynamics are apparent in the experiences of Khetagurovites who in letters, memoirs and official investigations remarked on sex and marriage in the "special conditions" of the Far East. Dormitory rooms shared by young women far from home, such as the ideal scene from Komsomol'sk-na-Amure in figure 16, "The Khetagurovite dormitory," were spaces where such issues were generally hammered out without much guidance from authorities.

The Bolsheviks, despite their penchant for social engineering, had actually created a vacuum to be filled by young people themselves as they set out to work far away from kin and home. In the late 1930s Communist party and Komsomol officials were preoccupied with exposing enemies and maintaining class purity. Orators and educators fused anxieties about class purity and vigilance with a discourse on morality enjoining women to uphold ideological and class boundaries in their choice of partners and associations. They did so while eliding more mundane but relevant questions about the meaning of marriage and useful advice on how to build longlasting relationships. For all their lectures on morality and anxious debates about the behavior of wayward young people, they were, in fact, unable to articulate valuable guidelines in the absence of influences that typically delineate normative boundaries for sexuality, selection of marriage partners, or conjugal responsibilities.[8] Although orators and educators reminded young audiences about their duties to uphold principles of Communist morality, the content of such principles offered little tangible advice for women as they navigated relationships outside of familiar contexts and in circumstances of extreme material hardship.

In the 1930s Communist morality offered guidance on how to avoid ideological contamination. Instead of prohibitions on confessional intermarriage, as had been the rule in Tsarist Russia, Soviet authorities tried to establish boundaries keeping those of the wrong class or political background from mingling with and potentially corrupting the laboring class. Komsomol activists across the Soviet Union operated under dictums such as the one published in the journal aimed at working women, *Rabotnitsa*, in March 1936: "What Does the Party Demand from a Communist in their Private Life?" *Rabotnitsa's* editors explained that although the party did not wish to dictate "whom someone can and cannot marry" or become involved in the details of personal affairs, Communists and Komsomol members had to choose partners carefully because "connections with the enemies of the laboring classes were unacceptable. This is the number one thing that the party demands from Communists in their private lives."[9] The editors quoted from Lenin himself: "Our morality comes out of the interests of the struggle of the proletariat." What the interest of the proletariat was at any one time when it came to sexual

---

[8] Besides the work of scholars like Dan Healey who have written on the subject of homosexuality, the field of Soviet sexuality studies and masculinity is in its infancy. See Dan Healey, *Homosexual Desire in Revolutionary Russia: The Regulation of Sexual and Gender Dissent* (Chicago: University of Chicago Press, 2001); Igor Kon and James Riordan (eds.), *Sex and Russian Society* (Bloomington: Indiana University Press, 1993); and Clements, Friedman, and Healey (eds.), *Russian Masculinities in History and Culture*. There have been several influential studies of masculinity and sex in literature of the 1920s. See Eliot Borenstein, *Men Without Women: Masculinity and Revolution in Soviet Fiction, 1917–1929* (Durham: Duke University Press, 2000), and Eric Naiman, *Sex in Public*. For a discussion of sexual practices in the mid-twentieth century, see Anna Rotkirch, "Traveling Maidens and Men with Parallel Lives – Journeys as Private Space During Late Socialism," in Jeremy Smith (ed.), *Beyond the Limits: The Concept of Space in Russian History and Culture*, (Helsinki: Studia Historica, 1999), 131–149.

[9] "Chego partiia trebuet ot kommunista v lichnoi zhizni," *Rabotnitsa* 9 (March 1936), 3. In the 1920s Aleksandra Kollontai attempted to engage the public in frank discussions of sexuality and the meaning of marriage in the context of socialism, but her work was suppressed and labeled debauched by other Bolsheviks. For fictional representations, meant for popular consumption, of women grappling with the choices facing them during the NEP period, see Kollontai, *Love of Worker Bees*, trans. Cathy Porter (Chicago: Academy Press Limited, 1978).

decorum was not always clear or enforceable. Valentina Khetagurova could offer patriotic fantasies to fire up imaginations and harsh rebukes for those who embarrassed the campaign, but little advice on how to reproduce the model family life she ostensibly built on the shores of the Pacific.

While the institution of marriage received official bolstering in 1936 and motherhood was heralded as a social duty, evidence from the Khetagurovite experiences demonstrates that young people treated marriage with a kind of casualness that threatened to make it a poor conduit for ensuring social stability and orderly reproduction. Memoirs, letters to authorities, and official investigations suggest that many young women flagrantly ignored the demands for sexual propriety out of material necessity or flaunted their sexuality as a way to express dissatisfaction with their lot. Their stories illuminate poorly understood aspects of everyday life for young people at the close of the 1930s. Here we see how conditions of material deprivation in the highly tense social atmosphere of the Far East created opportunities for others to exploit the vulnerabilities of migrant women. The documents generated by these women, their discussions of their misfortunes and their critiques of one another offer a fascinating window into young people's attitudes toward sex and marriage, as well as a grim portrait of just how vulnerable young women were to exploitation or abuse.

Coquettes

The consequences of noncommittal sexual relationships and casual attitudes toward marriage had taken on greater gravity for young women after the summer of 1936, when they lost access to legal abortion. Recognition of young women's autonomy and the plight of single mothers generated episodic and contradictory efforts to delineate sexual and marital behavioral norms. The main platform for airing these messages was *Komsomol'skaia pravda*, where young urban women's public and private behavior came under scrutiny in the second half of 1938. The newspaper insisted that progress toward socialism and national defense was in jeopardy because of seeming sexual disorderliness among young people. The signals from Moscow and attempts to censure young women indicate the relatively recent and concomitantly troubling recognition of young women as autonomous sexual beings. The tendency of the public debate to blame young women unduly for failed relationships and unplanned pregnancies simultaneously suggests that many people assumed that women were not simply victims of male lust but conscious actors who should have made the right decision.[10] This was a departure from Soviet and pre-revolutionary legal and social practices that absolved women of guilt for complicity in criminal or dissolute behavior and assumed that "individual autonomy remained a male preserve."[11]

These concerns were made apparent in a 1938 article, "A Young Woman's Honor", penned by a member of the Komsomol Central Committee's Sector for Work among Young Women. The text defined women's behavior as a problem and set the tone for subsequent discussions.[12] The author, Elena Kononenko, placed coquettes [*vertushki*] under fire. The opinion of the Komsomol leadership was represented by fictive elders in their interactions with fictive young people in need of correction. Kononenko opened her article with an imaginary scene in a female dormitory where young women were preparing to step out for the evening. One, described as "the leading fashion maven of the dormitory," stood at a mirror, slicking her plucked eyebrows and cutting short her once lovely long hair. A group of others, decked out in the latest "slit skirts and cocked hats," sauntered off, profane and dismissive of criticism from an older female roommate. The mature woman worker bemoaned the "nauseating" behavior of many women who were unduly concerned with fashion and the foxtrot, even though their accomplishments at the factory and activism were beyond reproach. They were missing something essential to Soviet womanhood. Although they were good workers and Stakhanovites, "[t]hey lack everything maidenly – neither modesty nor affability. No matter what you say, our young women have let themselves go."

---

[10] Sheila Fitzpatrick argues that "family propaganda" in the late 1930s was "anti-men. Women were consistently represented . . . as the nobler, suffering sex, pillars of the family . . . Men, in contrast, were portrayed as selfish and irresponsible." See Fitzpatrick, *Everyday Stalinism*, 143. The discussion in *Komsomol'skaia pravda* suggests that at least in messages aimed at a younger generation, women were not always the victims.

[11] Laura Engelstein, "Gender and the Juridical Subject: Prostitution and Rape in Nineteenth-Century Russian Criminal Codes," *Journal of Modern History* 60 (September 1988), 493. In the 1920s women were also not held fully responsible for their deviant actions. See Sharon Kowalsky, "Who's Responsible for Female Crime? Gender, Deviance and the Development of Social Norms in Revolutionary Russia," *Russian Review* 62 (July 2003), 366–386.

[12] Elena Kononenko, "Chest' devushki," *KP* August 28, 1938; subsequent further quotations taken from this article. Themes outlined in the article reappeared in other publications aimed at young people and at gatherings of Komsomol members throughout the country including the Far East in 1938 and 1939. Valentina Khetagurova in her speech at the Khetagurovite regional conference in September 1938 structured her criticism of young women in accordance with the criticisms outlined in the article and cited directly from the *Komsomol'skaia pravda* piece. See "Stenographic text of the regional Khetagurovite conference," September 18, 1938, Khetagurova, GAKhK P, f. 618, op. 1 d. 325, l. 332.

These "sorts" of women were also the kind that allowed lads to "speak indecently" to them and to "paw" them without consequence. While there were plenty of male rascals, the "coquettes" were to blame for falling into their hands. "They do not safeguard their honor." The story went on to present the mentality of one such hypothetical, easy-going coquette who having "lost her head" hooked up with a lad she hardly knew. As soon as she was pregnant, the man declared, "Our personalities are incompatible and whether I'm the father is still a question." The matronly commentator comforted and simultaneously berated the distraught girl, in her indignation pointing out the difference between women's lives before and after the Revolution. "How could you let him take your young life? You see this happened among us, necessity forced maidens to ruin their lives, to go with whomever was around. But why do you need to?" In the story the young woman also refused to turn to the state to force the man to take responsibility. She did not trust the courts to back her case and thought that the public hearings would only bring humiliation.

The lesson for the reader was that these were not private tragedies but dangerous failures in political consciousness. The immodest behavior of young women was playing into the hands of enemies. According to Kononenko, "when young women skid into the stinking swamp of meshchanstvo," the people's enemies rejoice. Those who argued that exemplary work and activism was all that was expected of them and that their personal life was their own affair were heading for trouble and probably politically suspect.

Kononenko explained that enemies were working to "detach the moral make-up of a young person from their ideological and political make-up so that they can corrupt them morally and drag them into their counter-revolutionary traps." Young women's freedom to choose their partners also meant freedom to make the kind of mistakes that appeared as manifestations of sexual and concomitant ideological disorderliness in the eyes of the Communist party. Kononenko reminded her readers that Lenin had rejected the "glass of water" attitude toward love and sex.[13] He and Stalin "taught" that the struggle for moral probity "was part of the struggle for communism."

Komsomol officials who wanted to draw young people into their alternative family in order to mold and discipline good citizens and future party members were unhappy with the way young people casually socialized in urban spaces. This concern is clear in another purportedly real

---

[13] The "glass of water theory" refers to the teachings of Aleksandra Kollontai, who wanted to liberate sexuality from the confines of bourgeois marriage and envisioned that sex would be as simple as drinking a glass of water in a society without private property.

letter from a young man who was asked to "describe young women today."
According to the author, women who were fine workers and activists were
using the anonymity of urban spaces to flaunt the sexual energy they kept
in check during work hours. While they

behave discreetly at work and at home, in the parks or outside town they act
provocatively, use obscenities . . . There are young women who only amuse themselves with dances, parties and romances, even cards and drinks. Many [women]
ask for vulgar treatment. There are gals who become acquainted right and left –
in the square, at the movies, theaters and even trams and buses. These acquain-
tanceships often lead to sad consequences because the young woman does not
know the young man, and he even gives her the wrong name.

To drive the point home, readers were provided with an insight into the
male psyche. "Let them know this! This behavior demeans them and
would a more or less decent young man behave well with her? Even
rascals who like these kind[s] of young women laugh at them when in the
company of men."

A final fictive case tackled the contentious meaning of meshchanstvo.
Concerned elders bewailed the accoutrements of modern womanhood
and urban pastimes as petty-bourgeois frivolities and contributors to
moral and political dissolution. In turn, young people portrayed in the
piece dismissed calls for discretion and female modesty as relics of petty-
bourgeois prudery. Grandparents who supposedly turned to the Komsomol to help them deal with an unruly teenager lamented that, "There
is much about our granddaughter that offends us . . . Her yearning to
dress according to fashion without regard to age, love of vulgar novels,
unconstrained behavior with young men. [There is] nothing maidenly
here." In response, the young woman teased her grandmother about nostalgia for "bridal veils and festoons" as well as a desire to "register her
as a bride." Grandmother dubbed heavy make-up and "erotic dances"
the real meshchanstvo and yearned to see "the resurrection of the word
bride." Kononenko sided with the grandmother and delineated what was
expected from a Soviet young woman. "She must be clean, loving and
honest. Let her fly an airplane, drive a tractor . . . She will be the most
wonderful bride in the world. Yes, bride . . . Why should we fear this
word?" Although this was a conspicuous indicator of an emphasis on
marriage as a natural course for all Soviet women, it was hardly a fully
elaborated handbook on how to manage the perils of single life. It was
also unlikely to provide much guidance for those who wished to know
how to combine marriage and flying an airplane.

A subsequent commentary ostensibly written by other young people also appeared in *Komsomol'skaia pravda* to continue the discussion

«Мировой парень».
Рис. В. БРИСКИНА и В. ФОМИЧЕВА.

17a. Cartoon from *Komsomol'skaia pravda*: "*First-Rate Lad.*"

of young women's behavior.[14] The letters to the editors published by the newspaper did not agree with Kononenko. Of the six published, five directly blamed the Komsomol for doing little to punish profligate men and for failing to provide supervision and activities for young people in general. Three of the six writers blamed male "scoundrels" for exploiting "flighty" young women with the connivance of the aloof Komsomol organization. Cartoons depicting the female and male version of the wrong kind of Soviet youth flanked the letters (figures 17a and 17b).

Most revealing was a letter sent by a junior commander serving in the Red Army.[15] K. Murashev wanted to argue that most Soviet young women, "like Khetagurova," were fine examples of honorable citizens. However, poor supervision from public organizations allowed certain weak elements to stumble into the hands of contemporary "Don Juans." "First-rate lads," as he called the foppish rascals ironically, were in fact threats to national defense because "[a]lmost every young man who goes

---

[14] "Chest' sovetskoi devushki. Pis'ma nashikh chitatelei. [A Young Soviet Woman's Honor. Letters from our Readers]," *KP*, September 12, 1938.
[15] K. Murashev, "Mirovye rebiata [First-Rate Lads]" *KP*, September 12, 1938.

«Мировая девочка».

Рис. В. БРИСКИНА и В. ФОМИЧЕВА.

17b. Cartoon from *Komsomol'skaia pravda*: "*First-Rate Gal.*" Illustrators V. Briskin and V. Fomichev.

into the army leaves behind a bride . . . While defending his great Motherland, he retains feelings for the girl he loves. Often under the influence of Don Juans the young woman brings pain to the person who loves her."

Murashev elaborated that "first-rate lads" had a simple attitude toward women: "Feelings for them are silly – a meshchanstvo . . . Wonderful Soviet young women are just girls to them who can be gotten drunk, insulted and tossed away."[16] One female reader, though, agreed with Kononenko and wrote in to support the portrayal of the flighty women, "the first-rate gals" whom she thought resembled the young women of her hometown. She was particularly vexed about the "foxtrot" on the dance floor where there was just too much physical contact and "vulgar" banter. Reflecting perhaps a disagreement among the Komsomol and party leadership on the ways to delineate who was responsible for sexual disorderliness, the letters together brought both the profligate man and the coquettish woman under the scrutiny of the public gaze.

[16] *Ibid.*

Family succor

This discussion of women's behavior in national newspapers proved well suited to the problems reported among Khetagurovites. Their debates at their regional conference in September 1938 mimicked to a significant extent the agenda set in the Kononenko piece. This was in part a result of the training received by the Komsomol organizers who orchestrated the event and who took the rostrum.[17] At the same time, not all the commentators were either sufficiently briefed or compelled to keep to a narrow interpretation on the roots of the supposed sexual disorderliness that plagued the reputation of Khetagurovites. The discussion that ensued and descriptions of behavior outlined in other exchanges with authorities divulge much more than just debates among policymakers or the representation of women. These stories are striking snapshots of lived experiences among young women. It is possible to ask how and whether messages from Komsomol authorities structured attitudes and how they collided with experiences. While these glimpses into practices, sensibilities, and coping strategies provide rich material for historians, they were distasteful revelations for contemporaries and exposed the limitations of their ability to mold young people according to plan.

Conditions in the Far East magnified the dynamics in many other parts of the Soviet Union where young people now lived and worked in unprecedented autonomy. Housed in dreary and inadequate barracks and dormitories, they had little to occupy them in their free time, for despite their numbers, venues and organizations where they could partake in activities under the supervision of authorities were poorly developed. Even when there were activities for them, these very same Komsomol clubs, summer camps, and weekend retreats for defense training provided ideal opportunities for unrestrained sexual exploration.[18]

Female Khetagurovites were selected for Far Eastern migration because they had proven themselves as activists in their home region and were expected to become exemplary leaders among women. They

---

[17] "Stenographic text of the regional Khetagurovite conference," September 18, 1938, Khetagurova, GAKhK P, f. 618, op. 1, d. 325, l. 333. At the conference Valentina Khetagurova read an excerpt from Kononenko's article, choosing the fictional young man's letter describing male views of coquettes. While she conceded that the publicized debate was not expressly about Khetagurovites, she thought that "[t]his to a large degree relates to the young women who have come here on the call-up. I have to tell you about these facts and that these facts are not unique."

[18] For instance, the aviation club in Khabarovsk had a reputation for debauchery as a storage room for parachutes provided congenial space for "drinking parties, orgies and the moral dissolution" of aviation club members in tandem with club leaders. See "Stenographic text of the regional Komsomol activists in Khabarovsk," January 4, 1939, GAKhK P, f. 618, op. 1, d. 321, l. 162.

arrived as part of a widely publicized campaign and were identified as a specific group, so the questionable behavior of some affected the reputation of all and provided fodder for those who sought to ostracize female workers and activists. Khetagurovite Murza offered her own estimates for the percentages of dissolute women among Khetagurovites to account for their bad reputation in the region: "I do not deny that among young women Khetagurovites 30–35 percent are corrupt. They must be taken on seriously. Concluding from these corrupt examples, people have decided that the rest are the same."[19] Her estimate of the number of bad apples was exceedingly high but underscores the power of reputation to shape the reception of all female migrants. She and others were anxious that such impressions about the migrants were making it difficult for all patriotic newcomers to acculturate and find respect in their new workplaces. They also thought that these behaviors undermined the tenuous authority of the Komsomol among other young people. As far as the authorities were concerned, this was a clear case in which sexual peccadilloes and failed marriages were not simply an embarrassment but obstructions to the larger goals of the government in the Far East.

Officials and other observers were disturbed by a number of tendencies. A common concern was a lighthearted attitude toward marriage. On the other hand, many observers were distressed that women were being forced into bad marriages by grave material need. There was also much trepidation about casual sex outside of marriage and the subsequent spread of venereal diseases and illegal abortions. Finally, there was more than one case of Khetagurovites choosing to socialize with and even marry politically suspect men and prisoners in the labor camps. All those who made bad decisions and besmirched the reputation of the Khetagurovite collective fell under the category of "unsteady." Some who transgressed beyond redemption were relieved of their title of Khetagurovite or forced to return home.

Observers and other Khetagurovites often complained that young women married only a few days after arrival. Female migrants were even called together to discuss the topic of hasty marriages in Komsomol'sk in 1938. Artiushina described the subsequent discussion. "The gals spoke openly about their own shortcomings, about their flighty attitudes toward love, family and marriage. Here of course you cannot only blame men. We need to respect one another. Half of the blame lies with the young

---

[19] "Memorandum on the work of the Committee for the reception of young people of the Khetagurovite call-up," November–December 1938, GAKhK P, f. 2, op. 6, d. 341, l. 163ob.

woman."[20] Couples who married a few days after meeting were bound to split up eventually after the birth of the child and then "abandoned it to its fate because the parents do not want to take responsibility."[21] The story of Baranenko became an example of loose morals and made its way into documents read by top regional and Komsomol officials at the highest rungs of the organization, and eventually by members of the Politburo:

> Some women get married three to four times. Baranenko arrived on January 2, 1939, got married on January 15th, on the 23rd she was divorced and that evening she married another man. On the 24th, they celebrated their wedding and the next morning they missed work and were being fired. Realizing her situation, she decided to poison herself. This incident was not fatal.[22]

The evidence from discussions of the Khetagurovites suggests that the problem for many was not that they rejected the institution of marriage – in fact, many were quick to enter into it. It was that marriage as an institution did not function as envisaged by Communist authorities attempting to bolster families and birth rates across the Soviet Union. Although many Khetagurovites were apparently eager to make their relationships official, such a step did little to protect them from abandonment or reputations ruined by male partners who continued to view marriage as a perfunctory ritual that suited their temporary interests and had few long-term repercussions. It is not even clear how the women themselves defined marriage.[23] Their discussions indicate that "marriage" could encompass informal marriages and transient states of cohabitation as well as an officially recognized union.[24]

Yet this consternation about hasty marriages is belied by other data. A report on the women's progress on the Far Eastern Railroad, compiled by

---

[20] "Protocol of the I Khabarovsk regional Komsomol conference," February 11–15, 1939, Artiushina, GAKhK P, f. 617, op. 1, d. 3, l. 145.

[21] *Ibid.*

[22] Copy of a Komsomol Central Committee report sent for comment to the First Secretary of the Khabarovsk Regional Party Committee. "Report prepared by the Komsomol Central Committee's Sector for Work among young Women," April 29, 1939, GAKhK P, f. 35, op. 1, d. 344, ll. 83–84.

[23] Sheila Fitzpatrick has examined popular attitudes on marriages in the 1930s. The concept of "free" marriage, inherited from the 1920s, was still shaping perceptions when the 1937 census showed that "one and a half million more women than men declared themselves to be currently married, implying that the same number of men were in relationships considered by their partners, but not themselves, to be marriages." See Fitzpatrick, *Everyday Stalinism*, 142.

[24] For an interesting comparison to a similar phenomenon in a context of geographic and social mobility, see Beverly Schwartzberg, "'Lots of Them Did That': Desertion, Bigamy and Marital Fluidity in Late Nineteenth-Century America," *Journal of Social History* 37:3 (2004), 573–600.

the Khetagurovite committee secretary Kuznetsova, noted that 14 percent of the women were married after one year in the area.[25] Evidence
from the memoirs of Khetagurovites also reveals no extraordinary rush
to marry. Most of the Khetagurovites married after one to two years in
the region. Like their age cohorts in the rest of the Slavic regions of
the Soviet Union, their age at first marriage ranged between twenty and
twenty-four.[26]

Anecdotal evidence from the memoirs provides a mixed picture of
mostly longlasting marriages but some unhappy unions. Kapitalina
Kostina methodically looked for someone who shared her interests and
would be a partner rather than a burden. Even the man she found attractive was a fellow *landsman* (a migrant from her region). While working
in the Komsomol, Kostina met an officer who also happened to be from
her own Kirov oblast. "We met again after two days and traded books.
He gave me *The Seagull* and I gave him *The Golden Noose* and that's how
I roped him in."[27] She even designed a trial period for their relationship:
"I told him that he had to live with me in my room, at that time I had a
nine-meter room with three other women. He had to live with me for one
month to try it out and then I would come to live with him. He agreed. To
this day he laughs about those terms."[28] Kostina's "test" proved effective and the couple stayed together. Kostina thought the marriage was
successful in the long term because

[W]e are both Communists and this is why our life together was interesting.
He was the party secretary for a long time and I was a member of the factory
committee or party group. More than anything, we loved public affairs, meetings,
conferences, and lectures. When our sons were still very young we left them alone
in our room and I found time for sports such as the volleyball team.[29]

Nevertheless, apparently hasty conjugality between people who barely
knew each other exasperated authorities who on the one hand wanted

---

[25] "Far Eastern Regional Communist Party Committee ORPO: Memorandum on the
question of the Khetagurovite movement – on the condition of Khetagurovite youth on
the Far Eastern Railroads as of March 10, 1938," GAKhK P, f. 2, op. 6, d. 358, l. 21.
Of those who married, "some" left with their husbands for other areas and of those who
stayed most who were married were still working. Thirteen "ran away" from work on
the Far Eastern Railroad (DVZhD).

[26] According to data collected by the Khetagurovite Committee after one year of migration,
most of the Khetagurovites were born between 1914 and 1919. Sergei Scherbov and
Harrie van Vianen have demonstrated that the mean age of marriage (among those who
were surveyed recently in the Russian Federation) slowly increased among those born
after 1910. For those born in 1910, the mean age was 23 years. It increased to 23.5 for
those born in 1917 then to 25.3 for those born in 1922 and 1923. The latter cohort
would have been too young to join the Khetagurovites. It was those born between 1920
and 1924 that "experienced a marriage delay" because of World War II. See Scherbov
and van Vianen, "Marital and Fertility Careers of Russian Women," 135–136, 139.

[27] Memoir of Kapitalina Kostina, GAKhK P, f. 442, op. 2, d. 282, l. 23.

[28] *Ibid.*, 25.   [29] *Ibid.*, 26–28.

to encourage family formation and on the other hand did not like their economic ramifications and the kind of family life that resulted from such unions. These marriages were considered anathema to the Khetagurovites' mission because they often ended in quick divorces and single motherhood, and because many of those who married quit their jobs, inadvertently subverting attempts to staff cadre-starved enterprises through the Khetagurovite campaign. For instance, when Khetagurovite Opryshko returned to her workplace after a long absence, she was dismayed to learn that all of the Khetagurovites at her factory had "[m]arried and dropped work. These are unsteady young women who consider that as a young woman they will work, but when they get married it is time to retire."[30] Valianskaia, who was sent with a hundred other women to train as mechanics and drivers, thought that it was a shame that only half of those who arrived finished their tractor-driving course. She connected this desertion to poor choices in family life:

They say that a family is also important. But in my opinion not the kind of families set up by Khetagurovites. There were such young women who did not deserve to carry the name of Valia Khetagurova. They brought disgrace to this name. What did things come to? Our Khetagurovites, not knowing the person, got married after one day. This at a time when we talk about permanent vigilance, one must get to know the person first and then decide on such a serious step in life such as marriage.[31]

When the women returned to the school "after one day" because their husbands "threw them out," they were turned away and rejected by other Khetagurovites. The rejected brides "returned from whence they came." A similar story about the dangers of marriage came from Khetagurovite Krynova from the Viazemsk Lespromkhoz (Timber Industry Enterprise). The most "unsteady" among her group had also married. "This is of course not bad, but there are facts such as when one of them married a man who already had three children and a wife. Then he was fired and he took off. Another one married an embezzler. This also undermined the authority of Khetagurovites to a certain extent."[32]

While hasty marriages or the impact of marriage and childbirth upon employment and activism were a topic of discussion, there was also plenty of concern about the proclivities of some women to engage in casual sex. The resulting pregnancies, rumors of venereal diseases, and ostracism were not construed as individual tragedies. The behavior was an embarrassment and a waste of funds spent on bringing the woman to the region.

---

[30] "Stenographic text of the regional Khetagurovite conference," September 17, 1938, Opryshko, GAKhK P, f. 618, op. 1, d. 325, l. 297.
[31] *Ibid.*, September 15, Valianskaia, 64.   [32] *Ibid.*, September 17, Krynova, 210.

One Khetagurovite who worked at BAMLag "simply frolicked herself a baby and then had to leave."[33] Many of the suicides, attempted suicides, and attempts to induce miscarriages among Khetagurovites were the products of such scenarios.[34] Kulakova from the Mikhailov district lamented too many unplanned pregnancies and abandoned mothers and argued that it was up to the women to take a good hard look at their potential partners. She sided with those who expected young women to be better judges of character and to maintain decorum:

We often have cases of unintentional pregnancies. You'll never see the father again, which means they were unintentional. Not all our young women understand the principles of communist morality . . . We are not judging those who are pregnant, but we must bring to the attention of young women that they should strive for some sort of family succor. In general, we women must approach our comrades more tactfully.[35]

Young women who were in the Komsomol and found themselves single mothers, either because their husbands left them or because they had never married, turned to the Komsomol for help. They usually asked for assistance with new housing or jobs and with aid in tracking down their errant partners. While some did receive help, many were rebuffed. As a consequence, a good number simply walked away from the youth league. Others became openly hostile to the Komsomol, especially if they felt that they were unfairly judged or blamed for their unhappy circumstances. One young Khetagurovite "refused to vote" for her district's deputy for the Supreme Soviet.[36] Raising a toddler and a newborn alone, she had attempted to abort her second child when no help was forthcoming from the Komsomol. When pressed by an activist to participate and conform, she forcefully drove away the busybody, informing her that "The Komsomol is irrelevant for me and I'll live the way I please."[37]

Finding a "good lad"

Confusion about how to recognize "a good lad" and trepidation about the lack of real security in marriage were further magnified by the tense political atmosphere of the late 1930s and the peculiarities of the Far East's social world. That was why poor behavior by individuals was a legitimate concern for the larger female collective and Khetagurova reassured her

---

[33] *Ibid.*, name inaudible, 179.
[34] For examples of women choosing suicide when they received no assistance from the Komsomol, see *ibid.*, Priakhova, 286, and *ibid.*, Belova, 249.
[35] *Ibid.*, September 16, Kulakova, 195–196.
[36] *Ibid.*, September 18, Khetagurova, 302–303.   [37] *Ibid.*, 315.

audience, "A collective can create great miracles on this issue."[38] One of the most common ways to exert pressure on those who ruined the reputation of the collective was through public exposure and punishment. Khetagurova was an ardent advocate of such tactics:

Lovers of all kinds of adventures, morally weak, even those smacking of a preference for risky ventures have wormed their way into the ranks of young patriots. We cannot let a few people ruin our wonderful collective. We must approach with greater strictness those who degrade our collective, [those] who bring in their own values and habits that are unnatural for Far Eastern Komsomol members.[39]

Collective supervision and correction were at the center of suggestions for improving the behavior of "unsteady" women and concerned activists surmised that "[a]s much as this or that young woman comes under fire of collective opinion then she will change."[40] At the 1938 conference someone brought up the example of Zina, confronted by other Khetagurovites when she garnered unseemly attention from men because she liked to attend dances. "We told her that if you do not find a job and work normally, then get out of here. She has now improved."[41] When collective censure did not work, Khetagurovites could be relieved of their titles. Stories of bad Khetagurovites losing their "titles" abounded at the Khetagurovite conference. Speaker after speaker introduced their own list of "unsteady" Khetagurovites whom they wanted expelled from their ranks and driven from the Far East.[42]

More than one female activist reveled in the success they had in deploying public humiliation as a means of social control. Saprykina, the secretary of the Nizhnii-Amur oblast Komsomol Committee, expressed disappointment that the Komsomol regional committee had done nothing to integrate "lessons about our morality" outlined in the Kononenko piece into mass agitation work among young people.[43] She had found her own way of dealing with "immoral" behavior on the part of new parents. "We

---

[38] *Ibid.*, 334.

[39] Valentina Khetagurova, "Organizovat' dvizhenie molodykh patriotov," *KP*, January 26, 1938.

[40] "Stenographic text of the regional Khetagurovite conference," September 16, 1938, Shukhman, 101. Kenneth Pinnow explains the uses and development of "collective opinion" in discussions of suicides. See Pinnow, "Violence against the Collective Self and the Problem of Social Integration in Early Bolshevik Russia," *Kritika* 4:3 (Summer 2003), 653–677. I translate *obshchestvennoe mnenie* as "collective opinion" rather than "public opinion" as suggested by Pinnow, *ibid.*, 662.

[41] "Stenographic text of the regional Khetagurovite conference," September 16, 1938, Shukhman, 97.

[42] Examples of requests to relieve others of the title are in *ibid.*, Feikhel'son, 112, and *ibid.*, Livshits, 121.

[43] "Protocol of the I Khabarovsk regional Komsomol conference," February 11–15, 1939, GAKhK P, f. 617, op., 1, d. 3, l. 164.

had a young woman who did not behave morally, and she gave birth to a baby. I personally wrote about this fact in our local newspaper."[44] The subject of the column subsequently stormed into her office demanding to know why Saprykina had "humiliated her across the whole oblast." The story had a happy ending and served to prove the effectiveness of such tactics. According to Saprykina, the same young woman returned to say, "Thank you. He came back to me." She proudly concluded, "Well, basically we married them." The transcript indicates laughter among the audience.

Humiliation was not necessarily thought to be the only way to deal with young women in difficult circumstances. Discretion and empathy were the techniques of Chumikhina and her group of Khetagurovites. She described how they dealt with

one Khetagurovite-mother, actually she was not married, so it happens. To create conditions for her and not drive her into a depressed mood, we did not ask her why, [or] how it happened, etc. We just treated her with absolute friendship . . . We gave her aid and said to her that she should be proud to be a mother and raise her child. We need cadres.[45]

This stress on getting peer groups involved was not only a function of the already widespread practice among Komsomol members of policing one another's political and personal lives. It was also a function of the absence of any communal forces of social control in a region teeming with a highly fluid population of young migrants. It had the potential to mitigate the social isolation experienced by women who had no way of evaluating their potential partner's suitability through more typical channels of social networks and gossip. Confusion about how to recognize "a good lad" and trepidation about the lack of real security in marriage were magnified by the tense political atmosphere of the late 1930s. This appeared in the observations of Khetagurovite Opryshko, who noted that a lack of social support and information led women into bad decisions. "And so it happens sometimes: a young woman, not having known the person, gets married. He turns out to be some kind of rascal and you get all kinds of moral and sexual corruption. If we work collectively this would not happen and it will be easier to know the lad that the young woman plans to marry."[46]

Sometimes little could be achieved, even when a seemingly innocent young woman made a mistake and a female collective came to her aid.

---

[44] Ibid., 165.
[45] "Stenographic text of the regional Khetagurovite conference," September 17, 1938, Chumikhina, 387.
[46] Ibid., Opryshko, 297–298.

The politically fashionable insistence that women had to be vigilant and were culpable for poor choices was used by some to absolve men from responsibility. Delegate Shukhman from Blagoveshchensk told the story of a Khetagurovite called Asia, who worked in a hair salon nicknamed "Khetagurovite" because all its employees had come in response to the call-up. Asia, a generally good girl, married a soldier but he "had many wives and was paying alimony."[47] When she became pregnant, he informed Asia that "you are not the only one I have, there are three of you." Asia tried to "poison herself three times. People heard that she lived with an *alimenshchik* [someone with alimony obligations]." Female Komsomol members were asked to intervene, but when they spoke to the man's commander he scoffed and blamed the girl for poor judgment.[48]

More than one female activist pointed out that it was material circumstances that pushed women into marriage rather than a dissolute life or empty heads. Khetagurovite Ivanova believed that women who came to the Far East without a profession or opportunities for training were "forced to get married because they earned only 200 rubles and it is difficult to live on this in the Far East. What does this lead to? Today she marries only out of material necessity and tomorrow she gets divorced."[49] Ivanova told the story of one young woman who could not live on 150 rubles, so she told everyone, "I am looking for a husband." The audience of Khetagurovites laughed. Ivanova, clearly agitated, excoriated those who thought there was something amusing about this scenario. What was there to laugh about when women were getting married because of material circumstances? "One young woman married and got a disease from him. Actually he was in the Komsomol and was punished for this and expelled. But she had to endure a great deal."[50]

A number of activists were not afraid to blame officials for the desperation that drove some women to make terrible choices. Apathetic and cynical bosses and local Communists were responsible for many bad decisions. Miagkaia, an accounts clerk in the Otrednenskii motorized tractor station (MTS), understood that women who were sent to the Far East without a good profession and channeled into tractor-driving schools were forced into compromising situations out of material need. "There is poor discipline in the Zverev auto colony. Gals are unbelievably promiscuous. How many have been sent away? How many reprimands have been given? Are these really Khetagurovites? Nothing happens. The

---

[47] *Ibid.*, September 16, Shukhman, 101.
[48] Men's status as payers of alimony was cited as a sign of dissipation in other discussions. See *ibid.*, Roshchina, 179.
[49] *Ibid.*, September 17, Ivanova, 223–224.   [50] *Ibid.*, 224.

district executive committee has decided: 'Let them live on 150 rubles, [let them] get married twenty times.'"[51]

Roshchina echoed this theme, complaining about the poor support women received from the Komsomol in Komsomol'sk-na-Amure and from the regional Komsomol committee. Particularly upset about incidents of "poisoning" (which usually implied either an attempted suicide or attempt to abort by ingesting quinine) in Komsomol'sk, she pointed to the lack of punishment for the men who drove women to desperate acts. "These *poshliaki* [lechers] have not been made responsible and our procurator has done nothing to punish them. Lads think this way: there are many young women. Today I can marry one, tomorrow another . . . But the procurators never once meted out justice in such a way as to crack all their ribs."[52]

Although Khetagurova took an unforgiving tone in the presence of Khetagurovites on the topic of those who married hastily, she displayed more sympathy in other contexts. At a regional conference of Komsomol activists in February 1939, she told the audience that the deplorable living conditions of many Khetagurovites led to other kinds of trouble and it was the fault of the Komsomol for letting their lives degenerate to such an extent:

We must remember that the young people who come here are just beginning an independent life, they are inexperienced. Then it is understandable that when some young woman comes, she ends up in a bad situation, a young man turns up and makes her an offer and she agrees to marry him not because she has some feelings for him but simply to get out of a difficult situation.[53]

The problem of hasty marriages became so urgent that Khetagurovites were officially discouraged from dating men and getting married in their first few months in the region. Women traveling to the Far East were explicitly warned "not to get married on the train."[54] Khetagurovites called on each other to make sure that new arrivals did not "suddenly get married after three days. This leads women into great distress."[55] However, such admonitions lacked the real assistance that young women needed in their new environment.

Calls for more restraint were ironically interpreted by some as official injunctions against marriage. This interpretation was so widespread that

[51] *Ibid.*, Miagkaia, 224.   [52] *Ibid.*, September 16, Roshchina, 183–184.

[53] "Protocol of the I Khabarovsk regional Komsomol conference," February 1939, GAKhK P, f. 617, op. 1, d. 3, l. 187.

[54] Memoir of Efrosina Mishalova, February 18, 1976, GAKhK P, f. 442, op. 2, d. 284, l. 95.

[55] "Stenographic text of the regional Khetagurovite conference," September 17, 1938, Ivanova, 224.

Khetagurova had to publicly rebuke proposals for abstinence. According to her, it was wrong to conclude, as some had surmised, that "[j]ust because you came to the Far East you should not meet lads or get married. You have come here not for one day, and you must create healthy families, but you should approach this issue seriously, having thought it over, create a good family, find yourself a good lad."[56] Khetagurovite Livshits remained hopeful that not all marriages were doomed to failure or likely to dilute the long-term contribution of young women to the defense of the Far East. She felt it necessary to defend marriage as a natural and positive phenomenon: "It happens that all young people, including Khetagurovites, meet young men. We have eight people who have gotten married and have settled in the Far East for a long time."[57]

Dubious people

Poor choices in sexual and marriage partners could carry a much heavier burden than a broken heart or single motherhood in the late 1930s. Conduct considered dissolute by authorities had been grounds for expulsion and censure among Komsomol and party members throughout this period and in all regions of the Soviet Union. Although Khetagurovites were acclaimed for their heroism and lavished with publicity, they were not immune from invasive probing into their personal lives and from loss of status.

As early as 1937, Khetagurova tried to encourage Khetagurovites to be suspicious and monitor one another. "Young women Khetagurovites, watch out, dubious people might be among us."[58] The members of the Khetagurovite Committee had a difficult time discerning whether they were inviting the right sort of person and later determined that many had come who did not "justify the [country's] trust."[59] In September 1938 Khetagurova ascribed the rash of what she considered to be unseemly behavior and flighty morals as indicators of enemy machinations. She thought it wise to launch an investigation to ascertain whether some might be trying to "intentionally undermine your authority with their behavior . . . There is no guarantee that the enemies are not carrying out their own deeds under the cover of the title Khetagurovite. [Enemies] could have used this undertaking and sent their own people here with special assignments to either corrupt or undermine the authority of Soviet patriotki."[60]

---

[56] *Ibid.*, September 18, Khetagurova, 332.   [57] *Ibid.*, September 16, Livshits, 121.
[58] *Ibid.*, September 15, Karlova, 53.   [59] *Ibid.*, Vochkova, 55.
[60] *Ibid.*, September 18, Khetagurova, 335.

Anxiety over the behavior of Khetagurovites seethed in part because of the presence of the labor camp system and the region's reputation as a wild cultural and ideological crossroads populated by remnants of pre-revolutionary society, the subjects of menacing neighboring countries, and colored by a rough male culture. Women were warned that they were leaving for a space teeming with enemies. Before Opryshko left Ukraine for the Far East, the secretary of her Komsomol committee warned the women: "Watch out! There are all sorts of elements there and they can use you any way they want for their alien aims."[61] Migrants were told that moral rectitude would buttress their political acumen and help them to avoid the machinations of enemies. Efrosina Mishalova remembered several lectures on vigilance and morality among women gathered for their trip to the Far East. At their hotel in Moscow, they listened to a special lecture on how to behave as women going to the Far East because their hotel had "foreign representatives"; they were told not to disclose why they had gathered and where they were going. During the journey, the women were reminded not to "gossip and [to] carry ourselves with dignity in the restaurant car" because they would be traveling with Chinese and Japanese passengers. "Anything" could happen en route. "Unknown people" might turn up in the carriage to "carry out some kind of agitation." These lectures had the desired effect, on Mishalova at least. "We were still young and inexperienced . . . But after this discussion on the train of course our minds started to work completely differently, we became more alert, and perhaps a tiny bit smarter."[62] The order to avoid disclosing their destinations to strangers in fact made little sense because their departures and the Khetagurovite campaign in general were highly publicized events. The insistence on secrecy as women gathered for the trip only made sense if it was employed as a test to observe their capacity to take matters seriously, follow instructions, and reinforce what was thought to be healthy paranoia.

The arrival of Khetagurovites in a border region populated by current and former prisoners, special settlers, and suspect groups plunged them into a social landscape where boundaries between "us" and "them" were simultaneously critical and hard to discern. Often, to the surprise and disdain of Khetagurovites, former prisoners and special settlers worked in positions of authority.[63] NKVD inspector Utkina worried about the milieu that surrounded Khetagurovites working in the city of Svobodny because there were many prisoners and former prisoners who worked and

[61] *Ibid.*, September 17, Opryshko, 297.   [62] Mishalova, 92ob–93ob, 95.

[63] One of these ex-prisoners who become an acclaimed author is the subject of Thomas Lahusen's *How Life Writes the Book: Real Socialism and Socialist Realism in Stalin's Russia* (Ithaca: Cornell University Press, 1997).

mingled among the free employees of the city. "The city of Svobodny is a large one but its conditions are special because a large part of the population is made up of prisoners. This means that we should approach the issue of youth with more seriousness. We must put the matter in such a way as to bring the young people closer to the Komsomol and not to those people who sit in our apparatus out of necessity."[64] Along with the potential for status confusion and "contamination" from "alien elements," the perception that Khetagurovites were available and must have arrived in search of male company tacked an extra layer of pressure on young women.

The authorities thought they had cause to be concerned. Stories of women accused of sexual dissolution were common among employees of the GULAG system and in enterprises that used prison labor in isolated circumstances. All these institutions and enterprises experienced extreme cadre shortages and indiscriminately hired large groups of Khetagurovites who were hard to place in any other jobs.[65] Starved of personnel, the NKVD also offered a generous salary as compensation for distasteful duties and regularly requested large numbers of employees regardless of education or skill level. Thus, unintentionally, the youngest, least experienced, and perhaps least politically "educated" found themselves in close proximity to the most "dubious" characters imaginable.

Young women who were sent to labor camps were more likely to personally witness another kind of truth about Soviet power and the plight of prisoners. None of those who volunteered to go to the Far East could have had any inkling that they would be assigned to work in the labor camp system or among convict laborers in the lumber and goldmining camps. Surviving copies of invitations sent by the Khetagurovite Committee to successful applicants demonstrate that migrants were not offered any specifics about their future employment.[66] Once the women were registered as residents and employees, there was little chance for them to abandon their jobs easily without serious consequences or at least excessive costs. Lack of alternatives forced women to endure conditions that were uncomfortable and potentially compromising. Khetagurovite Bloshkina reported that she was not provided with a place to live in when she went to work for the Dal'Lag NKVD. For months without her own

---

[64] "Stenographic text of the regional Khetagurovite conference," September 17, 1938, Utkina, 275.

[65] Utkina, herself an NKVD investigator, lamented that other Khetagurovites working in the NKVD were "very illiterate. They hardly know how to write" (*ibid.*, 272).

[66] A typical invitation came to a male accountant: "We invite you to work in one of our districts as an accountant if you have at least 2–3 years' experience and if you are single." See "Memorandum on the work of the Committee for the reception of young people of the Khetagurovite call-up," December 13, 1938, GAKhK P, f. 2, op. 6, d. 341, l. 137.

space, she was "compelled to sleep in a room with eight men. After this she was accused of having sex with someone under arrest."[67]

There is evidence that some recoiled from their duties in the administration of convict labor and as a result refused to live according to expectations, openly deriding the Komsomol. One of the channels for rebellion available to women in these conditions was to flaunt their sexuality. Khetagurovite Krynova, from the Viazemsk Lespromkhoz, explained that some among the first to arrive in the lumber camps "did not prove themselves. Honestly, a few of them were good gals, but felt themselves to be out of place. Other young women became loose – working badly."[68] When the "loose" women were fired and expelled from the league, they "wrote to comrade Stalin." The letter, sent without the knowledge of the Komsomol, backfired and they were "taken away by the organs of the NKVD."[69] Other women who were sent to the lumber camps quit and "now they are skipping from place to place."

Descriptions of Khetagurovites who refused to conform came from an employee of the Amur railroad. He explained that because convicts who worked for the railroad "regardless of their sentences" were poorly supervised, they had plenty of dangerous opportunities to fraternize with free employees, including the Khetagurovites.[70] This permitted Khetagurovite Mironenko to "get together" with a prisoner, convicted for counterrevolutionary activities. "They set up drinking bouts in her apartment." The young woman had "fallen so far" that she was also tried for counterrevolutionary activities and received a five-year sentence. Two other Khetagurovites regularly invited co-worker convicts into their homes. When they were asked to account for their behavior, they replied, "We have fallen in love with them."[71] The scandalized observer wondered, "What does it mean for a young woman Khetagurovite-Komsomolka to be drinking with counterrevolutionary criminals?"[72] He demanded that the women be expelled from the Komsomol. To his surprise, the Komsomol organization of BAMLag was unperturbed by such romances and the women were left to themselves.

Despite the financial enticements of work for the NKVD, certain "well-educated Khetagurovites" refused to "be of use."[73] Some tried to feign illness or a handicap to avoid working. A Khetagurovite employed in

---

[67] "Memorandum on the work of the committee for the reception of young people of the Khetagurovite call-up – Complaint of Bloshkina," December 19, 1938, GAKhK P, f. 2, op. 6, d. 341, l. 116.

[68] "Stenographic text of the regional Khetagurovite conference," September 17, 1938, Krynova, 209.

[69] *Ibid.*, 210.   [70] *Ibid.*, Davydov, 323.   [71] *Ibid.*, 324.   [72] *Ibid.*

[73] The NKVD paid arriving Khetagurovites 900 rubles as a lump sum and 700 rubles per month thereafter according to Utkina (*ibid.*, 273).

Dal'Lag told her bosses that she "could not work in Dal'Lag because it was hard for her to walk up to the fourth floor."[74] In more than one instance, women crossed the line between "us and them" at great personal cost, perhaps out of sheer rebellion and empathy. A highly qualified Khetagurovite, Abramchena, was sent to work in an NKVD department, but shortly after her appointment she expressed a desire to find another job. Unable to "get transferred" from the NKVD, she married a prisoner "and now walks around like, pardon me if this is rude, like a princess of fools."[75] She was not the only one to take this dangerous path. A nurse sent to work in a Kolyma labor camp, Aedita A. Sabot'ko, was fondly remembered by a former prisoner who was her subordinate in the medical ward. She was apparently "a sensitive and attractive woman, who for the sake of love and marriage to a former political prisoner 'dared' to lay it down, in other words, return her party card."[76] Yet among her colleagues she served as an inspiration, "with her calm and evenhandedness in the treatment of patients and medical personnel."[77]

Klava Novikova, the one-time Khetagurovite, who found herself in a labor camp for stealing food to feed her infant during World War II, did not seek to remarry after she was released from the camp because she "did not trust men. Besides, what kind of good one would I find with my biography?"[78] But in 1959 she noticed a quiet man with interesting manners who she thought might be a Buriat or a Kirghiz. It turned out that Japanese Iasaburo Khachiia was a former prisoner himself. He had served his sentence of ten years for "espionage" in the Magadan region after being picked up in North Korea in 1946 by the Red Army in a mass arrest of Japanese nationals. At the end of his sentence, a bureaucratic mix-up derailed his repatriation to Japan and he resigned himself to a marginal existence in the land of the Soviets. Klava and Iasaburo, with so much in common, eventually made a life for themselves in the small town of Progress in the Far East. Klava worked as an accountant and, after retirement, as a cleaning lady at the local court. Iasaburo, renamed Iakov Ivanovich, gained renown as the town's hairdresser and photographer, attracting a female clientele from across the Amur oblast.

---

[74] *Ibid.*, Belova, 255.   [75] *Ibid.*, Davydov, 325.
[76] Mstislav Tolmachev, "Takaia dolgaia poliarnaia noch'," glava 60, *Nizhegorodskii literaturnyi zhurnal. http://litzur.narod.ru/memory/tolmachev/s1/60.html* (1 and 2 of 6).
[77] *Ibid.*
[78] Ekaterina Sazhneva, "Zhili-byli samurai so starukhoi," *Moskovskii komsomolets*, November 16, 2005. *www.mk.ru*

"Rather odd customs"

While obtuse references to improper behavior and immorality peppered discussions among officials and Khetagurovites in their letters and at their regional conference, few details are discernible. The voices of the women in question are barely perceptible through the filters of those who used their stories for their own purposes. However, one accusatory summary sent by a procurator to the First Secretary of the Khabarovsk region's Communist Party Committee details the Khetagurovites' exploitation and sexual misadventures to a remarkable extent.[79] The procurator included excerpts of testimony from the accused, victims, and witnesses. In a follow-up note, the regional procurator also informed the First Secretary of other noteworthy revelations about the sexual misdeeds of men in responsible positions.[80] The level of detail, generously offered by the procurator to the First Secretary, indicates a desire to furnish titillating reading rather than information relevant to the addressee.

While this document provides the most explicit retelling of the fate that awaited young women who fell through the cracks of the Khetagurovite Committee's placement system, it has its limitations. Testimony was elicited from accused individuals who had every reason to prevaricate, while the victims and witnesses had their own reasons to present themselves as hapless victims or guiltless bystanders. Nevertheless, the document illustrates the way representatives of the state understood the power dynamics between men and women. The kind of accusations the procurators filed and their construction of the evidence reveals attempts to curb rampant abuses of women's vulnerabilities. The case also highlights the drive by judicial authorities to punish those who pursued what they construed to be "disorderedly sexual lives."[81] It exposes the responses of young women to the vast imbalance in power they encountered and tells us something about their attitudes toward sex and marriage. Finally, this source offers a partial glimpse into the realm of sexual relationships in settings where scarce material necessities, residential permits, and documents essential for employment depended on one's access to male-dominated patronage networks.

The Khetagurovites' misadventures began with the depressingly familiar-sounding story of poor conditions and poor morale in a lumber

---

[79] "Correspondence with the procuracy of the Khabarovsk region. Bill of indictment," June 1939, GAKhK P, f. 35, op. 1, d. 315, ll. 100–107.

[80] "Correspondence with the procuracy of the Khabarovsk region," August 5, 1939, GAKhK P, f. 35, op. 1, d. 316, ll. 62–63.

[81] "Correspondence with the procuracy of the Khabarovsk region. Bill of indictment," June 1939, GAKhK P, f. 35, op. 1, d. 315, l. 102.

camp system where many who were especially young and lacking in other skills were assigned. The group of women that eventually became the subject of an investigation had abandoned their jobs in the Oborsk Lespromkhoz. The enterprise exploited a significant number of convict prisoners, with more than 4,500 convict laborers working on the site in 1938.[82] Along with labor camp inmates, timber was processed by thousands of forced settlers.[83] The women in question, Klava S., twenty-one, Zina Sh., eighteen, and Nina U., seventeen, had good cause to look for something better at the end of 1938. In fact, the miserable state of affairs in the Oborsk Lespromkhoz was well known to the authorities even before details of this case came to light in the summer of 1939.

In 1938 Khetagurova received complaints about inept administrators and a lack of basic amenities there. She launched an investigation that may have improved conditions for some but did little to address the general malaise. Conditions continued to generate complaints and inquiries. In March 1939, several months before the case was investigated, Komsomol members working in the Lespromkhoz organized their own "light cavalry" to document their conditions and appeal for help. Poor supervision was at the root of the moral decay, according to two young male Komsomol members who wrote to the regional Komsomol committee and to *Tikhookeanskii komsomolets*. The self-appointed correspondents reported that 280 Komsomol members were left on their own, with little to do and little guidance, and conditions were driving young people away in a "panic." To underscore the extremes of disenchantment, they related that "[y]oung women have begun drinking wine, justifying it. 'There is nowhere to find amusement, we have to drink from boredom.' And in reality they are right, there are many young people here and at their stage of life they long for some kind of society and what happens, they start getting accustomed to what? To wine."[84]

---

[82] Convicts employed here came from the UshosstroiLag, one of five autonomous camp systems run in the region by the NKVD. See "Memorandum, information and reports of [the] political department and administration of the corrective labor camps NKVD in the Far East on the composition of the party organization, on its productive activities and on other questions," February 3–11, 1939, GAKhK P. f. 35, op. 1, d. 313, l. 3.

[83] It was a significant population: 7,780 individuals (4,473 of them adults) living in twenty-seven settlements in the forests that also happened to be less than 100 kilometers from the border with Manchuria. See "Reports and notes on the work of NKVD," January 11, 1939, GAKhK P, f. 35, op. 1, d. 313, l. 263. This was about the same number of special settlers as had been in the area as of January 1, 1934, when 8,821 individuals lived and worked around this timber enterprise. For conditions among these settlers, see E. N. Chernolutskaia, "Usloviia zhizni spetspereselentsev v Priamur'e v 1934 g.," in Argudiaeva (ed.), *Sem'ia i semeinyi byt v vostochnykh regionakh Rossii*, 171–177.

[84] "Requests, 1938–1939," GAKhK P, f. 35, op. 1, d. 339, ll. 8–11, and "Requests of a personal nature, Letter from Titov and Shchendaruk," March 1, 1939, GAKhK P, f. 35, op. 1, d. 347, l. 162.

These reports of panic, boredom, and dissolution had an uncanny prescience. The fate of those very same young people who ran away in a panic became grounds for the court case and judicial summary that landed on the desk of the Khabarovsk First Party Secretary in the summer of 1939. After fleeing the misery and monotony of the lumber enterprise, a group of young Khetagurovites found their way to Khabarovsk, where they expected to be temporarily housed and reassigned by the staff of the KhabarovskLes (Khabarovsk Forest Trust), an umbrella organization of the region's lumber industry. Demoralized by their experiences in the forests of the Khabarovsk region and probably hoping to find an easier life, the young women did not resist the unconventional offer made by the chief of the Trust, Goncharenko. Procurator Shevel'kov explained that when the young women arrived, "Instead of placing them in the dormitory, Goncharenko settled them in his own apartment, where he plied them with drink and used them in a sexual manner."[85]

A month later, Goncharenko evicted the women without "the ability to find a place in a dormitory and without a job." After Goncharenko expelled the Khetagurovites, one of his neighbors, an accountant for KhabarovskLes called Varkulevskii, took them in and "also plied them with drink, had sex with them and later threw them out of his apartment." The next move for the women was into the home of the chief of the military department of a party committee in the Kirov district (a neighborhood in Khabarovsk), Guliakov. He "kept them for more than one month, doing with them the same as Goncharenko and Varkulevskii." Court testimony corroborated what had been clear about KhabarovskLes operations from the numerous letters of complaints sent by others without any connection to this case. The organization had done nothing to provide decent living conditions while their administrators took advantage of the desperation they created. The procurator, in his correspondence with the Khabarovsk First Party Secretary, was simultaneously ironic and grave. "It must be concluded that there are rather odd customs at KhabarovskLes. [These] bring immense harm to the matter of fastening cadres in our region and to the matter of fulfilling the plans established for KhabarovskLes."[86]

The exposure of the way the Khetagurovites were treated by their bosses occurred only after authorities began to investigate an apartment occupied by three bachelors. Eventually, two were charged with having "organized a den of degeneracy into which they drew . . . a whole group of men and young women, among them Khetagurovites. [In their apartment]

---

[85] "Correspondence with the procuracy of the Khabarovsk region," August 5, 1939, GAKhK P, f. 35, op. 1, d. 316, l. 62.
[86] *Ibid.*, 62–63.

they put on systematic drunken orgies accompanied by group sex acts."[87]

One of those accused was Pavel Ianushevskii, a 32-year-old bachelor from a family of workers in the former Vitebsk guberniia (county). A member of the Communist party with only a village school education, Ianushevskii worked as the director of a Far Eastern construction enterprise (Dal'mestpromstroi). Another was Sergei D'iakov, a 29-year-old bachelor and Communist party member. D'iakov hailed from a working-class family in the Urals and had completed all seven years at school; he was the chief of the Regional Executive Committee's Housing Administration (Domoupravlenii). The third man was of much lower status and salary, a driver by the name of Ivan Shustov. Although he was a resident of the "den" and admitted participating in its revelry, his humble occupation and no doubt his collaboration during the interrogation and court proceedings absolved him from prosecution and placed him in the category of witness. In the final tally seven other men also took part in the events at D'iakov's home. Most were young and held positions far below those of the two hosts. For instance, Ianushevskii used his personal driver, Frolov, as a courier, "delivering drinks, food and women and taking part in the drinking and use of women."[88] A young music student was moved into the apartment at the behest of Ianushevskii and D'iakov to provide a ready source of musical accompaniment.

Ianushevskii, as chief of a large organization, had all the trappings of power and occasions for its abuse. An impressive salary, access to cars, and a slew of subordinates enabled him to structure a social world that fulfilled almost every kind of indulgence that a man of his education and background could invent. D'iakov had power over housing assignments and house wardens, which made it possible for him to provide apartment space that was immune from official scrutiny despite its occupants' persistently raucous behavior. The employment of such relatively young men with so few credentials as chiefs of large and powerful organizations resulted from the preceding series of purges that had devastated the region's experienced and older administrative cadres.

Ianushevskii and D'iakov had met in October 1938 and struck up a friendship. Shortly after, D'iakov moved Ianushevskii into his apartment in the building belonging to the Regional Executive Committee in the center of Khabarovsk. Once the two were flatmates, they started to socialize with a group of men and women who were not averse to heavy

---

[87] "Correspondence with the procuracy of the Khabarovsk region. Bill of indictment," June 1939, GAKhK P, f. 35, op. 1, d. 315, l. 100. Accusations against them were under statutes 150, 154 and 155 UK RSFSR.

[88] *Ibid.*, 105.

drinking and unconstrained sexual behavior. Without doubt a generous host, Ianushevskii also invited other male subordinates from work to join in his merrymaking.

Not every woman who participated in the parties or who had sexual relations with the men did so under duress or expressly out of need. Testimony from a female acquaintance and occasional lover of Ianushevskii, Elena L., suggests that she and other women welcomed invitations to attend the well-stocked parties. Notes from Ianushevskii such as "Come today for the evening and bring lots of women" suggests nothing unusual about the behavior of a group of single men other than the regularity with which they were able to offer such invitations.[89] Elena L. proved agreeable and came with numerous young women, including several, such as Elena K. and Liuba L. who became regular attendees.

Participants in the escapades understood that their carousing "would have been impossible to carry on for long had not D'iakov been the director of the Housing Administration and all house wardens were subordinate to him."[90] Shustov, the lowly driver, drew a distinct line between men like himself and the well-off bosses. He blamed all the drunken orgies on Ianushevskii because "he earned 2,500 rubles salary . . . and under these conditions the initiative for drinking with the participation of women belongs to Ianushevskii."[91]

The line between willing participation and exploitation was irrevocably crossed when Ianushevskii and D'iakov took in Khetagurovites "without employment and without residential permits." At any given time between October 1938 and April 1939, four or five women in such legal limbo lived in the apartment. All were young women who had fallen through the cracks of the Khetagurovite committee's job placement system. Besides those who had been traded as commodities by the bosses of KhabarovskLes – Klava S, Zina Sh., and Nina U. – there were other female Khetagurovites: Antonina M., Valia S., Nelia M., Vera T., and a few others not expressly named in the documents:

All of the named young women as a result of the criminal attitude on the part of the staff of the Oborsk Lespromkhoz, where they had been sent, were forced to leave it and return to Khabarovsk where they became temporarily homeless and without means of survival. Ianushevskii and D'iakov using their difficult situations pulled them into attendance of the den.[92]

The women's relationship with Ianushevskii and D'iakov began when Klava S. met them through the KhabarovskLes accountant, Varkulevskii,

[89] *Ibid.*, 102. Ianushevskii did not deny doing this.
[90] *Ibid.*, 100–107. Testimony of Kapko.   [91] *Ibid.*, 102. Testimony of Shustov.
[92] *Ibid.*, 101.

who was both a participant in Ianushevskii's social group and among the first to exploit the women's vulnerabilities when they first arrived in Khabarovsk. Klava S. admitted that on the very first day of her introduction to the Ianushevskii circle, she immediately took part in the drinking because "they had wine." She was sent to find her friends and the young women made themselves at home. Although Klava admitted to drinking wine, she also recalled being repulsed by Ianushevskii's behavior on the first night. She explained that "Ianushevskii propositioned Nina U., Vera T., and myself, in turn, but we tried to get away from him since he pestered us and wanted to have sexual intercourse." Considering that Klava and two of her friends had already spent some time being traded between employees of KhabarovskLes before their introduction to the Ianushevskii circle, Klava's shock at his propositions cannot be taken at face value.[93] Despite or because of the pestering, all the young women spent the night and continued to return to the house for the next several months.

The procurator included excerpts from the women's testimony to support his claim that the men's position of power and promises produced acquiescence to all manner of humiliations. Klava explained that "we stayed there since we lived without a residential permit, not having the documents for it or for getting a job."[94] The women had cause to believe that they would get assistance in finding legitimate employment and residential permits. After all, the men they met were more than capable of doing so and made numerous promises along those lines. Zina told the investigators:

When we ended up in the company of Ianushevskii, then we asked him and a series of others to get us a job. But they only made promises and using our helplessness forced us to enter with them into this filthy degenerate life. We were forced to have sex with the participants of this group. They presented themselves as decent people and said they were honest. Ianushevskii said that he was head of the Trust and D'iakov told me that if I lived with him then he would get me a job.[95]

The procurator made the point several times that the women had asked the men in responsible positions for help in finding work and they were given promises. The women's continuous pleading for legitimate work and the fact that the men promised to help them in exchange for sexual favors, seemed, in the eyes of the procurator, to absolve the women from any guilt and made the men all the more responsible.

---

[93] Another young woman told a similar story of initially thinking the men were respectable, until they began to drink and tell dirty jokes. *Ibid.*, 105. Testimony of Nelia M.
[94] *Ibid.*, 101. Testimony of Klava S.   [95] *Ibid.* 101. Testimony of Zina Sh.

Zina also claimed that she lived with Ianushevskii under the assumption that he would marry her. After a month of these promises, she finally realized that "it was impossible to live with him."[96] D'iakov succeeded in his sexual conquests by promising each woman marriage, and even "signed a promise." This kind of promissory note written late one night was presented to Zina. The contents of the note were used as evidence against D'iakov: "'As of October 14, 1938, 12 o'clock at night I am your husband and you are my wife.' Having issued this note D'iakov achieved intercourse with Zina Sh. after which he no longer spoke to her about marriage."[97] The procurator viewed these pledges of marriage to trick the women into sex as particularly sinister. "Having promised to marry them, giving them material aid [the men] were in fact pushing them on the path of prostitution."[98] The women knew that they were, in essence, "prostitutes. But there was nothing to be done, we had to make peace with it because we had nowhere to live and we had our own interest in it because they fed us and promised us work."[99]

After establishing that the women were forced into sexual acts by their circumstances, the procurator stressed that the sexual behavior in D'iakov's home took on extraordinarily "degenerate forms." After intentionally intoxicating the young women, the men, "As a rule fairly drunken, impudently divided the women among the men present . . . The men, shamelessly took the women and used them, finding places in the rooms, in the kitchen and in the corridor. Along with this they took turns using the women in an unnatural form on numerous occasions." Testimony about "unnatural forms" came from the female participants. Zina described the treatment of Klava, and a male hierarchy is discernible in the orchestration of sexual conquests. When D'iakov placed the drunken Klava on the bed and "used" her in front of the whole company of men and women, he then "recommended" her for "use" by Frolov, Ianushevskii's driver, and an accountant present at the party.

The women were also aware that after each night their performance was rated "for vigor during sexual intercourse." This rating system was particularly offensive to the procurator because it simultaneously "debased and compromised the movement of young women to the Far East." Drunken participants made fun of the Khetagurovite campaign, raising "derisive" toasts to the "kind of women who are coming here."[100]

None of this behavior actually qualified as offenses in the court case against Ianushevskii and D'iakov. The procurator had more to say about the way Ianushevskii treated his female employees and the women's

---

[96] *Ibid.*, 102.   [97] *Ibid.*, 106.   [98] *Ibid.*, 102.
[99] *Ibid.*, 101. Testimony of Nina S.   [100] *Ibid.*, 103.

responses to such manipulation. Eventually, the men were tried and convicted for forcing those under their authority in the workplace into sexual relationships, using their official cars and drivers for personal activities, and willfully spreading gonorrhea.

Two of Ianushevskii's secretaries gave testimony that was of direct relevance to the charges against the men. Their stories reveal attitudes toward sex and marriage. The procurator explained that a Khetagurovite who worked as Ianushevskii's secretary, Tatiana V., was "tricked and promised marriage, having received money from him, [and] went to his apartment where she stayed overnight. They were lovers for almost two months." Tatiana explained that Ianushevskii "offered to get together officially and [I would] live with him as a husband. I believed that he really wanted to marry me and his intentions were honest. This was the only reason that I agreed to be his lover."[101] When Ianushevskii grew tired of Tatiana, she was forced to quit her job.

Tatiana claimed that for the two months she was with Ianushevskii she firmly believed that they were engaged, though this was also when the apartment was the epicenter of ribald drinking and carousing. A large picture of a naked woman above his bed and the presence of random young women were not enough to discourage Tatiana's marriage plans. There were instances when Ianushevskii and his male compatriots tried to hide their behavior when Tatiana arrived unexpectedly.[102] Too drunk to move or perhaps simply apathetic, the nude Zina had to be wrapped in a blanket and spirited away into another room by loyal comrades. When Ianushevskii grew bored with Tatiana, he intentionally exposed her to his other diversions to end the relationship. Arriving at his house on a work-related errand, she found him sprawled on the bed in his underwear with a disheveled and barely dressed Nina U. Undeterred by the arrival of his bride-to-be, Ianushevskii continued kissing Nina. Tatiana did not recall much of a reaction to the situation until Ianushevskii began to compare Nina's body parts to those pictured in the photograph above his bed. "When he started to say these filthy things I could not take it and I hit him on the face and immediately left."[103]

After Tatiana quit under duress, the Khetagurovite Committee placed another young woman in the position of Ianushevskii's secretary on March 29, 1939. Ianushevskii "immediately erased professional boundaries." According to the new secretary, Vera D., her marital status came up at their first meeting and Ianushevskii told her that if she was a married woman "then you won't work here." When she was compelled to bring

---

[101] *Ibid.*, 103. Testimony of Tatiana V.   [102] *Ibid.*, 105.
[103] *Ibid.*, 103.

paperwork to his home after work, Vera always found him "intoxicated." On one of these visits, he locked the door and

started to hug and kiss me. When I began to resist, he started to persuade me not to be afraid and that I will not become pregnant and that I have a shabby skirt and that he will buy me a good suit and shoes. I resisted and wanted to scream but he closed my mouth and told me that it was pointless to scream because no one would hear me. He forced my hands behind my back and used me. Then he stood up and said, "Ugh, I thought you were a maiden."[104]

Having been raped and humiliated, Vera D. did not leave her job or refuse to have anything more to do with her assailant. Instead, she became a regular visitor to the apartment. Subsequently, the apparently naïve Vera overheard the men's banter about Zina, whom the men praised for having

"beautiful legs and a beautiful figure, she registers [oformliaetsia] well." I asked Ianushevskii where she was being registered, for what sort of work. He started laughing and said it means that she was adept in bed. Then I understood that he was also lovers with Zina. It became clear to me that Ianushevskii was not thinking of marrying me the way he promised but was simply using me and laughing at me.

The procurator was particularly galled by the group's irreverence for the language of officialdom and their puns on registration (oformlenie). "Not knowing the limits of shame, Ianushevskii in the presence of the young women selected one for himself and told her that 'I will register you today.' This means that the selected young woman had to lie down to sleep with him."[105] Because this point seemed so critical to him, the procurator introduced two other witness statements to document this particular impropriety and play with bureaucratic terminology.[106]

The procurator tried to reconstruct the convoluted list of lovers and relationships. He determined that at one time or another Ianushevskii was lovers with at least nine women. D'iakov was sleeping with at least six, including his former wife. The housemate, Shustov, and the music student admitted to sleeping with at least two. The final tally mattered because this "den of moral and political degeneracy" had become "a breeding ground of infection and transmission of venereal disease."[107] All the men who took part and all the women, along with the men who first abused the women's haplessness, Goncharenko and Guliakov, were diagnosed with gonorrhea.

---

[104] *Ibid.*, 104. Testimony of Vera D.   [105] *Ibid.*, 105.
[106] Klava S. told a similar story: "There were times when Ianushevskii selected one of us for him and proclaimed that he will be registering you today." *Ibid.*
[107] *Ibid.*, 106.

Ianushevskii was identified as the principal agent of transmission in this mini-epidemic. He had been diagnosed with gonorrhea as far back as 1937, "but because of incessant drinking and a degenerate sexual lifestyle the neglected gonorrhea took on a chronic form." When D'iakov was diagnosed and registered as a carrier of gonorrhea in February 1939, he continued to have "sexual intercourse" with his former wife. She in turn spread the disease to her new husband.

Ianushevskii admitted that men and women gathered in his apartment for the purposes of drinking and sex. He also admitted to sex with his secretaries and with using his subordinates for personal aims. He denied luring Khetagurovites into a den but "admitted that he did not take measures to stop them and instead provided the opportunity." He also denied being the source of the venereal disease and thought that his disease had been cured. D'iakov admitted that people gathered in his apartment to drink and to participate in a "disorderly sexual life." He also thought himself guilty of failing to assist Khetagurovites to find the "right path" and of having accepted their participation in this group. He admitted that the apartment was a breeding ground of venereal disease but denied having infected his former wife and claimed that he caught the infection from her. The men denied the most serious charges but their protestations had little effect. The court found Ianushevskii guilty as charged and sentenced him to five years. D'iakov received a four-year sentence in a labor camp.[108] No mention was made of the women's subsequent fate; they were fortunate that although Komsomol authorities were placing greater pressure on women to be responsible for their actions,

---

[108] *Ibid.*, 107.

The full accusations against Ianushevskii included:

1. Forcing sex from secretaries working for him in the Trust.
2. Organizing a den, drawing in "morally unstable youth" for drunken orgies with unnatural sexual acts.
3. Exploiting the temporarily difficult situation of those who came on the call-up: Klava S., Zina Sh., Nina U., Antonina M., and others.
4. Enticing the women into the den by promises of work and material aid but in fact putting them in the position of prostitutes.
5. Having brought his subordinates into the den and used them for delivery of wine and appetizers.
6. Having spread gonorrhea among the participants of the den.

D'iakov was charged as an accomplice who:

1. Provided the apartment to Ianushevskii by virtue of his position.
2. Was an active assistant in organizing the den of degeneracy.
3. Recruited men and women into the den for participation in drunken orgies and degenerate acts.
4. Achieved sexual relationships through dishonesty.
5. Knowing about his illness, nevertheless spread gonorrhea.

Soviet judicial practice still shielded them from full culpability in such circumstances.

This case was not covered in the local press and did not appear to have been orchestrated to transmit a cautionary tale to men or women. The fact that the men were prosecuted for nonpolitical crimes, mostly for gross abuse of their power over subordinates and for spreading venereal diseases, after the Great Terror had significantly subsided, suggests that this was not related to the vagaries of Stalinist mass repression. Given that anyone could fall into the hands of the NKVD on the flimsiest of evidence, it seems unlikely that the case against them was fabricated in such detail. The men also received fairly light sentences of four to five years if we consider that as a produce clerk Novikova received a sentence of seven and a half years for another nonpolitical crime several years later. There was no evidence of the men's subsequent fates or whether they tried to appeal their convictions.

One part of this story illuminates how conditions in the Far East could easily propel young women into compromising situations. Unbridled power in the hands of men like Ianushevskii to parcel out jobs, goods, and paperwork legitimizing residency easily translated into the ability to indulge every impulse. Offers of wine, food, and a roof over their heads were enough to entice more than one young woman into enduring humiliation and sexual exploitation. The other part reveals attitudes toward marriage. If the testimony of the two secretaries is to be believed, although they were not in the same desperate circumstances as the others, they, too, had very low expectations of love and respectful treatment from the men who promised to marry them. Marriage in this instance did not mean a partnership of like-minded comrades. Neither lover seemed to think of it as a long-term commitment. It was hardly understood by the women or men as a bond between two partners for reproduction and social stability. Rather, it was a temporary arrangement that at best brought some material rewards for women and sexual access for men. Although this may have been an exceptionally flagrant case of exploitation, it underscores the precarious position of many young women. On the frontier of Stalinism, the social dislocation inherent in migration dramatically increased women's vulnerabilities, pushing some to surrender to the economic and social power of men.

Conclusion

The campaign evident in *Komsomol'skaia pravda* to subdue sexual disorderliness by placing greater blame on young women provided ample opportunities for men to exploit women's sexuality. The consequences of sexual encounters fell into the domain of "women's problems." Women were held responsible for poor judgment while men were let off the hook. The extremes of disorganization, apathy, and shortages of housing and goods pushed many women into sexual exchanges or hasty marriages as a means of survival. Their behavior quickly became infamous among Far Easterners and sullied the reputation of all Khetagurovites for those prone to doubt the motivations of migrating women. Young women's geographic mobility and choice of professions offered an unprecedented spectrum in the officially demarcated realms of Soviet womanhood. No longer seen as passive victims of male lust, young women had also moved much closer to the realms of conscious personhood, endowed with the ability to make good and bad choices. This was part of the expansion in normative gender boundaries. At the same time, the politicization of their sexuality, and the expectations that as women they would be responsible for the success of marriages, crystallized a stark divide between the emotive attributes assigned to Soviet men and women.

The experiences of Khetagurovites demonstrate that many young people subverted the shift in state policies toward pronatalism and the concomitant elevation of marriage as an institution in the service of state interest. High geographic mobility and an overburdened court system made it easy for men to abandon wives or promise marriage as a ruse to cajole hesitant women into bed. The ban on abortions in the summer of 1936 added an extra layer of risk to sexual behavior while a marriage contract did little to tie down fathers who were unwilling to take responsibility. This meant hardships for women and quickly became a source of trouble for the Komsomol. The loss of well-trained and previously reliable cadres to the domestic hearth put marriage in a less than positive light from the perspective of Komsomol organizers, who worried about these losses. When partners abandoned them, young women made demands on the organization. If this assistance was not forthcoming, women were emboldened to openly reject the Komsomol and question socialist justice.

Marriage, far from representing an eternal institution, was a tenuous and potentially perilous predicament for young women in the late 1930s. Women's sexual autonomy and mobility generated a great deal of unease in the Far East. The realities of dislocation, anonymity, and material hardships produced what appeared to be disorderly sexual lives and a lighthearted attitude toward the institution of marriage. Among party and Komsomol officials, preoccupied with exposing enemies and maintaining class purity, there was an inability to articulate useful guidelines for behavior in a rapidly changing social world. This probably mattered very little to many of the young migrants faced with the necessities of basic survival or the desire to find some solace in the arms of a person they hardly knew. The ideal of marriage, epitomized by Khetagurova's status as Georgii's partner and *boevaia podruga* (girlfriend in struggle) proved elusive.

6   Snivelers and patriots

One resident of Komsomol'sk-na-Amure, fed up with conditions in the town, wrote directly to Stalin to "inform him" about life at Aviation Factory No. 126. He wanted Stalin to answer "several" questions. Tsvetkov thought comrade Stalin could at least explain, "Why housing conditions are so bad? Why is there a problem with regular salary payments? Why are there no goods or produce in the stores?" Tsvetkov sought answers for the perpetual shortages of toys, clothing, linens, and other merchandise despite the fact that a railroad link was in operation between Komsomol'sk and Khabarovsk. "I don't know why things are this way. If it is wrecking in retail then it must be investigated and measures should be taken . . . In this way they are creating class tensions among the working masses and all the laboring population of the city." Moreover, Tsvetkov was upset that having come to the city as a free employee and having married a Khetagurovite, he was still forced to share a room with two other young women. "I don't know what to do, as they say it is 'disgraceful' to run from here or [should I have] to live in inhuman conditions, but I did not come here to run . . . I'm asking you, comrade Stalin, to help the workers of Project 126, and me in particular."[1] Tsvetkov probably suspected what many officials knew very well. Many of the products sent to Komsomol'sk never made it because they were stolen from the train carriages. In 1939 thefts from trains going to the city totaled at least "640,000 rubles' worth of merchandise."[2]

While Tsvetkov was fuming, Anna Plaskina, who migrated as a teenager, also lived in one room with two families and a bachelor. However, years later she claimed that

[w]e did not feel the discomforts, everything was friendly and peaceful. There were enough kind words and space for everyone. We cared about each other

---

[1] Letter from Tsvetkov sent to Stalin from Komsomol'sk, May 25, 1938, and returned for investigation to the Komsomol'sk City Communist Party Committee. GAKhK P, f. 2, op. 1, d. 1349, l. 192.

[2] Lobanov, head of the Soviet cadre department of the regional Communist Party Committee. "Memorandum notes, 1939," GAKhK P, f. 35, op. 1, d. 172, l. 86.

when it was necessary. We did not have a kitchen or electric stoves. We cooked on primus stoves in a little corridor. Honestly, it was a bit more difficult in the winter, when we had to wash laundry on the streets at the pumps, but no one complained or decried their fates.[3]

Nina Asikritova, destined for work in a factory in Khabarovsk, had a good experience. In part, her successful transition was made possible by the fact that she stayed with a group of other young women in the city of Khabarovsk where it was more difficult for new migrants to sink into the oblivion of rural life or life in the GULAG. Asikritova remembered that the factory administration checked on how new migrants were living and went out of its way to make them comfortable when they found that Asikritova and others were living in a cold room:

When the factory's director, Vezvin, and the party bureau secretary Starostin came to visit (back then managers visited workers' apartments) they used to say, "Oh gals, we'll have to give you a different room." But we answered, "We are not cold. We were not expecting any better. You should make things comfortable for families." We put two cots together and the three of us slept close to each other [because] it was warmer that way. In the morning, we shattered the ice that had formed overnight in our bucket, tossed around icicles, and dashed off to the factory giggling the whole way.[4]

Valentina Khetagurova also kept to the story of helpful bosses when asked to recall the migration program.[5]

Obviously, not all Khetagurovites or other residents found enough kind words and space to keep their spirits up. In the spring of 1938, some of the women who had sailed with such fanfare to Komsomol'sk-na-Amure just one year earlier began to take their own lives. A series of copycat suicides, dubbed an "epidemic" by officials, began with the suicide poisoning of Khetagurovite Pavlova. Between February and April 1938, there were nine attempted suicides among Khetagurovites working at Aviation Factory No. 126. Three young women died.[6] Another fifteen Khetagurovites had tried or been successful in suicide attempts by September 1938.[7] In

---

[3] Memoir of Anna I. Plaskina, GAKhK P, f. 442, op. 2, d. 283, ll. 53–54.

[4] Memoir of Nina A. Asikritova, "Sorok odin god na Dal'nem Vostoke," October 1978, GAKhK P, f. 442, op. 2, d. 298, l. 6.

[5] "Just about all construction and industrial enterprises, retail, transport and administrative-economic institutions sent us requests, they happily took all arriving people, and gave them places to live which were hard to find at the time." See Valentina Khetagurova, "K 50-letiiu khetagurovskogo dvizheniia – Veriu v derzost' molodykh," *Dal'nii Vostok* 2 (1987), 132–133.

[6] "Protocol from the meeting of the Far Eastern Regional Komsomol Bureau, April 14, 1938: On isolated unhealthy phenomenon among young people at Factory No. 126," GAKhK P, f. 618, op. 1, d. 323, l. 10a.

[7] Letter from employees of Aviation Factory No. 126 sent to members of the Central Committee A. A. Andreev and to M. Kaganovich as the Commissar of Heavy Industry. The

all, there were thirty-six suicide attempts in Komsomol'sk that year among Khetagurovites.[8] The gulf between the descriptions of life by memoirists and the tragic stories of those who perished in the city of youth is one of the most troubling paradoxes of this history and the history of the Soviet Union generally.

"Special conditions"

When the Khetagurovites began to arrive in 1937, things were actually turning for the worse in the region. Life had not improved with the influx of funds and attention from Moscow. Thousands who had tried to make a life there found conditions unbearable and were leaving in droves.[9] Between 60 and 90 percent of workers departed shortly after arriving in the period of the First Five-Year Plan.[10] From 1930 to 1937 the pace of departures increased sharply among agricultural workers and workers in industries.[11] Only when resettlement programs were transferred out of NKVD jurisdiction in 1939 and the mass operations were curtailed did

letter was returned to the Khabarovsk Region Communist Party Committee. September 14, 1938, GAKhK P, f. 35, op. 1, d. 362, l. 3.

[8] "Memorandum, information and other documents of the Komsomol Central Committee and other organizations on the plans for work of the Khetagurovite committee – Report on the status of the Khetagurovite call-up by Tsyngalenok, Instructor of the Komsomol Sector for Work among Young Women," July 5, 1939, RGASPI f. M – 1, op. 23, d. 1351, l. 47.

[9] For more on the expansion of the use of convicts to develop the peripheries, beginning in 1929, see Ivanova, *Istoriia GULAGa, 1918–1958*, 158–221. As the NKVD erected its prison complex in the Far East from 1929, fewer and fewer voluntary settlers arrived and stayed. According to one People's Commissariat of Internal Affairs (NKVD) Resettlement Department document, between 1925 and 1937 approximately 175,638 individuals arrived for settlement as agricultural workers. Between 1925 and 1929, approximately 26 percent of those who settled in agriculture left after one year. See "On the necessity to organize in the region a prison camp for resettlement construction in agricultural kolkhozy, April 1938," GAKhK P, f. 2, op. 8, d. 192, ll. 9–10. Only 19.2 percent of those who arrived in 1925 were still living in the Far East in 1929. See "Memorandum on the summary of settlement in the Far East," July 19, 1936, RGAE, f. 5676, op. 1, d. 138, l. 4ob.

[10] In 1929–1930, 7,489 "industrial" settlers arrived and 5,496 left. The situation was so chaotic that "figures did not exist" for subsequent years among this category of settlers until 1937. Figures on "industrial" settlers taken from "Memorandum notes on the review of Far East settlement," July 19, 1936, RGAE, f. 5676, op. 1, d. 138, l. 7ob.

[11] In 1931 "16,000 persons arrived and 13,000 left." See "Stenographic record of the XII regional Communist conference of the Far East region," May 29, 1937, Comrade Vareikis, RGASPI, f. 17, op. 21, d. 5384, l. 54. The situation only grew worse the next year, mostly reflecting resistance to collectivization. "In 1932, 20,825 settlers left the regional collective farms, while only 8,234 arrived." See "On the necessity to organize in the region a prison camp for resettlement construction in agricultural kolkhozy," April 1938, GAKhK P, f. 2, op. 8, d. 192, ll. 9–10.

the numbers of voluntary settlers arriving and staying resume a steady growth.[12]

A large proportion of the patriotic migrants were destined to work in the administration of labor camps, where they were badly needed because the Great Terror generated a massive influx of prisoners. In just twelve months, the numbers of prisoners in the camps run by the Administration of Railroad Construction NKVD increased by 181,820.[13] No one was ready to house or feed these unfortunates. Every camp lacked barracks and warm clothing. There were never enough medical supplies. Nothing had been done to address the longstanding and debilitating food shortages. This deluge of prisoners, transported in overcrowded trains, with little or no food or water over a long period of time, exacerbated rates of infectious diseases, especially spotted fever. Convicts arriving at this time found themselves marching hundreds of kilometers in freezing temperatures. Mortality rates among this large contingent were especially high because it also had a higher proportion of people over the age of forty, "changing the age structure of the camp population" toward what one investigator called "an unfavorable balance."[14]

The type of convicts laboring in the region had also changed between 1937 and 1939. At the end of 1939, one of the other massive autonomous camp systems, Dal'Lag in the Khabarovsk region, contained about 65,000 prisoners, mostly convicted of "social" crimes rather than "counterrevolutionary activities" because a large number of those considered political prisoners had been removed from the camps near the border with Manchuria or summarily executed according to "orders from the

---

[12] The target plan for resettlement of agricultural workers in 1940 was 93,800 households. In the final tally 79,808 households were relocated. Out of this number 13,956, or 17.5 percent, quit the region within one year. The plan for assigning agricultural workers was fulfilled by 67.5 percent. Planners had ordered 93,500 houses built for new settlers but construction produced enough homes for only 63,938 families by the time they arrived, which was 68.4 percent of the plan. See "Memorandum: On the completion of plans for agricultural resettlement in the Far East and Siberia," April 28, 1941, RGAE, f. 5675, op. 1, d. 329, l. 42.

[13] A total of 48,335 people arrived between November and December 1937. In the first half of 1938, another 86,481 arrived, followed by another wave of 47,004 between August and December 1938. See "Memorandum: reports on the work of the corrective-labor camps NKVD USSR in the Far East: Borodin – Chief of Sanitation Department Administration of the Railroad Construction Camps (UZhDS) GULAG NKVD USSR for the Far East – Certificate on illness and mortality of the UZhDS camp population in 1938–1939," May 28, 1939, GAKhK P, f. 35, op. 1, d. 317, l. 9.

[14] *Ibid.*, "Certificate on illness and mortality . . . ," May 28, 1939, l. 8. Whereas at the start of 1937, 88 percent of the camps' population was made up of those aged nineteen to forty years of age, by January 1938 this cohort was now only 80.9 percent of the total population. The number of those over 41 grew from 11.8 percent to 18.6 percent by early 1938.

center."[15] Therefore many of the prisoners in the Khabarovsk region were more likely to be common criminals than intellectuals, professionals, or former Communist party members caught up in the Great Terror. This state of affairs would have confronted the new migrants from their very first days. It was euphemistically referred to as the "special conditions" of the Far East.

Importing young enthusiasts into a frontier region with no social support to buffer the transition required much more supervision than any official expected. Khetagurovites began to complain about their reception and about conditions they encountered from the very beginning of the campaign. NKVD camp employees, factory workers, tractor drivers, nurses, teachers, and librarians, along with local party and Komsomol personnel, pleaded for the authorities to investigate their situations. However, they discovered that local Komsomol and party cells could not or would not respond to them because they were in the midst of their own purge-induced turmoil.[16] The misfortunes encountered by a number of young migrants eventually led to the undoing of the Khetagurovite program as a whole.

Khetagurovites, heroic and selfless patriots, were supposed to serve as examples to encourage other migrants not only to move to the Far East but also to stay as permanent residents despite the obvious presence of convict laborers and hardships. Initial difficulties were to be expected and were supposed to be endured for the cause of national development. However, the misery and social isolation they encountered on a frontier of Stalinism came as a shock and fostered resentment among many formerly enthusiastic volunteers. Migrants' fantasies of finding friendly collectives where strong characters were formed in a winnable contest with natural forces could not have been more inappropriate to the kind of social and economic circumstances prevailing in the region in the late 1930s.

Migrants disembarked into a world rife with suspicion and hierarchies stacked against their interests. Local enterprise chiefs found the female migrants to be more of a liability than a benefit and devised ways to drive them out. Some newcomers, as we have seen, found themselves working in the administration of labor camps or in industries using convict labor. Reaction to these assignments depended on personality. Some achieved a sense of satisfaction from the power such positions offered while others

[15] "On the economic activities of Dal'Lag NKVD for 1938 and plans for 1939," GAKhK P, f. 35, op. 1, d. 313, l. 60.

[16] For more on the course of the purge and Great Terror in the Far East, see Steven E. Merritt, "The Great Purges in the Soviet Far East, 1937–1938," unpublished PhD dissertation, University of California, Riverside (2000); Stephan, *The Russian Far East*, 209–224 and Suturin, *Delo kraevogo masshtaba*.

looked for ways to escape. Many did not hesitate to demand better treatment and equality with men if they felt slighted, pointing to the officially sanctioned importance of women as defenders of the borderlands. The exigencies of coping in such a habitat not only did not bring forth qualities of self-sufficiency among the young people, they in fact reinforced quite opposite predilections and practices.

Unhappy migrants appealed to the Khetagurovite Committee and to Khetagurova. These were sympathetic ears to turn to but they were overwhelmed by the volume and variety of problems brought to their attention. Those invited to become Khetagurovites were explicitly told that they would be provided with living quarters.[17] Yet such promises were made by the Khetagurovite Committee staff without means to force bosses to live up to the arrangements once the workers were in the Far East. The best that Khetagurova could do was to compile a ten-page list of sixty-seven names and short descriptions of the complaints at the end of 1938, forwarding them to the Khabarovsk region Communist Party Committee.[18] Confusion, massive turnover, and general disgruntlement among those charged with monitoring the wellbeing of Khetagurovites exacerbated the migrants' suffering. The staff of the Khetagurovite Committee could do little to help most of those who wrote begging for assistance.[19] They achieved the resolution of only sixty-six cases out of the 1,015 complaints. In most cases, complaints were redirected to local organizations for investigation.[20] When the volume of letters from a single organization deluged the authorities, they turned materials over to the regional procurator as a last resort.[21]

---

[17] The letter of invitation spelled this out: "You will be provided with dormitory space but you should bring bedding from home." See "Memorandum on the work of the Committee for the reception of youth of the Khetagurovite call-up," December 13, 1938, GAKhK P, f. 2, op. 6, d. 341, l. 137.

[18] *Ibid.*, 179–188.

[19] It proved impossible to pay attention to the eventual resolution of complaint investigations in areas outside of the administrative centers. Not all the inspectors came back with reports finding conditions as described. For instance, one letter of complaint about "soulless treatment" turned out to have been written by an alcoholic who lived rent-free in his own room, did little work, and spent his money on drink. See "Reports to the secretary of the Khabarovsk Party Committee," 1939, GAKhK P, f. 35, op. 1, d. 359, l. 126. For another instance of unsubstantiated complaints, see "Stenographic text of the regional Khetagurovite conference," September 17, 1938, Mel'nikova, GAKhK P, f. 618, op. 1, d. 325, l. 305.

[20] "On the status of work on the Khetagurovite movement of youth to the Far East," April 11, 1939, GAKhK P, f. 35, op. 1, d. 344, l. 75.

[21] "Draft Decree – On the status of work on the reception of youth of the Khetagurovite call-up," December 1938, GAKhK P, f. 2, op. 6, d. 341, l. 199. The Regional Agriculture Administration (KraiZU) attracted the attention of the procurator because of its treatment of Khetagurovite employees and trainees in tractor-driving schools.

Party authorities agreed that something was awry with the way Khetagurovites were greeted and treated when they came to the Far East.[22] However, their abilities to enforce compliance with their resolutions, whether among factory bosses or the rank and file residents, were extremely limited. Their powers were circumscribed because of the distances between administrative centers and other towns and settlements, because there were too few party investigators and police to cover such a large area effectively, and because the region was already filled with people disinclined to obey officials and proclamations, having been brought there by force and stripped of their rights by this regime. The migrants' experiences, evoked in their letters of complaint, expose some of the zones where confrontations could take place between those who identified strongly with the state and those marginalized and victimized by the regime.

Individuals who wrote to the Khetagurovite Committee after their arrival did so because they were in trouble, and their letters reflect the most negative experiences. It would be unwarranted to assume that all Khetagurovites suffered the same treatment.[23] Of the approximately 25,000 who arrived, 90 percent did not file complaints. Many stoically suffered a certain amount of hardship in this poorly supplied and underdeveloped region. It was possible to find a niche in the cadre-starved area and lead an ordinary life, as Ania Alekseeva proved. Nevertheless, a significant number of locals treated Khetagurovites as unwelcome outsiders. Moreover, the Khetagurovite campaign never had much chance of real success because it was implemented in the midst of the chaos inflicted on the region by the Great Terror.

The unfortunate circumstances faced by many Khetagurovites were not recognized as the results of a dictatorial state or inevitable by-products of a dysfunctional system. From the migrants' perspective, the social

---

[22] "Far Eastern Regional Communist Party Committee ORPO: Memorandum notes, short reports, information sent to the Regional Communist Party Committee: On the status of the movement of youth of the Khetagurovite call-up to the Far East, March 20, 1938: Summary for eight months of 1937," GAKhK P, f. 2, op. 6, d. 358, l. 5. At the end of 1937, there had been 170 "serious" complaints. The staff of the Khetagurovite Committee reported complaints and their percent of the total sent to each industry. Thirty-two complaints were generated from the 1,200 women sent to work for the (KraiZU), which put them at a 2 percent complaint rate. The food industry had a 5 percent rate of complaints. Khetagurovites working in the Regional Department of People's Education (KraiONO) produced 13 complaints among 390 teachers and librarians. This put them at a 3 percent complaint rate.

[23] Letters of complaint should be considered as problematic cases whose authors were not necessarily typical. Sheila Fitzpatrick has described various genres of letters sent to authorities and noted that "[l]etters were written to solve problems, resolve disputes and settle scores." See Fitzpatrick, "Supplicants and Citizens: Public Letter-Writing in Soviet Russia in the 1930s," *Slavic Review* 55:1 (Spring 1996), 81.

power and political control wielded by incomprehensibly bitter, cruel, or blithely incompetent individuals were the sources of their misfortunes. Many of these conflicts revolved around the issues described for Stalin by Tsvetkov: poor housing or no housing at all, catastrophic shortages of goods, delayed pay or pay well below the minimum needed to survive, and quarrels with bosses and co-workers. The Khetagurovites shared many of the material deprivations and tribulations of others in the region. However, they were more likely to complain about their experience, to find a hearing if they persisted, and to attract unwanted attention from distant officials.

"Not our people"

The difficulties the Khetagurovites encountered emanated from separate but mutually reinforcing social and political dynamics. Some of these dynamics were peculiar to the Far East because of its distance from the center, the high cost of living, and its social makeup. Other problems encountered by the women Khetagurovites were emblematic of gender relations across the Soviet Union. Men greeted women's entry into the workforce with suspicion and at times open hostility. At the same time as women worked for wages, they remained responsible for all domestic chores and childcare in an economy of extreme shortages. They tended to have fewer options for finding a better situation. Out of desperation, many found themselves embroiled in nasty disputes with neighbors and co-workers over the few goods available.

In general, locals treated Khetagurovites with apprehension. Stories of former prisoners now in positions of authority refusing to cooperate with Khetagurovites were common. Obviously they were convenient scapegoats for all ills. However, the presence of so many individuals with plenty of cause to shun those they considered to be representatives of the regime figured repeatedly in the difficulties the women reported. When one former prisoner found out that he would have to work with a Khetagurovite, he refused. "He said that he must have a different person, someone local."[24] The general distrust of these new arrivals was not simply the purview of former prisoners. Other young people proved difficult to befriend. According to one activist Khetagurovite, "Gals at meetings

---

[24] Khetagurovite Shukhman, working for the Komsomol City Committee in Blagoveshchensk remarked, "It seems to me that in our city there are *otbyvateli* [former prisoners living under restrictions], although recently there has been [a] sweep of them thanks to politics." See "Stenographic text of the regional Khetagurovite conference," September 16, 1938, Shukhman, GAKhK P, f. 618, op. 1 d. 325, l. 94.

tried to avoid me. I said to them 'let's talk.' They refused and dashed away from me."[25]

Segments of the population, not sure what to make of the new arrivals and unable to fathom that people were moving voluntarily to this zone marred by the use of convict labor, suspected that the young women were somehow marginal figures forced to come to the Far East as a kind of punishment or for "reeducation." Such incomprehension and lack of admiration for the volunteers is apparent in a letter from a young Ukrainian medical student. Although in most of the text she tried to underscore how well she was coping with the new environment, she concluded with the following observation. "Everyone is rude here. I am not at all sorry that I came here, but I am sorry about one thing, it pains me that everyone is so rude to us, [treating us] as though we came here by force. Well, it's nothing. What occurred is now in the past; I'll see what happens."[26] Assumptions among locals that only convicts were heading to their region spoiled the resettlement of migrants in other kinds of settler programs in this period. A similar tense reception was the subject of a complaint from a large group of voluntary agricultural settlers in 1939. New arrivals in the Krasnaia Zaria kolkhoz encountered insufferable conditions and outright enmity from both the kolkhoz administration and other kolkhoz members. Nothing had been prepared for their arrival and they lived in cold, unfurnished huts. The Komsomol secretary was indifferent. The word in the kolkhoz was that no one should bother with them, since "[t]hese are not our people." The aggrieved letter writers wondered, "What are we, prisoners? Were we brought here to be tormented?"[27]

Others who encountered the Khetagurovites were so cut off from official culture that they could only watch with bewilderment the arrival of women with an exotic-sounding title. One Khetagurovite, sent to work in settlements populated by Old Believers working in the goldfields, explained that her new neighbors "had no idea about Khetagurovites and asked us what kind of nationality it was. We had to explain."[28]

In urban environments they were treated with contempt because locals dismissed Khetagurovites as unqualified dupes. The whole campaign and its namesakes were mocked and the women derisively nicknamed

[25] *Ibid.*, 94–95.
[26] "Memorandum on the work of the Committee for the reception of young people of the Khetagurovite call-up – Complaint of Galia Bondarenko," October 13, 1938, GAKhK P, f. 2, op. 6, d. 341, l. 113.
[27] "Requests received by the Regional Communist Party Committee, correspondence and information on their completion – Collective letter from settlers – 8 families with 47 individuals – 1939," GAKhK P, f. 35, op. 1, d. 350, l. 257.
[28] "Stenographic text of the regional Khetagurovite conference," September 16, 1938, Bondarenko, GAKhK P, f. 618, op. 1, d. 325, l. 168.

"Svistogurovki."[29] Khetagurovite Shukhman was proud that in the city of Blagoveshchensk, Khetagurovites made up 75 percent of the students in preparatory courses at a newly formed institute. Now there was some hope that things would change. "Previously, certain 'thinkers' here in Blagoveshchensk used to think that if it is a Khetagurovite that means she cannot write two words grammatically."[30] For Khetagurovites who considered the title a sign of heroic status and a designation reserved for the best of the crop, such lack of interest or outright hostility was a bitter pill.

Suspicions of migrant women may have stemmed, in part, from the women's unwitting insubordination to established settlement patterns among Slavs. The Tsarist and Soviet governments promoted settlement programs that relocated whole peasant families. Single men typically traveled to the region for temporary work or as scouts for households considering migration.[31] Through the 1930s, the planned settlement of demobilized soldiers relocated families under male tutelage.[32] Khetagurovites were "loose" women on the move who broke with this family-oriented tradition. Long-time residents of the Far East therefore suspected the women's intentions. Some, unaccustomed to seeing young women migrating on their own, may have assumed that they were "ruined" women who had been banished from their former places of residence by the police or village communes, a practice dating from the pre-revolutionary period. Many, as we have seen, deduced that these lone women were driven to the Far East by a rapacious reproductive instinct and were on the hunt for upwardly mobile husbands.[33] Such attitudes exposed more than one hapless migrant to a noxious brew of Russian patriarchal culture, bureaucratic ineptitude and the low regard for human life in the Stalinist system.

Family networks were not only the norm for women in the region but essential for everyday survival in an environment of shortages. Some of the conditions described by female Khetagurovites were not unique to

---

[29] *Svistit* means pointless and false. See "Protocol of the First Khabarovsk regional Komsomol conference," February 11–15, 1939, GAKhK P, f. 617, op. 1, d. 3, l. 164.

[30] "Stenographic text of the regional Khetagurovite conference," September 16, 1938, Shukhman, GAKhK P, f. 618, op. 1, d. 325, l. 98.

[31] On scouts and *landsmen* networks in resettlement, see Willard Sunderland, "Peasant Pioneering: Russian Peasant Settlers Describe Colonization and the Eastern Frontier, 1880s–1910s," *Journal of Social History* 34:4 (Summer 2001), 895–922.

[32] For more on this program see Stephan, *The Russian Far East*, 185, and Martin, "The Origins of Soviet Ethnic Cleansing," 840–842, 851.

[33] Anna Krylova underscored the same derisive reaction to women in combat during World War II when as early as 1942 a backlash "reinterpreted the meanings assigned to female fighting by official culture. In rumors and folk stories, the frontline women's effort was reduced to prostitution and husband-hunting." See Krylova, "Stalinist Identity from the Viewpoint of Gender," 650.

their status as migrants, though their isolated condition and lack of social support as outsiders no doubt exacerbated their burdens and undermined their ability to cope. For instance, the ability to pool resources such as basic food stocks in preparation for winter was not available to the single migrants. This lack of social networks made them all the more reliant on supplies that were parceled out according to hierarchies of privilege and personal connections they did not have.[34] Struggles over goods and their complaints to superiors only generated further friction and vengeful competitors.

With few allies, the women were more vulnerable to the power of community gossip. Intimations that the Khetagurovites were sexually voracious or carriers of venereal disease were effective in ostracizing the newcomers, who had no real defenders. In Arkhara, a rural area with a timber-processing enterprise and a railroad depot, there were rumors that Khetagurovite Iakovleva had a venereal disease. She expected the secretary of the local party committee to investigate and punish the gossips, but the party committee moved at a glacial pace to remedy the situation. Nothing was done and the guilty "narrow-minded" rumormongers remained anonymous and at liberty. Iakovleva then appealed to higher party officials. When they demanded to know why nothing had been done to track down the culprits, local party officials explained that it was impossible to follow up because their area lacked procurators and investigators. Although the excuses seem improbable, they have a ring of truth because of the persistent shortage of personnel to enforce the will of officialdom in Soviet (and Tsarist) rural areas.

Iakovleva's travails are a clear case of how the absence of social and kinship networks pushed women to rely on state authorities to protect their social status. Her attempts to get the party committee involved echoed the practice in Russian peasant communities of suing for restitution of a woman's reputation either by her or by her male relatives. In the Soviet case, there were no obvious legal avenues for a young woman to restore her reputation and the isolated single migrants had no family networks to mobilize for redress.[35] Unable to muster their own informal resources and connections to defend their interests and reputations in an unfamiliar context, Khetagurovites sought out and embraced intrusions from representatives of the regime. They pleaded with officials to police social relationships and protect them from their tormentors. In many cases,

---

[34] See Osokina, *Our Daily Bread*, and Lebedeva, *Russia's Economy of Favors*, for more on the way these distribution systems functioned.

[35] For a discussion of these practices among Russian peasants, see Christine Worobec, *Peasant Russia: Family and Community in the Post-Emancipation Period* (DeKalb: Northern Illinois Press, 1995).

authorities did respond, thus reinforcing the migrants' extreme dependence on the Communist party and the brute force of the state.

"Tough skin"

Women who already had plenty of experience as factory workers and activists in their home regions were surprised to find strong initial resistance to their entry into the Far Eastern workforce and communities. They were paid less for the same job, passed over for promotion, and ignored, if not taunted, by male co-workers. In the words of one female Khetagurovite, working in a remote northern outpost, "Some people treated us poorly and with great mistrust. Some of them said we came here especially to get married, to take away husbands, etc. Others said that we would not be able to handle our jobs."[36] Young women Khetagurovites who completed their training at schools for tractor drivers were told unequivocally that they were not wanted when they started work in the fields. When they insisted on working, they found that "[we] were not paid fully for our work. We women are ignored and they do not fully value the work of women drivers. They do not let us work assuming that young women will not work for long on a machine."[37]

Unequal treatment of women was widespread in the organization of the region's largest employer: the NKVD. Utkina, who worked as an NKVD investigator, criticized the prevailing double standards and employed the rhetoric of women's central role in impending total war to argue for a change. Although some of the Khetagurovites were exemplary employees, "Our young women are put into technical work. We have this kind of attitude. If it is a man – then please – he is offered to work as a *chekist* [police intelligence officer]. But if it is a young woman she is sent to a technical job."[38] Utkina questioned this practice not simply as a breach of promised equality but as a practice detrimental to national security in case of war. After all, "If we send men to the front then we will have to work as *chekists*."[39]

Discrepancies in pay based on gender and discriminatory work assignments figured prominently in complaints by the women sent to work in the factories of Komsomol'sk. A group of Khetagurovites, working at

[36] "Stenographic text of the regional Khetagurovite conference," September 16, 1938, Livshits, GAKhK P, f. 618, op. 1, d. 325, l. 118.
[37] "Memorandum, letters sent to the secretary of the Far Eastern Regional Komsomol Committee. Collective letter of complaint from the Molotov district, Pokrovskoe, 1938," GAKhK P, f. 618, op. 1, d. 326, l. 152.
[38] "Stenographic text of the regional Khetagurovite conference," September 17, 1938, Utkina, GAKhK P, f. 618, op. 1, d. 325, l. 276. "Technical work" implies typing or perhaps bookkeeping.
[39] *Ibid.*

the Komsomol'sk Aviation Factory No. 126, were unhappy because they earned 220 rubles per month. "The issue is not that it is impossible to live on 220 per month, but a colossal resentment builds up . . . There were many cases when gals were put to work in places where there was a man but they received a much smaller salary."[40] If the Great Retreat had initiated a period that naturalized women's subordinate positions, the women who went to the Far East were not quite ready to acquiesce to this kind of logic.

In other cases, it was clear that locals and male-dominated Komsomol organizations openly disputed the authority of young women. When Ol'ga Mel'nikova was sent to work as a secretary of the Komsomol Committee in the rural Mikhailov district, "the whole district started talking, all of the bosses started talking, 'This young woman has arrived and wants to order around all of the youth.'" Mel'nikova did not back down, having a good deal of organizing experience among youth in Ivanovo-Voznesensk and Kazakhstan. "I thought about it seriously and said, 'No, I have a tough skin and a head on my shoulders and an education.' And I do not want to order people around, but I want to work with young people and there was not a single kolkhoz where I did not go."[41] The resistance to her arrival produced an atmosphere so toxic that her treatment became grounds for the downfall of local authorities. The NKVD arrested the district committee Komsomol secretary and the district executive committee chairman on charges of maltreatment of Mel'nikova. The matter was so tightly connected to Mel'nikova that other women in the district pleaded with her to put an end to the proceedings against their men.

Men at all levels of authority put up a united front against the intrusions of young women in their workplace. Bosses of regional enterprises did not want the Khetagurovites because, as one director of a state shipping administration explained, "We don't know what kind of women are coming to the Far East. Let them come, and we'll look them over, see what they know how to do and then we will decide to take them or not."[42] Some bosses were threatened with criminal prosecution for refusing to cooperate. The acting secretary of the Khetagurovite Committee was convinced that managers not only failed to live up to their responsibilities but actively "worked to discredit the movement."[43] The

[40] "Stenographic text of the regional Khetagurovite conference," September 15, Iliukhina, GAKhK P, f. 618, op. 1, d. 325, l. 21.

[41] *Ibid.*, September 17, Mel'nikova, GAKhK P, f. 618, op. 1, d. 325, l. 312.

[42] Dubman, "Besplodnye razgovory. Blagoveshchenskie organizatsii ne gotoviatsia k vstreche molodykh patriotok," *TK*, April 10, 1937.

[43] "Far Eastern Regional Communist Party Committee ORPO: Memorandum on the question of the Khetagurovite movement – on the condition of Khetagurovite youth on the Far Eastern Railroads as of 10 March, 1938," GAKhK P, f. 2, op. 6, d. 358, l. 21.

chief of one corrective labor camp located near Komsomol'sk preferred to use engineers and other professionals from among former prisoners while "giving young specialist Khetagurovites second-rank tasks." He also proved uninterested in complaints from such Khetagurovites about their mistreatment at the hands of former prisoners.[44] Threats of arrests and public shaming of those who derided Khetagurovites did little to change attitudes.

Both tensions and the fluidity of gender roles are palpable in the stories of women who went to work in the most male-dominated industries of the Far East. Throughout her memoir, Iuliia Druzhevich, the locomotive driver, went to great lengths to prove that men on the railroad befriended her and treated her well.[45] Yet this insistence that there were no tensions between her and the men was subverted by her own stories. There were incidents when other employees refused to board her trains in disbelief that a woman was the driver. Druzhevich preferred to look like a man while at work; in all seasons she wore a man's railroad uniform and cap. "I did not like curious or surprised stares; I did not want to be different. Mid-height, thin, I [was] easily concealed among the men, you could only guess by my voice." We can assume that she avoided speaking in male groups. On days off she "tried to be herself." But this was not easy either. "I was upset that I could not clean my hands completely and it was unpleasant to feel calluses on the hands of a woman." She even developed a style and posture to hide her hands, keeping them under her jacket behind her back.[46] To emphasize her adherence to qualities associated with femininity, Druzhevich also interspersed her stories of mastering a male profession with bucolic vignettes about collecting flowers whenever her train slowed enough for a dash into a wildflower patch.

Animosity toward female workers in the Far East was acute in the late 1930s because it was a new phenomenon in a region that had no traditions of female industrial employment. Unlike areas of central Russia where women workers were visible, especially in the textile industry, the Far East had no substantial industrial base before the 1930s. In general, the region had fewer women in paid employment than was common in the rest of Russia before and after the Bolshevik Revolution. Many of the

---

[44] "Correspondence with organs of the NKVD on investigation and registration of persons for secret work. January 4, 1939 to October 21, 1939: Certificate on the Chief of the IugoVostLag NKVD Boris Kuznetsov," GAKhK P, f. 35, op. 1, d. 306, l. 172.

[45] Memoir of Iuliia Druzhevich, March 8, 1975, GAKhK P, f. 442, op. 2, d. 284, ll. 31–50. Druzhevich's progress as a trainee to become a locomotive driver received publicity in regional newspapers in October 1938. See Kashirin, "Devushki vedut paravoz," *TK*, October 22, 1938.

[46] Quoted in Dubinina, *Ty pozovi, Dal'nii Vostok!*, 151.

predicaments encountered by Khetagurovites in all spheres of production were expressions of workers' resistance to the entrance of women into previously male spheres of work, whether on the factory shopfloor, on the tractor, or even as NKVD personnel. Hostility to women in the workplace, sexual harassment, and the double burden of work at home were typical of women's experiences in the Far East just as much as in the Soviet Union more generally – but more intense.

"Dry bread and moldy herring"

To their surprise, many Khetagurovites found themselves at the bottom of goods distribution hierarchies because they were outsiders. This dynamic was most obvious in letters from migrants working in the countryside. Khetagurovites in agriculture were in a relatively privileged position because they were not bound to a kolkhoz. However, many found that they were regularly deprived of their pay or access to merchandise because they were outsiders in the patronage networks entrenched on state farms. For instance, in a group letter to Stalin, Khetagurovites described how things worked in their sovkhoz. "All material provisions first go to the mechanics, agronomists and so forth and they show them off and speculate in front of the workers." When distraught outsiders tried to change this system, they discovered that their competitors were not averse to using "physical reprisals."[47]

For the most part, this was a movement of people from urban areas to the countryside. Most of the Khetagurovites came from large and medium-size cities in central Russia, Ukraine, and Belorussia. Unlike the factory workers known as the "25,000ers" examined by Lynne Viola, sent to work as kolkhoz, sovkhoz, and rural soviet administrators, the Khetagurovites had no such official imprimatur and instant base of power. They arrived to drive tractors, to work as clerks, or to teach. Moreover, unlike the 25,000ers, most of the Khetagurovites were young women who were not going to find easy acceptance in the patriarchal countryside. Even those who were slated to work in Far East industries first went to construction sites that were only in the process of becoming urban.[48]

Those who had no previous experience of life in a state or collective farm seemed to be the most aggrieved and bewildered by their treatment.

---

[47] "Letters and requests of laborers received by the Regional Communist Party Committee from the Central Communist Party Committee, 1939," collective letter from Sredne-Vol'skii zernosovkhoz, Amur oblast, GAKhK P, f. 35, op. 1, d. 341, l. 217.

[48] This was not the rural-to-urban migration described by Stephen Kotkin in *Magnetic Mountain* and by others in the Soviet period. Rather, it had a number of similarities to the "25,000ers" campaign of the early 1930s discussed by Viola in *Best Sons of the Fatherland.*

Being assigned to work in agriculture was a step down in the social ladder of Stalinism. Although they were apt to tolerate some deprivations as acts of self-abnegation, they quickly became distraught to find themselves utterly destitute instead of applauded. Valianskaia, previously a factory worker in Kiev, trained to become a tractor driver in the Far East. Speaking to an audience of other Khetagurovites, she claimed that she did not mind the low pay she received in her first job as a tractor driver, but added, "It is a good thing that they feed us on credit at the canteen. Without money it turns out that you spend 150 rubles per month and when you get your pay, with your debts you get nothing in your hand. In my opinion this should not take place in the Soviet Union."[49] Young women living in a dormitory while studying to become tractor drivers lamented that they lived without bedding, hot water, or means to heat their rooms. They wrote sad letters to the person who initially fired up their enthusiasm for migration, Khetagurova. "Yes, Valia, we do not have a canteen, and without it our stomachs have swollen from dry bread and moldy herring."[50] At night drunkards stormed their dormitories. In another district, young women Khetagurovites were living in the basement of a cafeteria alongside barrels of slop meant for the pigsty.[51] The hardships they endured shocked even the experienced inspectors of the Komsomol. Under such circumstances, about a third of those sent to the state farm of the Amur oblast left after one year.[52]

Teachers were particularly vulnerable to initial mistreatment because they were sent on their own into the countryside where there was little supervision of local administrators, and wretched conditions.[53] Many found that they had nowhere to hold classes and nowhere to live after arduous journeys to remote areas. A good number did not have the

---

[49] "Stenographic text of the regional Khetagurovite conference," September 15, 1938, Valianskaia, GAKhK P, f. 618, op. 1, d. 325, l. 69.

[50] "Requests of members of the Communist party sent to the secretary of the Far Eastern Regional Communist Party Committee – excerpt from the letters of Khetagurovite Oreshkina and Vorobkova," January 13, 1938, GAKhK P, f. 2, op. 1, d. 399, l. 143.

[51] "Requests of a personal nature, March 4, 1939. Complaint letter from Kriuchkova, Kumar district," GAKhK P, f. 35, op. 1, d. 339, l. 80. Kriuchkova's letter had the desired effect and the Khabarovsk First Secretary ordered the Kumar district party committee to assist her.

[52] Valentina Khetagurova speaking at the First Khabarovsk Komsomol conference, February 11–15, 1939, GAKhK P, f. 617, op. 1, d. 3, l. 187.

[53] "Requests of a personal nature, May 18, 1939. Complaint letter from Andrionova," GAKhK P, f. f. 35, op. 1, d. 354, l. 131. Teachers were the only ones invited to go to the Far East with families and explicit promises of accommodation for all family members. Problems were not limited to teachers placed in rural schools. When Andrionova arrived with three children and a husband to work as a director of an adult literacy school in the Ordzhonikidze factory in Khabarovsk, her family was homeless for months and she was without daycare provisions for her own children.

funds to find their way home. For instance, two teachers sent to the Shmakov district became permanently homeless and went without work for months. Completely destitute, they survived by selling the contents of their luggage.[54] Local authorities in a rural district were blamed for the suicide of Gordeeva, a Khetagurovite teacher. Before she took her life, she had tried to rebuild her forlorn schoolhouse and obtain wood to heat the building. Numerous requests for funds produced no results. The Mikhailov district's Communist party First Secretary ignored her personal appeals for assistance and firewood. Cold and disillusioned, Gordeeva gave up on everything. Her end became grounds for the dismissal of the inattentive First Secretary.[55]

Letters make it clear that Khetagurovites were very sensitive to displays of hierarchies and systems of privileges that did not serve their interests. Anger about the difficulties endured by rank and file workers like the Khetagurovites and about the bosses of large construction projects crept into descriptions offered by memoir writers even when they did their best to avoid direct criticisms. Liubov' Kudriasheva, a railroad employee from Saratov, went to the Far East because she had "nothing to lose, I wanted to know much more, to see the unknown, to work and to be useful where there was a lack of working hands and particularly women's."[56] After a warm reception in Khabarovsk, she and a group of other women with experience working on the railroad were sent to work for the special construction project MPS-4. Letters of complaint from other Khetagurovites working for the same construction project support the impression that MPS-4 was one of the most dreadful assignments in the Far East.[57] While Kudriasheva stoically endured life on a site infamous for its misery and use

[54] "Far Eastern Regional Communist Party Committee ORPO: . . . March 20, 1938: Summary for eight months of 1937," GAKhK P, f. 2, op. 6, d. 358, l. 9.

[55] "On the completion of the resolution of the January Plenum of the Communist Party Central Committee on the mistakes of party organization during the expulsion of Communists from the party in the Mikhailov district," GAKhK P, f. 2, op. 5, d. 341, l. 9. For more on suicide among teachers, see E. Thomas Ewing, "Personal Acts with Public Meanings: Suicides by Soviet Women Teachers in the Early Stalin Era," *Gender & History* 14:1 (April 2002), 117–137.

[56] Memoir of Liubov' Kudriasheva, GAKhK P, f. 442, op. 2, d. 284, l. 4ob.

[57] "Protocols of the meeting of the Organizational Bureau of the Komsomol Central Committee of the Khabarovsk region," December 1938, GAKhK P, f. 618, op. 1, 324, l. 149; "Organizuite kul'turnyi otdykh molodezhi," *TK*, November 16, 1938, and "Stenographic text of regional Komsomol activists in Khabarovsk," January 4, 1939, GAKhK P, f. 618, op. 1, d. 321, l. 161. The archives and press coverage of this construction site document its well-known misery. Hundreds of young people had nothing to do. The poor conditions drove many to take up "drinking, fighting, card games in which Komsomol members often participate." To illustrate the dire situation, the speaker said that Komsomol members living in these conditions came to him to say, "I never drank in my life, but now I do."

of convict labor, she could not avoid illustrating an obvious and no doubt remarked-upon gulf in accommodation between the voluntary workers and the bosses:

The construction site was a desolate wasteland. There was not a single place to live, just wagons for the bosses. We were given tents and we lived in these until the deepest frosts when they transferred us first into *fanzy* [Korean huts] and then into railroad cars where we lived about a year or two until temporary barracks were built.[58]

In one of the many tussles over living space in which Khetagurovites found themselves on the losing end, an observer noted, "You see we have this situation that if a person has a rank [*chin*] a bit higher – then one apartment is not enough for him, he needs five, but if a Khetagurovite has come with a lower rank then she can be left without an apartment."[59] Another young woman had a similar reaction to a conflict over living quarters: "It is amazing that when some lowly boss arrives their apartments are oil-painted but they won't even whitewash them for Khetagurovite young women."[60] Venting these kinds of frustrations could easily produce further animosities and tussles that the women would never win on their own.

Enemies in our midst

Migrants were explicitly warned to be wary of strangers they met in the Far East – the authorities worried that young women would become corrupted from overexposure to questionable characters. They instilled in many a tendency to suspect those they met and question the way things were done from their very first days. Khetagurovites took their responsibilities to put things in order so seriously that they indiscriminately launched attacks on the local power structure from the start. Khetagurova recalled that at the Far Eastern Regional Komsomol Committee plenum in July 1937, a third of the members were female Khetagurovites. She thought it was a good thing that "[t]hey spoke knowledgeably and put questions acutely. I marveled: after all, hadn't they just come here and now they have managed to figure out everything?"[61] While she "marveled" approvingly, many others found this proclivity annoying, if not downright threatening.

---

[58] Kudriasheva, 4ob–5.
[59] "Stenographic text of the regional Khetagurovite conference," September 16, 1938, Prisekina, GAKhK P, f. 618, op. 1, d. 325, l. 122.
[60] *Ibid.*, Feikhel'son, 115.   [61] Khetagurova, "K 50-letiiu," 133.

Although they were newcomers, some of the Khetagurovites acted as experts on enemy machinations. Shestoperova, working in a Komsomol'sk factory, perhaps epitomized the airs some adopted toward co-workers in this tension-filled environment:

In every factory we had enemies who interfered not only with the Khetagurovite movement but also in the growth of our industry. You all know what sort of military significance the region has for us, this is not a secret. This is why we must be vigilant and alert, we must be on guard [*na cheku*]. But we look through our fingers. The enemy is masking very well since he shows himself active in work, completes all activities but as a result he can wreck. That is why before starting work, we must look around. We must approach comrades next to us with vigilance. We must study him in production and in life.[62]

Many of the activists took such warnings to heart and further eroded their chances of building friendships and alliances. Some of the Khetagurovites did not even wait to get to their destination before pointing fingers. An attempt on the part of a stranger to caution the young librarian Loseva about the difficulties ahead was taken as an act of sabotage:

On the train with us was a woman, imploring us, "Where are you going? In the Far East there are no vegetables, nor fruits, you will perish." We told another Komsomol member about this incident and he called in an NKVD group on the train to investigate. Perhaps this was not even our own person, it could have been a spy who sneaked in and spread this kind of agitation.[63]

There were other "tasks" that some of the women apparently did not question. Ogleblina, with seven other young women Komsomol members, participated in "agitational" work among residents on an island off the coast of Vladivostok. Sent to proclaim the party line to workers in their homes, she later "marveled how back then the people listened to us young gals and that we were not afraid to go there with very serious topics." Besides participating in the preparation for the election for the Supreme Soviet, Ogleblina also carried out an even more grave assignment. She briefly recalled her "work in connection with the deportation of Koreans to Kazakhstan." The Khetagurovites were ordered to go to "every Korean family to explain to them where, why, and what awaited them in Kazakhstan." Simultaneously, they were to take away their documents and to "prevent panic":

This was a difficult assignment, not only morally but physically. Imagine for yourself a Korean *fanza* with their infamous [single] room. There are no chairs

[62] "Stenographic text of the regional Khetagurovite conference," September 16, 1938, Shestoperova, 143.
[63] *Ibid.*, September 17, Loseva, 201.

or benches, nor tables. They somehow fold their legs and we have to do the same. So the distressing conversation begins, there are many questions, they do not notice, but our legs are going numb . . . But regardless, we completed our work well, gathered them on time for departure and they all left the island on one flotilla.[64]

Unfortunately, this was all she had to say about her participation in the deportations. It appears that she found the assignment distasteful but could not or would not elaborate on what she thought of the whole affair. Her stress on the physical discomforts the Russians suffered while ordering the Koreans to depart illustrates how some absolved themselves of moral dilemmas by shifting focus to mundane details and exotic settings. It is little wonder that many in the region gave the Khetagurovites a less than an enthusiastic reception.

Other young women took an even more active role in speaking for the state or implementing the worst aspects of the regime's policies in the Far East. Mariia Konopleva, a Khetagurovite who headed a Cultural-Education Sector (KVCh) in a labor camp, played an unwitting role in the survival of historian Anton Antonov-Ovseenko. The "pleasant-looking" blond unexpectedly selected him to join a music and choral ensemble in the midst of death and suffering. Antonov-Ovseenko speculated on the apparent insouciance in Konopleva, who just as easily dismissed talented artists, returning them to a sure death from overwork. He reasoned that

[y]oung Mariia Konopleva really believed that Komsomol members were remaking the Far East. But there, on the spot, she understood something else, that it was all done by the hands of prisoners, they, the victims of the terror, built Komsomol'sk-na-Amure. Konopleva ended up among prison guards, and once she was in the GULAG system, she could not leave voluntarily. She came to know life in the Small Zone, learned to swear, and this young creature was transformed into a practiced camp commander. Power, it can ruin anyone. The feeling of unlimited power over people . . . over many prisoners awakened cruel instincts in the young Khetagurovite.[65]

It would be unwarranted to label all Khetagurovites willing participants in the inhumane and repressive practices of frontier Stalinism. Clearly, women like Novikova were not immune from the vagaries of the Soviet justice system. The relentless arrests and search for wreckers in this tumultuous period tossed some Khetagurovites from the ranks of the revered to the stratum of the reviled. The Khetagurovites' tussles with

---

[64] Memoir of L. S. Ogleblina, GAKhK P, f. 442, op. 2, d. 282, ll. 135–136.

[65] Anton Antonov-Ovseenko, *Vragi naroda* (Moscow: Intellekt, 1996), 61. Antonov-Ovseenko is the son of a famous Bolshevik who perished in the Great Terror. A history student and later a Soviet dissident historian, he spent eleven years in the camps starting from 1941.

superiors and locals often backfired and the hapless patriots found themselves sentenced to labor in the Far East camps. In one case, very similar to Novikova's, an eighteen-year-old Khetagurovite was hired, "without informing the Komsomol," to work in a store. The store burned down. When an investigation found that 20,000 rubles were missing, she was tried for negligence and sentenced to two years in prison. The story was particularly pitiful in the eyes of the observer, who wrote about her case to dramatize the treatment of Khetagurovites as a group, because the girl was from an orphanage and "needed help." Instead, she was "taken like a criminal under a convoy."[66] Meanwhile, although the store manager's wife was accused of losing 1,000 rubles, the procurator "quashed" further investigations. This was not a lone case of young, inexperienced Khetagurovites sent to work in the retail industry finding themselves in a prison cell thanks to the accusations of hostile locals working in collusion with the militia.

Complaints were most bitter and stories of suffering and marginalization most harrowing from those who were sent to areas and organizations that had been recently devastated by police repression. Locals were understandably fearful of those they suspected of being "minions of the bosses" or simply "snotty," as some called the Khetagurovites.[67] An anonymous letter of protest sent to party officials illustrates how Khetagurovites came to symbolize the hated regime. The letter heaped abuse on the country's "mindless and illiterate" leadership made up of "Jews and Georgians." The anonymous authors warned the official addressee, the First Secretary of the Khabarovsk region's Communist Party Committee, that he did not have

[l]ong to enjoy your sweet life and entertain yourself with lies to millions of people who are suffering naked and cold . . . Look around and look into the depths of the masses, everyone is dissatisfied . . . You're breeding lots of Stakhanovites [and] Khetagurovites. It is all lies, the people see it but keep silent because you have the weapons, there is no freedom of speech or press, you control everything.[68]

---

[66] "Requests of a personal nature," March 4, 1939, complaint letter from Kriuchkova, Kumar district, GAKhK P, f. 35, op. 1, d. 339, l. 80.

[67] A comment on "minions" made in the city of Birobidzhan among garment workers. See "Stenographic text of the regional Khetagurovite conference," September 17, 1938, Gracheva, 231. The "snotty" comment came from the railway division in the city of Svobodny, also an administrative center of the GULAG. See *ibid.*, September 16, name inaudible, 179.

[68] Anonymous letter of protest signed by "a group of Khasanovites," March 16, 1939, GAKhK P, f. 35, op. 1, d. 347, l. 138. Khasanovites were soldiers who fought the Japanese at Lake Khasan in 1938. For more on this episode, see V. A. Afanasev, "The Fighting at Khalkin-Gol in 1939 in the Context of World War II," *Otechestvennaia istoriia* 5 (September–October 1999), 181–185.

Khetagurovites also stepped into jobs when bosses, union chiefs, and party or Komsomol secretaries at every level were inexplicably disappearing, swept away by the purges. Many Khetagurovites were assigned to work in organizations and industries where their supervisors had no clear use for their labor or where things were so disorganized that no one could give them comprehensible directions. It was a situation destined to produce failures. Ovchinnikova explained why and how she was demoted in her new place of work from financial inspector to a technical secretary: "I was sent to where an enemy had ruined all matters. The supervisor was also a new employee. Whenever I asked him something he would answer, 'I don't understand anything myself. They sent you here, so you work.'"[69]

Blurred lines between prisoners, former prisoners, and voluntary workers produced perilous situations for young women. Khetagurovite Irina Gordeeva was expelled by her local Komsomol organization for "connections with a prisoner." In her appeal Gordeeva explained that when she went to work for the Dal'Lag NKVD in Khabarovsk, she struck up a friendship with a driver for one of the construction project's bosses. As far as she was concerned, he was just another employee. The young man informed her only much later that he was a prisoner. Those investigating her appeal concluded, "She could not have known this earlier because she had no cause to consider him a prisoner since he ate in the canteen of the free employees." Her "connection" with the prisoner consisted of him "driving her in the automobile home and to work." When the construction project was moved to another city, he was transferred and they continued to see one another on occasion, "because she found him attractive." Gordeeva was apparently fortunate to find a sympathetic audience among Komsomol activists at the regional level. She was reinstated by the regional Komsomol Committee and given a strong warning for "relations with a convict."[70]

"We do not snivel"

Although complaints came from a variety of people and professions, they shared assumptions about their "rights" as patriots. Khetagurovites expected special rights as patriots and tended to rely on party and Komsomol organizations for the basic necessities of life, whether or not they had any reasonable grounds to insist on such aid. The migrants were

---

[69] "Stenographic text of the regional Khetagurovite conference," September 15, 1938, Ovchinnikova, 44.

[70] "Protocol from the meeting of the Far Eastern Regional Komsomol Bureau," December 21, 1938, Appeal statement of Gordeeva, GAKhK P, f. 618, op. 1, d. 324, l. 230.

utterly dependent on the organizations that hired them for allocation of living quarters as well as for provisions of social services, merchandise, and places of recreation after work. Yet regional managers ignored their obligations to these newcomers and intentionally let this resettlement problem grind to a halt because the Khetagurovite campaign encroached upon their prerogatives to choose and control their employees.

A dearth of social organizations and community structures was one of the characteristics of frontier Stalinism. There were precious few spaces for newcomers to build relationships and resolve disputes. This contributed significantly to the high rates of complaints and the high turnover among the general population. The kind of voluntary organizations that developed in other settler societies in response to the extremes of social and personal dislocation experienced by migrants were mostly missing from the Soviet Far East. Venues for forging relationships among strangers, other than the workplace, were almost nonexistent because of personnel turnover and the general antipathy of the regime to forms of association outside of officially prescribed boundaries.[71] To make matters worse, because Khetagurovites were given work assignments rather than selecting them themselves, they could not fall back on the bonds of *zemliachestvo* (place of origin) with those they knew from home even if they arrived together. Moreover, for factory workers and laborers, state-controlled unions were unable to function as a locus of identity and collective action.

Efforts to create occasions and spaces for activities after work were often rejected by enterprise bosses who held the purse strings and had little interest in such projects. Things were especially tough in lumber camps and remote fishing operations with thousands of employees and prisoners yet no libraries, theaters, or buildings available for public use. Even when there were occasions for relaxation and socializing, they took place in the open and dusty margins of factories and construction sites. This lack of "cultured" diversions was one of the most common themes in letters from young people and observers of conditions.

Young people, for the most part, arrived from cities and had come to expect at least one theater, radio stations, and public spaces. They presumed that their new bosses would welcome their efforts to stem the tide of "dissolution, drinking and desertion." However, when Komsomol activists asked their lumber camp administrator to launch a club, he answered, "I do not have the funds and no time to deal with this issue.

---

[71] For an overview of the debate about violence and social dislocation in New Zealand's early settler period, see Graeme Dunstall, "Frontier and/or Cultural Fragment? Interpretations of Violence in Colonial New Zealand," *Social History* 29:1 (February 2004), 59–83.

I must fulfill the cubic meter plan. I don't need people, I need cubic meters."[72] When Komsomol members tried to press the issue further, he branded them "fiends."

Everything was out of the ordinary for a young newcomer. Although the Far East had the largest proportion of young people in the country, the Komsomol was relatively small.[73] The thousands of young men who milled about this frontier evinced little interest in joining the Komsomol or the Communist party.[74] Such organizations, especially in the late 1930s, were also hardly a welcoming space for newcomers and especially for young women. The purges, continuing arrests, expulsions, and revolving door in such organizations made them unlikely places to build relationships of mutual support. Komsomol members often lamented that the mass of non-Komsomol young people had the upper hand in isolated settlements and poorly organized industrial towns such as Komsomol'sk-na-Amure where they regularly taunted and shunned activists.

Some patriotic migrants fulfilled their promises to become instigators of "cultured" activities in their new homes and created their own venues for sociability. Particularly popular and nonthreatening to authorities were sports clubs and the already existing network of military training courses for civilians. The role of sports before and after Khetagurovites moved to the Far East facilitated the development of affinity networks. Many of the Khetagurovites who later wrote about their experiences emphasized sports in their stories of their first years on the frontier. These outlets were so important to newcomers that young people devoted their free time to clearing space and building facilities as a priority after arrival. While Robert Edelman, a specialist on the history of sports in the Soviet Union, has argued that sports, and soccer in particular, functioned as an outlet for expressing dissatisfaction with the regime or at least a way to channel one's energies into seemingly nonideological pursuits, for Khetagurovites sports were a way of fitting in and fulfilling the Communist party's expectations.[75]

---

[72] "Requests of a personal nature," March 1, 1939, letter from Titov and Shchendaruk, GAKhK P, f. 35, op. 1, d. 347, l. 162.

[73] In 1939 the Khabarovsk region had 72,000 Komsomol members (21,400 women). See "Protocol of the Khabarovsk regional Komsomol," February 11–15, 1939, GAKhK P, f. 617, op. 1, d. 3, l. 55.

[74] For more on the rift between Bolshevik official culture and youth culture, see Gabor T. Rittersporn, "Formy obshchestvennogo obikhoda molodezhi i ustanovki sovetskogo rezhima v predvoennom desiatiletii," in Timo Vikhavainen (ed.), *Normy i tsennosti povsednevnoi zhizni: Stanovlenie sotsialisticheskogo obraza zhizni v Rossii, 1920–1930-e gody* (St. Petersburg: Zhurnal "Neva," 2000), 347–367.

[75] For more on Soviet sports, see Robert Edelman, "A Small Way of Saying 'No': Moscow Working Men, Spartak Soccer, and the Communist Party, 1900–1945," *American Historical Review* 107:5 (December 2002), 1441–1476.

This was the case for Ogleblina from Moscow, who arrived with thirty-four other young women in June 1937 to work for the Far Eastern State Fishing Trust. The group was sent to a remote island in the Pacific to work in a fish-processing plant. No one had any idea of what to expect. "I must say that after Moscow the fish plant's depressing appearance had an effect. Some began to cry but we kept this all among ourselves and we did not show our disappointment."[76] The party and Komsomol relied on the new arrivals to improve social and cultural conditions on the island, and indeed the Khetagurovites supplied all sorts of labor. They turned a storage room in a barrack into a club and "ended up with a decent club for that time and place." They organized a drama circle and "even performed in other fishing plants." Although she was not overly confident about the "artistic merit" of these performances, "nevertheless the fishermen and residents of the island now had somewhere to go in their free time. The club was never empty. We considered that we were being of benefit. Residents used to say 'We're going to the club today, the Muscovites are performing,' as they used to call us." Besides the drama circles, the Khetagurovites labored to organize sports on the island. The authorities had offered Khetagurovites an empty field and one horse, so they "dug up the field, took away the rocks, built a fence and built two rows of benches and the stadium was ready." With two volleyball courts, the migrants organized a volleyball team. Again their creation was an instant hit. The benches were always packed, "probably because there was nowhere else to go."[77]

Khetagurovites used a variety of techniques to ameliorate their situations and confront their superiors. Some wrote multiple letters to the Khetagurovite Committee and Khetagurova. The letters of complaint demonstrate the tendency of young people to think that they were worthy causes and deserved special consideration. When they were not treated humanely (*po-chelovecheski*), by their immediate supervisors, they turned to other organizations with stories that pointed a damning finger at locals unwilling to treat them with deference. A Khetagurovite sent to work as a librarian was initially promised a salary of 350 rubles per month but received only 240. Because the cost of living was higher in the Far East and because Loseva also had to support her elderly mother, she turned to her director to ask for more pay. In response the director taunted her, "Oh, so you came here to earn money?" Loseva thought that her

[76] Ogleblina, 133. Ogleblina was sent to work as a senior pioneer leader in a summer camp where half the children were Russian and half were children of people native to the island. At the end of the summer, she began work as a secretary of the district party committee's political department.
[77] *Ibid.*, 134.

experience epitomized the kind of "soulless style" of running things that "has made many Khetagurovites leave for home."[78]

Khetagurovites wondered about the "rights" of patriots. A group of young women sent to work in a sovkhoz wanted Khetagurova either to dispatch a committee to investigate their situation or to transfer them to another sovkhoz where they "could work and where we would be treated as Khetagurovites, as people, and especially as cadres." They also inquired whether Khetagurovites had any "rights" and whether there were any special exemptions for them. "Or does it all end up that they come here to work and no one has to worry about them or help them?" The letter was signed "Khetagurovki orphanage graduates."[79] Others took their cases directly to Stalin and the editors of *Komsomol'skaia pravda*. Still others gave up and tried to end their suffering in the most dramatic way possible.

One way to navigate unpleasant situations was to become a nuisance. Some of the Khetagurovites were either unable or unwilling to carry out odious tasks. There are indications from comments made by Khetagurovites that women from the first wave of Khetagurovites were not enthusiastic employees of the labor camps. A large number of young women who had been assigned to work for the railroad construction administration turned to socializing with prisoners. One young woman threw herself out of a second-floor window in desperation, breaking her hand "for unknown reasons."[80] Their poor performance was blamed on wreckers who supposedly selected weak-willed Khetagurovites intentionally for work in a Baikal-Amur railroad construction camp. These shrewd enemies,

[w]anting to disgrace the title of Khetagurovite, selected the kind of young women who did not have strength of will, a strong temperament. These were the types to quickly fall under the influence of those people who wanted to disgrace them in front of the whole construction site, in front of the Soviet nation. There were young women who fell on this hook, but the Komsomol noticed them in time and pulled these gals out.[81]

[78] "Stenographic text of the regional Khetagurovite conference," September 17, 1938, Loseva, GAKhK P, f. 618, op. 1, d. 325, l. 203.
[79] Collective letter of complaint from the Krasnoiarsk rice sovkhoz, GAKhK P, f. 2, op. 1, d. 399, l. 114.
[80] "Report on the conditions in the military guard of the UZhDS GULAG NKVD in the Far East: Report on conditions in BurLag," September 1939, GAKhK P, f. 35, op. 1, d. 314, l. 173.
[81] "Stenographic text of the regional Khetagurovite conference," September 16, 1938, Utkina, GAKhK P, f. 618, op. 1, d. 325, l. 107.

Forcing the management and Komsomol to "pull" them out of their assignment was probably the only sure way to extricate oneself from employment in the GULAG system.

The coping strategies revealed in letters of complaint and suggestions at the Khetagurovite conference illustrate differences in the way men and women reacted to their situation and how they approached state authorities. Women factory workers called for the formation of special commissions or female brigades that could monitor the treatment of Khetagurovites and other women in their factories. Male Khetagurovites did not opt for the formation of such groupings. The reason is clear. Organizing men into groups with demands and agendas was a dangerous business. Women's groups, however, had completely different connotations. Special groups and sections for women were staples of Soviet and party institutions, beginning with the Zhenotdel in the 1920s.

Women conceived collective responses to their problems and sought official status for their groups. At the Khetagurovite conference in September 1938, Khetagurovite Karlova enumerated stories about soulless bureaucrats who did nothing to address the needs of the 155 Khetagurovites living in Spassk. However, she wanted the audience to know that "[w]e do not snivel. Our district Khetagurovite conference has already set up its own Committee." Khetagurovites had already drawn up a plan of action for their Committee for Life, Education and Labor for the Khetagurovites of Spassk:

We will observe the condition and life of young women Khetagurovites. If there are questions concerning the party committee then we will resolve them there, if the questions are concerning the district executive committee then we will make the managers answer. These bureaucrats to this day still have not understood that young women Khetagurovites carry a big political significance especially for the Far East.[82]

At Factory No. 199 in Komsomol'sk-na-Amure, young women organized a similar committee that included Khetagurovites and women who came during Komsomol mobilizations of 1933–1934. They selected seven members of what they called their "initiative group" intended to observe and review women's complaints. However, the project proved short-lived when neither the bosses nor the unions supported them, so "our work in this sector died out."[83]

Some proposed that young women should be placed together so that it would be "more fun. And they would be more persistent."[84]

---

[82] *Ibid.*, September 15, Karlova, 51.   [83] *Ibid.*, September 16, Gordeeva, 154.
[84] *Ibid.*

Opryshko also suggested that the Khetagurovite Committee send "courageous" young women into the countryside where they "must work with kolkhozniki" and where it is "more difficult than in the cities. Weaker young women can be sent [into cities] and they can pull them along."[85]

Opryshko was right. Those who came and stayed in groups or immediately found a network of like-minded compatriots fared much better in the region. Aleksandra Vorob'eva did not come alone to the Shmakov district, but arrived with her thirteen-year-old son and adult sister. She went to work according to her training as a senior inspector for state insurance. In their very first days, the sisters created a good situation by seeking out potential patrons and *landsmen* groups. Because they had been devoted members of Ukrainian choral groups, dating back to their childhood in church choirs, it seemed natural to ask about choirs. As luck would have it, there was a Ukrainian choir sponsored by a local lumber mill. Taking matters into their own hands, the sisters tracked down the choirmaster, a fellow Ukrainian. That very same day, with his help, the Vorob'eva sisters were given "a sunny room with a view of the river." When the women came back to their hostel and announced to the other residents that they were getting a room, everyone was incredulous. "They said that the procurator and the investigator already lived for two months in a small room and so how was it possible for you gals to get an apartment so fast?"[86]

In contrast, male Khetagurovites did not underscore their helpless status in their letters of complaint. In part, they felt more empowered because they were older than the women Khetagurovites and tended to be professionals with more options. One man wrote to the Khetagurovite Committee secretary to "Notify you" that if conditions did not change he would quit "and go to another organization where I will receive an apartment or dormitory."[87] A male teacher wrote to Khetagurova after fruitless attempts to force his superiors to provide him with an apartment. He told Khetagurova, "I received 2,400 rubles to resettle but they will not provide me with housing and I will be forced to return to Odessa . . . Help me to receive an apartment so that I will not be accused of wasting government funds."[88] A Komsomol member called Bliskunov wrote an irate letter to the Khetagurovite Committee. It was his sixth letter of complaint. The first five had gone unanswered so he concluded, "If you

---

[85] *Ibid.*, September 17, Opryshko, 296.
[86] Memoir of Aleksandra Vorob'eva, GAKhK P, f. 442, op. 2, d. 282, l. 104ob.
[87] Letter of complaint from Ivan Nechaev, October 5, 1938, GAKhK P, f. 2, op. 6, d. 341, l. 126.
[88] Letter of complaint from Nikita Kravets, December 19, 1938, GAKhK P, f. 2, op. 6, d. 341, l. 129.

had treated me in this way when I wrote to volunteer to come here, then I wouldn't have agreed to come."[89]

Khetagurovites were adept at laying bare the gulf between the propaganda about their life and the reality in order to elicit attention from authorities. As has been described, some pointed to the dangerous implications of the inequality they encountered and argued for an expansion in women's roles as total war drew closer. Others employed the rhetoric of women's mission as caregivers and cultured consumers to press their demands. Karlova explained that although women were keeping up with young men in their earnings, in Komsomol'sk there was nothing to be done with all this money because the stores were empty. Like everyone else, she and her Khetagurovite friends had "desires to improve, to beautify one's life. First of all to dress well. At the factory we do not see [merchandise] and our organizations cannot provide for the youth. It is an outrage. People travel to Moscow just to buy a suit."[90]

Numerous speakers at the September 1938 conference of Khetagurovites in Khabarovsk expressed dissatisfaction with the quality of life they found in places like Komsomol'sk and their expectation that as members of the Komsomol they were entitled to goods. Vochkova connected the lack of merchandise and provisions in Komsomol'sk stores with the roadblocks facing Khetagurovites in their mission to "develop and strengthen" their new communities. "Here in Khabarovsk there is a party network [providing] bedding for young women, etc. You would think this was a trifle. However, if you're looking at a room to make it attractive and to create a permanent place of residence, this is missing."[91]

Women claimed that their aspirations to become happy mothers were obstructed by conditions in the Far East. Speakers at the conference highlighted the fact that 1,050 children had been born in Komsomol'sk in 1937. Vochkova chimed in that although it was wonderful to see so many newborns, this also meant that 1,050 families had to make do without proper nutrition and with a crippling lack of daycare facilities that forced women to leave their jobs. There were only one hundred places for children in the Komsomol'sk kindergartens, so she reasonably wondered, "Where are we going to put the other 950 children? We have taken to building this city, the capital of the Far East and here in this large population we do not have even one store. Furthermore, things are terrible

---

[89] Letter of complaint from I. E. Bliskunov, 1938, GAKhK P, f. 2, op. 6, d. 341, l. 130. Bliskunov noted several times that he was sending a copy of his letter to the Komsomol Central Committee in Moscow.

[90] "Stenographic text of the regional Khetagurovite conference," September 15, 1938, Karlova, 53.

[91] *Ibid.*, Vochkova, 58.

with services for young mothers." All this was especially problematic in Komsomol'sk because young people had come on their own and could not rely on support, advice, and babysitting from parents and grand-parents. Vochkova knew of one young mother who returned to Moscow because she could not find household help in Komsomol'sk. She did not hesitate to enumerate other deficits. "I must say something about the specific circumstances in the city. There is a lack of fresh vegetables and fresh food, [and] this produces a certain effect on overall health. Many have stomach problems. The factory's one doctor has to deal with every kind of illness, starting with the teeth and ending with the feet."[92]

Although more than one speaker broached the subject of special priv-ileges like extended vacations to visit parents and forms of organizing Khetagurovites, others roundly criticized their suggestions. Gordeeva was against the idea of forming a special committee to protect their rights and push for special privileges, while neglecting the needs of other women. "While workers at our factory receive a two-week vacation, Khetagurovites demand a three-month vacation and payment for travel expenses. Comrades, this is not right."[93] She argued that if they had read Khetagurova's call-up letter, they should have known that they would encounter difficulties. "Why should we demand better conditions?"

Belova, from Okha on Sakhalin, concurred with those who rejected the idea that Khetagurovites should be provided with special privileges such as longer vacations. She pointed out that although she lived on the island, where conditions were more difficult than in Khabarovsk, "Our women are not crying the way they are here. All of us are citizens of the Soviet Union and should have the same rights . . . It is silly to bring up the question of special vacations. We came here and then begin to snivel – this is intolerable."[94] Utkina also claimed that poor living conditions did not justify feelings of resentment and disillusionment. Young employees of BAMLag were not given rooms and slept in tents for four months in the winter. "But these young women did not get scared and did not cry."[95]

The officials of the Khetagurovite Committee and Khetagurova her-self shot down all discussions of special committees and privileges. Mel'nikova, acting secretary of the Khetagurovite Committee at the time, explained that Khetagurovites were not entitled to any special benefits. "We all know that we receive salaries according to the law, no one is going to pay you anything above the law. We are eligible for the same vacations

[92] *Ibid.*, 59.   [93] *Ibid.*

[94] *Ibid.*, September 17, Belova, 252. This rejection of special privileges was echoed by several other speakers. *Ibid.*, September 15, Vochkova, 61.

[95] *Ibid.*, 107.

[as] all other laborers of the Soviet Union."[96] Some of the Khetagurovites were obviously aware that special privileges had in fact existed for other workers in the form of *l'goty*, aimed at attracting and retaining those with special skills in certain industries and northernmost regions. This system of incentives fostered expectations that could not be fulfilled and had the potential to embitter those who were left out. It seemed that acts of sacrifice in the name of patriotism produced conditions and terms of employment less advantageous than those garnered by other Soviet workers who openly sought out better deals and made decisions based on monetary calculations.

The Khetagurovites volunteered to make sacrifices and work in difficult conditions for the sake of the Motherland. Their status as patriots who supposedly eschewed base monetary incentives separated them from other migrants in the region who did not deny the allure of better salaries and incentives from the government. This distinction between Khetagurovites and other migrants weakened their case when complaining to their immediate superiors. When young women suggested that they be given special consideration and material support once they realized the importance of such incentives for survival, other young women and officials dismissed them as "snivelers."

Liquidation

Complaints, mishaps, and outright demands made by migrants who went to the Far East through the Khetagurovite system burdened an already dysfunctional organization. The Khetagurovite Committee was riddled with problems from its very inception. It was originally conceived as an organization strictly concerned with the selection and placement of volunteers, but conditions in the region, conflicts of interest with local enterprises, and its own convoluted system made the Khetagurovite resettlement program ultimately unworkable.

The problems stemmed in part from the haphazard genesis of the campaign. There was no actual plan to facilitate migration of patriotic female volunteers and ensure an orderly resettlement before Khetagurova's letter appeared in *Komsomol'skaia pravda*. Once responses began to flood in, the Central Committee of the Komsomol and the newspaper's editors scrambled to process the applications and find a way to expedite

---

[96] Of course, there were categories of workers who were paid different salaries and had special vacation time under the incentive programs in effect during the 1930s. However, these incentives did not apply to the southern zones of the Far East where most of the young women were working. See *ibid.*, September 17, Mel'nikova, 313.

the migration. A disconnect between the editorial staff of *Komsomol'skaia pravda*, who produced bombastic pieces inviting young people to rush to the frontier where everyone was supposedly needed, and those who actually had to place volunteers in a region with limited housing and uncooperative employers, was never resolved.

A major cause of failure was the reluctance of regional enterprise chiefs to let the Khetagurovite Committee select employees on their behalf. Bosses avoided using the Khetagurovite program shortly after it began operations, though there was a labor shortage in the region and many of those volunteering were qualified. Georgii M. Statsevich, secretary of the Far Eastern regional Communist Party Committee, pointed to problems surrounding this migration program as early as October 1937:

Certain administrators of regional and oblast soviet and economic institutions and organizations and the directors of enterprises (sovkhoz administrators of Khabarovsk, Ussuriisk, and Amurskaia oblasts, administrators of the Far Eastern and Amur railroad, the Blagoveshchensk pastry factory, and a series of others) did not understand the political and economic significance of the movement of youth to the Far East. [They] have demonstrated a soulless and bureaucratic attitude toward the Khetagurovites, especially on the question of living conditions.[97]

The Khetagurovites quickly became a nuisance for regional managers who probably treated them like any other worker but soon realized that enthusiastic patriots were more likely to complain and seize the attention of top party officials. The resulting scrutiny was not simply a matter of annoyance. In 1937 such inquiries could quickly snowball into denunciations costing individuals their jobs and lives. The best way to avoid such unfavorable mention and bothersome employees was to sidestep the Khetagurovite Committee by failing to provide the organization with requests for labor.

By 1939, the organization for greeting new arrivals had severely deteriorated. The new male head of the Khetagurovite Committee, Lapshin, admitted that its office did not make a great first impression. "Young people having just arrived from a ten- to twelve-day train ride stand in a narrow hallway filling out forms."[98] There was nowhere to rest or even sit down. Initial conditions were so bad that on their first few days the young people were taking matters into their own hands. "Things have come to

---

[97] "Protocols 48–56: Far Eastern Regional Communist Party Committee, January 4, 1938 to February 25, 1938: Addendum to protocol 41 from October 14, 1937, RGASPI f. 17, op. 21, d. 5444, l. 48.

[98] "Memorandum, information and other documents of the Komsomol Central Committee and other organizations on the activities and plans of the Khetagurovite Call-Up Committee – Report from the chair of the Khetagurovite Committee," March 11, 1939, RGASPI f. M – 1, op. 23, d. 1351, l. 41.

the point that without the knowledge of the Committee or Komsomol organizations, arriving patriots have independently convened meetings in their dormitories and resolved issues about the disgusting reception they received."[99] The financing of the migration was also convoluted.

In April and May of 1939, the dysfunctional state of the Khetagurovite Committee came to the attention of Central Committee VKP(b) member A. A. Zhdanov and became a subject for discussion in the bureau of the Komsomol Central Committee.[100] At the end of April, a report by an investigator for the Council of People's Commissars went to Zhdanov, the Komsomol Central Committee, and the Khabarovsk region's party First Secretary Donskoi detailing the shortcomings. The report's author, one Sergeev, criticized the Committee's propensity to improperly reject applicants possessing highly desirable qualifications. "Rejections are sent to welders, drivers, and a whole series of other specialists."[101] His conclusion was categorical. "Despite the large political and economic meaning of the Khetagurovite movement of youth and the large number of letters received from those wishing to come to the Far East, the organization of this movement and the processing of arrivals is in an exceptionally poor state."[102]

An investigation by the Komsomol Central Committee resulted in a similar finding.[103] The Communist Party Central Committee resolved in November 1939 that the Khetagurovite Committee, rather than facilitating migration, actually presented "an artificial barrier to the patriotic movement of youth." While 300,000 individuals had expressed interest in migration through the program, the number of arrivals stood at around 25,000. The resolution noted that the Khetagurovite Committee was not able to process all the applications and to coordinate its activities with regional industries in a way that would expedite the appropriate placement of thousands in a timely manner. Top party officials considered it unacceptable that applicants waited for eight to ten months for an answer.

---

[99] *Ibid.* "Report to Comrade Mishakova from Lapshin, chair of the regional committee for the reception of youth in the Far East," April 15, 1939, RGASPI f. M – 1, op. 23, d. 1351, l. 27–28.

[100] Zhdanov became involved because the Komsomol had been put under his control in November 1938. See "Protocol No. 66 PB Communist Party Central Committee, November 27, 1938: 3. Supervision and control of Komsomol organs to be placed with the Secretary of the Communist Party Central Committee, Comrade Zhdanov," RGASPI f. 17, op. 3, d. 1004, l. 2.

[101] Correspondence with the Communist Party Central Committee. "On the status of work on the Khetagurovite movement of youth to the Far East," April 11, 1939, GAKhK P, f. 35, op. 1, d. 344, l. 76.

[102] *Ibid.*, 74.

[103] *Ibid.*, 91. On April 29, 1939 Tsyngalenok, an instructor in the TsK Komsomol Sector for Work among Young Women addressed a report that reiterated these findings to the secretaries of the Komsomol Central Committee, Mikhailov, Gromov, and Mishakova.

Moreover, "[s]tate funds had been squandered. We considered that young people can get the opportunity faster to work for enterprises, kolkhozy, and institutions of the Far East directly through economic and soviet organizations, with the help of Komsomol organizations."[104] Although interest from people across the Soviet Union in becoming a Khetagurovite continued to be strong, the Khetagurovite Committee was "liquidated" at the end of 1939.

The Khetagurovite program had succumbed to the bad planning and chaos engendered by the Great Terror within the top leadership of the Communist Youth League and Far Eastern officialdom more broadly. Shortcomings in the resettlement program exposed fissures between party authorities and local enterprise chiefs who eventually managed to circumvent efforts to intervene in their prerogatives in the selection and treatment of employees. The end of the program also relieved local Komsomol and Communist party authorities from the chore of having to pay special attention to requests from unhappy newcomers.

Conclusion

On the frontier of Stalinism, enterprise managers and organizational chiefs operated in an autarchic system that they prized and guarded. They had exaggerated powers for a number of reasons. Most enterprises were in some way connected directly or indirectly to the secretive and insular NKVD system of labor camps. Their distance from Moscow also shielded them from a certain amount of scrutiny when it came to working conditions for free employees. Without a preexisting urban infrastructure on the frontier, the enterprise chiefs were also expected to act as both industrial managers and civic planners. They predictably chose to channel their energies into boosting industrial output quotas, which were easier to quantify and dangerous to ignore, at the cost of a high labor turnover which could be blamed on amorphous factors such as a difficult climate or the laborers' underdeveloped sense of patriotic duty. The Khetagurovite Committee interfered in the administrators' ability to select their own employees and parachuted meddlesome Komsomol activists into their operations. In the end, regional industrial managers got their way as a new generation of officials and managers began rebuilding their authority and security after the chaos of the Great Terror.

---

[104] "Memorandum, information and other documents of the Komsomol Central Committee and other organizations on the status and plans for the activities of the Khetagurovite Committee to mobilize youth for construction projects of the Far East: Draft Resolution of the Communist Party Central Committee: On the Khetagurovite Committee," November 21, 1939, RGASPI f. M – 1, op. 23, d. 1351, l. 73.

Khetagurovites were well aware and proud of the fact that they were representatives of the Communist party and Soviet state. They also expected reciprocal support from the state they represented and pledged to defend. When they found deplorable conditions, they were especially offended by the fact that hardships were not shared equally. The façade of socialist equality was easily shattered in the conditions of the Far East, where basic survival was so highly dependent on access to kin or patronage networks and incentive programs designed to retain workers. The realities of life for women in the region transformed many idealistic patriot-heroines into isolated "snivelers."

Yet the period was remembered as one of equally shared burdens and supportive collectives even by women like Novikova who subsequently spent more than seven years in the labor camps. One reason the memoirists did not include harrowing stories of early difficulties was that complaining had been so severely stigmatized among them. Having volunteered in an act of self-abnegation, many women had to accept their deprivations as a matter of course for a greater good or face being denied the exalted status of patriot.

The high turnover rates among settlers in the region and the unhappy experiences of some suggest that although convict and special settler labor was a central component in the development of infrastructure and industries, their exploitation and presence also gave rise to a social landscape that drove away potential permanent settlers. Those who came voluntarily in this period were often taken for forced settlers and treated as such by locals who had begun to assume that everyone arriving came under a cloud if not under convoy.

Of course, in general, insufficient investment in housing and social services pushed people to abandon the area throughout the Soviet period. Furthermore, having programs that rewarded certain categories of workers while mobilizing others through ideals of self-sacrifice and patriotism was bound to lead to disgruntlement among patriots. The system of material and patriotic incentives developed to entice and keep workers in the region belies the myths of Siberian self-sufficiency. The frontier of Stalinism, in fact, fostered a highly dependent relationship with the state among new migrants. Although the myths of Siberia and the Far East promised spaces of personal freedom (*volia*), in reality the dynamics of frontier Stalinism offered greater license and control for those already in power as local enterprise chiefs and party functionaries.

Conclusion

Seeing women as active agents and not as inanimate props in propaganda exposes sources of support for the Communist regime. The willingness of thousands to go and to withstand horrendous conditions and distasteful obligations underscores the regime's ability to build loyal support without recourse to violence or material rewards. On the other hand, those they encountered on the frontier of Stalinism were just as likely to see everything as a charade of a repressive system, never accepted the regime as legitimate, and never cared to refashion themselves or learn to "speak Bolshevik." Both ways of relating to the state existed at the same time.

This resettlement campaign and the migrants' self-perception do not support the argument that the second half of the 1930s ushered in a limited vision of women's roles as mothers and housewives. Their aspirations and limitations were certainly products of the imperfectly realized dreams of radical egalitarianism among Russian revolutionaries, and their choices were no doubt impacted to some extent by pronatalist policies. However, their lives after the supposed Great Retreat were not more troublesome nor were women's roles in society more circumscribed. The sources of their very real burdens and perils were more heterogeneous than a supposed turn by the regime toward emphasizing domesticity. Arguably, their lives were more profoundly impacted by the dissonance between the prospects of an expanded vision of their roles and recognition as frontier builders on the one hand, and on the other, the mass repressions and the GULAG system on the frontier of Stalinism.

The Khetagurovite story underscores the differences between Soviet empire-building practices and those of Western European powers. One of the primary driving forces motivating Soviet women was a desire to partake in the unfolding epic of Soviet conquests in the harsh but supposedly bountiful natural world of the Far East. They were not seeking to function as guardians of racial boundaries nor enjoined to think of themselves as embodiments of ethnic traditions. Valentina Khetagurova's marriage exemplified the melding of ethnic groups into one patriotic Soviet identity and was praised and rewarded by the regime. This sanction, rather than punishment for mixing ethnic groups, reflects the desire of Communists, as well as many pre-revolutionary intellectuals, to facilitate, as Vera Tolz has argued, the "integration and fusion of Russia's different nationalities into a single nation [*edinyi narod*] within the current state borders, united above all by a common history of living together."[1] The vision of a Russian and Ossetian coming together on the shores of the Pacific Ocean in a productive and reproductive relationship operated as a metaphoric and actual realization of this fusion.

The lively response to the Khetagurovite campaign points to the popularity of frontier myths among the Soviet public. It also illustrates the ascent of a new female archetype born out of the needs and fantasies of the Soviet state as a Eurasian power. This New Woman of the Soviet empire was much more than a compliant helpmate or a huntress of upwardly mobile grooms.

Unfortunately, the darkest of themes associated with the frosty East reflected the realities of frontier Stalinism. What awaited the migrants on the frontier were the gruesome products of the Communists' utopian quests to catapult the Soviet Union into a modern industrial society and mold a new Soviet person. Once in the region, volunteers could find themselves unwitting and often unwilling wardens in the labor camps or their bewildered prisoners.

The realities of frontier Stalinism mercilessly exploited those who were so willing to help in securing Soviet power in the peripheries. The tragic stories of some migrants illustrate women's ill-fated endeavors to acculturate in a frontier long accustomed to male preponderance and visibility. They also expose the perils for women of living outside of the sometimes confining but also protective web of kinship networks. The social dislocation and hardships they endured dramatized the ongoing failures of the state to encourage permanent settlement in a vulnerable region despite material incentives for badly needed professionals and patriotic appeals directed at young people.

As the female migrants arrived in the region, many found themselves in isolated circumstances, sometimes without housing or a salary sufficient for basic survival. More than one patriotic migrant was ostracized and shunned by co-workers and neighbors simply because she was a woman who made claims to authority and special status. Others were dropped in a sea of aggrieved agricultural workers and special settlers, or in organizations that employed a large number of current and former

---

[1] Vera Tolz, "Orientalism, Nationalism, and Ethnic Diversity in Late Imperial Russia," *Historical Journal* 48:1 (2005), 150.

convict laborers. Their status as representatives of the state made the Khetagurovites anathema to those who abhorred the regime.

The migrants' unrealistic expectations, fed by literature, film, and journalistic accounts of Far Eastern adventures, further intensified their disappointment and unhappiness when they discovered that life in the Far East replicated the same drudgery that they apparently sought to escape. When conditions were less than ideal and when locals were not impressed with the arrival of ostensible heroes, the young people interpreted their reception as personal rejection and malicious attempts to discredit them. Some were quick to see in their misadventure evidence of enemy machinations. Their tendency to suspect all those they met further ensured that locals treated them as intruders and made them targets of abuse and reprisals.

The tenacious association of women with sexuality and petty materialism, dating back to the pre-revolutionary period and the 1920s, cast a shadow over their voluntarism and sacrifices. Regardless of their motivations for migrating, they had to justify themselves before they ever boarded their trains for the Far East. Forty years later, insinuations about their intentions still haunted participants. Their experiences presaged the difficulties women encountered when they were denied equal recognition for their wartime exploits after World War II.

A number of female migrants, in trying circumstances, gravitated toward sexual unions and marriages as their only opportunity to find companionship and build social networks. At the same time as authorities decried the sexual reputation of some Khetagurovites, they were also unable to articulate clear guidelines for a uniquely Soviet sexual morality. Irrespective of official injunctions, marriages or liaisons with men they hardly knew became the only means to gain access to goods or a place to live for a number of young women. This part of their story illustrates a point of similarity between the Khetagurovites and single women migrants in other historical and national contexts. In the Soviet case, however, marriage itself was not necessarily viewed as a positive step among Communist party and Komsomol members because it depleted the ranks of activist women. These losses were especially obvious in the Far East where the project of enticing activist women to take up badly needed positions was undermined by the eagerness of some new arrivals to get married. Issues of sexuality and the choice of marriage partner were particularly politicized in this period of the Great Terror in a region with thousands of prisoners and former prisoners.

It is unwarranted, though, to assume that everyone found themselves in the same circumstances. Despite the unhappy stories of some, there were plenty of migrants who created longlasting relationships on the frontier and did not drop out of public life. Marriage appeared in Ania Alekseeva's memoirs as an unproblematic stage in men's and women's lives which did not eclipse other pursuits.[2]

The generation to which most Khetagurovites belonged, born between 1910 and 1922, had grown up almost entirely in the Soviet system. Some were deeply traumatized by the series of cataclysms that began with World War I. Others, like Efrosina Mishalova, knew only Soviet power and the apparent sustenance and education that the state offered to women like themselves. With nothing to lose and no idyllic childhood to recall, they were keen to connect their interests wholly with the national collective. The appeal of party organizations that promised and often delivered a sense of belonging and visible recognition for loyalty was a powerful inducement for the most socially isolated.

While those migrants who experienced quick promotions and social recognition for their sacrifices on the Soviet frontier epitomized promises fulfilled for some women in Soviet society, generally the frontier also exaggerated some of the most difficult aspects of the Soviet system for women and their children. The lack of proper nutrition, the dearth of essential merchandise, and the absence of labor-saving devices were far worse in this region than in major European cities of the Soviet Union. These deficiencies sapped the energies of women already committed to work and public activism. Although many were quickly promoted, their duties at home in such circumstances derailed the momentum of whatever upward mobility they initially found.

Whatever life courses were in store for the migrants in the Far East, everyone's life took an unforeseen turn in 1941 with the Nazi invasion. Mishalova and many other Khetagurovites volunteered to fight the enemy in any capacity. When Alekseeva's husband departed for the front, leaving her alone with an infant, "I did not become glum; [after all] I was in the same situation as thousands of others."[3] During the war, she worked in Komsomol'sk, collected warm clothing to send to the front, and organized ski trips for local teenagers. Although she worried terribly during the war, her husband returned one day in the spring of 1946. "This was probably the happiest day of my life."[4] Alekseeva's and Klava Novikova's husbands also miraculously survived their service on the front, unlike millions of other soldiers.[5] Being in the Far East spared the women the torments of

---

[2] Alekseeva described a happy marriage of equals with shared interests, especially in sports: "When our first daughter was born in 1942, our life became even fuller . . . Despite the fact that there was no one around to help us with raising our children, this did not especially burden us. We helped each other and took our daughter with us to our workouts." See Memoir of Ania Alekseeva, GAKhK P, f. 442, op. 2, d. 283, l. 32.

[3] *Ibid.*, 32.   [4] *Ibid.*, 33.

[5] In the course of the Nazi assault on the Soviet Union, German forces occupied 400,000 square miles with 65 million inhabitants. Hitler's extermination detachments liquidated

German occupation or bombardment – but not hunger, worry, loss of loved ones, or grueling labor regimes.[6]

When the war ended, women, many of whom had lost husbands, children, and the potential to marry because of the high male mortality during the war, became even more encumbered by the demands of economic recovery and reconstruction. They were also called upon to heal the physical and psychological wounds of the men who came back from the front. The stories of women who fought on the fronts or survived disasters like the siege of Leningrad were subsumed by the regime into a generic narrative about the sacrifices of the Soviet people and eclipsed by an emphasis on the heroism of male soldiers.[7]

The Soviet population, having expected greater liberalization and the trust of their regime as rewards for their loyal service during the war, instead faced ever more rigid labor discipline. The use of slave labor grew to unprecedented levels. Stalin was determined to collect reparations from the Germans and other Axis powers. German and Japanese war prisoners, like Novikova's second husband Iasaburo, were forced to help in rebuilding cities and industries. Consumer and agricultural production lagged chronically as intense investment in heavy industry and construction continued. Draconian policies brought growth in industry and military capacity. Meanwhile, Soviet living standards were among the lowest in Europe.

After the war, Alekseeva continued to work, raised her children, and remained active in public organizations. In retirement she belonged to a club of former Khetagurovites and was the chairwoman of the local Red Cross and of a women's committee at her factory. She regularly

not just Communists but two million Jews and millions of other Soviet citizens, most of whom were women and children. The number of losses among the Soviet armed forces and civilians is staggering. Of the 196.7 million Soviet citizens in 1941, close to 26 million were dead by 1945 as a direct result of the war, either in the fighting forces or as civilian casualties. On women in the Leningrad siege, see Cynthia Simmons and Nina Perlina, *Writing the Siege of Leningrad: Women's Diaries, Memoirs and Documentary Prose* (Pittsburgh: University of Pittsburgh Press, 2002).

[6] For studies on Soviet society during the war, see Robert W. Thurston and Bernd Bonwetsch, (eds.), *The People's War: Responses to World War II in the Soviet Union* (Urbana and Chicago: University of Illinois Press, 2000), and Amir Weiner, *Making Sense of War: The Second World War and the Fate of the Bolshevik Revolution* (Princeton: Princeton University Press, 2002).

[7] Art and literature focused exclusively on the trauma and heroism of returning male soldiers. Recently, Western scholars have drawn attention to women in the postwar years. See Anna Krylova, "'Healers of Wounded Souls': The Crisis of Private Life in Soviet Literature, 1944–1946," *Journal of Modern History* 73:2 (June 2001), 307–331; Greta Bucher, "Struggling to Survive: Soviet Women in the Postwar Years," *Journal of Women's History* 12:1 (Spring 2002), 137–159; and Lisa Kirschenbaum, "Gender, Memory, and National Myths: Ol'ga Berggol'ts and the Siege of Leningrad," *Nationalities Papers* 28:3 (2000), 551–564.

visited Komsomol'sk-na-Amure's schoolchildren to tell them about her own "lively youth and to offer advice to young people about life."[8]

After demobilization from the Far Eastern fleet, Mishalova was hired as the head of the cadre department of the Far Eastern Coal Exploration Trust and soon thereafter she "was called to work in the KGB." In 1947, because her husband, Dimitrii, was transferred to Penza, 625 kilometers southeast of Moscow, she abandoned her own career track and the couple left the Far East.[9] They finally settled in Kiev after Dimitrii left the Ministry of Internal Affairs (MVD) USSR in 1952. Mishalova felt that she "did not have time to complete special feats. I lived and worked like everyone else and then the war muddled up everything."[10] She exemplified the gratification derived from having participated in the settlement of the Far East, despite the cynicism of others:

We know that our life had substance and was rich from the spirit of completed exploits and romanticism (although, it seems we did not know the word "romantic" at the time) . . . We were not petty, envious, or lazy. At the same time, we lived under great deprivation: we did not have splendid apartments, nor beautiful clothes, shoes and other things. But, on the other hand, we possessed a powerful love for the Motherland! We felt indebted to her and we yearned for the Motherland to become rich, free, strong, and beautiful! And things were always good and joyful for us because we knew we were needed! People who have never known anything of the kind won't believe the story of our lives! They could even suspect that it is dreamed up to "show off as a heroes." But we know: our life was marvelous.[11]

In the 1970s former Khetagurovite Nina Ermakova viewed the history of Far Eastern development through a prism of solidarity with other women. "You know, the hands of women have done so much in these thirty-seven years in Komsomol'sk-na-Amure that it cannot all be described."[12] Parimova was very conscious of the significance of women's labor. "I saw with my own eyes and not by reading it in literature, what enormous roles women played in the Great Patriotic War! How can it be possible not to be proud of them?"[13]

Surveying her life's work, Ermakova felt that it was the right time to answer a question she posed to herself before she migrated. As a young

---

[8] Alekseeva, 26.
[9] For a discussion of women in the post-World War II period and the choice many made to focus on family rather than on their careers, see Greta Bucher, *Women, the Bureaucracy and Daily Life in Postwar Moscow, 1945–1953* (Boulder, CO: Eastern European Monographs, 2006).
[10] Memoir of Efrosina Mishalova, February 18, 1976, GAKhK P, f. 442, op. 2, d. 284, l. 112.
[11] Dubinina, *Ty pozovi, Dal'nii Vostok!*, 159–160.
[12] Memoir of Nina Ermakova, April 8, 1974, GAKhK P, f. 442, op. 2, d. 283, l. 7.
[13] Memoir of Valentina Parimova, GAKhK P, f. 442, op. 2, d. 283, l. 70.

person, she wondered if she was strong enough to withstand whatever lay ahead. Now she could say, "Yes, I withstood! I have lived and worked in our city for thirty-seven years. I have been awarded medals for outstanding labor during the Great Patriotic War. My children live here."[14] Anna Plaskina concluded her memoir by summing up the pleasure she gained from the achievements of her family and her own record as a patriot and party member. "I am proud of my sons, I'm proud that along with my husband, I raised a worthy replacement for myself, teaching them to love the Far East and our own city . . . It seems life was not lived in vain."[15] Mishalova's memories of the Far East assuaged the pains of growing old and a hard life. "Now when we are already almost sixty, we often talk about our ailments, the bad luck and grief we endured, but we remember our youth with a warm smile and joy: we lived the right way!"[16]

These women were deeply invested in the Soviet system and viewed its achievements, such as healthcare and urban amenities, as the products of their individual and collective labor. As they surveyed their circumstances, they could compare the often imperfect but functional late Soviet system with the waves of calamities they had withstood. They not only found a place where they felt needed but could take personal satisfaction in the achievements of a Soviet Union that had come a long way from the days of hunger and wars. Having made very public sacrifices, former Khetagurovites looked back at a life that had meaning beyond the mundane and private. For women like the memoirists, the Communist regime fulfilled its pledges to promote and educate them, the truly "wretched of the earth."[17]

Soviet authorities proved unable to design a system for the Far East that could transform migrants into residents. However, while the high turnover continued, one of the Far East's problems resolved itself. After World War II, the region no longer suffered from a glaring or debilitating shortage of women and skilled female professionals. The sex ratios evened out for several reasons. First, the massive loss of men in the fighting forces during the war meant that women predominated in the population across the Soviet Union even in places formerly dominated by men. Second, by the 1970s the Far East's population was reproducing itself rather than relying solely on male migrant laborers. With the development of local universities and technical schools, and the almost universal involvement of women in the paid labor force in the post-World

14 Ermakova, 7.
15 Memoir of Anna I. Plaskina, GAKhK P, f. 442, op. 2, d. 283, l. 55.
16 Quoted in Dubinina, *Ty pozovi, Dal'nii Vostok!*, 160.
17 A phrase from the Soviet National Anthem, originally from the song of the First and Second International.

War II period, Far Eastern institutions had less difficulty finding employees for female-identified professions.

Even in the late Soviet period, life in the Far East was not easy. In 1978–1979 life expectancy was two years lower than in the rest of the country – as much as four years lower in the Far East's northern regions. The rift between the life expectancy of men and women was more than eleven years.[18] Lack of decent housing was the primary motivating force behind decisions to leave the region in the 1960s and 1970s as much as in the 1930s.[19]

By 1990, the population of the Far East had reached almost eight million. Demographers were projecting an increase by another million for the year 2000. In fact, after the collapse of the Soviet Union, the Far Eastern region experienced a decline in population. Whereas the area had a population of 7,941,000 in 1989, in 1998 there were 7,367,000 individuals registered. The region is currently sparsely populated, with an average population density in 2003 of 3.7 people per square kilometer compared with the Russian Federation's overall average population density of 8.61 and the USA's of 29.77 people per square kilometer.[20] As their own population forsakes the region, Russians bewail the influx of Asian migrant laborers into all sectors of the Far Eastern economy. Fear of invasion, not by military forces but by Chinese laborers and companies from Korea and Japan, is pervasive in the political discourses of regional politicians, the state-dominated media, and ordinary Far Easterners of Slavic descent.[21]

The story of the Khetagurovites has not wholly disappeared from post-Soviet consciousness. On occasion, elderly Khetagurovites such as Novikova have been interviewed by local newspapers and television stations. In one such interview Valentina Udalova told a reporter that "Khetagurovite was an honorable title for the first builders of the Far East." Her explanation and self-image in 2004 did not differ from those invoked in 1937 or 1978, illustrating the effectiveness of official Komsomol culture in building group and personal identities. She went to

---

[18] Rybakovskii, *Naselenie Dal'nego Vostoka*, 166.

[19] "Between 1959–1970 the tempos of arrival increased by 14.6%[;] at the same time, tempos of departures jumped by 16.1%." See N. V. Abramova, "Problemy formirovaniia naseleniia i trudovykh resursov v dal'nevostochnom regione Rossii (1965–1985 gg.)," in Chernolutskaia (ed.) *Voprosy sotsial'no-demografichskoi istorii*, 176. For more on efforts to stimulate migration and permanent settlement to Siberia and the Far East in the post-World War II period, see John Sallnow, "Siberia's Demand for Labour: Incentive Policies and Migration, 1960–85," in Alan Wood and R. A. French (eds.), *The Development of Siberia: People and Resources* (London: Macmillan, 1989), 188–207.

[20] Sue Davis, *The Russian Far East: The Last Frontier?* (London: Routledge, 2003), 24–27.

[21] For more on this, see Elizabeth Wishnick, "Russia in Asia and Asians in Russia," *SAIS Review* 20:1 (2000), 86–101.

the resource-rich land because it was necessary for socialism and, "[a]fter all, I was a Komsomol member. All of us Komsomol members were energetic, young and capable."[22]

The Khetagurovites and their enthusiasm for grand feats on the Far Eastern frontier resurfaced in the national consciousness when Aleksei Arbuzov's 1938 acclaimed play, *Tania*, made a sensational comeback on the Moscow stage of RAMT (Russian Academic Youth Theater) in March 2003. Arbuzov integrated motifs from Alexander Pushkin, especially the figure of Tatiana from *Evgenii Onegin*, with "myths of Soviet womanhood."[23] The first part of the play dramatizes the illusions of purely personal happiness. The story begins in 1934 when Arbuzov's heroine, Tania, lives with her husband in accordance with supposed petty-bourgeois gender norms. Tania is naïve and utterly dependent on her man. As the play progresses, she finds out that he is having an affair. Eventually, he leaves her without knowing that she is pregnant. A single mother and a lackluster medical student, Tania is unable to save her child several years later and is subsequently plagued by guilt. In the second part, Tania travels to the Far East as a Khetagurovite. Having become a selfless and competent doctor, she comes to the aid of her ex-husband and his new wife to save their child (they also happen to be living in the region). She overcomes her personal tragedy by dedicating herself selflessly to the collective good and the project of constructing a Far Eastern city of youth. Through service to the Soviet people she finds real happiness. Because women's interests were previously associated with the narrow realms of family life, Tania's fealty to national goals epitomizes the transformative power of socialism.

Some theater critics reacted negatively to the resurrection of this "naïve" play because they considered it a tired relic of Socialist Realism and one that obfuscated the tragedies of the 1930s. Others placed the production and its success among audiences in a larger context of a creeping nostalgia among Russian audiences for this past. One critic explained that she found the play topical because "[e]very one of us shares a suppressed memory of our ancestors with its mixed feelings of love and hatred for the happiest and the simultaneously most frightening epoch in modern Russian history."[24] Tania's discovery of authentic happiness and overcoming of personal tragedy through participation in

---

[22] "Khetagurovka," *Provintsiia*, March 4, 2004. Fans of the contemporary singer Valerii Leont'ev were reading about Khetagurovites because the secretive Leont'ev revealed details of his background, including the fact that his grandmother was a Khetagurovite. See Ramazan Ramazanov, "I tainyi plod liubvi neschastnoi . . . ," *Pravda.ru*, November 15, 2003. *www.pravda.ru/culture/2003/11/15/57283_.html.*

[23] Oleg Zintsov, "Iakutskaia istoriia," *Vedomosti*, March 14, 2003.

[24] Alena Karas', "I tak, ona zvalas' Tat'ianoi . . . ," *Rossiiskaia gazeta*, March 11, 2003.

the Khetagurovite call-up made another theater critic, Irina Alpatova, "a little sad that [today] nobody calls upon you or takes you someplace."[25] Contemporary Russian audiences were ostensibly increasingly aware that women like the Khetagurovites epitomized not simply a naïveté, but a timeless quest to live for something that transcends the mundane and the personal. And as Alpatova surmised, "The only thing that could rescue people from their private woes was the romance of the collective. Actually, it was the only thing that could. The lesson is that one cannot live without dreams. Is this passé? How is one to know?"[26]

As for Novikova, more heartaches and unexpected turns were in store. She outlived her alcoholic son, who perished in his sixties. But Baba Klava took great care of her husband during their thirty-seven years together. As soon as he turned sixty, Baba Klava insisted that he retire because "[i]f you don't take care of a man, he won't make it for very long . . . You can't find a man like Iasha in this region. The other women envied me . . . he didn't drink, didn't smoke and performed acupuncture."[27] Having heard of the unusual couple's story, a Russian journalist explained to his readers that Klava loved her Japanese husband "in-Russian, in other words she felt sorry for him. She never sat down to eat without him; the first ripe berry went to him. He never raised his voice, and God forbid, never laid a finger on her."[28]

When Mikhail Gorbachev's reforms opened the Far East to foreign tourists, a visiting Japanese group learned about Novikova and Iasaburo Khachiia and eventually put him in touch with the Japanese wife and daughter he thought had perished. Eventually, Baba Klava insisted that Iasaburo return to his ailing first wife in Japan. She was left alone in her little house in Progress, where she waited by the phone for her weekly call from her "Iasha" in Japan. Subsequently, such generosity of spirit attracted the attention of Japanese journalists and the public. Novikova became a celebrity and the subject of a book and film documentaries in Japan. People across Japan donated money to a fund to bring her to their country in 2003 for a tour and a brief reunion with Iasaburo.[29]

---

[25] Irina Alpatova, "Tat'iany milyi ideal," *Kul'tura* 10, March 13–19, 2003. *www.kultura-portal.ru/tree/cultpaper/arc.jsp?number=480*

[26] *Ibid.*

[27] Sazhneva, "Zhili-byli samurai so starukhoi," *Moskovskii komsomolets*, November 16, 2005. *www.mk.ru*

[28] Aleksandr Iaroshenko, "Klaudia i Iasaburo," *Amurskaia pravda*, March 25, 2004. *www.amurpravda.ru/articles/2004/03/25/4.html?print* (3–4 of 8).

[29] In 2003 Iasuko Murao, a Japanese journalist, took an intense interest in the story, having visited both Iasaburo and Novikova in the Far East. She subsequently published *Kuraudia kiseki no ai* (*Claudia and Her Miraculous Love*) and organized the fundraising to take Novikova on a tour of Japan.

Appendix 1

Table 1: Distribution of Khetagurovites in industries and organizations for 1937.

Agriculture	1546
Far Eastern Railroad	1016
Industrial enterprises	937 (701 in Komsomol'sk factories)
Special Far Eastern Army	791
NKVD	773 (primarily to the cities of Khabarovsk and BAMLag in Svobodny)
State Fishing Trust	629 (Vladivostok)
Fishing industry	509 (Kamchatka and Nikkolaevsk-na-Amure)
Coalmining	440 (towns of Artem and Suchan)
Regional Agriculture Department	374
Goldmining	246
Sakhalin (employment not specified)	219
Other regional industries and organizations	200
Party organizations	167
Regional Health Department	108
Komsomol organizations	104
Public baths	49

Source: "Far Eastern Regional Communist Party Committee ORPO: Memorandum notes, short reports, information sent to the Regional Communist Party Committee: On the status of the movement of youth of the Khetagurovite call-up to the Far East, March 20, 1938: Summary for eight months of 1937," GAKhK P, f. 2, op. 6, d. 358, l. 3.

Appendix 2

Table 2: Places of origin of Khetagurovites arriving in 1937.

Ukraine	2700
Moscow oblast	865
Azov-Black Sea oblast	395
Ordzhonikidze oblast	320
Leningrad oblast	305
Belorussia	280
Saratov oblast	250
Ivanovskaia oblast	230
Sverdlovsk oblast	210
Voronezh oblast	205
Oblasts: Gor'kovskaia, Zapadnaia, Kurskaia, Kalininskaia, Stalingradskaia, Kiubishevskaia, Iaroslavskaia, Cheliabinskaia, Orenburg, Novosibirsk, Republic of Azerbaijan	100–200 per oblast

Source: "Far Eastern Regional Communist Party Committee ORPO: Memorandum notes, short reports, information sent to the regional Communist Party Committee: On the status of the movement of youth of the Khetagurovite call-up to the Far East, March 20, 1938: Summary for eight months of 1937," GAKhK P, f. 2, op. 6, d. 358, l. 2.

Appendix 3

"До свиданья, девушки!" ("Goodbye, Young Women!"), 1938
Song dedicated to departing Khetagurovites.

Наступает очередь звонкой весны.	Here comes the turn of the resounding spring.
Юный собирайся поток!	A young torrent gathers!
Преданные дочери нашей страны	Loyal daughters of our country
Едут на Дальний Восток.	Are traveling to the Far East.
Припев:	Chorus:
До свиданья, девушки! Поезд скоро, девушки.	Goodbye, gals! The train is leaving soon, gals.
Слышится прощальный гудок.	One can hear the farewell whistle.
Напишите, девушки, как живете, девушки,	Do write, gals, how you're living, gals,
Как вас встретил Дальний Восток.	How the Far East greeted you.
Много будет пройдено новых дорог,	Many new roads will be traversed,
Много километров путей.	Many kilometers of track.
Провожает Родина вас на Восток,	The Motherland is sending you off to the East,
Славных своих дочерей.	Her glorious daughters.
До свиданья, девушки, до свиданья, девушки!	Goodbye, gals, goodbye, gals!
Слышится прощальный гудок.	One can hear the farewell whistle.
Поезд скорый, девушки, он домчит вас, девушки,	The fast train, gals, will rush you, gals,
В наш советский Дальний Восток.	To our Soviet Far East.
Сквозь края и области мимо полей	Through regions and counties past fields
Двухнедельный путь ваш далек.	Your two-week journey is long.
Славою и доблестью песни своей	With your glorious and heroic song
Радуйте Дальний Восток.	Bring joy to the Far East.
Припев.	Chorus

Source: *www.sovmusic.ru/english/text.php?fname=dosvida3*. Author's translation.
Music by Isaak Dunaevskii, lyrics by L. Levin.

234

Appendix 4

"На восток" ("To the East")
Poem published in a Far Eastern newspaper to welcome arrivals.

Чайкой через горы,	The call-up of
Через Байкала зыбь	Valia Khetagurova
Вали Хетагуровой	Soared like a sea-gull over mountains
Полетел призыв	Across the swells of the Baikal
Совершил весною	This distant flight
Дальний перелет	Was completed in the spring
От границ восточных	From the eastern border
И амурских вод	And the waters of the Amur
Сердце зажигал он	This call-up of fiery days
Клич горячих дней	Flared up hearts
К девушкам цветущей	Of the gals in this flowering
Родины моей	Motherland of mine
Отрывались девушки	They tore themselves away
От душевных строк,	From heartfelt lines,
Уезжали девушки	The gals went
К Вале, на Восток	To Valia, to the East
Край к победам двигать,	To propel the region to victories,
Высь науки брать.	To take up the heights of science.
С парашютом прыгать,	To jump with a parachute,
Выше всех летать.	To fly higher than anyone.
Из лазурной дали,	From the sky-blue distance,
Сел и городов	Villages and cities
Отвечают Вале	Hundreds of voices
Сотни голосов:	Answered Valia:
«Вместе с солнцем мая	"Together with the May sun
Ждите нас к себе	Wait for us
Мощь большого края	To lift the power of the large region
Поднимать в труде.	In labor.
Стройными рядами	In neat ranks
Улицей пройдем,	We will stroll the street,
В первый раз мы с вами	For the first time singing
Песню пропоем.	A song with you.
Так, чтоб нас слыхали	So that we will be heard
Сёстры дальних стран,	By sisters in distant countries,
Чтоб любимый Сталин	So that beloved Stalin
Улыбнулся нам.	Smiles at us.

Aleksandr Nishchev (soldier of the Red Army), *Tikhookeanskii komsomolets*, December 6, 1937. Author's translation.

Appendix 5

"Khetagurovka"
Poem by a female migrant published in a Far Eastern literary journal.

Я из сердца Союза – из цветущей столицы	From the Union's heart – from the blossoming capital
На далекий восток принесла свой привет.	I bring to the Far East my greetings.
Пусть под небом восточным моя песня промчится	Let my song race across the eastern sky
Ураганом весенним, песней наших побед.	Carried by the storm of spring, our victory song.
Я – такая, как все, как десятки задорных	I am just like all of them, those tens of fervent
Юных девушек нашей великой страны.	Young women of our great Motherland.
Будем с песней веселой трудиться упорно, -	We will work diligently with a happy tune –
Мы здоровья, энергии, силы полны!	We are full of health, energy and strength!
А на дальний Восток нас стремится немало –	And there are not a few who hurry to the Far East –
Педагогов, поэтов, актеров, врачей:	Pedagogues, poets, actors, doctors:
Мы хотим, чтобы всюду страна расцветала,	We want the country to blossom everywhere
Чтобы пенилась счастьем, как горный ручей.	So that it bubbles with joy, like a mountain brook.
И несем мы от шумной, цветущей столицы	And we carry from the bustling, flowering capital
На далекий восток свой горячий привет.	To the Far East our heartfelt greeting.
Наша молодость песнею звонкою мчится,	Our youth rushes with a resounding song,
Песней, ярче которой не сыщет поэт!	A song, more dazzling than any poet can uncover!

Anna Boriss, *Na rubezhe. Zhurnal khudozhestvennoi litereatury i publitsistiki* (May–June 1937), 22. Author's translation.

Appendix 6

"Песня девушек-дальневосточниц" ("Song of Young Women – Far Easterners")
Song published in the largest journal for women workers, *Rabotnitsa*.

Дышит прохладной	A refreshing evening
Ночной ветерок...	Breeze is in the air...
Мы, девушки, едем	We, gals, are traveling
На Дальний Восток.	To the Far East.
Мы счастливы, – всюду	We are thrilled –
Мы радость найдём:	We will find happiness:
И в тундре холодной	In the cold tundra and
И в краю глухом!	In a remote region!
В диких, суровых	In wild harsh
Сибирских лесах,	Siberian woods,
В знойных, пустынных	In burning hot
Горячих песках...	Desert sands...
Мы нашу родную	We will recognize
Страну узнаем	Our native country
И песни о родине	And songs we will
Нашей поём!	Sing about our Motherland!
Лети, паровоз наш,	Fly our train,
Быстрей и быстрей!	Faster and faster!
Мы едем туда,	We are going there,
Где курганы степей	Where burial knolls in the steppe
Память хранят	Guard memories of days past
О минувших днях,	Of great heroes
О славных героях,	Of terrible battles,
О грозных боях!	We are going to that region
Мы едем в тот край	Of the Soviet land
Советской земли,	Where in battles with enemies,
Где в битвах с врагами	Our fathers had fallen...
Отцы слегли...	
Там мы совхозы,	There sovkhozy,
Заводы построим,	Factories we will build
Устроим каналы,	Set up canals,
Тоннели пророем...	Dig out tunnels...
Мы парки на вечных	Parks on timeless swamps
Болотах взрастим,	We will cultivate
И край тот огромный	And we will transform
Мы в сад превратим!	That huge region into a garden!
Это не радость ли?	Isn't this happiness?
Счастье не это ли?	Isn't this fortunate?
Жизнь созидать,	To create life,
Где лишь песню ветра	Where the song of the wind
Слушал бурливый	Was heard only by the
И грустный Амур,	Sad turbulent Amur,
Край тот был вечно	That region eternally
Печален и хмур...	Wistful and sullen...
Мы счастливы тем,	We are lucky that
Что в сталинский век	In the era of Stalin
Нет выше цены,	There is no higher value
Как цена – человек!	Than the value of – a person!
И если сердца наши	And if our hearts
Счастьем полны	Our full of joy
Такое же счастье	This same joy
У всей страны!	Is in the whole country!
Так спой веселее	So breeze, sing
Ты нам, ветерок!	More cheerfully to us!
Мы, девушки, едем	We, gals, are traveling
На Дальний Восток	To the Far East

Виктор Митин (Viktor Mitin) *Rabotnitsa*, June 1937, 18. Author's translation.

Appendix 7

"Едущим на восток – Напутствие" ("Parting wishes – For travelers to the East")
Poem by a famous Soviet writer dedicated to the Khetagurovites and published in the Komsomol national newspaper in the month when a large contingent of young women set off for the Far East.

Много в Союзе Далеких дорог, Самая дальняя – Дальний Восток.	In the Union there are many Long roads, The longest of them To the Far East.
Шел эшелон – Бесконечный состав – К тихим домам Пограничных застав.	The echelon ran – An endless train – To the quiet houses To the border posts.
Строить заводы, Растить города Наши друзья Отправлялись туда.	To build factories, To grow cities Our friends Have gone there.
Только успеем Им руки пожать, – Новых идем На вокзал провожать.	We just managed To clasp their hands, – Then we go to See off new ones at the station.
Парень, возьми На прощанье цветок! Девушки едут На Дальний Восток.	Lad, take with you A flower for the farewell! Gals are traveling To the Far East.
Родины голос Туда их позвал Снова наш Севереный Дымный вокзал.	The Motherland's voice Has called them there Again our Severnyi Smoky station.
Колеса стучат, Словно сердце в груди: Все впереди! Все впереди!	The wheels pound, Like a heart in your chest: Everything is ahead! Everything is ahead!

(*Continued*)

Знойное лето,	The sultry summer,
Седые снега,	The grey snows,
Тихое море,	The Pacific sea,
Глухая тайга.	The solitary taiga.
Слышишь, друзья	Do you hear it, friends
О Байкале поют.	They sing about the Baikal.
Дай на прощание	Give me your hand
Руку твою!	To say farewell!
Помни! Далеко	Remember! You must carry
Должна ты пронесть	A long way
Нашего города	Our city's
Славу и честь.	Good name and honor.
Чтобы сквозь версты,	So that through miles,
Через Байкал	Past the Baikal
Голос подруги	The voice of our girlfriend
До нас долетал.	Will reach us.
Если ты встретишь там	If you meet there
Друга души,	A soulmate,
Ты не стесняйся –	Don't be shy –
И прямо пиши.	Just write.
Просто, подробно	Simply, in detail
Скажи нам о нем,	Tell us about him,
Мы над письмом	We will sigh carefully
Осторожно вздохнем.	Over the letter.
Вот тебе, девушка,	Here are the hands
Руки друзей.	Of your friends for you, gal.
Книги читай,	Read books,
Память лелей!	Cherish the memory!
Няньчи детей,	Fuss over children,
Паровозы води!	Drive trains!
Все впереди!	Everything is ahead!
Все впереди!	Everything is ahead!
Что же грустят	Why are the voices
Голоса запевал? –	Seeming sad as they sing? –
«Славное море	"Glorious sea
Священный Байкал».	Holy Baikal."
Белый платок,	A white scarf,
Краткий свисток,	A short whistle,
Дальний Восток,	Far East,
Дальний Восток!	Far East!

Evgenii Dolmatovskii, *Komsomol'skaia pravda*, April 9, 1937. Author's translation.

Appendix 8

"Лейся, песня, на просторе" ("Song – Go Flutter Through the Air")
This song from a 1936 film was popular among young women traveling by ship to Komsomol'sk-na-Amure in 1937.

Лейся, песня, на просторе,	Song – go flutter through the air,
Не скучай, не плачь, жена!	Do not be lonely, do not cry, wife!
Штурмовать далеко море	Our country is sending us
Посылает нас страна.	To storm the distant sea.
Курс – на берег невидимый,	The course to the shore is invisible,
Бьется сердце корабля.	The boat's heart beats.
Вспоминаю о любимой	At the obedient helm
У послушного руля.	Remembering the loved one.
Буря, ветер, ураганы –	Gales, winds, hurricanes –
Ты не страшен, океан:	Ocean, you are not frightening:
Молодые капитаны	Young captains
Поведут наш караван.	Will steer our caravan.
Мы не раз отважно дрались,	We fought bravely more than once,
Принимая вызов твой,	Taking up your challenge,
И с победой возвращались	And returning victorious
К нашей гавани домой.	To our harbor, home.
Лейся, песня, на просторе,	Song – go flutter through the air,
Здравствуй, милая жена!	Greetings, darling wife!
Штурмовать далеко море	Our country sent us
Посылала нас страна.	To storm the distant sea.

From the film *Semero smelykh* (*The Brave Seven*), 1936. Music by Venedikt Pushkov, lyrics by Andrei Apsolon.
Source: www.sovmusic.ru/text.php?fname=leisya2 Author's translation.

Selected bibliography

ARCHIVES

Russian State Archive of the Economy (RGAE) – Moscow
Russian State Archive of Film-Photographic Documents (RGAKFD) – Krasnogorsk
Russian State Archive of Literature and Art (RGALI) – Moscow
Russian State Archive of Socio-Political History (RGASPI) – Moscow
State Archive of the Khabarovsk Region (GAKhK) – Khabarovsk
State Archive of the Russian Federation (GA RF) – Moscow

NEWSPAPERS AND JOURNALS

Amurskaia pravda
Dal'nii Vostok
Izvestiia
Komsomol'skaia pravda (KP)
Krasnaia zvezda
Krasnoe znamia
Kul'tura
Moskovskii komsomolets
Na rubezhe. Zhurnal khudozhestvennoi litereatury i publitsistiki
Pravda
Pravda.ru
Provintsiia
Rabotnitsa
Rossiiskaia gazeta
Tikhookeanskaia zvezda (TZ)
Tikhookeanskii komsomolets (TK)
Vedomosti

PUBLISHED PRIMARY SOURCES

Antonov-Ovseenko, Anton. *Vragi naroda*. Moscow: Intellekt, 1996.
Aziatskaia Rossiia. Vol. 1. Sankt-Petersburg, 1914.
Fedorova, T. V. *Naverkhu Moskva*. Moscow: Sov. Rossiia, 1975.

Gerchikov, Leonid. *Eto nash gorod, gorod na zare. Moskva-Komsomol'sk: Dalekoe i blizkoe.* Moscow: Moskovskii rabochii, 1982.

Iaroshenko, Aleksandr. "Klaudia i Iasaburo." *Amurskaia pravda,* March 25, 2004. *www.amurpravda.ru/articles/2004/03/25/4.html?print*

Khetagurov, Georgii. *Ispolnenie dolga.* Moscow: Voenizdat, 1977.

Khetagurova, Valentina. "Priezzhaite k nam na Dal'nii Vostok!" *Komsomol'skaia pravda,* February 5, 1937.

—."Zdravstvui, iunost' 30-kh!" *Rabotnitsa* 8 (1967).

Khlebnikov, Gennadii and Efim V. Dorodnov. *Muzhestvo Komsomol'ska, Adres Podviga – Dal'nii Vostok, Kn. 3.* Khabarovsk: Khabarovskoe knizhnoe izdatel'stvo, 1974.

Kiparenko, A. V. "Na stroitel'stve goroda iunosti," in A. V. Artiukhina et al. (eds.), *Uchastnitsy velikogo zasedaniia.* Moscow: Gos. politizdat, 1962, 145–156.

Petrov, Evgenii. "Khetagurovki," in G. Akopian (ed.), *Zhenshchiny strany sotsializma.* Moscow: OGIZ, 1939, 46–51.

"Rezoliutsii i soveshchaniia po rabote domov Krasnoi Armii i Flota, February 4–7, 1929: Resolution 121 – Rabota s sem'iami: Rabota sredi zhen," in *Vsearmeiskie soveshchaniia politrabotnikov, 1918–1940 (rezoliutsii).* Moscow: Izdatel'stvo Nauka, 1984, 275–276.

Sazhneva, Ekaterina. "Zhili-byli samurai so starukhoi." *Moskovskii komsomolets.* November 16, 2005. *www.mk.ru/numbers/1912/article64683.htm* (2 of 9).

Tolmachev, Mstislav. "Takaia dolgaia poliarnaia noch'," glava 60, *Nizhegorodskii literaturnyi zhurnal. http://litzur.narod.ru/memory/tolmachev/s1/60.html* (1 and 2 of 6).

Vershigora, Peter. *Liudi s chistoi sovest'iu.* Moscow: Moskovskii rabochii, 1946.

Volovich, Hava. "My Past," in Simeon Vilensky (ed.), *Till My Tale is Told,* trans. John Crowfoot et al. Bloomington: Indiana University Press, 1999, 241–276.

Vsesoiuznoe soveshchanie zhen khoziaistvennikov i inzhenerno-tekhnicheskikh rabotnikov tiazheloi promyshlennosti – stenograficheskii otchet. Moscow: Partizdat, 1936.

Vsesoiuznoe soveshchanie zhen komandnogo i nachal'stvuiushchego sostava RKKA. Moscow: Gos. voennoe izdatel'stvo, 1937.

SECONDARY SOURCES

Abrams, Lynn and Karen Hunt (eds.). "Borders and Frontiers in Women's History." *Women's History Review* 9:2 (2000), 191–200.

Afanasev, V. A. "The Fighting at Khalkin-Gol in 1939 in the Context of Word War II." *Otechestvennaia istoriia* 5 (September–October 1999), 181–185.

Alexopoulos, Golfo. *Stalin's Outcasts: Aliens, Citizens and the Soviet State, 1926–1936.* Ithaca: Cornell University Press, 2003.

Argudiaeva, Iuliia V. (ed.). *Sem'ia i semeinyi byt v vostochnykh regionakh Rossii.* Vladivostok: Dal'nauka, 1997.

—. *Krest'ianskaia sem'ia u vostochnykh slavian na iuge Dal'nego Vostoka Rossii (50e-gody XIX v. – nachalo XX v.).* Vladivostok: DVO RAN, 1997.

—. *Staroobriadtsy na Dal'nem Vostoke Rossii.* Moscow: Institut etnologii i antropologii RAN, 2000.

Armstrong, John. *Nations Before Nationalism*. Chapel Hill: University of North Carolina Press, 1982.

Attwood, Lynne. "Rationality Versus Romanticism: Representations of Women in the Stalinist Press," in Linda Edmondson (ed.), *Gender in Russian History and Culture*. New York: Palgrave, 2001, 158–176.

Baker, Mark. "Rampaging Soldatki, Cowering Police, Bazaar Riots and Moral Economy: The Social Impact of the Great War in Kharkiv Province." *Canadian-American Slavic Studies* 35:2–3 (Summer–Fall 2001), 137–155.

Ball, Alan. "The Roots of Besprizornost' in Soviet Russia's First Decade." *Slavic Review* 51:2 (Summer 1992), 247–270.

Bassin, Mark. "Turner, Solov'ev, and the 'Frontier Hypothesis': The Nationalist Significance of Open Spaces." *Journal of Modern History* 65:3 (1993), 476–511.

—. *Imperial Visions: Nationalist Imagination and Geographical Expansion in the Russian Far East, 1840–1865*. Cambridge: Cambridge University Press, 1999.

Batsaev, Igor D. and A. G. Kozlov. *Dal'stroi i Sevvostlag OGPU-NKVD SSSR v tsifrakh i dokumentakh*. Magadan: SVKNII DVO RAN, 2002.

Bergmann, Linda. "Women Against a Background of White: The Representation of Self and Nature in Women's Arctic Narratives." *American Studies* 34:2 (Fall 1993), 53–68.

Bernstein, Frances L. "Envisioning Health in Revolutionary Russia: The Politics of Gender and Sexual-Enlightenment Posters of the 1920s." *Russian Review* 57:2 (April 1998), 191–217.

Bone, Jonathan A. "Who Really Built Komsomol'sk-na-Amure, and Why?" *Rev. Etud. Slaves* 71:1 (1999), 59–92.

Bonnell, Victoria. *Iconography of Power: Political Posters under Lenin and Stalin*. Berkeley: University of California Press, 1997.

Borenstein, Eliot. *Men Without Women: Masculinity and Revolution in Russian Fiction, 1917–1929*. Durham: Duke University Press, 2000.

Botev, Nikolai. "The Ethnic Composition of Families in Russia in 1989: Insights into the Soviet 'Nationalities Policies.'" *Population and Development Review* 28:4 (December 2002), 681–706.

Boxer, Marilyn J. "Rethinking the Socialist Construction and International Career of the Concept 'Bourgeois Feminism.'" *American Historical Review* 112:1 (February 2007), 131–158.

Breyfogle, Nicholas, Willard Sunderland, and Abby Schrader (eds.). *Peopling the Russian Periphery: Borderland Colonization in Eurasian History*. London: Routledge, 2007.

Brooks, Jeffrey. *Thank You, Comrade Stalin!: Soviet Public Culture from Revolution to Cold War*. Princeton: Princeton University Press, 2000.

Bucher, Greta. *Women, the Bureaucracy and Daily Life in Postwar Moscow, 1945–1953*. Boulder, CO: Eastern European Monographs, 2006.

Buckley, Mary. "The Untold Story of *Obshchestvennitsa* in the 1930s." *Europe-Asia Studies* 48:4 (1996), 569–586.

—. *Mobilizing Soviet Peasants: Heroines and Heroes of Stalin's Fields*. Lanham, MD: Lexington Books, 2006.

Burton, Chris. "Minzdrav, Soviet Doctors, and Policing of Reproduction in the Late Stalinist Years." *Russian History* 27:2 (Summer 2000), 197–221.

Cavanaugh, Catherine. "'No Place for a Woman': Engendering Western Canadian Settlement." *Western Historical Quarterly* 28:4 (Winter 1997), 493–518.

Chatterjee, Choi. *Celebrating Women: Gender, Festival Culture, and Bolshevik Ideology, 1910–1939*. Pittsburgh: University of Pittsburgh Press, 2002.

Chernolutskaia, Elena. "Protivorechivost' migratsionnoi politiki na Dal'nem Vostoke SSSR v 20–30-e gody (na primere Primor'ia)," in *Istoricheskii opyt osvoeniia vostochnykh raionov Rossii*. Kniga II. Vladivostok: DVO RAN, 1993, 89–92.

— (ed.). *Voprosy sotsial'no-demograficheskoi istorii Dal'nego Vostoka v XX veke*. Vladivostok: DVO RAN, 1999.

Chirkov, Petr Matveevich. *Reshenie zhenskogo voprosa v SSSR (1917–1937)*. Moscow: Izdatel'stvo Mysl', 1978.

Clancy-Smith, Julia A. and Frances Gouda (eds.). *Domesticating the Empire: Race, Gender and Family Life in French and Dutch Colonialism*. Charlottesville: University Press of Virginia, 1998.

Clark, Katerina. *The Soviet Novel: History as Ritual*. Bloomington: Indiana University Press, 1981.

Clements, Barbara Evans. *Bolshevik Feminist: The Life of Aleksandra Kollontai*. Bloomington: Indiana University Press, 1979.

—. "Baba and Bolshevik: Russian Women and Revolutionary Change." *Soviet Union* 12:2 (1985), 161–184.

—. "The Utopianism of the Zhenotdel." *Slavic Review* 51:2 (Summer 1992), 485–496.

—. *Bolshevik Women*. Cambridge: Cambridge University Press, 1997.

—, Rebecca Friedman, and Dan Healey (eds.), *Russian Masculinities in History and Culture*. New York: Palgrave, 2002.

Conquest, Robert. *The Great Terror: A Reassessment*. New York: Macmillan, 1990.

David-Fox, Michael, Peter Holquist, and Marshall Poe (eds.). *The Resistance Debate in Russian and Soviet History*. Bloomington, IN: Slavica Publishers, 2003.

Davies, Sarah. *Popular Opinion in Stalin's Russia: Terror, Propaganda and Dissent, 1934–41*. Cambridge and New York: Cambridge University Press, 1997.

— and James Harris (eds.). *Stalin: A New History*. New York: Cambridge University Press, 2005.

Davis, Sue. *The Russian Far East: The Last Frontier?* London: Routledge, 2003.

DeHaan, Heather. "Engendering a People: Soviet Women and Socialist Rebirth in Russia." *Canadian Slavonic Papers* 41:3–4 (September–December 1999), 431–455.

Devereux, Cecily. "New Woman, New World: Maternal Feminism and the New Imperialism in the White Settler Colonies." *Women's Studies International Forum* 22:2 (1999), 175–184.

Diment, Galya and Iuri Slezkine (eds.). *Between Heaven and Hell: The Myth of Siberia in Russian Culture*. New York: St. Martin's Press, 1993.

Dobrenko, Evgeny. *The Making of the State Reader: Social and Aesthetic Contexts of the Reception of Soviet Literature*. Stanford: Stanford University Press, 1997.

Dubinina, Nina I. *Dal'nevostochnitsy v bor'be i trude. Istoricheskii ocherk, 1917–1941.* Khabarovsk: Khabarovskoe knizhnoe izdatel'stvo, 1982.
—. *Ty pozovi, Dal'nii Vostok!* Khabarovsk: Khabarovskoe knizhnoe izdatel'stvo, 1987.
Dunham, Vera S. *In Stalin's Time: Middle-Class Values in Soviet Fiction.* Cambridge: Cambridge University Press, 1976.
Dunstall, Graeme. "Frontier and/or Cultural Fragment? Interpretations of Violence in Colonial New Zealand." *Social History* 29:1 (February 2004), 59–83.
Edelman, Robert. "A Small Way of Saying 'No': Moscow Working Men, Spartak Soccer, and the Communist Party, 1900–1945." *American Historical Review* 107:5 (December 2002), 1441–1476.
Elantseva, O. P. *Obrechennaia doroga, BAM (1932–1941).* Vladivostok: Dal'nevostochnyi gos. universitet, 1994.
—. *Stroitel'stvo No. 500 NKVD SSSR: Zheleznaia doroga Komsomol'sk-Sovetskaia Gavan' (1930–1940 gg.).* Vladivostok: Dal'nevostochnyi gos. universitet, 1995.
—. "Stroitel'stvo zheleznykh dorog na vostoke Rossii v 1930-e gody." *Rev. Etud. Slaves* 71:1 (1999), 93–112.
Engel, Barbara Alpern and Anastasia Posadskaya-Vanderbeck (eds.), Sona Hoisington (trans.). *A Revolution of Their Own: Voices of Women in Soviet History.* Boulder, CO: Westview Press, 1998.
Engelstein, Laura. "Gender and the Juridical Subject: Prostitution and Rape in Nineteenth-Century Russian Criminal Codes." *Journal of Modern History* 60:3 (September 1988), 458–495.
—. *The Keys to Happiness: Sex and the Search for Modernity in Fin-de-Siècle Russia.* Ithaca: Cornell University Press, 1992.
Ershova, El'vira B. "Garnizonnye zhensovety v Sovetskoi Armii v 60-e–80-e gody," in *O nas i nashem dele 3–4* (September 1999). *www.womnet.ru/aboutus/3-4/index.htm.*
Evans, John L. *Russian Expansion on the Amur, 1848–1860: The Push to the Pacific.* Lewiston, NY: Edwin Mellen Press, 1999.
Ewing, Thomas E. "Personal Acts with Public Meanings: Suicides by Soviet Women Teachers in the Early Stalin Era." *Gender & History* 14:1 (2002), 117–137.
Farnsworth, Beatrice. *Aleksandra Kollontai: Socialism, Feminism and the Bolshevik Revolution.* Stanford: Stanford University Press, 1980.
—. "The Rural Batrachka (Hired Agricultural Laborer) and the Soviet Campaign to Unionize Her." *Journal of Women's History* 14:1 (Spring 2002), 64–93.
Figes, Orlando. *Peasant Russia, Civil War: The Volga Countryside in Revolution, 1917–21.* Oxford: Clarendon, 1989.
Fitzpatrick, Sheila. "Sex and Revolution: An Examination of Literary and Statistical Data on the Mores of Soviet Students in the 1920s." *Journal of Modern History* 50:2 (1978), 252–278.
— (ed.). *Cultural Revolution in Russia, 1928–1931.* Bloomington: Indiana University Press, 1984.
—. *The Cultural Front: Power and Culture in Revolutionary Russia.* Ithaca: Cornell University Press, 1992.

—. *Stalin's Peasants. Resistance and Survival in the Russian Village After Collectivization.* New York: Oxford University Press, 1994.

—. "Supplicants and Citizens: Public Letter-Writing in Soviet Russia in the 1930s." *Slavic Review* 55:1 (1996), 78–105.

—. *Everyday Stalinism: Ordinary Life in Extraordinary Times: Soviet Russia in the 1930s.* New York: Oxford University Press, 1999.

— and Iuri Slezkine (eds.). *In the Shadow of Revolution: Life Stories of Russian Women from 1917 to the Second World War,* trans. Slezkine. Princeton: Princeton University Press, 2000.

—. "The World of Ostap Bender: Soviet Confidence Men in the Stalin Period." *Slavic Review* 61:3 (Autumn 2002), 535–557.

—. *Tear Off the Masks!: Identity and Imposture in Twentieth-Century Russia.* Princeton: Princeton University Press, 2005.

Fuqua, Michelle V. *The Politics of the Domestic Sphere: The Zhenotdely, Women's Liberation, and the Search for a Novyi Byt in Early Soviet Russia.* Seattle: Henry M. Jackson School of Internationl Studies, University of Washington, 1996.

Galliamova, L. I. *Dal'nevostochnye rabochie Rossii vo vtoroi polovine XIX–nachale XX vv.* Vladivostok: Dal'nauka, 2000.

Gatrell, Peter. *A Whole Empire Walking: Refugees in Russia during World War I.* Bloomington: Indiana University Press, 2000.

Getty, J. Arch. *The Origins of the Great Purges: The Soviet Communist Party Reconsidered, 1933–1938.* Cambridge: Cambridge University Press, 1985.

—. and R. T. Manning (eds.). *Stalinist Terror: New Perspectives.* Cambridge: Cambridge University Press, 1993.

—. and Oleg V. Naumov. *The Road to Terror: Stalin and the Self-Destruction of the Bolsheviks, 1932–1939.* New Haven: Yale University Press, 1999.

—. and Oleg V. Naumov. *Stalin's "Iron Fist": The Times and Life of N. I. Yezhov.* New Haven: Yale University Press, 2008.

Gibson, James R. "Russian Imperial Expansion in Context and by Contrast." *Journal of Historical Geography* 28:2 (2002), 181–202.

Goldman, Wendy Z. "Freedom and its Consequences: The Debate on the Soviet Family Code of 1926." *Russian History* 11:4 (Winter 1984), 362–388.

—. *Women, the State, and Revolution: Soviet Family Policy and Social Life, 1917–1936.* Cambridge: Cambridge University Press, 1993.

—. "Industrial Politics, Peasant Rebellion and the Death of the Proletarian Women's Movement in the USSR." *Slavic Review* 55:1 (Spring 1996), 46–77.

—. *Women at the Gates: Gender and Industry in Stalin's Russia.* Cambridge: Cambridge University Press, 2002.

Goodman, Phil. "'Patriotic Femininity': Women's Morals and Men's Morale during the Second World War," *Gender & History* 10:2 (August 1998), 278–293.

Gorsuch, Anne E. "'A Woman is Not a Man': The Culture of Gender and Generation in Soviet Russia, 1921–1928." *Slavic Review* 55:3 (Fall 1996), 636–660.

—. *Youth in Revolutionary Russia: Enthusiasts, Bohemians, Delinquents.* Bloomington: Indiana University Press, 2000.

Gregory, Paul R. and Valery Lazarev (eds.). *The Economics of Forced Labor: The Soviet GULAG*. Stanford: Hoover Institution Press, 2003.

Halfin, Igal. *From Darkness to Light: Class Consciousness and Salvation in Revolutionary Russia*. Pittsburgh: University of Pittsburgh Press, 2000.

—. *Terror in My Soul: Communist Autobiographies on Trial*. Cambridge, MA: Harvard University Press, 2003.

Hall, Catherine. *Civilizing Subjects: Metropole and Colony in the English Imagination, 1830–1867*. Chicago: University of Chicago Press, 2000.

Harvey, Elizabeth. *Women and the Nazi East: Agents and Witnesses of Germanization*. New Haven: Yale University Press, 2003.

Hayden, Carol Eubanks. "The Zhenotdel and the Bolshevik Party." *Russian History* 3:2 (1976), 150–173.

Healey, Dan. *Homosexual Desire in Revolutionary Russia: The Regulation of Sexual and Gender Dissent*. Chicago: University of Chicago Press, 2001.

Hellbeck, Jochen. "Fashioning the Stalinist Soul: The Diary of Stepan Podliubnyi, 1931–1939." *Jahrbücher für Geschichte Osteuropas* 44:3 (1996), 344–373.

—. *Revolution on My Mind: Writing a Diary under Stalin*. Cambridge, MA: Harvard University Press, 2006.

Hirsch, Francine. "Race without the Practice of Racial Politics." *Slavic Review* 61:1 (Spring 2002), 30–43.

—. *Empire of Nations: Ethnographic Knowledge and the Making of the Soviet Union*. Ithaca: Cornell University Press, 2005.

Hoffmann, David. "Mothers in the Motherland: Stalinist Pronatalism in Its Pan-European Context." *Journal of Social History* 34:1 (Fall 2000), 35–54.

—. *Stalinist Values: The Cultural Norms of Soviet Modernity, 1917–1941*. Ithaca: Cornell University Press, 2003.

Holquist, Peter. *Making War, Forging Revolution: Russia's Continuum of Crisis, 1914–1921*. Cambridge, MA: Harvard University Press, 2002.

Hurtado, Albert L. *Intimate Frontiers: Sex, Gender, and Culture in Old California*. Albuquerque: University of New Mexico Press, 1999.

Ilic, Melanie. *Women Workers in the Soviet Interwar Economy: From "Protection" to "Equality."* New York: St. Martin's Press, 1999.

Ivanova, Galina M. *Istoriia GULAGa, 1918–1958: Sotsial'no-ekonomicheskii i politiko-pravovoi aspekty*. Moscow: Nauka, 2006.

Jameson, Elizabeth and Susan Armitage (eds.). *Writing the Range: Race, Class, and Culture in the Women's West*. Norman: University of Oklahoma Press, 1997.

Kabuzan, V. M. *Dal'nevostochnyi krai v XVII-nachale XX vv. (1640–1917): Istoriko-demograficheskii ocherk*. Moscow: Nauka, 1985.

Kaufman, A. A. *Pereselenie i kolonizatsiia*. Sankt-Petersburg: Obshchestvennaia pol'za, 1905.

Kharkhordin, Oleg V. *The Collective and the Individual in Russia: A Study of Practices*. Berkeley: University of California Press, 1999.

Khlevniuk, Oleg. *The History of the GULAG: From Collectivization to the Great Terror*, trans. Vadim Staklo. New Haven: Yale University Press, 2004.

Khodarkovsky, Michael. *Russia's Steppe Frontier: The Making of a Colonial Empire, 1500–1800*. Bloomington: Indiana University Press, 2002.

Kirschenbaum, Lisa. "Gender, Memory, and National Myths: Ol'ga Berggol'ts and the Siege of Leningrad." *Nationalities Papers* 28:3 (2000), 551–564.

Koenker, Diane P. "Men Against Women on the Shop Floor in Early Soviet Russia: Gender and Class in the Socialist Workplace." *American Historical Review* 100:5 (1995), 1438–1464.

Kollin, Susan. *Nature's State: Imagining Alaska as the Last Frontier.* Chapel Hill: University of North Carolina Press, 2001.

Kon, Igor and James Riordan (eds.). *Sex and Russian Society.* Bloomington: Indiana University Press, 1993.

Kotkin, Stephen. *Magnetic Mountain: Stalinism as a Civilization.* Berkeley: University of California Press, 1995.

— and David Wolff (eds.). *Rediscovering Russia in Asia: Siberia and the Russian Far East.* Armonk, NY: M. E. Sharpe, 1995.

Krivelevich, E. B. et al. (eds.). *Ot shamanskogo bubna do lucha lazera (Ocherki po istorii meditsiny Primor'ia)*, Chast' 1. Vladivostok: Vladivostokskii gosudarstvennyi meditsinskii universitet, 1997.

Krylova, Anna. "'Healers of Wounded Souls': The Crisis of Private Life in Soviet Literature, 1944–1946." *Journal of Modern History* 73:2 (June 2001), 307–331.

—."Stalinist Identity from the Viewpoint of Gender: Rearing a Generation of Professionally Violent Women-Fighters in 1930s Stalinist Russia." *Gender & History* 16:3 (November 2004), 626–653.

Kuhr-Korolev, Corinna (ed.). *Sowjetjugend 1917–1941: Generation zwischen Revolution und Resignation.* Essen: Klartext, 2001.

—. *Gezähmte Helden: Die Formierung der Sowjetjugend.* Essen: Klartext, 2005.

Lahusen, Thomas. *How Life Writes the Book: Real Socialism and Socialist Realism in Stalin's Russia.* Ithaca: Cornell University Press, 1997.

Lebedeva, Alena. *Russia's Economy of Favors: Blat, Networking and Informal Exchange.* Cambridge: Cambridge University Press, 1998.

Levine, Philippa (ed.). *Gender and Empire.* Oxford: Oxford University Press, 2004.

Lewin, Moshe. *The Making of the Soviet System: Essays in the Social History of Interwar Russia.* New York: New Press, 1994.

—. "Russia/USSR in Historical Motion: An Essay in Interpretation." *Russian Review* 50:3 (1991), 249–266.

Lih, Lars. *Bread and Authority in Russia, 1914–1921.* Berkeley: University of California Press, 1990.

Limerick, Patricia Nelson. *Something in the Soil: Field-Testing the New Western History.* New York: W. W. Norton, 2000.

Maier, Robert. "Sovety Zhen as a Surrogate Trade Union: Comments on the History of the Movement of Activist Women in the 1930s," in Kevin McDermott and John Morison (eds.), *Politics and Society Under the Bolsheviks: Selected Papers from the Fifth World Congress of Central and East European Studies 1995.* New York: St. Martin's Press, 1999, 189–198.

Malia, Martin. *The Soviet Tragedy: A History of Socialism in Russia, 1917–1991.* New York: Free Press, 1994.

Marks, Steven G. *Road to Power: The Trans-Siberian Railroad and the Colonization of Asian Russia, 1850–1917.* Ithaca: Cornell University Press, 1991.

—. "Conquering the Great East: Kulomzin, Peasant Resettlement and the Creation of Modern Siberia," in Stephen Kotkin and David Wolff (eds.), *Rediscovering Russia in Asia: Siberia and the Russian Far East.* Armonk, NY: M. E. Sharpe, 1995, 23–29.

Marsh, Rosalind. "Women Writers of the 1930s: Conformity or Subversion?," in Melanie Ilic (ed.), *Women in the Stalin Era.* New York: Palgrave, 2001, 173–191.

Martin, Phyllis M. "Celebrating the Ordinary: Church, Empire and Gender in the Life of Mère Mari-Michelle Dédié (Senegal, Congo, 1882–1931)." *Gender & History* 16:2 (August 2004), 289–317.

Martin, Terry. "The Origins of Soviet Ethnic Cleansing." *Journal of Modern History* 70:4 (December 1998), 813–861.

Matsusaka, Yoshihisa Tak. *The Making of Japanese Manchuria, 1904–1932.* Cambridge: Cambridge University Press, 2001.

McCannon, John. "Positive Heroes at the Pole: Celebrity Status, Socialist-Realist Ideals and the Soviet Myth of the Arctic, 1932–39." *Russian Review* 56:3 (1997), 346–365.

—. *Red Arctic: Polar Exploration and the Myth of the North in the Soviet Union, 1932–1939.* New York: Oxford University Press, 1998.

McClintock, Anne. "Family Feuds: Gender, Nationalism and the Family." *Feminist Review* 44 (Summer 1993), 61–80.

Merritt, Steven E. "The Great Purges in the Soviet Far East, 1937–1938." Unpublished PhD dissertation. University of California, Riverside, 2000.

Midgley, Clare (ed.). *Gender and Imperialism.* Manchester: Manchester University Press, 1998.

Mil'bakh, V. S. "Repression in the Red Army in the Far East, 1936–1939." *Journal of Slavic Military Studies* 16:4 (2003), 58–130.

Montrose, Louis. "The Work of Gender in the Discourse of Discovery." *Representations* 33 (Winter 1991), 1–41.

Mostov, Julie. "Sexing the Nation/Desexing the Body: The Politics of National Identity in the Former Yugoslavia," in Tamar Mayer (ed.), *Gender Ironies of Nationalism: Sexing the Nation.* London: Routledge, 2000, 18–100.

Naiman, Eric. "When a Communist Writes Gothic: Aleksandra Kollontai and the Politics of Disgust." *Signs* 22:1 (1996), 1–29.

—. *Sex in Public: The Incarnation of Early Soviet Ideology.* Princeton: Princeton University Press, 1997.

Neary, Rebecca Balmas. "Mothering Socialist Society: The Wife-Activists' Movement and the Soviet Culture of Daily Life, 1934–41." *Russian Review* 58 (July 1999), 396–412.

Nobles, Gregory H. *American Frontiers: Cultural Encounters and Continental Conquest.* New York: Hill and Wang, 1997.

Northrop, Douglas. *Veiled Empire: Gender and Power in Stalinist Central Asia.* Ithaca: Cornell University Press, 2004.

Oja, Matt F. *From Krestianka to Udarnitsa: Rural Women and the Vydvizhenie Campaign, 1933–1941.* Pittsburgh: Center for Russian and East European Studies, University of Pittsburgh, 1996.

Osokina, Elena A. *Our Daily Bread: Socialist Distribution and the Art of Survival in Stalin's Russia, 1927–1941* (The New Russian History, ed. Kate Transchel), trans. Transchel and Greta Bucher. Armonk, NY: M. E. Sharpe, 2001.

Pallot, Judith. "Forced Labor for Forestry: The Twentieth-Century History of Colonization and Settlement in the North Perm Oblast." *Europe-Asia Studies* 54:7 (2002), 1055–1083.

Park, Hyun Ok. "Korean Manchuria: The Racial Politics of Territorial Osmosis." *South Atlantic Quarterly* 99:1 (2000), 193–215.

Perry, Adele. "'Fair Ones of a Purer Caste': White Women and Colonialism in Nineteenth-Century British Columbia." *Feminist Studies* 23:3 (1997), 501–524.

Petrone, Karen. "Masculinity and Heroism in Imperial and Soviet Military-Patriotic Cultures," in Barbara Evans Clements, Rebecca Friedman, and Dan Healey (eds.), *Russian Masculinities in History and Culture*. New York: Palgrave, 2002, 172–193.

Phillips, Richard. *Sex, Politics and Empire: A Postcolonial Geography*. New York: Palgrave, 2006.

Pickles, Katie. *Female Imperialism and National Identity: Imperial Order Daughters of the Empire*. Manchester: University of Manchester Press, 2002.

Pikalov, Iurii V. *Pereselencheskaia politika i izmenenie sotsial'no-klassovogo sostava naseleniia Dal'nego Vostoka RSFSR (noiabr' 1922–iiun' 1941 gg.)*. Khabarovsk: KhGPU, 2004.

Pinnow, Kenneth M. "Violence Against the Collective Self and the Problem of Social Integration in Early Bolshevik Russia." *Kritika* 4:3 (Summer 2003), 653–677.

Polian, Pavel. *Ne po svoei vole: istoriia i geografiia prinuditel'nykh migratsii v SSSR*. Moscow: OGI-Memorial, 2001.

Reagin, Nancy. "The Imagined Hausfrau: National Identity, Domesticity, and Colonialism in Imperial Germany." *Journal of Modern History* 73:1 (March 2001), 54–86.

Reid, Susan E. "All Stalin's Women: Gender and Power in Soviet Art of the 1930s." *Slavic Review* 57:1 (Spring 1998), 133–173.

Rieber, Alfred J. and Masha Siefert (eds.). *Extending the Borders of Russian History: Essays in Honor of Alfred J. Rieber*. Budapest: Central European University Press, 2003.

Rittersporn, Gabor T. "Formy obshchestvennogo obikhoda molodezhi i ustanovki sovetskogo rezhima v predvoennom desiatiletii," in Timo Vikhavainen (ed.), *Normy i tsennosti povsednevnoi zhizni: Stanovlenie sotsialisticheskogo obraza zhizni v Rossii, 1920–1930-e gody*. St. Petersburg: Zhurnal "Neva," 2000, 347–367.

Rosenberg, William and Lewis Siegelbaum (eds.). *Social Dimensions of Soviet Industrialization*. Bloomington: Indiana University Press, 1994.

Rossman, Jeffrey. "The Teikovo Cotton Workers' Strike of April 1932." *Russian Review* 56:1 (1997), 44–69.

Rotkirch, Anna. "Traveling Maidens and Men with Parallel Lives – Journeys as Private Space During Late Socialism," in Jeremy Smith (ed.), *Beyond the*

Limits: The Concept of Space in Russian History and Culture. Helsinki: Studia Historica, 1999, 131–149.

Rybakovskii, Leonid L. *Naselenie Dal'nego Vostoka za 150 let.* Moscow: Nauka, 1990.

Sallnow, John. "Siberia's Demand for Labour: Incentive Policies and Migration, 1960–85," in Alan Wood and R. A. French (eds.), *The Development of Siberia: People and Resources.* London: Macmillan, 1989, 188–207.

Sanborn, Joshua A. *Drafting the Russian Nation: Military Conscription, Total War, and Mass Politics, 1905–1925.* DeKalb: Northern Illinois University Press, 2003.

Scherbov, Sergei and Harrie van Vianen. "Marital and Fertility Careers of Russian Women Born Between 1910 and 1934." *Population and Development Review* 25:1 (March 1999), 129–143.

Schrader, Abby M. "Unruly Felons and Civilizing Wives: Cultivating Marriage in the Siberian Exile System, 1822–1860." *Slavic Review* 66:2 (Summer 2007), 230–256.

Schrand, Thomas. "The Five-Year Plan for Women's Labour: Constructing Socialism and the 'Double Burden,' 1930–1932." *Europe-Asia Studies* 51:8 (December 1999), 1455–1478.

—. "Soviet 'Civic-Minded Women' in the 1930s: Gender, Class, and Industrialization in a Socialist Society." *Journal of Women's History* 11:3 (1999), 126–150.

Schwartzberg, Beverly. "'Lots of Them Did That': Desertion, Bigamy and Marital Fluidity in Late Nineteenth-Century America." *Journal of Social History* 37:3 (2004), 573–600.

Serduk, M. B. "Religioznye pereseleniia na iuge Dal'nego Vostoka Rossii," in A. I. Krushanov and V. L. Larin (eds.), *Dal'nii Vostok Rossii v kontekste mirovoi istorii.* Vladivostok: DVO RAN, 1997, 241–244.

Shulman, Elena. "Soviet Maidens for the Socialist Fortress: The Khetagurovite Campaign to Settle the Soviet Far East, 1937–1939." *Russian Review* 62:3 (July 2003), 387–410.

Siegelbaum, Lewis H. *Stakhanovism and the Politics of Productivity in the USSR, 1935–1941.* New York: Cambridge University Press, 1988.

— and Ronald Suny (eds.). *Making Workers Soviet: Power, Class and Identity.* Ithaca: Cornell University Press, 1994.

Simmons, Cynthia. "Lifting the Siege: Women's Voices on Leningrad (1941–1944)." *Canadian Slavonic Papers* 40:1–2 (March–June 1998), 43–65.

— and Nina Perlina. *Writing the Siege of Leningrad: Women's Diaries, Memoirs and Documentary Prose.* Pittsburgh: University of Pittsburgh Press, 2002.

Slezkine, Iuri. *Arctic Mirrors: Russia and the Small Peoples of the North.* Ithaca: Cornell University Press, 1994.

Stark, Meinhard. *Frauen im GULAG: Alltag und Uberleben, 1936–1956.* Munich: DTV, 2003.

Starks, Tricia. "A Fertile Mother Russia: Pronatalist Propaganda in Revolutionary Russia." *Journal of Family History* 28:3 (July 2003), 411–442.

Stephan, John J. *The Russian Far East: A History.* Stanford: Stanford University Press, 1994.

Stites, Richard. *The Women's Liberation Movement in Russia: Feminism, Nihilism, and Bolshevism 1860–1930*. Princeton: Princeton University Press, 1978.

Stockdale, Melissa K. "'My Death for the Motherland is Happiness': Women, Patriotism, and Soldiering in Russia's Great War, 1914–1917." *American Historical Review* 109:1 (February 2004), 78–116.

Stoff, Laurie. "They Fought for Russia: Female Soldiers of the First World War," in Gerard J. DeGroot and Corinna Peniston-Bird (eds.), *A Soldier and a Woman: Sexual Integration in the Military*. New York: Longman, 2000, 66–82.

Stoler, Ann Laura. "Making Empire Respectable: The Politics of Race and Sexual Morality in Twentieth-Century Colonial Cultures," in Anne McClintock, Aamir Mufti, and Ella Shohat (eds.), *Dangerous Liaisons: Gender, Nation and Postcolonial Perspectives*. Minneapolis: University of Minnesota Press, 1997, 344–373.

—. *Carnal Knowledge and Imperial Power: Race and the Intimate in Colonial Rule*. Berkeley: University of California Press, 2002.

Strobel, Margaret. *European Women and the Second British Empire*. Bloomington: Indiana University Press, 1991.

Sunderland, Willard. "Peasant Pioneering: Russian Peasant Settlers Describe Colonization and the Eastern Frontier, 1880s–1910s." *Journal of Social History* 34:4 (Summer 2001), 895–922.

—. "Empire Without Imperialism? Ambiguities of Colonization in Tsarist Russia." *Ab Imperio* 2 (2003), 101–114.

—. *Taming the Wild Field: Colonization and Empire on the Russian Steppe*. Ithaca: Cornell University Press, 2004.

Suny, Ronald and Terry Martin (eds.). *Empire and Nation-Making in the Age of Lenin and Stalin*. New York: Oxford University Press, 2001.

Suturin, Aleksandr. *Delo kraevogo masshtaba: O zhertvakh stalinskogo bezzakoniia na Dal'nem Vostoke*. Khabarovsk: Khabarovskoe khizhnoe izdatel'stvo, 1991.

Tauger, Mark B. *Natural Disaster and Human Actions in the Soviet Famine of 1931–1933*. Pittsburgh: Center for Russian and East European Studies, University Center for International Studies, University of Pittsburgh, 2001.

Thurston, Robert W. and Bernd Bonwetsch (eds.). *The People's War: Responses to World War II in the Soviet Union*. Urbana and Chicago: University of Illinois Press, 2000.

Timasheff, Nicholas S. *The Great Retreat: The Growth and Decline of Communism in Russia*. New York: E. P. Dutton, 1946.

Tolz, Vera. "Orientalism, Nationalism, and Ethnic Diversity in Late Imperial Russia." *Historical Journal* 48:1 (2005), 127–150.

Treadgold, Donald W. "Russian Expansion in the Light of Turner's Study of the American Frontier." *Agricultural History* 26:4 (1952), 147–152.

—. *The Great Siberian Migration: Government and Peasant in Resettlement from Emancipation to the First World War*. Princeton: Princeton University Press, 1957.

Turton, Katy. "After Lenin: The Role of Anna and Mariia Ul'ianova in Soviet Society and Politics from 1924." *Revolutionary Russia* 15:2 (December 2002), 106–135.

Uspenskaia, V. I. (ed.). *Aleksandra Kollontai: Teoriia zhenskoi emansipatsii v kontekste rossiiskoi gendernoi politiki: materialy mezhdunarodnoi nauchnoi konferentsii* Tver', March 11, 2002. Tver': Zolotaia bukva, 2003.

Vashchuk, A. S. (ed.). *Adaptatsiia etnicheskikh migrantov v Primor'e v XX v.* Vladivostok: DVO RAN, 2000.

Vasil'chenko, El'vira A. (ed.) *Nauchno-metodicheskie problemy gumanitarnykh nauk*, vol I. Komsomol'sk-na-Amure: Komsomol'sk-na-Amure gos. tekhn. universitet, 1999.

—. *Sovetskaia gosudarstvennaia politika po preobrazovaniiu sotsial'nogo statusa zhenshchin v usloviiakh Dal'nego Vostoka (1917–1940 gg.).* Komsomol'sk-na-Amure: Komsomol'sk-na-Amure gos. tekhn. universitet, 2000.

Vibert, Elizabeth. "Real Men Hunt Buffalo: Masculinity, Race and Class in British Fur Traders' Narratives." *Gender & History* 8:1 (1996): 4–21.

Viola, Lynne. "Bab'i Bunty and Peasant Women's Protest During Collectivization." *Russian Review* 45:1 (1986), 23–42.

—. *The Best Sons of the Fatherland: Workers in the Vanguard of Soviet Collectivization.* New York: Oxford University Press, 1987.

—. *Peasant Rebels under Stalin: Collectivization and the Culture of Peasant Resistance.* New York: Oxford University Press, 1996.

—. "The Other Archipelago: Kulak Deportations to the North in 1930." *Slavic Review* 60:4 (Winter 2001), 730–755.

—, V. P. Danilov, N. A. Ivnitskii, and Denis Kozlov (eds.). *The Tragedy of the Soviet Countryside: The War Against the Peasantry, 1927–1930.* New Haven: Yale University Press, 2005.

—. *The Unknown GULAG: The Lost World of Stalin's Special Settlements.* Oxford: Oxford University Press, 2007.

von Geldern, James and Richard Stites (eds.). *Mass Culture in Soviet Russia: Tales, Poems, Songs, Movies, Plays and Folklore, 1917–1953.* Bloomington: Indiana University Press, 1995.

Vysokov, M. S. *Slaviane na Dal'nem Vostoke: Problemy istorii i kul'tury. Doklady i soobshcheniia nauchnoi konferentsii.* Iuzhno-Sakhalinsk: Sakhalinskii tsentr dokumentatsii noveishei istorii, 1994, 99–104.

Waters, Elizabeth. "The Modernization of Russian Motherhood, 1917–1937." *Soviet Studies* 44:1 (1992), 123–135.

Webster, Wendy. "Domesticating the Frontier: Gender, Empire and Adventure Landscapes in British Cinema, 1945–1959." *Gender & History* 15:1 (2003), 85–107.

Widdis, Emma. "Borders: The Aesthetic of Conquest in Soviet Cinema of the 1930s." *Journal of European Studies* 30:4 (December 2000), 401–411.

—. *Visions of a New Land: Soviet Film from the Revolution to the Second World War.* New Haven: Yale University Press, 2003.

Wildenthal, Lora. *German Women for Empire, 1884–1945.* Durham: Duke University Press, 2001.

Wishnick, Elizabeth. "Russia in Asia and Asians in Russia." *SAIS Review* 20:1 (2000), 86–101.

Wood, Alan. "Sex and Violence in Siberia: Aspects of the Tsarist Exile System," in John Massey Stewart and Alan Wood (eds.), *Siberia: Two Historical*

Perspectives. London: GB-USSR Association and School of Slavonic and East European Studies, 1984, 35–61.

— (ed.). *The History of Siberia: From Russian Conquest to Revolution*. London: Routledge, 1991, 117–139.

Wood, Elizabeth. *The Baba and the Comrade: Gender and Politics in Revolutionary Russia*. Bloomington: Indiana University Press, 1997.

—. "The Trial of the New Woman: Citizens-in-Training in the New Soviet Republic." *Gender & History* 13:3 (November 2001), 524–545.

Woollacott, Angela. *Gender and Empire*. New York: Palgrave, 2006.

Worobec, Christine. *Peasant Russia: Family and Community in the Post-Emancipation Period*. DeKalb: Northern Illinois University Press, 1995.

Young, Louise. *Japan's Total Empire: Manchuria and the Culture of Wartime Imperialism*. Berkeley: University of California Press, 1998.

Yuval-Davis, Nira. *Gender and Nation*. London: Sage, 1997.

— and Floya Anthias (eds.). *Woman-Nation-State*. New York: Macmillan, 1989.

Zeliak, V. G. *Piat' metallov Dal'stroia*. Magadan: Kordis, 2004.

Zemskov, V. N. *Spetsposelentsy v SSSR, 1930–1960*. Moscow: Nauka, 2003.

Zhiromskaia, V. B. *Demograficheskaia istoriia Rossii v 1930-e gody: Vzgliad v neizvestnoe*. Moscow: ROSSPEN, 2001.

Index